Digressive Voices in Early Modern English Literature

Digressive Voices in Early Modern English Literature

ANNE COTTERILL

OXFORD
UNIVERSITY PRESS

Great Clarendon Street, Oxford OX2 6DP

Oxford University Press is a department of the University of Oxford.
It furthers the University's objective of excellence in research, scholarship,
and education by publishing worldwide in

Oxford New York

Auckland Bangkok Buenos Aires Cape Town Chennai
Dar es Salaam Delhi Hong Kong Istanbul Karachi Kolkata
Kuala Lumpur Madrid Melbourne Mexico City Mumbai Nairobi
São Paulo Shanghai Taipei Tokyo Toronto

Oxford is a registered trade mark of Oxford University Press
in the UK and in certain other countries

Published in the United States
by Oxford University Press Inc., New York

First published 2004

British Library Cataloguing in Publication Data
Data available

Library of Congress Cataloging in Publication Data
Data available

ISBN 0–19–926117–2

1 3 5 7 9 10 8 6 4 2

Typeset by Hope Services (Abingdon) Ltd.
Printed in Great Britain
on acid-free paper by
Biddles Ltd.,
King's Lynn, Norfolk

In memory of my brother,

Charles Fogle Cotterill

Acknowledgements

Many have helped me along the way of this book, and I can only begin to thank them here. First, *Digressive Voices* exists because Steven Zwicker at Washington University introduced me to the world of Restoration England and to Marvell, Milton, and Dryden. An extraordinary, and extraordinarily generous, scholar and teacher, Steve has encouraged my ideas, followed my digressions, tirelessly strengthened my prose, and for over ten years offered the sustained guidance and friendship that have helped me to reshape an intellectual and literary life. I continue to learn from his creative energy. In my initial semester of graduate school, after years of living overseas, I was hooked into literary study again by Joseph Loewenstein who became the English Renaissance for me in all of its *copia* and complexity. I am indebted particularly to his pointing me to the study of rhetoric. Derek Hirst first showed me how superbly a historian can read literary texts and the range and interest of seventeenth-century historical materials. He has been most generous and steady with his encouragement.

I am grateful to Rutgers University and to Rutgers's Department of Literatures in English for a year's sabbatical to pursue this project. Many colleagues have read patiently and critically portions or all of the manuscript and helped me to pull the thread that leads through these digressions: Emily Bartels, Wesley Brown, Chris Chism, Ann Coiro, Stacy Klein, Ron Levao, Bridget Lyons, Michael McKeon, Jackie Miller, and Carla Yanni. Mary Bly corrected many pages and has been an example of scholarly and personal warmth and strength. With his knowledge of seventeenth-century natural philosophy John Shanahan has helped me to rethink the chapter on Sir Thomas Browne. For Chris Chism's years of insightful advice and of wide-ranging talk by the Raritan canal, which has inspired and clarified my thinking, I am most grateful. Nika Hedges prepared my bibliography with resourcefulness on short notice and with scrupulous care. Jean Ensminger provided me with beautiful surroundings and encouragement during several important years and graciously housed me one spring so that I could work at the Huntington. Thráinn Eggertsson has enlarged my understanding and encouraged me in many ways, not least through his Icelandic gift for narrative. While coming from another language and professional discipline, Thráinn's sharp ear and good taste in English, demonstrated by his own writing and cultivated by wide reading, exceed the sensibilities of many native speakers and have taught me about my own language as well as his own.

I want to thank Sophie Goldsworthy, my attentive and most patient editor at Oxford University Press, Elizabeth Prochaska, Assistant Commissioning Editor, Frances Whistler, In-house Editor, Jackie Pritchard, my copy-editor, and the press's two anonymous readers whose interest in my project and astute suggestions helped guide me through my final revisions. An earlier version of Chapter 6 appeared as 'The Politics and Aesthetics of Digression: Dryden's *Discourse Concerning the Original and Progress of Satire*', in *Studies in Philology*, 41/4, copyright © 1994 by the University of North Carolina Press. That material is used here by permission of the publisher. Versions of Chapter 2 and Chapter 5 appeared earlier as, respectively, 'Marvell's Watery Maze: Digression and Discovery at Nun Appleton', *ELH* 69 (2002), 103–32; and 'Parenthesis at the Center: The Complex Embrace of *The Hind and the Panther*', *Eighteenth-Century Studies* 30/2 (1996–7), 139–58.

Finally, to my mother I owe my first knowledge of the pleasures of reading, my love of books, and an appreciation for good writing—and, in the seventeenth-century sense, for good wit. She has lived a full life of reading and required me to be clear-eyed and articulate to keep up with her. I am grateful to my remarkable family—of brothers and sister, in-laws, nieces, and nephews—who have inspired and supported me in conversations and letters with their talents, wisdom, and achievements. This book is dedicated to Charles who from the perspective of six feet seven taught us about the gentle uses of self-deprecation as well as self-esteem, about the importance of teaching, and about the generosity and transport of humour.

A.C.

Contents

Introduction: To Wander 'out of the Common Road'

> Then he was more happy in his digressions than any we have nam'd. I have always been pleas'd to see him, and his imitator, *Montaign*, when they strike a little out of the common road: For we are sure to be the better for their wand'ring.
>
> (John Dryden, 'The Life of Plutarch', 1683)[1]

Digressive Voices in Early Modern English Literature begins and ends with the intellectual and imaginative pleasures of narrative wandering. Famous for his digressions and eloquent about their pleasures, John Dryden sounds the themes of this book even more exactly, however, a decade after 'The Life of Plutarch' when he links 'sweet' digressiveness to self-defence. In his dedicatory epistle to Francis, Lord Radcliffe, prefixed to the miscellany *Examen Poeticum* (1693), the poet turns aside to defend himself and English drama from recent attacks and acknowledges his excursion twice before he returns reluctantly to the miscellany's contents: 'This, my Lord, is, I confess, a long digression, from Miscellany Poems to Modern Tragedies: But I have the ordinary Excuse of an Injur'd Man, who will be telling his Tale unseasonably to his Betters'; two pages later he announces, 'I will not give my self the liberty of going farther; for 'tis so sweet to wander in a pleasing way, that I shou'd never arrive at my Journeys end'.[2] My subject is how writers transformed the sweet liberty of digression, the insubordinate 'Straggler' of *The Arte of English Poesie* (1589), to create a complex form of underground writing and of self-definition in some of the richest non-dramatic texts of seventeenth-century England.[3] Such a pointed use of digressiveness in the period has not been recognized.

[1] John Dryden, *The Works of John Dryden*, vol. xvii, ed. Samuel Holt Monk (Berkeley and Los Angeles: University of California Press, 1971), 277.

[2] John Dryden, *The Works of John Dryden*, vol. iv, ed. A. B. Chambers and William Frost (Berkeley and Los Angeles: University of California Press, 1974), 367, 369.

[3] George Puttenham, *The Arte of English Poesie: A Facsimile Reproduction* (Kent State, Oh.: Kent State University Press, 1970), III. xix. 240.

My study follows the digressive voices of Donne's *Anniversaries*, Marvell's *Upon Appleton House*, Sir Thomas Browne's *The Garden of Cyrus*, Milton's *Paradise Lost*, and two late works by Dryden: his mysterious, three-part beast fable *The Hind and the Panther*, and his longest preface, *The Discourse of Satire*. By the beginning of a new century and new era of politics and print, Jonathan Swift's *A Tale of a Tub* registers the digressive voice not as a straggler but as a monstrous, quintessentially 'modern' sound with no substance or past: a rootless figure for the professional pen, emerged from the shadows of poverty and transformed to a national threat. To such sensational press and to Swift's anxiety for the future, I then leave these voices whose transformations in the eighteenth century and beyond constitute another story.

By underground writing I mean the veiled expression of political doubt and enmity together with an exploration of hidden and unruly or disturbing parts of the speaker's self. Through their fluent, aggressive narrators capable of powerful rhetorical complexity, the writers whose texts I examine also explore the experience of vulnerability, marginality, loss, and anger. The unconventional progress of these texts also becomes an indirect analysis of and resistance to political and cultural forces—not least, to an intellectual and moral rigidity suspicious of learning and of aesthetic ornament and amplitude. These writers use digressions to stake out intellectual territory and form powerful personae.

My book has grown from an interest in the connection between the rhetorical sophistication of early modern writers, particularly their display of an abundance of intellectual riches productive of digressive *copia*, and their sense of threat. The texts of this study reflect a competitive, agonistic world of writing and reading shaped in part by the writers' inheritance of a classical rhetorical tradition of oral persuasion and by the necessity to negotiate a maze of demands for literary survival dictated by politics and patronage. As sensitive readers and auditors, these writers reflect on the dangers of being invaded and transformed or otherwise consumed and silenced by others' words. The writing here acts both offensively and defensively, advancing over the page and into less visible spaces such as the labyrinthine inner ear that leads to the mind's judgement. In these texts, the human body behind the text's figurative one of paper and ink becomes the central landscape *in absentia* on which a drama about speaking and the deferral of ends is played, as Swift's *A Tale of a Tub* exposes.

Part of the dangerous, consuming nature of the world of these texts and voices becomes the straight narrative line to an end, to death's or censorship's breathlessness. In these works often addressed to aristocratic patrons, direct linear progression of thought also becomes aligned subtly with the direct descent of privilege through a lineage designed to continue the life and power of bloodlines beyond death. Digressions could function within writing's alternative form of reproduction as lines of important generation that are hidden from vision and from attack until they emerge as complex and enduring.

The writers considered here employ a figure of speech, *digressio*, as a figure *for* speech and mental, interior, movement. The Latin root of digression, *digressio*, translates a Greek rhetorical term, *parecbasis*, that means 'to step or go aside or depart';[4] and digressions have stepped 'alongside the subject' in poetry and oratory, in fiction and in historical and critical writing since antiquity.[5] The movement of stepping aside has proved richly allusive yet by definition elusive: digressions have been read as lightly pleasurable and darkly sinuous, as the harmless vehicles of gossip and romance and the heroic wandering of epic liberty. The words 'discourse' and 'digress' share the Latin prefix 'dis-', which means apart, prompting some to argue that 'the closed structure of story' with a beginning and an end 'is in permanent tension with the proclivity' of all

[4] Digressio consists of the prefix 'dis-' which means 'apart', plus the word 'gradus' meaning 'step' or 'degree'. The severing motion of 'dis-' cuts through such unsettling verbs as disaffect, disestablish, disable, disagree, while the related Greek prefix 'di-' or 'two', audible in the 'dis-' of 'digression', suggests a divided yet not disconnected road or will. Most recently, Ross Chambers's *Loiterature* (Lincoln: University of Nebraska Press, 1999) thoughtfully explores the action of literary digression. The author surveys practices of digressive narrative since Laurence Sterne and makes a persuasive connection between the practice of digression and the interests and perspectives of modern cultural studies. On the kinds of intersection or divided road that generate digressions, see ch. 1, 'Divided Attentions (On Being Dilatory)', 10–16, and his image of the 'three-way' crossing, the *trivium*, and especially the Y-shaped division 'in which digression is the only option' (11).

[5] The reference to digression as stepping 'alongside the subject' is from Longinus, *On the Sublime*, translated with commentary by James A. Arieti and John M. Crossett (New York: E. Mellon Press, 1985), 77, section 12.5. The translators note that Longinus' word for digression 'is a technical term of Old Comedy . . . and denotes that part of the play in which the chorus came forward and addressed the audience in the poet's name. It also means "straying", "overstepping", "illusion", and "transition".' For a discussion of digression in classical epic and romance and its relation to Renaissance literature, see Bernard Weinberg, *A History of Literary Criticism in the Italian Renaissance*, 2 vols. (Chicago: University of Chicago Press, 1961); for the 16th-century Italian theorists of vernacular *copia* and digressiveness, see esp. vol. ii. On the tradition of digression in fiction, see David Morrison Kirk, 'The Digression: Its Use in Prose Fiction from the Greek Romance through the Eighteenth Century', (Ph.D. theisis, Stanford University, 1960); and in narrative from the 19th to the 20th century, see Joel Dana Black, 'The Second Fall: The Laws of Digression and Gravitation in Romantic Literature and their Impact on Contemporary Encyclopaedic Literature' (Ph.D. thesis, Stanford University, 1979).

discourse to digress.[6] Hobbes warned that the power of the mind's 'Fancy' to invent, including the invention of metaphor and simile, needed to be directed toward a strong use or application, for 'without Stedinesse, and Direction to some End, a great Fancy is one kind of Madnesse; such as they have, that entring into any discourse, are snatched from their purpose, by every thing that comes in their thought, into so many, and so long digressions, and Parentheses, that they utterly lose themselves'.[7] Each narrator in these texts meets or evokes a spectre of speechlessness or ineffectual speech, as well as of loss of direction and self.

Through a figurative descent to the body's unstable underworld associated with a female or with effeminate weakness, the narrators unravel a winding thread into a labyrinth that conceals, yet confronts them with, speechless death. On the occasion of Elizabeth Drury's death, Donne's aggressive anatomist descends to the horror of physical death and dissolution before he ascends in voice and vision; Marvell's tutor dives through meadows and floods past images of sacrificed young into physical pain and abandon, while his narrative extends between two virgins sacrificed to marriage and the family line; Milton's epic speaker falls through Eve's body in her attempt to swallow the world whole and, past death, to interiority and conscience; *The Hind and the Panther*'s confessional narrator descends into the hide and claws of female beasts to expose his own deadly predators; Dryden's historian of satire swims 'into my depth' to decapitate the courtly, effeminate sycophant that threatens to have been himself; and Swift's Hack descends by digressions into the sexless impotence of lonely fragmentation and madness. Browne's garden excursions follow his descent, in *Hydriotaphia, or Urne-Buriall*, into the underground of the voiceless dead where the equal horror of human

[6] See Chambers, *Loiterature*, 86 and n. 4. The departures of digression always postpone ends: 'The complication of the detour is related to the danger of short-circuit', writes Peter Brooks, 'the danger of reaching the end too quickly, of achieving the im-proper death'. Peter Brooks, *Reading for the Plot: Design and Intention in Narrative* (New York: A. A. Knopf, 1984), 103–4. See also Chambers, *Loiterature*, 25: 'That we don't and can't lose sight of them [Tristram Shandy's reasons for sadness] completely is predicted, however, by both the oddly two-sided or ambiguous structure of the narrative discourse as a simultaneously dilatory and end-oriented phenomenon and the very condition of digression which is, as etymology proposes, a stepping away from—but a stepping away from that's sutured to that away from which it steps . . . beguiling narrative—or better still: beguiling narration as an alternative to narrative closure—isn't a bad phrase with which to characterize loiterature generally'.

[7] Thomas Hobbes, *Leviathan*, ed. Richard Tuck (Cambridge: Cambridge University Press, 1991), book I, ch. 8, 51.

corruption and sexual reproduction mingles in images of wombs and tombs. Instead of Maria Fairfax or Eve, in his paradise Browne invokes nature's art, the 'Elegancy of her hand' and her 'Conjugall' number five whose intersection of odd and even becomes a figural alternative to sexual generation and mortality—the quincunx becomes a pattern for the eternal intersection and branching of all life, including thought.

Notably absent from *Digressive Voices* is the voice of a female writer. In the last two decades, excellent single-author studies, anthologies, and print publication series of the work of early modern British women writers have begun to shape a new literary landscape for the period and recover these important voices.[8] Much work on the relation of Lanyer, Cavendish, Hutchinson, Behn, and others to issues of literary figuration and digression waits to be done. My focus is on texts by male writers whose relative privileges of gender then, and canonicity today, need not obscure for us the paradox of the loquacious speakers they produced when they found themselves in weakened and powerless or dangerously ambiguous social and political positions. Their narrative voices, mimicking the experience of many kinds of de-centredness, wind digressively around the danger of being silenced through a landscape of the dead or silent that are frequently women or a figure of male effeminacy and submission. Gender studies and the work of historians of sex like Thomas Lacqueur have broadened, surely, the investigation of gender beyond biology and its binary oppositions in order to complicate ideas of the feminine and masculine and an awareness of their interaction within the imagination, language, and bodies of both sexes.

This study does not aim to exhaust the subject of early modern digressions or to include every digressive text of the period. In the second half

[8] I can only suggest the richness of the variety and quality of materials on early modern women writers, beginning with the Brown University Women Writers in English 1580–1850 series. Collections that have introduced their work include (from the 1980s) Moira Ferguson (ed.), *First Feminists; British Women Writers 1578–1799* (Bloomington: Indiana University Press, 1985), Germaine Greer et al. (eds.), *Kissing the Rod: An Anthology of Seventeenth-Century Women's Verse* (New York: Farrar Straus Giroux, 1988); and Elspeth Graham et al. (eds.), *Her Own Life; Autobiographical Writings by Seventeenth-Century Englishwomen* (London: Routledge, 1989); (from the 1990s) Louise Schleiner (ed.), *Tudor and Stuart Women Writers* (Bloomington: Indiana University Press, 1994); James Fitzmaurice (ed.), *Major Women Writers of Seventeenth-Century England* (Ann Arbor: University of Michigan Press, 1997); and (from 2000–) Jane Stevenson and Peter Davidson (eds.), *Early Modern Women Poets: An Anthology* (Oxford: Oxford University Press, 2001); Stephanie Hodgson-Wright (ed.), *Women's Writing of the Early Modern Period, 1588–1688: An Anthology* (New York: Columbia University Press, 2002). See also, for example, Paula McDowell, *The Women of Grub-Street: Press, Politics, and Gender in the London Literary Marketplace, 1678–1730* (Oxford: Clarendon Press, 1998).

of the sixteenth century, Montaigne withdrew onto his family estate and over the next twenty years composed essays that theorize digression as the liberty and art of self-exploration. His *Essais* (1588) and Robert Burton's *The Anatomy of Melancholy* (1621) hover over the century and over the texts of this book as highly self-conscious models of digressive writing. Montaigne and Burton, however, removed themselves from the public sphere to think, write expansively, and revise at their leisure, whereas the authors I examine produce and situate their digressive writing within a dense, conflicted political world under the pressure of a patron's or public's religious, social, or ideological expectations. I focus on a group of canonical works whose central emotional interests have been disputed and which men composed when they were displaced or exiled from a centre of power or when the location of that centre was unclear. These writers slipped by digression into obscurity, that time-honoured cover of the satirist and of the political minority and disenfranchised, and, under that cover, into political comment and autobiography.

Donne, Browne, Marvell, Milton, and Dryden were schooled in rhetorical arts and techniques of amplification as well as in ancient and Christian models of heroic, labyrinthine wandering—models of life and of the human mind as a labyrinth, a journey full of unexpected turns and byways. These writers used their learning and the disciplined turning of tropes to seek the safety and liberties of literary obliqueness: they gained the artful freedom to step aside from their public theme into a deeper, more personal subject, to expand the notion of a subject in relation to subjectivity, and to create a narrative voice that appears to wander. They adopted the narrative practice of stepping away from the subject in order to step into subjectivity. The amphibian was a popular seventeenth-century motif for survival in ambiguous times and divided worlds; and like a tortoise or like the salmon-fishers hooded in canoes at the end of Marvell's long poem, the writers here often needed to obscure their heads. Under the descent of darkness, the head, whether as crown, palace, prison, or madhouse, becomes a crucially mobile space for Shakespeare's homeless King Lear at the beginning of the century, for Milton's Satan, and for a whole amphibious age. The image of a tortoise or snail with a home on its back—the 'Oeconomic Virtues' of Lovelace's 'Snayl' (l. 38)—captures the precarious life of the mind wandering in internal exile, as if underground or underwater: a hidden world into which an exiled patriarch or a disenfranchised poet might retreat.

What makes these texts 'digressive' for the purposes of this book is the narrator's circuitous, distended progress shaped by pressures to defend, to complicate and resist, and to attack—pressures that appear to kidnap his narrative away from the conventional expectations of his genre. At the same time these artful voices also digress to recollect; the narrators have a pressing past and draw our attention to their ability to manœuvre with the thread of the past through a landscape that has become too intensely, bewilderingly present. Montaigne had characterized his essays as grotesquely 'composed of so many monstrous bodies, patched and huddled up together of divers members'; and these voices divert attention in a 'slyly subversive' way that allows them to remember—to collect and connect together even into a monstrous body—disparate fragments of experience.[9]

THE THREAD OF DESIGN

For a Renaissance writer familiar with Ovid since grammar school, the maze of political and personal dislocation or of a richly stocked mind could hardly fail to evoke the Cretan labyrinth in book 8 of the *Metamorphoses.*[10] We enter Ovid's story as King Minos of Crete returns home from military victory; his queen, Pasiphae, has committed adultery with a bull and gives birth to a monster, half-man and half-beast, whose double form casts shame and infamy on the royal household. Like any head of state with a family scandal, Minos must save face, and to conceal this monstrous progeny he employs the famed craftsman and inventor Daedalus, an artist and exile from Athens. The cover-up is both an engineer's miracle and a deadly work of art. Daedalus closes Pasiphae's bastard deep inside an architectural maze that George Sandys glosses as

[9] *The Essayes: or Moral, Politicke, and Militarie Discourses of Lo: Michaell de Montaigne*, trans. John Florio, 3 vols. (1603; repr., London: J. M. Dent and sons, 1965), i. 29, 195, quoted in William E. Engel, *Mapping Mortality: The Persistence of Memory and Melancholy in Early Modern England* (Amherst: University of Massachusetts Press, 1995), 116. The characterization of digression as 'slyly subversive' comes from a recent discussion of digression as a rhetorical tool for Renaissance women writers. See Boyd Berry, ' "Pardon . . . though I Have Digrest": Digression as Style in "Salve Deus Rex Judaeorum" ', in Marshall Grossman (ed.), *Aemilia Lanyer: Gender, Genre, and the Canon* (Lexington: University Press of Kentucky, 1998), 212–33.

[10] See 8. 152–82. All references to Ovid's text are to the Loeb Classical Library edition, trans. Frank Justus Miller, rev. G. P. Goold (Cambridge, Mass.: Harvard University Press, and London, 1994). Ovid's *Metamorphoses* supplied Renaissance classrooms with figures and fragments for rhetorical training in a wide range of textbooks, and it circulated in complete translations by Arthur Golding (1567) and George Sandys (1632). See, for example, Richard J. DuRocher, *Milton and Ovid* (Ithaca, NY: Cornell University Press, 1985), 23–4; and Jonathan Bate, *Shakespeare and Ovid* (Oxford: Clarendon Press, 1993).

'a prison under the earth'.[11] Sandys's terse, brilliant translation of the *Metamorphoses* from 1632 was reprinted in almost every decade of the seventeenth century:

> *Minos* resolves his marriage shame to hide
> In multitude of roomes, perplext, and blind.
> The work t'excelling *Daedalus* assign'd.
> Who sence distracts, and error leads a maze
> Through subtill ambages of sundry wayes.
> As *Phrygian Maeander* sports about
> The flowrie vales; now winding in, now out;
> Himselfe incounters, sees what followes, guides
> His streames unto their springs; and, doubling, slides
> To long mockt seas: so *Daedalus* compil'd
> Innumerable by-waies, which beguild
> The troubled sense; that he who made the same,
> Could scarce retire: so intricate the frame
> When in this fabrick *Minos* had inclos'd
> This double forme, of man and beast compos'd;
> The Monster, with *Athenian* blood twice fed,
> His owne, the third Lot [Theseus], in the ninth yeare, shed.
> Then by a Clew reguided to the doore
> (A virgins counsel) never found before.[12]

Daedalus builds an extravagant 'fabrick' for the bastard, of only one door but many rooms, of such bewildering dimensions with passageways that always seem to digress rather than go forward that he is almost trapped there himself. He transforms King Minos' private marital shame into a sinister edifice of power. Conquered Athens must send periodic human sacrifices to wander the labyrinth and fall prey to the beast at the centre. When Athenian prince Theseus arrives in Crete as a sacrifice, he captures the heart of Minos' eldest daughter, Ariadne. Her linen 'clew' or thread enables her lover to negotiate the labyrinthine twists of art and passion: to penetrate the domestic maze, kill the monstrous perversion deep within, and emerge intact. The military hero returns only to abduct and abandon her.

[11] *Ovid's 'Metamorphoses', Englished, Mythologized, and Represented in Figures by George Sandys*, ed. Karl Hulley and Stanley Vandersall (Lincoln: University of Nebraska Press, 1970), 'Upon the Eighth Booke of Ovids Metamorphosis', 289. In his interpretation of the labyrinth, Sandys continues, 'By a Labyrinth the Antient deciphred the perplexed condition of man, combred and intangled with so many mischiefs: through which impossible to passe without the conduct of wisdome, and exercise of unfainting fortitude'.

[12] Ibid. 358. Translation of Latin ll. 162–8.

Angus Fletcher has elaborated on Northrop Frye's sense of the labyrinth as an image of 'lost direction' in this world, 'often with a monster at its heart', as opposed to 'the apocalyptic way or straight road, the highway in the desert for God prophesied by Isaiah'. Fletcher notes how the image of a labyrinth 'geometrizes some problems of state of mind':

> Losing the 'straight road' can occur for various reasons, but common to all is a psychological component. . . . The loss of direction is a lost *sense* of direction. The reader is asked to share in this mental experience, with all its attendant anxiety. We are not misled when sometimes the experience is vaguely pleasant or titillating as when, in the Renaissance and the seventeenth and eighteenth centuries, landscape becomes a high art and the maze becomes an adjunct to the formal garden. The literature describing this art, and using its associations for metaphoric purposes, tends always to emphasize the wandering, meandering, errant aspect of passage through the labyrinth. . . . One does not pass through a mazy scene unless one thinks one's way through it. The thinking of the labyrinth is the problem of the labyrinth. It is not so much a trial of strength as a kind of perceptual skill. The meandering passage promotes always a thinking into one's state of mind. To a degree the labyrinth leaves its traveler with nothing much but state of mind.[13]

The digressive writing in this book focuses our attention on the textual speaker's state of mind and process of thought, particularly on the evidence that the speaker does not forget. What contributes to a failed sense of orientation and direction in the midst of a labyrinth is a failure of memory, which is to say the absence of a place of perspective on the present—a discontinuity or disconnection between outside and inside the labyrinth, between past and present. 'The literature and art of the labyrinth (of virtually any type)', writes Fletcher, 'indicates that a sense of direction implies a continuous linkage with the past. The "faculty" that fails to work in the maze is memory'.[14] Hence, Ariadne's 'clue' or thread was less a device to help Theseus trace his way back out of the maze than his line of continuity with her and the outside. 'The maze it would seem, has an excessive presentness; it is a scene of too many instants, too much linear complexity', and the disorientation comes from losing an outside view on that complexity. The texts in this study unravel, to represent and view from the outside, a complexity within.

The ritual equestrian re-creations of a maze described at the close of the funeral games in Virgil's *Aeneid* 5. 588–95 or the intricate labyrinth

[13] Angus Fletcher, 'The Image of Lost Direction', in Eleanor Cook et al. (eds.), *Centre and Labyrinth: Essays in Honour of Northrop Frye.* (Toronto: University of Toronto Press, 1983), 330.

[14] Ibid. 339.

dances of Renaissance France and England duplicated the terrifying experience of loss of direction as 'a loss of clarity as to what "forward" means'. To move forward, Theseus was forced 'to keep reversing his direction, that is, he must go backward. The tighter the arc as he approaches the center, the more frequent will be this enforced "undoing" of the idea of forward motion'.[15] The dances emphasized as playful this progress built on repeatedly turning back before turning forward, a sinuosity whose danger Thomas Greene calls 'the Meander effect *in malo*':

> Not only does retro-progression frustrate all progress toward a goal, but its peril can also be perceived as distorting all the straight Aristotelian lines by which our western culture has taught us to organize our lives: . . . The peril of reversals, which can be described as the Meander effect *in malo*, diverts and entangles these lines, thus rendering explicit a half-conscious fear that human experience is indeed an entanglement of lines, of progressions, of sequences, we had been led to expect to remain distinct.[16]

Greene's discussion of labyrinth dances and their antecedents emphasizes the sense of joy and delight they induced both in dancers and spectators, a joy in the performance of human virtuosity as a symbolic representation of 'the superiority of human skill to the traps of contingency'.[17] The texts I discuss encourage a reader to sense the writer's energy and celebration of his skill. They are texts that celebrate the triumph of rhetorical turning and a connection to the past that allow the writers to tread safely the meanders of dangerous states of mind and sometimes of a national state lost for direction.

Of the twenty-four lines of Ovid's Latin text (152–76), from the return of King Minos to Theseus' transport of Ariadne to the island of Dia (Naxos), Ovid slows and dilates for ten lines to describe the labyrinth. Ovid's epic simile becomes a dallying, pastoral moment of digression: he compares Daedalus in the process of building a maze to the river Maeander that teases a straight line and 'seemes to play' and run races with 'himselfe' and 'his streame', changing direction as if never to reach the sea, the 'retro-progression' Greene describes of alternately turning back and forward. For the duration of Ovid's simile, to lose oneself making a complex artefact like a labyrinth or an epic poem resembles the play

[15] Angus Fletcher, 'The Image of Lost Direction', in Eleanor Cook et al. (eds.), *Centre and Labyrinth: Essays in Honour of Northrop Frye*. (Toronto: University of Toronto Press, 1983), 336.

[16] Thomas M. Greene, 'Labyrinth Dances in the French and English Renaissance', *Renaissance Quarterly*, 4 (2001), 1403–66, 1419–20.

[17] Ibid. 1458.

of nature that delights in change and the unpredictable. That over, six abrupt lines dispatch the rest of the plot (171–6)—from the appearance of Theseus to the abduction and abandonment of Ariadne. Ovid's narrative captures the casual, swift violence of martial Theseus to both minotaur and Ariadne, and the hero's efficiency contrasts with the pleasantly dilatory moments of the artisan, a homesick exile, unwinding the labyrinth from his brain.

Arthur Golding's heptameters from 1567 further expand the simile and edge the builder's dawdling, playful leisure with hints of danger of the loss of direction and self:

> And as with trickling streame the Brooke *Mæander* seemes to play
> In *Phrygia*, and with doubtfull race runnes counter to and fro,
> And meeting with himselfe doth looke if all his streame or no
> Come after, and retiring eft cleane backward to his spring
> And marching eft to open Sea as streight as any string,
> Indenteth with reversed streame: even so of winding wayes
> Unnumerable *Dædalus* within his worke convayes.
> Yea scarce himselfe could find the meanes to wind himselfe well out:
> So busie and so intricate the house was all about.[18]

The Renaissance translations by Golding and Sandys highlight that moment of play with Maeander; but such phrases as 'subtill ambages of sundry wayes' and 'Innumerable by-waies, which beguild | The troubled sense' do not allow us to forget the dark connections between the artist's labyrinth and the secret man-beast and death which Daedalus contains at the core. The labyrinth becomes an opportunity for Theseus, with Ariadne's help, to regain a heroic national identity; but for those who enter unaided the labyrinth quickly changes the potentially pleasant experience of meandering as if infinitely free to the frightening experience of losing one's way and one's self. The innumerable rooms within and the stifling domestic nature of the shame, menace, and power enclosed at their heart draw a parallel between the mazy human interiors of architecture and psyche, of prison, home, and the mind. Within elaborate textual architecture writers complexly housed and similarly controlled access to themselves, while displaying their power. Along passages of a literary labyrinth, the reader might wander in delight yet become bewildered.[19]

[18] *The. xv. Bookes of P. Ovidius Naso, entytuled Metamorphosis, translated oute of Latin into English meeter, by Arthur Golding Gentleman* (London: W. Seres, 1567), 8. 216–24.

[19] The palace of Whitehall in the 17th century housed and protected the king's body in London within a famous chaotic maze, 'a great rabbit warren of apartments, cubby holes and corridors maybe two thousand rooms in all', that kings manipulated to control access

Golding's rhyme of 'astray' and 'play' above (ll. 215, 216) reminds readers that Ovid has transported us astray with his simile. In this brief story of kings and family secrets locked 'In multitude of roomes, perplext, and blind', of subversive minors ('a virgins counsel') and a foreign conqueror, Ovid weaves a rich web of connections among power and obfuscation, gender and interiority. This labyrinthian suspension between delight and danger or transgression, between interiority and politics, between home and nation structures the digressive works of Donne, Browne, Marvell, Milton, and Dryden. These writers catch us in an uneasy space between the intense discomfort of Hobbes with digressions, noted earlier, and the pleasure of Dryden, in the epigraph, for wandering 'not always in the open field' but over a winding trail scattered with intellectual riches. The writers considered here play with a loss of direction and self in their texts, solicit the figure of a woman or a feminine nature to negotiate their twists and turns, and finally wrest a powerful, even a prophetic, voice from the depths of the maze.[20]

The past decade has seen a sharp revival of interest in rhetoric and rhetorical training among scholars across a number of disciplines—literature and composition, classics, art and architecture, history, even economics.[21] Yet while poets and scholars have long contemplated the

to themselves. See Brian Weiser, 'From Whitehall to Winchester: Charles II's Palaces', in Eveline Cruickshanks (ed.), *The Stuart Courts* (Striud: Sutton, 2000). The quoted description of Whitehall is from John Miller, *James II: A Study in Kingship* (Hove: Wayland, 1977), 38, cited in Professor Weiser's article.

[20] On early modern subjectivity and conceptions of the self, see Jonathan Sawday, 'Self and Selfhood in the Seventeenth Century', in Roy Porter (ed.), *Rewriting the Self: Histories from the Renaissance to the Present* (New York: Routledge, 1997), 29–48; Linda Gregerson, *The Reformation of the Subject: Spenser, Milton, and the English Protestant Epic* (Cambridge: Cambridge University Press, 1995); and Roger Chartier (ed.), *A History of Private Life, III: Passions of the Renaissance*, trans. Arthur Goldhammer (Cambridge, Mass., Belknap Press 1989).

The internal monologue of digression translates visual gaps and dramatic asides into non-dramatic texts and a very private form of spectatorship. Katharine Eisaman Maus has explored a rhetoric of inwardness, 'that within which passes show', in English Renaissance drama. See Katharine Eisaman Maus, *Inwardness and Theater in the English Renaissance* (Chicago: University of Chicago Press, 1995). She distinguishes her project, however, from an interest in subjectivity *per se* or the self and from psychoanalytic ways of thinking. Maus documents the distinction made between 'inside' and 'outside', between surface and depth, in the late 16th and early 17th centuries and argues that the Renaissance stage seems to 'foster theatergoers' capacity to use partial and limited presentations as a basis for conjecture about what is undisplayed or undisplayable. Its spectacles are understood to depend upon and indicate the shapes of things unseen'. Maus, *Inwardness*, 32.

[21] For a survey of approaches to rhetoric by contemporary disciplines, see John Bender and David Wellbery (eds.), *The Ends of Rhetoric: History, Theory, Practice* (Stanford, Calif.: Stanford University Press, 1990), 'Rhetoricality: On the Modernist Return of

figural power of metaphor, and John Lennard's *But I Digress* illumines brilliantly the rhetorical use of parenthetical statement in English verse, no one has studied the ancient figure of *digressio* that was attacked in the seventeenth century as expressive of moral, intellectual, and political weakness, of self-indulgence, in Swift's eyes finally of modernity's mad emptiness.[22] *Digressive Voices* explores how this rhetorical figure helped to focus around speech and eloquence the social and political anxieties of an age, exactly when a variety of historical forces were effecting a gradual, long-range shift from oral to print and market culture—from the prestige of oral performance and the immediacy of speaking and singing voices to a new public consciousness of the disembodied voices of books.[23] Donne, Marvell, Milton, Browne, and Dryden all learned

Rhetoric', 3–39. See also Renato Barilli, *Rhetoric*, trans. Giuliana Menozzi (Minneapolis: University of Minnesota Press, 1989), 102–29; and Brian Vickers, *In Defence of Rhetoric* (Oxford: Clarendon Press, 1988), esp. 435–79. On architecture as 'the rhetoric of building', see Lee Morrissey, *From the Temple to the Castle: An Architectural History of British Literature, 1660–1760* (Charlottesville: University Press of Virginia, 1999). Michael Hawcroft demonstrates the productivity of rhetoric to the reading of French literature in *Rhetoric: Readings in French Literature* (Oxford: Oxford University Press, 2000). See also Ronald H. Carpenter, *History as Rhetoric: Style, Narrative, and Persuasion* (Columbia: University of South Carolina Press, 1995); Richard A. Cherwitz, (ed.), *Rhetoric and Philosophy* (Hillsdale, NJ: L. Erlbaum Associates, 1990); Clifford Geertz, *Works and Lives: The Anthropologist as Author* (Stanford, Calif.: Stanford University Press, 1988); Donald N. McCloskey, *The Rhetoric of Economics* (Madison: University of Wisconsin Press, 1985).

[22] John Lennard, *But I Digress: The Exploitation of Parentheses in English Printed Verse* (Oxford: Clarendon Press, 1991).

[23] I refer to digression as a rhetorical 'figure', for it is included among the 'Figures Auricular' discussed by George Puttenham in *The Arte of English Poesie* (1589) and called a figure in other rhetorical handbooks of the period. Exactly what constitutes a figure as opposed to a scheme or a trope has vexed rhetoricians since antiquity; those questions will not constitute part of my study. See, for example, Quentin Skinner, *Reason and Rhetoric in the Philosophy of Hobbes* (Cambridge: Cambridge University Press, 1996), 50–1; Richard Lanham, *A Handlist of Rhetorical Terms*, 2nd edn. (Berkeley and Los Angeles: University of Clarendon Press, 1991), 154–7; and Erich Auerbach, 'Figura', in *Scenes from the Drama of European Literature: Six Essays* (Gloucester, Mass.: P. Smith, 1973). With Quintilian, I call the digression tentatively a figure of thought and, like Cicero, recognize that it qualifies as well as a rhetorical embellishment and as one of the parts of a classic oration. Among the ancients Quintilian cautiously calls digression a figure of thought, although he adds, 'some authorities regard it as forming one of the parts of a speech' (9. 2. 55). But later he notes that while Cicero included digression as a figure in *De Oratore* 3. 52: 201, in his later work, *Orator* 9.1.37, Cicero relegates digression to a stylistic embellishment (9. 3. 90). The main divisions of a speech vary in number according to authorities. Quintilian names five: the *exordium* or *prooemium*, the narration, the proof, the refutation, and the peroration (3. 9. 1 ff). The author of the *Rhetorica ad Herennium* adds a *divisio* or division which sets out the points agreed upon and those to be contested and which occurs between the narration and the refutation. The digression may come after the narration or after the division. *Paradiegesis* is a narrative digression often used to introduce an argument.

classical stylistics and languages as the basis of English composition; and Donne, Marvell, and Dryden wrote to win powerful patrons as had their classical predecessors, Virgil and Ovid. They worked as political and social minors—as hired tutors, secretaries, translators, eulogists, and political mythologists—for nobility, military generals, and kings. Yet for all of these writers their humanist training in rhetoric and multiple languages enabled them to create labyrinthine texts that could reach far above the heads of their patrons or of all but the most skilled readers.[24] Donne, Marvell, and Dryden worked to build complexity on command like the artisan Daedalus, who used his commission to test his skills and create a fabulous, bewildering artifice but who created also an underground home that reflected his geographic prison and emotional exile and entrapment. Like Ariadne they all stepped around authority and used the digression's meandering line to thread a labyrinth of passion.

I suggest further that the voluble male eloquence I examine seems to expand in the shadow of female or effeminate figures who, through associations with death, melancholy, or sacrifice, receive and absorb the poet's fears of weakness and marginality.[25] For a concrete historical parallel, one might turn to the traditions of ritual sexual inversion in early modern Europe, which allowed men to assume the disguised persona of disorderly females, as symbols of incapacity and insubordination but also of fertile power, for the purpose of social protest.[26] In the texts I consider,

[24] See, for example, John Hale, *Milton's Languages: The Impact of Multilingualism on Style* (Cambridge: Cambridge University Press, 1997). More generally, the scholarship of J. G. A. Pocock and Quentin Skinner has offered a useful methodology of reading early modern texts by suggesting a set of practices that illuminate the interrelations among linguistic and literary and political events and authority. Rosalie Colie's inclusionism and paradox can be read in relation to what Pocock and others have taught us about attention to the historicity and rhetoricity of language, its vocabularies and idioms. Of the extensive work by Pocock and those he has influenced, one might note Pocock's *Politics, Language, and Time* (New York: Atheneum, 1971); Kevin Sharpe and Steven N. Zwicker, 'Texts as Events: Reflections on the History of Political Thought', in *Politics of Discourse: The Literature and History of Seventeenth-Century England* (Berkeley and Los Angeles: University of California Press, 1987), 21–34, and, in that same volume, Michael McKeon, 'Politics of Discourses and the Rise of the Aesthetic in Seventeenth-Century England', 35–51. See also Kevin Sharpe, *Remapping Early Modern England: The Culture of Seventeenth-Century Politics* (Cambridge: Cambridge University Press, 2000), esp. 38–123. Of Quentin Skinner's work, see most recently *Liberty before Liberalism* (Cambridge: Cambridge University Press, 1998) and *Reason and Rhetoric*.

[25] Interestingly, in his translation of Ovid, Golding links King Minos and Ariadne with the word 'pollicie', with reference to his decision to build the labyrinth and her device of the 'clew' to navigate it. Father and daughter are both politic, he to ravel and she to unravel.

[26] Natalie Zemon Davis, 'Women on Top: Symbolic Sexual Inversion and Political Disorder in Early Modern Europe', in Barbara A. Babcock (ed.), *The Reversible World: Symbolic Inversion in Art and Society* (Ithaca, NY: Cornell University Press, 1972), 147–90.

young females or effeminate figures repeatedly enable the writer to reflect and deflect—through all the rhetorical complexity of digression—the political and emotional danger in the occasions for and into which he must compose his work.

Towards the end of the sixteenth century in the privacy of his estate, Montaigne warned his reader, 'I go out of my way, but rather by license than carelessness' and with 'no goal but a domestic and private one'.[27] In the seventeenth century, writers such as Marvell and Dryden had to serve themes of state and patron; yet other, more private, perspectives expand through their digressions 'rather by license than carelessness' and, like the labyrinth in Ovid's story, carry a disproportionate balance of the richness and authority of these texts. Narrative tactics of digression and excess, associated in traditional misogynist views with foolish or dangerous female speech, that of an Alisoun of Bath or a Duessa, prove to have less to do with biology than with vulnerability, uncertainty, and the need for subterfuge that crosses gender and class.[28] Within an embattled age, the underground movements of these passionate, strategically digressive narrators subtly control and shape their texts even as they appear to fragment them. After the Glorious Revolution brought William III and his printing press, and after Parliament's refusal in 1694 to extend the Licensing Act, 'the underground polemics, which had been available only to the daring as part of the extensive clandestine circulation of books and manuscripts during the Restoration, now joined the aboveground cultural mix'.[29] When the most intense religious polemic and fears of civil war, plots, and popery began to recede, replaced by the moral crusade of the Collier controversy and the battle between the ancients and moderns, the digressive, garrulous narrator seemed to emerge above ground in the

[27] Michel de Montaigne, *The Complete Essays of Montaigne*, trans. Donald M. Frame (Stanford, Calif.: Stanford University Press, 1958), 'To the Reader', 2.

[28] For the way that commonplace associations of women's public speech with promiscuity and their silence with chastity (wandering speech a reflection of dangerously promiscuous or foolish behaviour) exerted pressure on medieval and early modern women writers and public speakers to 'speak like a man', see two recent sourcebooks: Carolyne Larrington (ed.), *Women and Writing in Medieval Europe: A Sourcebook* (London: Routledge, 1995), and Kate Aughterson (ed.), *Renaissance Woman: A Sourcebook Constructions of Femininity in England* (London: Routledge, 1995). See also Carole Levin and Patricia A. Sullivan (eds.), *Political Rhetoric, Power, and Renaissance Women* (Albany, NY: SUNY Press, 1995).

[29] 'For example, a good portion of polemical poetry stretching back to the 1660s began to be printed in a virtually official set of volumes called *Poems on Affairs of State*'. Leo Braudy, 'Untuning the Century: The Missing Decade of the 1690s', in Elaine Scarry (ed.), *Fins de Siècle: English Poetry in 1590, 1690, 1790, 1890, 1990* (Baltimore: Johns Hopkins University Press, 1995), 72.

eighteenth century, with a larger, more self-conscious, stylized profile to help shape the miscellany, interiority, and broad appeal for both sexes of the modern novel.

TEXTS AS BATTLEFIELDS

The digression becomes a weapon of both aggressive and defensive force in the texts studied here. Earlier we recalled that George Puttenham, in *The Arte of English Poesie*, characterizes *digressio* as the 'Straggler', which could mean vagabond or a disorderly foot soldier 'that marches out of his array';[30] and the military character of Puttenham's *digressio* reminds us of the historically close, widely documented connection between the strategies of oratory and those of physical combat and conquest or war.[31] In the classical world, the crucial male disciplines for survival were the art of speaking, or rhetoric, and the art of fighting.[32] Achilles was trained as 'a rhetor of speech and a doer of deeds' (*Iliad* 9. 443)—'the earliest extant mention of "rhetor" in Homer's works'.[33] Drawing on the close link between epic fighting and speaking, classical rhetoricians identified and assembled figures of speech, their battery of weapons, from epic and other narrative fiction.[34] Quintilian urges the student of eloquence to

[30] Puttenham, *The Arte of English Poesie*, III. xix. 240.

[31] See, for example, Wayne A. Rebhorn, *The Emperor of Men's Minds: Literature and the Renaissance Discourse of Rhetoric* (Ithaca, NY: Cornell University Press, 1995), esp. ch. 1, 'Bound to Rule', 23–79.

[32] See, for example, M. L. Clarke, *Rhetoric at Rome: A Historical Survey* (New York: Routledge, 1996), p. ix. See especially Skinner, *Reason and Rhetoric*, 48–51. Figures from medieval sagas, such as the warrior-poet Egill Skallagrímsson of *Egils saga*, also come to mind.

[33] Cheryl Glenn, *Rhetoric Retold: Regendering the Tradition from Antiquity through the Renaissance* (Carbondale: Southern Illinois University Press, 1997), 20.

[34] Primary models of narrative, and of narrative wandering, such as Homer's *Iliad* and *Odyssey*, not only open in the middle of an action, which challenges the sense of a cohesive, closed, structure of a story with a clear beginning and end, but also use digressions to supply background and information in a system of 'interlocking concentric circles' that represent in a given moment the intersection of multiple dimensions of time and, in the history of men, 'a pattern of contingencies'. Kirk, 'The Digression', 18. 'Evidently . . . for the ancient reader the epic digressions or introduced tales suggestively or allusively referred to a body of tradition so that the presence of the digression brought about a confluence of associations which added greatly increased significance and dimension'. Early in the Western tradition, therefore, poets used digressions to open up time in order to bring together, or orchestrate, into resonance the simultaneous, multiple associations of a single moment. Later digressive Greek romances best known to Renaissance writers date from the Alexandrian period, at about the beginning of the Christian era, and include *Aethiopica* by Heliodorus, *Leucippe and Clithophon* by Achilles Tatius, and *Daphnis and Chloe* by Longus. Also to the early Christian era belong the anti-heroic or picaresque Roman tale, the *Satyricon* of Petronius and *The Golden Ass* of Apuleius. Kirk, 'The Digression', 21–6.

study Homer carefully for 'his similes, his amplifications, his illustrations, digressions, indications of fact, inferences, and all the other methods of proof and refutation which he employs'.[35] The term *ornatus*, used by Cicero, Quintilian, and the author of the *Ad Herennium* to refer to rhetorical ornament or the ornate quality of language, was also 'the word ordinarily used to describe the weapons and accoutrements of war. To be properly *ornatus* was to be equipped for battle, powerfully armoured and protected. The rhetoricians claim that the "ornaments" characteristic of the Grand Style are *not* mere decorations or embellishments; they are weapons an orator must learn to wield if he is to have any prospect of winning the war of words'.[36] Quintilian writes of the young orator whom his handbook addresses, 'in view of the fact that the battles of the forum that await him are not few, let him strive for victory in the schools and learn how to strike the vitals of his foe and protect his own' (5. 12. 22).

Cicero claimed that the ability to amplify a speech with ornament represented the highest measure of distinction in eloquence, for amplification was the most effective weapon for arousing emotion—the pre-eminent achievement of the great orator (*De Oratore* 3.104–5). The word *ornatus* could refer also to an ornament of dress or attire, so that it points in the direction of battle but also of luxury, to the masculine but also conceivably to the effeminate or feminine. In book 8 of the *Institutio Oratoria*, where Quintilian discusses rhetorical ornament, he emphasizes that the ornament of eloquent speech must 'be bold, manly and chaste, free from all effeminate smoothness and the false hues derived from artificial dyes, and must glow with health and vigour' (8. 3. 7).[37] He compares a shapely horse and shapely athlete to an elegant speech in order to make the point that 'true beauty and usefulness always go hand in hand' (8. 3. 11)—beauty has the power of skilled, victorious action. When discussing the use of history for orators, Quintilian finds it 'permissible to borrow the graces of history', which he considers 'a kind of prose poem'

[35] Quintilian adds about Homer, 'the majority of writers on the principles of rhetoric have gone to his works for examples of all these things' (10. 1. 49). Cicero called reading 'the well-spring of perfect eloquence' (*Brutus*, 322). Cicero, *Brutus*, trans. G. L. Hendrickson, Loeb (London: W. Heinemann, 1971).

[36] Skinner, *Reason and Rhetoric*, 49.

[37] Quintilian's Latin reads, 'Sed hic ornatus (repetam enim) virilis et fortis et sanctus sit nec effeminatam levitatem et fuco ementitum colorem amet, sanguine et viribus niteat'. Citations of the Latin text and English translation of Quintilian refer to the Loeb edition of the *Institutio Oratoria*, trans. H. E. Butler (Cambridge, Mass.: Harvard University Press, 1995–8).

('Est enim proxima poetis et quoddammodo carmen solutum', 10. 1. 31), 'to embellish our digressions, provided always that we remember that in those portions of our speech which deal with the actual question at issue we require not the swelling thews of the athlete, but the wiry sinews of the soldier, and that the cloak of many colours which Demetrius of Phalerum was said to wear is but little suited to the dust and heat of the forum' (10. 1. 33). Quintilian's concern to distinguish true eloquence, 'manly' and 'bold' ('virilis et fortis'), from 'effeminate smoothness' ('effeminatam levitatem'), a distinction important to seventeenth-century writers as well, underlines rhetoric's beginning in ancient poetry as the noble male warrior's intangible power: a skill in words as with swords to effect action. To ensure that the difference between tangible weapons of steel and airy weapons of breath, between exterior and interior powers, does not reflect the binary of gender, the interior skill is modelled on a hero's readiness for physical combat. The poet may need 'to take refuge in certain by-ways of expression' (Quintilian gives the poet greater freedom with figures of speech), but 'the orator stands armed in the forefront of the battle, fights for a high stake and devotes all his effort to winning the victory. . . . I would not have his weapons defaced by mould and rust, but would have them shine with a splendour that shall strike terror to the heart of the foe, like the flashing steel that dazzles heart and eye at once, not like the gleam of gold or silver, which has no warlike efficacy' (10. 1. 29–30). Yet along with steely words, the orator wields figurative weapons that combine power and sweetness in order to arouse and capture the listener's emotions, a subject we return to later.

Like their classical predecessors, Renaissance rhetoricians considered language a weapon. In the dedicatory epistle of Henry Peacham's *Garden of Eloquence* (1593), for example, the writer calls figures of speech 'martiall instruments both of defence & invasion', good weapons to have 'always readie in our handes'. Published in Hanover in 1608, Bartholomew Keckermann's *Systema Rhetorices* refers to a good argument as 'like an *aries*, or "battering ram" (*Systema*, 144), and the right disposition of one's arguments like an *acies*, a battle formation' (121).[38] Early modern writers, who combined Quintilian's poet and orator, conscripted figures of speech, including digression, to defend themselves on what they steadily represented as textual battlefields: 'For a wise poet, like a wise General', writes Sir William Davenant in 1650, 'will not shew his

[38] The citations from Peacham and Keckermann appear in Rebhorn, *Emperor of Men's Minds*, 41. For further examples of Renaissance rhetoricians who use imagery of war to characterize the work of eloquence, see his 41–5.

strengths till they are in exact government and order, which are not the postures of chance, but proceed from Vigilance and labour'.[39] In his gloss on Ovid's tale of the Cretan maze, George Sandys observes that the minotaur was a symbol for the Roman army's most strategic and dangerous secrets wrapped in labyrinthine 'darknesse':

> the Romans bore a Minotaure in their ensignes, to declare that the counsels and stratagems of a General should be muffled in the unsearchable darknesse of secresy, such as not to be traced or discovered by the Enemy—nay often to be concealed from their neerest friends, according to that saying of Metellus. If I thought that my shirt knew my purpose, I would teare it from my body.[40]

The digressions in seventeenth-century texts similarly enfold and lead to a variety of 'counsels and stratagems'. Moreover the arts of combative oratory and of preaching had become entwined, so that Puritan William Chappell would urge that preachers learn to 'insinuate something either hiddenly or openly, whereby we may possess the hearers affections, and by them, as by setting scaling ladders invade the fort of the mind'.[41]

In the Renaissance, when the learning of Latin and rhetoric usually meant the removal of the male child out of the home into the masculine world of school, of mental toughening, the arts of speaking and fighting were twinned early in life. As Juliet Dusinberre argues, the

> teaching of rhetoric through disputation encouraged combative habits of mind which could later be fed into practical skills on the battlefield. Even in a peacetime environment the persuasive arts of rhetoric were part of a structure of competitive public display which the young male child learnt as soon as he entered school and which became as natural to him as breathing.[42]

Part of competitive rhetorical training, in antiquity and in Renaissance England, was to learn to argue both sides of a case, what Cicero called *argumentum in contrarias parte* or *in utramque partem*.[43] Milton's Latin

[39] Sir William Davenant, 'Preface to *Gondibert*', in Joel E. Spingarn (ed.), *Critical Essays of the Seventeenth Century*, vol. ii (Oxford: Clarendon Press, 1908), 25.

[40] Sandys, *Orid's 'Metamorphoses'*, 289.

[41] As Wayne Rebhorn has argued, by the Renaissance those to be persuaded and defeated were less other rhetors and judges than a broad audience of listeners whose hearts and minds might be ruled. See Rebhorn, *Emperor of Men's Minds*, 42–3, who cites William Chappell, *The Preacher, or The Art and Method of Preaching* (London: Edw. Farnham, 1656), 145.

[42] Juliet Dusinberre, *Virginia Woolf's Renaissance: Woman Reader or Common Reader?* (Iowa City: University of Iowa Press, 1997), 47–8.

[43] See Skinner, *Reason and Rhetoric*, 9–10, 97–9; Skinner, 'Moral Ambiguity and the Renaissance Art of Eloquence', *Essays in Criticism*, 44 (1994), 267–92; and Thomas O. Sloane, 'Schoolbooks and Rhetoric: Erasmus's *Copia*', *Rhetorica*, 9 2 (Spring 1991), 117.

prolusions belong to the tradition of such exercises that test the persuasive brilliance, not the truth, of an argument. The moral ambiguity of the rhetorical arts, available like mercenaries to fight any cause, had troubled thinkers since Plato, and not least in sixteenth- and seventeenth-century England.[44] Yet two-faced Janus was a popular Renaissance emblem 'of a person, usually a skeptic, who can see both sides of any question'.[45] In an age fraught by the polarization of ideology and the demand to take sides, the usefulness of digression's stepping aside may have resided, as Ross Chambers has emphasized about the figure, in the way the movement facilitates a shift to another or third perspective: out of the knowledge of one's lack of knowledge, and out of scepticism or irony about the constructed, ideological nature of all discursive positions.[46] Digression in the texts I examine, for example in Sir Thomas Browne's prose or Marvell's poem, facilitates an oblique way of seeing, an alternative perspective and hidden or peripheral or forbidden vision—a kind of voyeurism.[47] At once a camouflage of movement but also of vision, digression leads both reader and spectator into and through a mental landscape to the crux of the composing mind. Landscapes under threat of attack abound in seventeenth-century literature, and digression and divergence serve as devices for psychological, political, and poetic survival—and attack.[48]

The digressive literary landscapes of the seventeenth century become battlefields where the dazzling but pragmatic power of rhetorical art can effect a writer's figurative and literal survival. When the male poets whom I study wrote from positions of vulnerability, disfranchisement, or subservience, their training gave them a crucial competitive edge: their

[44] See Skinner, *Reason and Rhetoric* and 'Moral Ambiguity'. Thomas Sprat, author of *The History of the Royal Society of London* (London: J. Martyn etc., 1667), would banish the ornamental armoury of deceitful eloquence from 'all civil Societies' if it were not for the fact that eloquence 'is a Weapon which may be as easily procur'd by bad men as good, and that, if these should onely cast it away, and those retain it, the naked Innocence of vertue would be upon all occasions expos'd to the armed Malice of the wicked'. Spingarn (ed.), *Critical Essays of the Seventeenth Century*, 116.

[45] Sloane, 'Schoolbooks and Rhetoric', 117.

[46] Chambers, *Loiterature*, particularly ch. 10, 'Reading and Being Read (On Being Pedestrian)', 270–92.

[47] James Elkins, *The Poetics of Perspective* (Ithaca, NY: Cornell University Press, 1994), has reminded us that Renaissance perspective, rather than the solemn unifying principle of pictorial (and literary) space of later theory, was rather a collection of methods, a plural and playful concept concerned with drawing objects rather than 'excavating space'.

[48] See, for example, Geoffrey Hill, *The Enemy's Country: Words, Contexture, and other Circumstances of Language* (Stanford, Calif.: 1991). See also Steven N. Zwicker, *Lines of Authority: Politics and English Literary Culture, 1649–1689* (Ithaca, NY: Cornell University Press, 1993), esp. ch. 1, 9–36.

textual mazes created spaces in which they might anatomize safely their political enemies and simultaneously introduce and conceal personal concerns. In the seventeenth century, not only does the garden of England become a battlefield, as Marvell mourns in *Upon Appleton House*, but so does the printed page. The 'flowers' of rhetoric, the figures and ornaments of speech, including digression, become conscripted for aggressive and defensive manœuvres. Puttenham's delinquent 'Straggler' becomes a surprising dark horse whose apparent weakness proves a source of authority. His English epithets for other 'Figures Auricular' suggest the dangerous arena of listening, spying, speaking, and silence into which writers circulated their texts: the poet may call on 'Hiperbaton, or the trespasser', 'Prozeugma, or the ringleader', 'Antitheton, or the quarreller, otherwise called the overthwart or rencounter', 'Noema, or the figure of close conceit', 'Prosopopeia, or the false impersonation', and 'Periphrasis, or the figure of ambage', to name a few.[49]

Digressions diffuse the pressure to act precipitously, yet they precipitate action obliquely forward. In resisting time's urgency, allowing breathing room, and opening up a field of play that indirectly enables survival, the digressive texts of these chapters employ strategies of pleasure reminiscent of those of Scheherazade, 'for whom', according to Richard Regosin, 'speaking alone forestalled death'.[50] Indeed digressions have been associated in literature less with battlefields than with play and time out, like the moment described earlier of Ovid's Daedalus dallying within the evolving labyrinth or Dryden's sweet pleasure, with which we began, of wandering among the variety of a richly stocked mind. The impulse to prolong the delights of thought by moving not forward but laterally or obliquely characterizes, too, the voice of *The Garden of Cyrus* at the beginning of the fourth chapter: 'As for the delights, commodities, mysteries, with other concernments of this order, we are unwilling to fly them over . . . and shall therefore enlarge with additional ampliations'.

49 Puttenham, *Arte of English Poesie*, 318–20.

50 Richard Regosin has observed of Montaigne that he 'always writes in the face of death . . . he is always writing to face up to death in the form of absence and in a sense to face it down. I am reminded in this context of Scheherazade, for whom speaking alone forestalled death. As long as there were words there was breath, and the teller of tales—both speaker and writer—was able to postpone the inevitable silence and nothingness of the end. . . . Foucault saw the self-reflexive nature of language itself as the hedge against death'. Richard L. Regosin, *Montaigne's Unruly Brood: Textual Engendering and the Challenge to Paternal Authority* (Berkeley and Los Angeles: University of California Press, 1996), 39, who refers to Foucault's essay 'Language into Infinity', in *Language, Counter-Memory, Practice: Selected Essays and Interviews*, ed. D. F. Bouchard, trans. D. F. Bouchard and S. Simon (Ithaca, NY: Cornell University Press, 1977).

Digressions promise the expansive pleasures of variety and a 'sweet surplus of truth' where less would not be enough, or the freedom to expand illogically 'under the guise of a pause, a rest, or delay'.[51] Note the playful flight of the extended simile that opens Robert Burton's 'Digression of the Air' in *The Anatomy of Melancholy* whose image of 'ample fields of Ayre' highlights the connections among digression, breathing room, and mental airspace, between long-winded and long-winged travel. The hawk 'for his pleasure' circles before he plunges:

> As a long-winged Hawke when hee is first whistled off the fist, mounts aloft, and for his pleasure fetcheth many a circuit in the Ayre . . . so will I, having now come at last into these ample fields of Ayre, wherein I may freely expatiate and exercise my selfe, for my recreation a while rove, wander round about the world, mount aloft to those aethereall orbes and celestiall spheres, and so descend to my former elements againe.[52]

Digression and pastoral have been paired at least since Virgil's *Eclogues*.[53] Here Burton evokes meandering country play while he transmutes narrative roving to a brief moment of natural, even epic, freedom.[54] But after the hawk takes his pleasure in first mounting and circling about, he descends swiftly to kill.

Pressures of disjunction in the public sphere may become inflected as the private disjunctions of literary forms that appear deliberately hard to grasp and attack. Literary digression thus functions to evade the confines and dead ends of political and social dichotomy. To dodge the breathlessness of verbal exhaustion or entrapment on polemical matters and

[51] A 'sweet surplus of truth' refers to the splendidly digressive, encyclopedic volumes composed by Franciscus Junius while librarian to Thomas Howard, Earl of Arundel, in the 1620s and 1630s; see the introduction to Franciscus Junius, *The Painting of the Ancients (De Pictura Veterum)*, ed. Keith Aldrich et al. (Berkeley and Los Angeles: University of California Press, 1991), p. liii. For the second quoted reference to digression, see Paul M. Curtis, 'Byron's *Beppo*: Digression and Contingency', *Dalhousie Review*, 73 1 (1993), 18–33, 21.

[52] Robert Burton, *The Anatomy of Melancholy*, ed. Thomas C. Faulkner et al., 3 vols. (Oxford: Clarendon Press, 1989), ii. 33.

[53] Dryden, the Restoration's great student of Virgil, continues after the passage that is my epigraph, 'The best quarry lies not always in the open field: And who would not be content to follow a good Huntsman over Hedges and Ditches when he knows the Game will reward his pains?' See also his preface to *Fables Ancient and Modern* for reference again to Montaigne's digressiveness and to the mind's wandering as the delightful hunt for game within an overstocked mind. *The Works of John Dryden*, vol. vii, ed. Vinton A. Dearing (Berkeley and Los Angeles: University of California Press, 2000), 24–47, esp. 31 and 37.

[54] Raymond Williams, *The Country and the City* (New York: Oxford University Press, 1973), 260. Paul Alpers (*What is Pastoral?* (Chicago: University of Chicago Press, 1996), 241) discusses 'inclusiveness' as 'the hallmark of the major first-person pastorals' of the 17th century.

not be silenced, to show infinite linguistic resources and authority, could mean literary and political life instead of death's breathlessness.

These digressions work their life-giving power by incorporating the disorder and loss of self against which they strive. They redress the pressures of the political over-world by soliciting an underworld, as does the tutor of *Upon Appleton House* who descends to the meadows and woods or the *Anniversaries*' narrator to death's dissolution. *Paradise Lost* is a model for their anticlimactic, paradoxical experience of the digression whose step aside into physical dissolution or humiliation perpetuates movement and breath. There is a near death, mortality looms, but life also continues. The immediate end anticipated by Adam and Eve, and Satan, does not come, although innocence has died.

DIGRESSION AND EFFEMINACY

Inflections of gender subtly colour the characterization of these speakers and their narrative movements. The constant care of rhetoricians and speakers to distinguish and distance bold and manly speech from Circean seduction and the effeminate run from antiquity through the Renaissance. Equally consistent across time are the potential associations of highly figurative poetry and prose, along with the amplification of digression and other modes of copious speech, with the feminine. Cicero's contemporaries who claimed to imitate the terse Attic school of oratory attacked his highly ornamental Grand Style, in Quintilian's words, as 'bombastic, Asiatic, redundant, given to excessive repetition . . . sensuous, extravagant and (an outrageous accusation!) almost effeminate in his rhythm' (12. 10. 12–13). (Note the emotional parenthesis with exclamation point that the translator adds to open but strictly contain what he marks as a potentially digressive eruption of passion.[55]) Miriam Brody notes that Quintilian composed his *Institutio Oratoria* on the education and training of orators for the bar when the Senecan declamatory style of the period 'promoted a florid, excessively gestured and nuanced delivery that Quintilian . . . reviled'.[56] In book 5, where he discusses argumentation and proof, Quintilian creates the spectre of a eunuch to represent the decadent, heavily ornamented, painted, and effeminized style of declamation against which he proposed a manly, vigorous art of words:

[55] John Lennard has explored brilliantly the digressive life of parentheses in *But I Digress.*

[56] Miriam Brody, *Manly Writing. Gender, Rhetoric, and the Rise of Composition* (Carbondale: Southern Illinois University Press, 1993), 14.

> indeed, declaimers are guilty of exactly the same offence as slave-dealers who castrate boys in order to increase the attractions of their beauty. For just as the slave-dealer regards strength and muscle, and above all, the beard and other natural characteristics of manhood as blemishes, and softens down all that would be sturdy if allowed to grow, on the ground that it is harsh and hard, even so we conceal the manly form of eloquence and power of speaking closely and forcibly by giving it a delicate complexion of style and, so long as what we say is smooth and polished, are absolutely indifferent as to whether our words have any power or no. . . . Consequently, although this debauched eloquence (for I intend to speak with the utmost frankness) may please modern audiences by its effeminate and voluptuous charms, I absolutely refuse to regard it as eloquence at all: for it retains not the slightest trace of purity and virility in itself, not to say of these qualities in the speaker. . . . Shall we then, who are endeavoring to mould the ideal orator, equip eloquence not with weapons but with timbrels? (Book 5. 12. 17–21)

For Quintilian effeminate speech like 'timbrels', represented by the slave eunuch, and the speech of a vigorous and virtuous man were two kinds of language. The student must be aware of the dangers of the use of ornamentation to seduce and soften both speaker and listener.

Besides heavy use of ornamentation, another dangerously effeminate habit of speech to Quintilian is talk in an uncontrolled, disorderly stream. Quintilian emphasized that an orator's inspired improvisation, whose orderly, ornate fluency reflected long rhetorical study, was distinct from 'a continuous flow of random talk, such as I note streams in torrents even from the lips of women when they quarrel' (10. 7. 13). In Shakespeare's *I Henry IV* Northumberland scolds his son Hotspur for provoking King Henry by self-indulgent railing in his angry 'woman's mood, | Tying thine ear to no tongue but thine own' (I. i. 236–7). In the seventeenth century when politics and stylistics could become almost indistinguishable, writers often reflect an uncertainty or defensiveness about the relative power of even the most masterful language, which must unfold over time, to act with a force comparable to the split-second force of a blow. One thinks of Hamlet's anguished attempt to play word against deed, speak daggers against real ones, and his condemnation of womanish words and himself that 'Must like a whore unpack my heart with words | And fall a-cursing like a very drab' (II. ii. 571–2). His similes of disgust reflect how a too open mouth might signal the dangerous sexual openness and appetite, or weakness before male violence, of which he accused his mother and Ophelia. His military double, Fortinbras, appears at the end ironically to 'Bear Hamlet like a soldier to the stage' and play 'the soldiers' music and the rites of war' (V. ii. 385, 388).

Quintilian's concerns about excessive ornamentation resurface in the Renaissance when the explosion of English style manuals in the sixteenth and seventeenth centuries reflected an intense interest and debate around the use of rhetorical ornamentation in the vernacular.[57] Although dominated by masculine equestrian figures that climax in the poet astride Pegasus, Sir Philip Sidney's *A Defence of Poesy* (1595) employs images of two contrasting women—the classical matron Lady Rhetoric and the courtesan—to distinguish true eloquence from eloquence dressed with excessive, borrowed, or shopworn ornaments: 'So is that honey-flowing matron Eloquence apparelled, or rather disguised, in a courtesan-like painted affectation', and the gaudy ornaments that follow include 'far-fet words', excessive alliteration, and 'figures and flowers, extremely winter-starved'.[58] Puttenham cautions, for example, about the use of *metalepsis* which he calls 'the Far-fet' or far-fetcher, one of the figures like digression and metaphor which simulate physical transport: 'And it seemeth the deviser of this figure, had a desire to please women rather than men: for we use to say by manner of Proverbe: things farrefet and deare bought are good for Ladies'.[59]

That writing appropriate for, and mimetic of, female softness and love of the far-fetched is distinct from writing described as 'vigorous' and 'sinewy', appropriate for manly men, becomes a commonplace of seventeenth-century stylistics. Fifty years ago Donald Davie drew attention to the distinction made by seventeenth-century poets and critics, from Jonson through to Dryden, between 'strength' and 'ease' of poetic lines and the associations of these two terms with masculine and feminine qualities and readers, respectively—also with the masculine labour and fertility of a professional writer and the effeminate idleness of a dilettante.[60] In this seventeenth-century revision of the noble ease of Castiglione's and Sidney's *sprezzatura*, strong, manly lines become abrupt, even dissonant, and fiery, while smoothly flowing lines and soft sounds come to be associated with a feminine or an effeminate, often courtly and compromised, world, or with lower-class pretensions to high

[57] See, for example, Wayne A. Rebhorn (ed.), *Renaissance Debates on Rhetoric* (Ithaca, NY: Cornell University Press, 2000) and *Emperor of Men's Minds*; and Vickers, *In Defence of Rhetoric*, 294–339. For further references on this topic, see Ch. 1 n. 42.

[58] Sir Philip Sidney, 'Defence of Poesie', in *Sir Philip Sidney*, ed. Katharine Duncan-Jones (Oxford: Oxford University Press, 1989), 246, ll. 1397–8. On Renaissance iconography of Lady Rhetoric, see Rebhorn, *Emperor of Men's Minds*, 64.

[59] Puttenham, *Arte of English Poesie*, 193.

[60] Donald, Davie, *Purity of Diction in English Verse* (Oxford: Oxford University Press, 1953), 199–206.

style. Jonson sneered at shallow versifiers, 'Womens-Poets they are call'd; as you have womens-Taylors. . . . You may sound these wits, and find the depth of them, with your middle finger. They are Creame-bowle, or but puddle deepe'.[61]

Donne aspired to a poetic line of sinewy strength yet practised digressions and courted and transcended associations with feminine weakness by claiming God's Word as his model. Ensnared in the toils of illness, Donne defended the godly mystery of rhetorical amplification, the 'voyages' and 'peregrinations' and 'extensions' of high style, against Puritan distrust of figurative language:

my God, thou art a direct God, may I not say a literal God, a God that wouldst be understood literally and according to the plain sense of all that thou sayest? But thou art also (Lord, I intend it to thy glory, and let no profane misinterpreter abuse it to thy diminution), thou art a figurative, a metaphorical God too; a God in whose words there is such a height of figures, such voyages, such peregrinations to fetch remote and precious metaphors, such extensions, such spreadings, such curtains of allegories, such third heavens of hyperboles, so harmonious elocutions . . . such sinews even in thy milk, and such things in thy words, as all profane authors seem of the seed of the serpent that creeps, thou art the dove that flies.[62]

The physical representation of gender in language as 'sinews' and 'milk' is startling. The masculine two-syllable word bends and shapes, while the feminine flows and feeds; God becomes an androgynous yet transcendent creator, 'the dove that flies'. Thomas Carew's elegy on Donne (1633) likewise joins images of vast inner wealth and fertility and hard physical labour in his praise of a manly Donne who, despite all of his addresses to and ventriloquy of women, opened and mined his own strain of 'rich and pregnant fancy' to write lines 'Of masculine expression'. His strong, sinewy wit bent into poetry the 'stubborn' and 'tough thick-ribbed' English vernacular, while the present bankrupt 'libertines in poetry' only lisp 'soft, melting phrases'. Copious invention, productivity, and hard labour were signs of masculine fertility and vigour as well for Dryden, who consistently praised and aligned his personal taste with the fiery 'masculine' originality and potency of Homer and Juvenal. Yet his references to the poets he translated most—chiefly Virgil but also Horace and Ovid—express paradoxically a more complex attraction to a mixture of

[61] 'Timber, or, Discoveries', ll. 707–30, in Ben Jonson, *Ben Jonson*, ed. Ian Donaldson (Oxford: Oxford University Press, 1985), 540–1.

[62] John Donne, *Devotions upon Emergent Occasions, Together with Death's Duel* (Ann Arbor: University of Michigan Press, 1959), opening lines of XIX Expostulation, 124.

strength and weakness, the masculine and feminine. He appeared to locate male and female in himself as the styles of other poets whom he admired or criticized; yet behind the cover of these literary 'fathers', his late digressive style pushed against and redrew the sharp lines of gender, allowing personal grievance and confession of weakness to sit beside bold critical authority.[63]

Dorothy Stephens observes that in the Renaissance 'the unquestioning assumption' of Aristotle's long-favoured conception of 'woman's unstable intellect, morals and body' as wanderers had begun to wane. Yet

> the very fact that the nature of woman was more genuinely disputed than it had been for millennia seemed in a sense to emphasize that women were indeed erratic, making them the perfect representation of a man's inner turmoil and self-evasion. And the fact that Elizabethans' obsessions with secrecy and spying extended to a paranoia about what women thought or talked about when men weren't around meant that the male poet's relationship with his feminine inner self, who was largely hidden even from himself, involved complexities of voyeurism, desire, wooing, and teasing.[64]

I examine male authors whose digressions suggest an 'inner self' that inhabits the perspective of the weak and marginal, and they take as a subject or speak for a host of female or weakened male figures: for example, Donne and Elizabeth Drury; Marvell and Isabel Thwaites, Mary Fairfax, and most mysteriously 'the subtle' nun; Milton and the Lady of *Comus*, Eve, and later the seduced, humiliated Sampson; Dryden and Anne

[63] In his dedicatory letter to Sir Robert Howard preceding 'Annus Mirabilis', Dryden is most contradictory about Virgil whom he claims to be his 'master in this poem' and whose mixed qualities of heroic grandeur and softness appear crucial to the young English poet's presentation and defence of his own writing. Comparing Ovid's and Virgil's ability to render characters', and especially women's, turbulence of mind and passion, he notes, 'Virgil speaks not so often to us in the person of another, like Ovid, but in his own; he relates almost all things as from himself, and thereby gains more liberty than the other to express his thoughts with all the graces of elocution, . . . and to confess as well the labour as the force of his imagination'. Liberty, force, and labour of imagination, characterize the art of masculine Virgil. In the next paragraph, he discusses a writer's choice among styles of imagery and sets up a dichotomy as he compares Juvenal's with Virgil's. He notes, 'if some of them are to be like those of Juvenal, *stantes in curribus aemiliani*, heroes drawn in their triumphal chariots, and in their full proportion; others are to be like that of Virgil, *spirantia mollius aera*: there is somewhat more of softness and tenderness to be shown in them'. Virgil's softness becomes promptly woven into Dryden's defence against critics that 'I did *humi serpere*' in his verses to the Duchess of York; he argues that he 'affected the softness of expression' and 'smoothness of measure' exactly appropriate to address a lady. John Dryden, *John Dryden*, ed. Keith Walker (Oxford: Oxford University Press, 1987), 27, 29.

[64] Dorothy Stephens, *The Limits of Eroticism in Post-Petrarchan Narrative: Conditional Pleasure from Spenser to Marvell* (Cambridge: Cambridge University Press, 1998), 10.

Killigrew, Eleonora, Anne Hyde, the Duchess of Ormonde, and those eloquent female beasts, the Hind and the Panther, whose ladylike composure struggles to subdue animal instinct. The feminine subject that the male writer may address, praise, or ventriloquize appears to allow him access to otherwise inexpressible feelings of sadness and loss, vulnerability and threat, rage and transgressive freedom. These feelings are then folded through digression into complicated masculine tones of hostility, condescension, and competition.

Psychoanalytic and feminist critics from Freud and Lacan to Kristeva have made us aware of gender in the psychology of melancholy and mourning.[65] Juliana Schiesari's *The Gendering of Melancholia: Feminism, Psychoanalysis, and the Symbolics of Loss in Renaissance Literature* and Lynn Enterline's *The Tears of Narcissus: Melancholia and Masculinity in Early Modern Writing*, for example, suggest ways to think about the aggressively voluble, digressive writing that I examine in relation to the Renaissance convention articulated by Marsilio Ficino of the male artist as *homo melancholicus*, a talking subjectivity based on the cultivation of suffering and lack—'the privileged site for a nobility of spirit whose specialness is distinguished by the gift of illness'.[66] The melancholy nobleman offered a dignified model for the masculine expression of feelings of loss and sorrow: the Renaissance melancholic, most exquisitely embodied in Schesari's book by Torquato Tasso and Hamlet, mourned 'a finitude whose expression presupposed its reconnection to an exhilarating infinitude, coupled with a heightened awareness of the self as "different" from the common *vulgus* and by virtue of this difference, extraordinary'.[67] Donne, Marvell, Milton, and Dryden claimed emotional and intellectual distinction from the '*vulgus*' and wrote around a lack—if not literally of a father, then of recognition or adoption by a patriarch or of a distinction within a competitive patriarchal culture. Their voices wound around the danger of being silenced, a fate often represented as the silence of dead or sacrificed women.

According to Schiesari, the '*discourse* of melancholia has historically designated a topos of expressibility for men and has accordingly given them a means to express their sorrows in a less alienated way, while rele-

[65] See Julia Kristeva, *Black Sun: Depression and Melancholia*, trans. Leon S. Roudiez (New York: Columbia University Press, 1989) and *The Kristeva Reader*, ed. Toril Moi (New York: Columbia University Press, 1986).

[66] Juliana Schiesari, *The Gendering of Melancholia: Feminism, Psychoanalysis, and the Symbolics of Loss in Renaissance Literature* (Ithaca, NY: Cornell University Press, 1992), 261.

[67] Ibid. 19.

gating women to an inexpressive babble' or the 'utter inarticulateness' of depression. Especially those women who lacked a husband—maids, nuns, and widows—were presumed to lack the phallus of a tongue, 'a place in the symbolic order's prime system, language'.[68] Luce Irigaray and Helène Cixous have argued that formal rhetorical features, like digression, that disrupt expectations of linear logic and narration have been essential to female speech and the female interrogation of patriarchal discourse.[69] Recalling, however, that Kristeva early wrote of the 'feminine' that 'it is only in relation to meaning and signification, positioned as their excessive or transgressive other that it [the feminine] *exists, speaks, thinks* (itself) and *writes* (itself) for both sexes',[70] I examine here texts by male writers who found themselves in relatively powerless or dangerously ambiguous social and political positions. The study of digression and literary figures generally is an opportunity to continue to complicate our understanding of gender to include a range or panoply of rhetorical attitudes, perceptions, and gestures associated with interiority, indirection, and passive aggression.

Disjunction and displacement are digressive moves and common seventeenth-century themes; but they are also psychological concepts.[71] Freud's essays not only on mourning and melancholy but on the interpretation of dreams and on jokes and the unconscious have sharpened and complicated our sense of the mind's essential indirection and androgyny.[72] A literary form of stepping aside to another subject and subjectivity may reveal disturbing connections among physical, psychological, and

[68] Ibid. 15.

[69] Luce Irigaray, *Speculum of the Other Woman*, trans. Gillian C. Gill (Ithaca, NY: Cornell University Press, 1985); Hélène Cixous in Cixous and Catherine Clément, *The Newly Born Woman*, trans. Betsy Wing, foreword by Sandra M. Gilbert (Minneapolis: University of Minnesota Press, 1986).

[70] Kristeva, *The Kristeva Reader*, 11.

[71] A standard reference for psychoanalytic terminology is still J. La Planche and J.-B. Pontalis, *The Language of Psycho-analysis*, trans. Donald Nicholson-Smith (New York: Norton, 1973). On the relations between digression and aggression, see, for example, Sandra Schor, 'Reclaiming Digression', in Louise Z. Smith (ed.), *Audits of Meaning: A Festschrift in Honor of Ann E. Berthoff* (Portsmouth, NH: Boynton/Cook, 1988), 238–47.

[72] In *The Standard Edition of the Complete Psychological Works of Sigmund Freud*, trans. James Strachey and Anna Freud (London: Hogarth Press, 1953–74), see *Jokes and Their Relation to the Unconscious*, vol. viii; *On Dreams*, v. 629–86; 'Remembering, Repeating and Working-Through', xii. 147–56; 'Mourning and Melancholia', vol. xiv. See also Freud's 'Creative Writers and Day-Dreaming', ix, 141–54; William Kerrigan, 'The Articulation of the Ego in the English Renaissance', in Joseph H. Smith (ed.), *Psychiatry and the Humanities*, iv: *The Literary Freud: Mechanisms of Defense and the Poetic Will*, ed. Joseph H. Smith (New Haven: Yale University Press, 1980), 261–308.

syntactic violence.[73] Digressive speaking appears to tap and channel the energy of forbidden, disruptive emotions, while it toys with the tension between exposure and concealment. Patricia Parker's work on dilation, secrecy, and spying has suggested connections between the circumlocution and voyeurism of an Iago or of the restless narrators of Marvell and Swift and the genre of anatomy which I address in Chapter 1. As theorists of Renaissance anatomy have observed, anatomy handbooks and their illustrations seemed systematically to tear and plumb surfaces, to disintegrate wholes, as if to expose a forbidden sight buried underneath the skin: death itself or the human interior as criminal, as feminine, or as monstrous.[74]

DIGRESSION AND DESIRE

Traditionally the practice of digression has been linked to the capture of a listener's desire for forbidden pleasure: the delight in escape from time's inexorable forward movement and in passion's transport out of time. In his discussion of the placement of digressions in book 4, Quintilian notes that the current fashion originating 'in the display of the schools of declamation' was to digress as soon as the initial statement of facts of a case was made 'with a view to securing the utmost amount of favour from their audience' (4. 3. 1–2). The digression represented an enormously pleasurable moment that rhetoricians inserted as soon as possible to hook their listeners: 'I imagine that they feared that if the slender stream of concise statement, such as is generally required, were followed by the pugnacious tone inevitable in the arguing of the case, the speech would fall flat owing to the postponement of the pleasures of a more expansive eloquence' (4. 3. 2). In the fifteenth century, Rudolph Agricola associates the digression with a surreptitious, indirect approach to the pleasurable subject one

[73] The connections between logic and grammar were noted by Aristotle and elaborated in this century, for example, by Northrop Frye in *Anatomy of Criticism: Four Essays* (Princeton: Princeton University Press, 1957). See more recently Lennard, *But I Digress* (1991). For the relations between narrative, psychology, and epistemology see Brooks, *Reading for the Plot.*

[74] Patricia Parker, '*Othello* and *Hamlet*: Spying, Discovery, Secret Faults', in *Shakespeare from the Margins* (Chicago: University of Chicago Press, 1996), 229–72; 'Shakespeare and Rhetoric: "Dilation" and "Delation" in *Othello*', in Patricia Parker and Geoffrey Hartman(eds.), *Shakespeare and the Question of Theory* (New York: Methuen, 1985), 54–74. On Renaissance anatomy, see Jonathan Sawday, *The Body Emblazoned: Dissection and the Human Body in Renaissance Culture* (London: Routledge, 1995); and Devon Hodges, *Renaissance Fictions of Anatomy* (Amherst: University of Massachusetts Press, 1985).

wants to expand upon. He describes how a speaker with a 'somewhat harsh and sad' subject would want to 'slip quite freely toward [more pleasant things] in a digression, which is done most conveniently when, by means of a deceptive transition, we arrive at those things in such a way that we do not seem to have pursued them, but to have been forced to go to them'.[75] After detailing how to shift stealthily from praise of music to a full-blown description of spring, Agricola adds that many writers, especially Plato and Lucian, employ such techniques and concludes, 'we see how, having begun with an introduction quite removed from the subject proposed, they creep little by little and with stealthy steps to that which they are aiming at'.[76] Digressions seem to promise a forbidden, 'stealthy' pleasure in the freedom of stepping not only aside from, but also out of, stated bounds. Digressions also seem to be necessary when one's subject cannot be stated directly but must be arrived at 'little by little'.

The Greek *parecbasis* carried the sense of moral transgression in the *Oresteia* and in Aristotle, although elsewhere Aristotle uses the word in the formal literary sense of leaving the subject.[77] The Roman rhetoricians translated *parecbasis* variously as *digressio*, *excursus*, and *egressio*, which generally refer to a strategically 'digressive or interpolated tale' within an oration;[78] among other functions, the digression in classical oratory served as a formal transition and in this capacity became incorporated into medieval and Renaissance arts of preaching.[79] For Quintilian a digression 'outside the five divisions of the speech' reflected an emotional detour (4. 3. 15); and indeed, from the early rhetoricians, digression was associated with the extra breath of the 'furor poeticus', the inspired passion which excites emotion in the listener, which touches and persuades.[80] Both Cicero and Quintilian attempted to answer Plato's objections to the dangerous effect of rhetoric by claiming that rhetoric's most

[75] Rudolph Agricola, *De Inventione Dialectica Libri Tres* (*Three Books Concerning Dialectical Invention*), book III, ch. IV, cited in Rebhorn (ed. and trans.), *Renaissance Debates on Rhetoric*, 2000), 54.

[76] Ibid. 55.

[77] Aristotle employs the term to refer to an overstepping of the law, in *Athenian Constitution* (7. 1), Black 'The Second Fall', 12–15. See the *Nichomachean Ethics* (4. 5. 13).

[78] See, for example, Lanham, *Handlist*, 54.

[79] It was chiefly Augustine 'who adapted the classical arts of discourse to serve the purposes of a redeemed culture'. John S. Chamberlin, *Increase and Multiply* (Chapel Hill: University of North Carolina Press, 1976), 3. See Th.-M. Charland, *Artes Praedicandi* (Paris: J. Vrin, 1936), 213 ff.

[80] Cicero, *De Oratore*, trans. E. W. Sutton, Loeb Classical Library (Cambridge, Mass.: Harvard University Press, 1996), 2. 76. 311–12.

profound and affective eloquence depended as much on the high moral character and passion of the speaker as on his technical skills.

In the hands of a great orator and master of feeling like Cicero who, according to Quintilian, excited audiences to frenzied seizures and 'a perfect ecstasy of delight' (8. 3. 4), the humble but flexible digression expanded and soared.[81] H. V. Cantor counted at least fifty-five substantial examples in the speeches of Cicero.[82] In his later pedagogical works, Cicero enlarges on the importance of digression for eulogy, satire, and invective. As *apoplanesis*, or the evasion of a difficult issue, a digression could take the form of an irrelevant answer or a pleasing and strategic diversion from a prosecutor's proofs.[83] As an overflow of passion, improvised digressions such as Cicero's became 'emollients' to soothe and soften the harder elements of a case and the unreceptive ears of an audience.[84] They also provided opportunities for autobiography and self-characterization, self-fashioning and self-defence; James May has surveyed what he calls *ethica digressio* which Cicero used to establish antithetical character portraits of client and opposition as well as to describe and defend his own character.[85] Above all, Ciceronian oratory was theatre: Quintilian describes how Cicero altered his tone and manner of presentation to suit and even impersonate the characters of his client's drama.[86] A Roman audience recognized and expected to be moved by digressions, and one of the most celebrated digressions in the history of oratory was Cicero's dramatic and extended plea for citizenship for the

[81] See Clarke, *Rhetoric at Rome*, 79.

[82] H. V. Cantor, '*Digressio* in the Orations of Cicero', *American Journal of Philology*, 52 (1931), 351–61.

[83] A related Greek term noted by Quintilian (9. 2. 107), and in the Renaissance by Peacham as a special form of *insinuatio*, is *paradiegesis*, which means 'incidental narrative' and is a narrative digression specifically used to introduce an argument. *Apoplanesis* was much used by Cicero. Peacham cites the example of Cicero's '*fabula*' on Metullus' death in the *Pro M. Caelio*. See Henry Peacham, *The Garden of Eloquence* (2nd enlarged ed. London, 1593), ed. William G. Crane (Gainesville, Fla.: Scholars' Facsimiles and Reprints, 1954) for his discussion of *apoplanesis*, 117.

[84] 'Hic igitur velut fomentis, si quid erit asperum, praemolliemus, quo facilius aures iudicum quae post dicturi erimus admittant, ne ius nostrum oderint'. Quintilian, *Institutio Oratoria* 4. 3. 10.

[85] James M. May, *Trials of Character: The Eloquence of Ciceronian Ethos* (Chapel Hill: University of North Carolina Press, 1988). May traces this type of digression back to Antiphon's 'On the Murder of Herodes' in the 4th century BC, to Gorgias' defence of the mythical Palamedes, and to Plato's portrayal of Socrates in the *Apology* which includes the philosopher's long digression, immediately preceding the epilogue, on his own character and divine mission.

[86] Quintilian, *Institutio Oratoria* 11. .1. 39.

Greek poet Archias, which became an exalted defence of education and culture (AD 62).[87]

This classical training of both speakers and audiences in the pleasures of digression is both upheld and redirected in the first century AD by the unknown author whom we call 'Longinus'. The sublime discourse praised by Longinus proceeded from and celebrated the moral elevation of both speaker and listener whose passion could result in disjunction and digression. Longinus repeatedly allows himself digressions: 'I digressed into this topic [the *Iliad* and *Odyssey* compared], as I said, to illustrate how easy it is for great genius to be perverted in decline into nonsense' (9. 14); 'So much, my dear Terentianus, by way of digression on the theory of the use of those figures which conduce to sublimity' (29. 2), and, again, when he distinguishes mediocre writers, no matter how accomplished, from those of genius (32. 8–36).[88] Longinus distinguished sublimity's height from the more pedestrian rhetorical ability to amplify quantities of words, just as Quintilian had distinguished between the prepared yet inspired eloquence of an orator speaking extempore and the angry verbal flood of a shrew. In so doing, Longinus distinguished mere amplitude, which extends discourse and piles up details, from the rich expansiveness that lifts passages to verbal grandeur. In a famous digression, Longinus contrasts the 'abrupt sublimity' and elevated fire of Demosthenes, which stuns and amazes the listener like lightning, with the diffusive grandeur, if not sublimity, of Cicero whose eloquence he compares to a 'spreading conflagration. His huge fires endure' (12. 4–5). Longinus notes that Cicero's profusion is appropriate in '*loci communes*, epilogues, digressions', among other places (12. 5). With the influential translation of Nicholas Boileau (1674), *On the Sublime* became a crucial influence on late seventeenth- and eighteenth-century aesthetics.[89] The

[87] Harold Gotoff has remarked, 'Cicero delivered his orations to audiences intimately concerned with the issues and ramifications of each case, audiences whose attention, credence, and support were essential for his own success as a public figure'. *Cicero's Eloquent Style: An Analysis of the Pro Archia* (Urbana: University of Illinois Press, 1979), 8–9. Cicero, *Pro Archia*, trans. N. H. Watts, Loeb Classical Library (Cambridge, Mass.: Harvard University Press 1923, 1993), 2.

[88] Quotations of 'Longinus' are from the translation by D. A. Russell of *On Sublimity*, in D. A. Russell and M. Winterbottom (eds.), *Classical Literary Criticism* (Oxford and New York: Oxford University Press, 1989)See also n. 5.

[89] In 'The Author's Apology for Heroique Poetry and Poetic License' (1677), and later in the 1690s, Dryden will draw on Longinus' distinction between a free and fiery, elevated fury of invention and a more pedestrian, restricted spirit to argue his taste for the superior fire of exiled Juvenal over the sycophantic Horace and for Homer's 'more copious' invention and 'heat' compared with Virgil's 'confined' powers and 'sedate' temper. See Ch. 6.

text was an example of stylistic analysis that elevated certain literary practices of representing passionate and disjunctive speech.[90]

Quintilian's concern that the orator-lawyer not be lost for words in mid-speech, like a ship that has lost its wind, or be unable to improvise a new direction in order to meet an unexpected line of attack, and Longinus' praise, while subtly qualified, for the rich extended fluency of Cicero reflected the classical interest in an aesthetic of *copia*: the ability to command large and various stores of words. Copious discourse, if successful, traditionally avoided two forms of breathless depletion: *inopia* or poverty of diction, and hollow prolixity or '*copia* without *varietas*'.[91] Both theoreticians of rhetoric distinguish between empty loquacity and rich fluency, and they distinguish *digressio*, a particular device that extends a discourse, from the broad notion of rich, plentiful eloquence referred to by the word *copia*. For the seventeenth-century writers represented in this book, the classical notion of *copia*, particularly as interpreted by Erasmus early in the sixteenth century, offered a model for the association of fertile literary power with the production of abundant, protean language whose plentitude and playful productivity gives pleasure. In her study of memory in medieval culture, Mary Carruthers observes that for pre-modern writers who composed by drawing appropriate words and phrases for a particular topic out from their large memory stores, 'Ethical truths especially are expressed not singly but "copiously" ' and that 'copiousness, like decorum, is an essential part of a rhetorical understanding of the nature of human speech'.[92] In the Renaissance the practice of *copia* came to reflect a release of vernacular expression from the aesthetic strictures of the Ciceronian period and ancient notions of decorum and a reorientation of the figures of invention, including *digressio* and *egressio*, toward the generative power of words themselves. My study of the digressive voice in early modern England is indebted to Terence Cave's brilliant account of the rediscov-

[90] In the *Theaetetus*, for example, Plato contrasts the leisurely, speculative philosopher who enjoys the truancy of the contemplative life with the publicly engaged and restricted orator. 'The contemplative philosopher, in other words, allows himself the liberty of digression in order to reach his goal. . . . In contrast, the orator in the high-pressured court cannot permit himself to indulge in digressions. . . . Digressions evidently lend themselves to leisurely, philosophical discussions or diatribes, often in an idyllic, pleasant setting', like a garden. The original garden of transgression, however, hovers behind all such contemplative gardens in the Renaissance. See Black, 'The Second Fall', 44–5.

[91] Terence Cave, *The Cornucopian Text: Problems of Writing in the French Renaissance* (Oxford: Clarendon Press, 1979), 22.

[92] Mary Carruthers, *The Book of Memory: A Study of Memory in Medieval Culture* (Cambridge: Cambridge University Press, 1990), 26.

ery by Renaissance humanists of the rhetorical concept of *copia* and its transformation into an ideal of verbal fecundity through Erasmus' popular textbook *De Copia verborem ac Rerum* (1512).[93] Cave describes the importance for sixteenth-century vernacular writing—but also for seventeenth-century digressions—of the emergence of a literary aesthetic of textual productivity and authority out of the conjunction and revitalization of the classical notions of imitation, improvisation, and the breath of inspiration.

As Cave and others have emphasized, the full title of Erasmus' book, *De Duplici Copia Verborum ac Rerum Commentarii Duo*, admits to an essential doubleness in, a split between, words and things highlighted by the division of the text into part I on 'Copia of Words' and part II on 'Copia of Thought'. In Erasmus' text, however, '*Res* and *verba* slide together to become "word-things"; the notion of a single domain (language) having a double aspect replaces that of two distinct domains, language and thought'. Cave uses a tantalizing image for the words with which Erasmus directs students how to generate more: words become like windows or lattices through which we see the world, as the lattices open to release 'word-things'.[94] As an example Cave draws our attention

[93] Cave, *The Cornucopian Text*. On the Ciceronian and Anti-Ciceronian period, see the work of Morris W. Croll from earlier in the century, *Style, Rhetoric, and Rhythm* (repr. Woodbridge, Conn.: Ox Bow Press, 1989); more recently, see, for example, 'The Periodic Style and the Running Style' in Richard Lanham, *Analyzing Prose* (New York: Scribner, 1983), 53–76. On the ancient notions of decorum, see G. L. Hendrickson, 'The Origin and Meaning of the Ancient Characters of Style', *American Journal of Philology* 26 3 (1905), 249–90; on the Renaissance discussion, see references to decorum in Weinberg, *A History of Literary Criticism in the Italian Renaissance*; and the entry for decorum in Marjorie Donker, *Dictionary of Literary-Rhetorical Conventions of the English Renaissance* (Westport, Conn.: Greenwood Press, 1982). Michael Baxandall has made a similar argument about the influence on Renaissance painting of shifts in attitude toward the Ciceronian period. Baxandall has written eloquently about the transition from Latin to vernacular artistic theory and practice with respect to painting. He points to a link between digressive modes of perception and shifts in the use of the rhetorical terminology that had served to talk about painting as well as verbal composition. Alberti, for example, employed the language of invention and disposition, and of inspiration and ornament, in the fifteenth century to construct a powerful but rigidly neoclassical model of painting as an organization much like Cicero's periodic sentence. Yet as the prestige of Latin syntax and its categories of experience yielded to the energy, expressiveness, and worldly authority of the vernacular, those same humanist terms opened into an aesthetic of abundance for painting. See *Giotto and the Orators* (Oxford: Clarendon Press, 1971), esp. chs. i and iii. See David Summers, *Michelangelo and the Language of Art* (Princeton: Princeton University Press, 1981), on Michelangelo's ethics and aesthetics of ambiguity and his Neoplatonic *licenza* and *fantasia* to uncover things not seen.

[94] Cave, *The Cornucopian Text*, 29, 31. Similarly, in *The Garden of Cyrus*, Browne refers to networks of relation among words and within the physical, natural world as expressive, like lattices that both reveal and conceal, of a vast principle of fertility that leads those who see clearly from visible to invisible dimensions of existence.

to a passage in Part II of *De Copia*, in Erasmus's discussion of various methods of amplification of matter. The fifth method consists of vivid description, *evidentia*, *enargeia*, ecphrasis: 'painting the picture of things', or describing people, places, and moments in time in such vivid detail that the reader or hearer can see them in imagination, be drawn 'outside himself as in the theatre'.[95] Erasmus quotes an example from Quintilian to demonstrate how a phrase like 'a city captured', once lifted from abstraction, opens into a complex scene of enormous sounds and sights: ' "if someone should say that a city was captured, he doubtless comprehends in that general statement everything that attends such fortune, but if you develop what is implicit in the one word, flames will appear pouring through homes and temples; the crash of falling buildings will be heard, and one indefinable sound of diverse outcries" '[96] Cave notes that 'not perhaps entirely by chance' the next section, the Sixth Method of amplifying, concerns '*egressio* or *digressio*: terms which carry etymologically the sense of an excursion or deflection. In such instances, *res* seem to be less the source of production than a by-product; they are revealed by the autonomous proliferation of language'.[97] Following Quintilian closely, Erasmus finds digressions to be appropriate both near the beginning of the speech to secure the audience with some pleasurable diversion and near the end when the listener needs to be refreshed, although then Erasmus lists a series of occasions when a digression midway may be called for, as after the narration or after the proof or whenever weariness needs to be dispelled.

Cave notes a connection between an interest in the productivity of individual words and the fragmenting pressures exerted on the unifying force of language in sixteenth-century Europe by textual and linguistic scholarship:

> immense pressures were being exerted on the epistemological status of language by the intensive reappraisal of Scripture and of classical culture, that is to say, the whole corpus of consecrated writing; the fissures which began to appear in long-established theological and ethical structures provoked an urgent desire, in all camps, to seal the leaks and prevent the fragmentation of the *logos*. The figures of Babel—whether the Old Testament *topos* itself, Proteus, Mercury, or the dismemberment of Orpheus—proliferate at this time. . . . Theoretical and semi-theoretical writing of this period repeatedly expresses its inability to produce a

[95] Desiderius Erasmus, *On Copia of Words and Ideas (De Utraque Verborem ac Remum Copia)* (Milwaukee: Marquette University Press, 1963), 47.

[96] Ibid. 48.

[97] Cave, *The Cornucopian Text*, 31.

coherent account of the relationship of language to 'world', 'thought', and 'truth'.[98]

Indeed, early modern stylistics, such as *The Arte of English Poesie*, natural philosophers such as Bacon and Sprat, and literary texts themselves confirm that readers and writers in England were interested in and disturbed by the problem of the ambiguous relationship between words and things and by the moral valence of rhetorical figures and *copia*. Language use reflected a variety of cultural pressures, including strident religious and political controversy that turned on the meaning of God's Word, pressures increased by military and ideological conflicts in Europe and the emergence of new paradigms for thinking about the world created in the early modern ferment of scientific thought. The ancient epic bond between arms and the muse took on a new ironic life as rhetorical training in techniques of *copia* that emphasized the various 'feast of the mind' and a garden or garland of figurative flowers required that writers set that distracting feast and fruitful garden into competition with real battlefields.[99] Recall, for example, at mid-century the opening of Marvell's 'An Horatian Ode upon Cromwell's Return from Ireland', whose speaker—if he is 'The forward youth'—feels he 'must now forsake his muses dear' as Cromwell left 'his private gardens'. If he wants to act on the public stage, or even survive, he must don rusty armour—yet perhaps as well the ancient ornaments and shield of rhetorical combat—and leave with the garden and pastoral the romance of poesie's figures as a posy of flowers. While debating the sacrifice of poetry to arms, the speaker slips into a poem about arms an exquisitely shielded marching tension between muse and Mars that looks backwards and forwards simultaneously in order to capture the horror and excitement of that unstable moment. The speaker does not forsake the muses, rather stealthily returns them to the battlefield. Soon afterwards, in *Upon Appleton House*, Marvell thinks more deeply about the movement for England and poetry between garden and battlefield.

Out of a complex rhetorical heritage, the digression in seventeenth-century England becomes available as a strategic and ambiguous figure.

[98] Cave, *The Cornucopian Text*, 157.

[99] For copious writing as a various 'feast of the mind', a sensuous movable feast, see ibid. 25. On the 'hunger' for 'a fictional feast' of talk, of dialogue, see 103–4 in Cave's chapter on Erasmus' *Convivium religiosum*. Rebhorn, *Emperor of Men's Minds*, 176–7, discusses the relationship between Renaissance rhetoric and food that goes back at least to Plato's attack on rhetoric as cookery in the *Gorgias*. On the medieval metaphor of reading, rumination, and memory as a process of eating and digestion, see Carruthers, *The Book of Memory*, 44, 164–9, and elsewhere; see the general index under 'Digestion-rumination metaphor'.

According to the *OED*, the earliest recorded use of the English noun 'digression' appears in the fourteenth century and means 'a departure or deviation from the subject in discourse or writing'.[100] In the sixteenth and seventeenth centuries examples of the noun 'digression' and the verb 'to digress', used figuratively to mean divergence other than formal literary deviation from an announced topic, begin to proliferate: for example, a swerve from a 'right' rule or path.[101] In the sixteenth and seventeenth centuries the word 'digress' is used to describe the wandering path of human and astronomical bodies, but also the wandering of the mind, the soul, and affections as well as political allegiance. Like the winding brook Maeander in Ovid's simile, discussed earlier, which portrays Daedalus' mind playfully creating the labyrinth, digressive minds are often figured as mazy streams. In *Richard II*, v. iii. 66, King Henry denounces the Duke of York's traitorous 'digressing' son as the muddy, wandering stream of his father's pure spring.[102] (Hence, Milton teases the reader with God's creative delight that sends four streams 'wand'ring' through Paradise with innocent 'mazy error', IV. 239). Digression may mean transgression, that is, 'moral deviation or going astray' and divergence from a rule or 'right' course; Shakespeare's Tarquin anticipates his rape of Lucrece as 'my digression' (l. 202).[103] At the approach of the English civil wars Gilbert Watts retranslates Bacon's *De Dignitate et Augmentis Scientiarum* (1640), where we find 'So man, while he aspired to be like God in knowledge, digressed and fell' ('Homo, dum ad Scientiam divinae parem aspiraret, praevaricatus est et lapsus', VII. iii).[104] Rhetorical figures carried

[100] *The Oxford English Dictionary* cites Chaucer's *Troilus and Criseyde*:

> But how this town com to destruccion
> Ne falleth naught to purpos me to telle,
> For it were a long digression
> Fro my matere, and yow to long to dwelle. (I. 141–5)

[101] The *OED* quotes from James Ussher (1611) in John Gutch, *Collectanea Curiosa; or Miscellaneous Tracts, Relating to the History and Antiquities of England and Ireland, the Universities of Oxford and Cambridge, and a Variety of Other Subjects*, 2 vols. (Oxford: Clarendon Press, 1781), i. 39: 'The [Irish] subjects rebelled, and digressed from their allegiance'.

[102] The ambiguous, mazy stream of Spenser's allegory and later of Milton's Eden (whose serpentine underground river serves Satan's transgressive purpose) appears here as the transgressive and digressive Aumerle.

[103] 'Then my digression is so vile, so base, / That it will live engraven in my face' (*The Rape of Lucrece*, ll. 202–3).

[104] Gilbert Watts retranslated the Latin of *De Dignitate et Augmentis Scientiarum*, Bacon's expansion to *Of the Advancement of Learning*, into *Of the Advancement and Proficience of Learning, or, The Partitions of Sciences, IX Bookes*... (Oxford: Lichfield, 1640), vii. iii. 362.

moral and political weight, and digressions appeared to reflect dark unruly wandering, illicit pleasure, and aggressive amplification.

In Henry Peacham's *The Garden of Eloquence* (1577, rev. 1593), *digressio* is defined as 'the handling of some matter going out from order, but yet for profit of some pertinent cause'. But Peacham follows these opening remarks with an unusually long statement of caution about an orator's need to control the potential for darkness of *digressio*:

> The first [care] is to see some cause why we should digress, that is, that the same digression may some manner of way profit, commend, and garnish the cause that we have in hand, for the digression ought in some respect to pertain and agree to those matters which we handle, and not to be strange or far distant from the purpose. The second is to provide a forehand a perfect and readie way to goe forth aptly and making no long stray out, likewise to foresee a fit entrance for our returne. The third is to take good heed that we do not darken our main cause and principall matter: we darken it if we goe forth abruptly, tarie too long abroad, tell thinges strange, distant, or disagreeing to the purpose, or returne into the cause overthwartly.[105]

The unease in Peacham's repetition of the words 'strange' and 'far distant', with their suggestion of an obscure alien (from *estrange* and *extraneus*) associated with a foreign, unfamiliar place, is heightened by the repetition of 'darken', as opposed to clarify. He characterizes the digression as potentially disruptive, suspicious behaviour which diverges and returns 'overthwartly', that is, obliquely or adversely, even perversely, and which tarries too long talking about 'strange' matters. Thomas Wilson in *The Arte of Rhetorique* (1553, 1560) similarly warns that the digression not be long but 'bee so set out that it confounde not the cause, or darken the sense of the matter devised.[106] When Peacham comes to the specific uses of *digressio*, he recommends the figure on the condition that the writer strictly circumscribe it by 'wariness'. Once again he breaks into strong moral language to warn against its potential for disorder:

> if warinesse and good heed be taken, this figure is a vertue whereby the oration is amplified, garnished and wel commended: otherwise it is a vice which doth violate both order and art, and doth greatly deforme the Oration by patching it, as it were with shreds and broken peeces.[107]

[105] Peacham, *The Garden of Eloquence*, ed. Crane, 154.

[106] Thomas Wilson, *The Arte of Rhetorique*, ed. Thomas J. Derrick (New York: Garland, 1982), 182.

[107] Peacham, *The Garden of Eloquence*, 154.

Peacham's image of an oration reduced by too many digressions to a deformity of shreds and patches suggests the potential of the figure to trigger the fear of fragmentation. A century later Swift dramatized exactly that fear with *A Tale of a Tub*'s chaotic narrator.

Peacham and Wilson associate the digression with vice, with wayward delinquency and abrupt disappearance and absence, with dark disorder and literary and even psychological deformity. And the connections they perceive among moral, social, political, and aesthetic disorder shadow the practice and perception of digressive writing throughout the seventeenth century. The associations of digression with disorder in a century of deep civic disorder and incessant debate about government suggest the centrality and provocative nature of this figure as an expressive mode of both poetry and prose.

In the seventeenth century not only poets but natural philosophers digressed and debated about the morality of digression. Thomas Sprat opens *The History of the Royal-Society of London* (1667) with a call for members to purify and regulate English speech and writing and, first, to abjure dependence on rhetorical arts and figurative language so that 'the whole spirit and vigour' of the Society's purpose and experimental work be not 'eaten out by the luxury and redundance of speech'. In the second part, s. xx, he whips himself into a righteous fury, as passionate as any orator, against the respect that all educated men hold for the 'seeming Mysteries' of rhetorical devices, including digression:

> Who can behold without indignation how many mists and uncertainties these specious Tropes and Figures have brought on our knowledg? How many rewards which are due to more profitable and difficult Arts have been still snatch'd away by the easie vanity of fine speaking? For now I am warm'd with this just Anger, I cannot with-hold my self from betraying the shallowness of all these seeming Mysteries upon which we Writers and Speakers look so bigg. And, in few words, I dare say that, of all the Studies of men, nothing may be sooner obtain'd than this vicious abundance of Phrase, this trick of Metaphors, this volubility of Tongue, which makes so great a noise in the World. But I spend words in vain, for the evil is now so inveterate that it is hard to know whom to blame, or where to begin to reform. We all value one another so much upon this beautiful deceipt, and labour so long after it in the years of our education.[108]

Sprat demands of educated men a moral discipline of the tongue and manly rigour to resist 'this beautiful deceipt' of rhetorical figures, 'this vicious abundance of Phrase'. He calls angrily to cut down with the

[108] See Spingarn (ed.), *Critical Essays of the Seventeenth Century*, ii. 117.

executioner's blade the pleasures of extraneous language: to put 'in execution the only Remedy' which is to reject 'all amplifications, digressions, and swellings of style'. Sprat associates digressions with self-indulgence and with seductive, vicious self-enlargement.

In the seventeenth century the negative associations of literary digression with getting out of line and autonomous mobility—with stylistic, social, political, and psychological disorder—and with the non-linear progress of untrained, female speech, resemble contemporary representations of what Erasmus called that 'Ambivalent Organ', the unruly tongue.[109] Renaissance grammars and conduct books portray the tongue, like the unruly, dilating phallus, as in need of constant restraint. Carla Mazzio has documented the early modern period's nervousness about the tongue's agency and ability to swell and extend even beyond the body's borders; that 'wilde member'—'the insubjectible subject'—among other spectres of monstrous orality erupts as a problem 'precisely when questions about instability of reference seem to be moving from mouth to hand, or more precisely, from tongue to pen to press'.[110] Mazzio has noted as well, however, nostalgia for the fluidity and pre-eminence of oral speech and concern for fluent voices being silenced by the speech of print in Shakespeare's *Love's Labour's Lost* where 'the melancholy of love articulates a melancholy of speech in a world dominated by technologies of writing and print'. The competition in that play between oral speech and books of speech registers 'the oral and psychic self-estrangement of speakers living in a culture in transition to print'.[111]

In their address to a reader-listener, the written voices of my study evoke the tensions, immediacy, and authority of oral speech while exploiting the more protected, leisurely access to the reader's attention of writing. The relevance for literary skills of training rooted in classical schooling for the political theatre of oratory was that the pressure of partisan politics on aesthetic careers in the seventeenth century, not least the threat of censorship, meant that a writer might expect to write into a reception almost as immediate as that of a live performance.[112] And, as

[109] Erasmus, *Lingua*, trans. Elaine Fantham, in *Collected Works of Erasmus*, ed. Elaine Fantham and Erika Rummel (Toronto: University of Toronto, 1989), 365. Cited on p. 53 of Carla Mazzio, 'Sins of the Tongue', in David Hillman and Carla Mazzio (eds.), *The Body in Parts: Fantasies of Corporeality in Early Modern Europe* (New York: Routledge, 1997), 53–79.

[110] Mazzio, 'Sins of the Tongue', 65.

[111] Carla Mazzio, 'The Melancholy of Print: *Love's Labour's Lost*', in Carla Mazzio and Douglas Trevor (eds.), *Historicism, Psychoanalysis, and Early Modern Culture* (New York: Routledge, 2000), 188.

[112] See Steven Zwicker, 'Early Modern Reading: Habits and Practices, Protocols and Contexts', *Eigo Seinen*, 148/2 (May 2002), 78–81.

historians of reading have emphasized, a text of this period was as likely to have been read aloud and among company as in silence and solitude:

In the sixteenth and seventeenth centuries the reading style implicit in a text, literary or not, was still often an oralization of the text, and the 'reader' was an implicit auditor of a read discourse. The work, which was addressed to the ear as much as to the eye, plays with forms and procedures that subject writing to demands more appropriate to oral 'performance'.[113]

These works indeed address the ear, especially in the writers' mastery of the subtle registers of tone.

The writers in *Digressive Voices* need to speak but not orally; they use the relative safety and space for manœuvre of complicated textual voices to sidestep but compete with the more directly polemical voices and controversies of their time. Bruce R. Smith has documented superbly the soundscape of early modern England and has urged that we not allow our postmodern distance from the sixteenth and seventeenth centuries, crossed largely through scrutiny of surviving written and printed documents, to make us deaf to the importance and resonance of speaking and singing voices, even within print.[114] Smith reminds us to read the written signs of sounds for the bodies they represent. The digression capable of at least two stylistic profiles—one high and powerfully male, the other low and weakly feminine or effeminate—allowed writers to open a space on the page for a written voice of otherwise unspeakable reflection and complexity, even androgyny. More, literary digression, as a figure of indirect yet aggressive movement—away from or at an angle to the announced subject but toward a personal subject—becomes a figure for the indirection of writing itself that stands in for a silenced tongue, for an undeliverable physical blow, and for the vulnerable body of a writer who inhabits political or social margins yet whose breath may yet reach to the centre of power.

In 1700 a physician named Richard Boulton, who shared Sprat's impatience with rhetorical ornament and digressions, 'epitomiz'd' in three

[113] Roger Chartier, *The Order of Books: Readers, Authors, and Libraries in Europe between the Fourteenth and Eighteenth Centuries*, trans. Lydia G. Cochrane (Stanford, Calif.: Stanford University Press, 1994), 9.

[114] 'In hindsight, it is easy for us to talk about the "triumph" of printing in early modern Europe. What we are apt to miss is the resistance of voice to the new medium. In a culture that still gave precedence to voice—in legal practice, in rhetorical theory, in art made out of words, in the transactions of daily life—we should be looking, not for evidence of the hegemony of type technology, but for all the ways in which that newly discovered resource was colonized by regimes of oral communication'. Bruce R. Smith, *The Acoustic World of Early Modern England: Attending to the O-Factor* (Chicago: University of Chicago Press, 1999), 128.

volumes the works of the seventeenth-century aristocrat and scientific virtuoso Robert Boyle.[115] In a 'Preface to the Reader', Boulton defends the price of his epitome. His volume cannot be judged by the common rule, that is 'to estimate the Value of a Book by the Bulk'. While Boyle was prone to 'long digressive Excuses', 'too frequent Excursions', and a 'Prolix and Complaisant Way of Writing', the epitome has cleared away clouds of 'Ornaments' and 'Additions of Art or Rhetorick'. Boyle would interrupt himself with digressions that made it difficult for 'Vulgar Readers' to 'carry his Sense along with them'. But the epitome has extracted 'a System of Philosophy' and set it 'almost before the Eye at once' to be 'more easily swallow'd and digested'.

Boulton's distaste for the rhetorical arts and his preference for an easily digestible 'system' reflect over a century of debate on the practice and consumption of English literary style and rhetorical ornament. Moreover, his characterization of digression as 'Complaisant' expresses an intriguing prejudice: the roots of the word complaisant are in pleasure and geniality; to be complaisant in the seventeenth century is to be obliging and polite, flexible and yielding. The noun 'complaisance' may also carry overtones of dissimulation.[116] Boulton hints that the great Boyle, brother to Richard, the second Earl of Cork, and to Roger Earl of Orrery, aristocratically indulges and accommodates only himself. His digressions are reflections of nobility's ease and extravagance. The texts of *Digressive Voices*, although by non-aristocrats, claim exactly such privileged space to please the complaisant self and, like the voices they embody, resist epitome.

[115] Richard Boulton, *The Works of the Honourable Robert Boyle, Esq; Epitomiz'd*, 4 vols. (London: Thomas Bennet etc., 1700).

[116] The noun 'complaisance' which entered the language in the mid-17th century suggested a politely obliging act of accommodation and courtesy, although *The Art of Complaisance or the Means to oblige in Conversation* by S.C. (London: John Starkey, 1673) linked complaisance and dissimulation. With 'obscurity' as 'the best Sanctuary from envy or censure', the deliberately nameless author writes especially for 'those who place themselves in the Court where conversation is most difficult, and appears with greatest variety . . . to assist them in their designs of advancement in the pursuit of which, they will find so many oppositions'. The Latin epigraph reads 'Quis nescit dissimulare, nescit vivere' (He who does not know how to dissimulate does not know how to live), while the second chapter opens, 'Dissimulation is part of the essence of Complaisance, without which 'tis impossible that a Courtier or any other person should be able to conduct himself with safety amidst the malice and contrivances of men' (8).

THE TEXTS

I have ordered my six chapters chronologically by text yet arranged them into sections that reflect the two broad themes of this book. The first and third sections headed 'Strategic Voices' examine a text by Donne from early in the century and two texts by Dryden from the final decades, respectively, which highlight digressiveness turned outward for purposes of self-defence and self-portraiture. Their narrators address a sceptical or hostile readership and situate the writer's abilities and ambitions strategically within a competitive urban landscape. These chapters on the writer's contest to be heard embrace a more contemplative middle section whose voices, although equally sensitive politically, turn notably inward to figure the mind or psyche as a garden or natural landscape. 'Sounding Interior Gardens at Mid-Century' represents, at the core of this book, a flowering of texts in the 1650s about gardens, which cultivate digressiveness as a trope for exploring inner wandering. They reflect the central importance in seventeenth-century literary culture of gardens, specifically the biblical gardens of Eden and Canticles and the embattled garden of England, to represent inner landscapes and mazes and the intersecting conflicts of private and public worlds.

Chapter 1 addresses the eccentric length and the authoritative, aggressive narrator of Donne's *Anniversaries* (1612). Donne uses the public occasion of lamenting a deceased girl he never knew to anatomize his own fears of loss—including the loss, with life's breath, of the breath of inspiration—and, miraculously, to return to poetic life, rising imaginatively in his poem with Elizabeth to a superior vantage. The symbolic arc of past descent 'represented', climaxed by the grotesque beheaded man (II. 9–17), and future ascent of the 'low' 'contemplated', climaxing in the violence of a burst abscess (II. 474–82), suggests not least the poet's consuming drama of failed opportunities and talents and his determination to rise with his new patron, Sir Robert Drury. Donne's brooding lament over physical and psychical imprisonment, depletion, and dissolution—and his competitive ambition that drives him to speak even beyond the requirements and understanding of his patron—propel the inordinate length of *The Anniversaries.* Lament and anger also shape the digressive, serpentine mode of praise for his subject, which combines a lurch forward of hyperbole with backward twists and detours into vicious social satire.

In Chapter 2, I suggest that the narrator of *Upon Appleton House* (*c.*1651) reflects on and responds to intense pressures of contemporary and personal occasions characterized by loss or uncertainty. While a lowly family tutor, the voyeuristic narrator dares to range far and deep over the Fairfax estate and history and into the psyche apparently of Lord Fairfax but perhaps more profoundly of himself. The narrator's digressive tour of the landscape progresses through time but also dives out of time to explore an ambiguous self exposed at the depths of a landscape of drowning, watery labyrinths and trauma. The poem aligns the male narrator and the startlingly predatory voices of the 'subtle' nun and 'bloody Thestylis', only to highlight the dead silence of youth including Isabel Thwaites and Mary Fairfax.

In 1658 physician Thomas Browne protests not only the 'brutall terminations' of death but also the silencing of individual voices and cultural and religious institutions by civil war and the republican government. In a challenge to literal-minded readers of 'this ill-judging age' suspicious of literary ornament and rhetorical flowers, he follows his subterranean exploration of death and burial customs, *Hydriotaphia, or Urne-Buriall*, with his prose ode to light, *The Garden of Cyrus*, a learned celebration of the five-pointed pattern of planting called a quincunx, and the subject of Chapter 3. No Eve or Mary Fairfax walks these garden paths, but their absence allows the narrator liberty to range in an intellectual and sensual freedom as if enacting alone the invisible 'plastick principle' of generation contained in seeds, which becomes the diminutive hero of the visible and the invisible universe. He cultivates a rich Paradise that juxtaposes an elegant quincuncial order with digressions 'into extraneous things' and 'collaterall truths', in contrast to the geometrical gardens and utilitarian, nationalistic horticultural schemes being devised in the 1650s to promote England's economic flowering.

The argument of my fourth chapter is that Milton's epic presents the 'grateful digressions' (VIII. 55) of unfallen Adam and Eve, like the angels' divine labyrinth dances, and the mazes and branching lines of Paradise, as examples of heavenly playfulness, pleasure, and natural order. In contrast, the rigidity of Satan's transgressive desire for power is an unswerving line of envious pride that will dead-end. The fallen angels are unable to navigate diversion, much less dance it, but are lost in hell in mazes of thought and wandering. God's plan for man is full of long, delaying byways and steps backward (to fallen perception) in order to go forward. Digression is not transgression when the psychological and literal stepping aside steps away from the desire to master divine mystery and seeks no end except to tread that complex harmony. The turning aside into delight diffuses the destructive impulse of God's creatures to equal God in knowledge. Yet another labyrinth, besides the diversionary mix of talk and caresses of Adam and Eve and besides the angelic dance of 'Eccentric, intervolved' motions, 'yet regular | Then most, when most irregular they seem', treading out 'mazes intricate', is the ear whose inner labyrinth is capable of delaying and diffusing, but also masking, the hard edges of anger, hate, and sin. The ever-wakeful, permeable ear as the soul's gateway, whose mazy inner folds or labyrinth delay, defer, and temper the voice, was a Renaissance commonplace; and no one was more sensitive than Milton to the pressures on thought and the psyche created by a multitude of persuasive voices entering the brain through the ear—from the classical tongues of education to contemporary polemic—and their potential to inhibit the cultivation and integrity of ones own voice or the ability to hear the divine speak within. From her first delighted moment alone at the pool with the world's reflected surfaces, and from the first experience of having her vision corrected at her ear, the poet dramatizes through Eve a process of falling into self-knowledge. She falls through inexperienced, shallow self-reflection down to the bottom of despair and, paradoxically, from that state of feeling, or desiring to be, invisible, into an experience of deepest reflection. Like *Upon Appleton House*, *Paradise Lost* plunges the reader 'within', but specifically within the ear, and within a garden where Eve, a human garden, will sound alone the depths of her fallen knowledge. Milton who ventriloquizes all of the voices suggests the difficult experience of finding one's own.

In Chapters 5 and 6, I examine the disguise and threat of the feminine or effeminate in two of Dryden's least understood works, representative of his renewed interest in digressive forms as he probably foresaw and then began a career of speaking from outside the court. He wrote the long and bewildering beast fable *The Hind and the Panther* (1687) apparently to defend James II's Edict of Toleration and certainly to offer the curious public their long-awaited story of his conversion to Roman Catholicism. But Dryden bursts every convention of fable and public relations and offers a reading public hungry for blood an unflattering self-image. He invokes the feminine symbol of Eastern mystery and anti-Catholic propaganda, the Scarlet Whore of Babylon and Beast of the Apocalypse, to create protective mystification: against an ominous setting of violent menace, he creates not one but two female voices, predator and prey, two beastly mother churches that eerily resemble each other. The narrator's voice intrudes as well, a third party that introduces digressions of self-reflection. The lady beasts tensely match wits and exchange dark prophetic fables late into the night to forestall the end of their fabular encounter where they only consume salad—to forestall a return to physical violence. The *Discourse Concerning the Original and Progress of Satire* (1692) is Dryden's longest dedication and critical essay. It is addressed to Dryden's old patron, the Earl of Dorset, who unlike the poet had profited by the Glorious Revolution. Dryden uses the occasion of writing a history of satire as introduction to a volume of translations of satires of Juvenal and Persius to create a potentially unflattering portrait of Dorset and William III's court, carefully lodged at the centre of the essay in the oddly prolonged trial of critical judgement between Horace and Juvenal. The length and difficult progress of this essay simultaneously signal and conceal the personal story that Dryden unfolds behind the announced history of satire. To the figure and satire of Horace, Dryden assigns qualities of effeminate sycophancy and compromised accommodation to a usurping monarch, Augustus Caesar, qualities that the poet must distance from himself, once the hired pen of the Stuarts, and possibly attaches by the subtlest association to Dorset, like Horace the courtier of a usurper. Dryden gives the first prize of satire to Juvenal, the satirist in exile, whose masculine freedom of rage and digression he claims as his own.

I conclude with an epilogue on Swift's *A Tale of a Tub* (1704). In his anger at, yet sensitive mimicry of, the discursive freedom of Dryden and other 'moderns' who represented authority in the market place, Swift heightens the self-authorizing voice of digression into an explosive new form of fragment and miscellany that will become absorbed into the market's greatest literary success, the novel. Swift understood exactly the dangerous disruption of digression that threatens not only lines of narrative and logic but also other traditional lines of authority and hierarchy. He angrily conflates Dryden's liberties in his digressive prefaces and the laureate's claims in his late work for an alternative family of fathers and sons based on textual offspring, an exclusive genealogy of fathers and heirs, with the iconoclastic religious and sexual liberties of sectarian zealots and with the wildly digressing, orphaned sons of the allegory. The digression becomes synonymous in Swift with the Hack's chaotic writing voice that keeps talking, a mind disconnected from any body—disinherited from the parent narrative of the ancients and in permanent exile of modernity on the popular page.

PART I

Strategic Self-Sounding: Voices Raised from the Dead

1

The 'Motion in Corruption' of Donne's *Anniversaries*

Thou shalt not peepe through lattices of eies,
Nor heare through Laberinths of eares, nor learne
By circuit, or collections to discerne.
(*The Second Anniuersarie. Of the Progres of the Soule*, ll. 296–8)[1]

In my epigraph, Donne's narrator reminds us that knowing everything 'straight' characterizes perception in heaven. Earthly eyes and minds struggle laboriously for partial vision gained indirectly through lattices, labyrinths, circuitous routes, and collections—images throughout this book for human perception and progress. As Donne's first published verse, *The Anniversaries* have appeared indeed more like another puzzling detour in a circuitous career than as the self-announced achievement of clear vision and a voice of prophetic authority. The rambling length of 'such an eccentric long poem' of 'coarse, prosaic features and comical and satirical deformities', as one scholar has described 'An Anatomie of the World', is particularly curious for this poet of exquisite songs and sonnets and of the most nuanced verse epistles.[2] Neither these features nor Donne's preceding work conspicuously suggests the Old Testament poet and prophet mediating in these poems between heaven and earth. Ever since the 'many censures' of 1612 and Jonson's famous quip that 'if it been written of ye Virgin Marie it had been something', *The Anniversaries* and Elizabeth Drury herself have retained an aura of

[1] John Donne, *The Variorum Edition of the Poetry of John Donne*, gen. ed. Gary A. Stringer, vol. vi: *The Anniversaries and the Epicedes and Obsequies*, ed. Paul A. Parrish et al. (Bloomington: Indiana University Press, 1995), 8. All citations to *The Anniversaries*, to the two elegies 'upon the Death of Mrs. Bulstrode', and to the 1625 letter 'To Sir Robert Carr' accompanying 'A Hymne to the Saynts and To the Marquesse Hamilton' will refer to the Variorum edition.

[2] Arthur F. Marotti, *John Donne, Coterie Poet* (Madison: University of Wisconsin Press, 1986), 242.

extravagant, esoteric mystery.[3] Donne may claim to summon 'the people', but these Mosaic songs or hymns are not for everyone. Coleridge found them 'the strangest caprices of genius upon record'.[4]

The Anniversaries saw three editions in Donne's lifetime (1612, 1621, 1625), appeared in six collections of his work between 1633 and 1669, and were read and mined by the century's poets.[5] Dryden cited them in 1692 as a model for 'Eleonora'.[6] Yet the first audience of *The Anniversaries* wondered why he had 'said so much' in response to the death of a 14-year-old girl of no acquaintance or relation.[7] One of Donne's elegists in 1633 praised his 'Anniverse' for being 'so farre above its Reader, good,

[3] For Jonson's remark and Donne's answer, see 'Conversations with Drummond of Hawthornden', in *Ben Jonson*, ed. C. H. Herford and Percy and Evelyn Simpson, 11 vols. (Oxford: Oxford University Press, 1952), i. 133. T. S. Eliot observed that Donne is 'often saying something else, something poignant and personal, and yet, in the end, incommunicable to us'. *Selected Essays, 1917–1932* (New York: Harcourt, Brace and Company, 1932), 292. H. L. Meakin, *John Donne's Articulations of the Feminine* (Oxford: Clarendon Press, 1998), opens with an epigraph from 'An Anatomy of the World', 'Nor could incomprehensibleness deter | Me, from thus trying to imprison her' (ll. 469–70). Meakin explores 'incomprehensibleness' of the feminine for Donne and 'the ways in which the poet constructs a shelter for himself out of or indeed against the female body, leaving the feminine in what is sometimes recognized as "*internal exile*"' (22). See the summary of general critical commentary 1612–1989 in *Variorum: The Anniversaries and the Epicedes and Obsequies*, 239–365.

[4] Samuel Taylor Coleridge, *Coleridge's Miscellaneous Criticism* (Cambridge, Mass.: Harvard University Press, 1936), Lecture X, 143.

[5] For a discussion of the poems' life in the 17th century, see Barbara Kiefer Lewalski, *Donne's Anniversaries and the Poetry of Praise: The Creation of a Symbolic Mode* (Princeton: Princeton University Press, 1973), 335; also Lewalski, *Protestant Poetics and the Seventeenth-Century Religious Lyric* (Princeton: Princeton University Press, 1979).

[6] 'Doctor Donn, the greatest Wit, though not the best Poet of our Nation, acknowledges, that he had never seen Mrs. Drury, whom he has made immortal in his admirable *Anniversaries*; I have had the same fortune, though I have not succeeded to the same Genius. However, I have follow'd his footsteps in the Design of his Panegyrick, which was to raise an Emulation in the living, to Copy out the Example of the dead'. See Dryden's letter of dedication, 'To the Right Honorable the Earl of Abingdon &c'., preceding his 'Eleonora; A Panegyrical Poem Dedicated to the Memory of the Late Countess of Abingdon', in John Dryden, *The Works of John Dryden*, vol. iii, ed. Earl Miner (Berkeley and Los Angeles: University of California Press, 1969), 233.

[7] A letter of April 1612 from Donne to George Garrard includes this passage: 'But for the other part of the imputation, of having said so much, my defence is, that my purpose was to say as well as I could: for since I never saw the Gentlewoman, I cannot be understood to have bound my self to have spoken just Truth:' See John Donne, *Letters to Severall Persons of Honour (1651): A Facsimile Reproduction*, introd. M. Thomas Hester (Delmar, NY: Scholars' Facsimiles & Reprints, 1977), 255. Donne's letter from Paris to Sir Henry Goodyer in the spring of 1612 reports this and other criticisms he hears of *The Anniversaries* in England: 'I doubt not but they will soon give over that other part of that indictment, which is that I have said so much; for no body can imagine, that I who never saw her, could have any other purpose in that, then when I had received so very good testimony of her worthinesse, and was gone down to print verses, it became me to say, not what I was sure was just truth, but the best that I could conceive;'. Donne, *Letters*, 75.

| That wee are thought wits, when 'tis understood'.[8] In the miracles of scholarship, Donne's protean 'Shee' has metamorphosed into the mother of God, the Roman Catholic Church, the Logos, Christ, Astraea, Queen Elizabeth, *sapientia creata*, 'the archetypal woman as symbolized in the cabala's Shekinah', a 'poetic symbol' of the Protestant regenerate soul, and 'a stand-in for male loss'.[9]

Are *The Anniversaries* a well-wrought urn or 'a movement through tension to pleasure', a plot 'bound to time'?[10] Critics have differed on their formal success. 'No one has tried to put himself in the poet's place', complained Rosalie Colie in 1971, 'to work at the literary reason for the many "peeces" of the poems. Why *are* they so oddly and so persistently disjunctive?'[11] Among scholars who have pursued a literary solution to the poems' complexity, Barbara Lewalski brilliantly assembled the puzzle of their generic pieces, exhaustively documenting the literary modes on which Donne draws, each with its range of diction, gestures, and expectations.[12] Yet the rich mix of generic traditions and the various literary postures of elegist, satirist, confessing penitent, preacher, and politic counsellor with which the poet plays help *The Anniversaries* and their poet resist a death grip and an anatomy of interpretation.

Protesting that a critical industry has reduced these poems to 'hermeneutical barometers', Edward Tayler offered to 'set the record straight: about what John Donne meant when he said that "he described

[8] 'On Dr. Donnes death: By Mr. Mayne of Christchurch in Oxford', in *Poems by J.D. with Elegies on the Authors Death* (London: John Marriot, 1633), 393.

[9] The quoted reference to Elizabeth Drury as the cabala's Shekinah comes from Richard E. Hughes, *The Progress of the Soul: The Interior Career of John Donne* (New York: Morrow, 1968), 208. For the other figures see, most recently, Jennifer Donahue, 'Elizabeth Drury as Testimony: A Thomistic Analysis of Donne's "*Anniversaries*"', *Ben Jonson Journal*, 5 (1998), 133–48. See also Ronald Corthell, 'The Obscure Object of Desire: Donne's "*Anniversaries*" and the Cultural Production of Elizabeth Drury', in Arthur F. Marotti (ed.), *Critical Essays on John Donne*, (New York: G. K. Hall, 1994), 123–40, from whose essay come the last two quoted phrases, 132 and 135. Frank Manley's introduction to *John Donne: The Anniversaries* (Baltimore, 1963) includes a synopsis of the interpretations of Elizabeth Drury as well as a detailed explanation of his own identification of her with various traditions of the feminine principle of Wisdom. For a recent review of the commentary on 'She', see the *Variorum edition* of *The Anniversaries*, 293–317.

[10] James Andrew Clark, 'The Plot of Donne's "*Anniversaries*"', *SEL* 30 (1990), 64.

[11] Rosalie L. Colie, 'All in Peeces: Problems of Interpretation in Donne's Anniversary Poems', in Amadeus P. Fiore (ed.), *Just So Much Honor* (University Park: Pennsylvania State University Press, 1971), 197–8.

[12] See Lewalski, *Donne's Anniversaries*. The relevant genres she reviews include the poetry of praise and the poetry of compliment, the devotional meditation, the funeral sermon and the obsequie, the formal complaint, the elegy, and satire, and medieval philosophical traditions already assimilated in poetry organized in debate-form, *contemptus mundi* and *consolatio philosophiae*.

the Idea of a Woman and not as she was", and about the structure and the meaning, of The Anniversaries'.[13] The poems' meaning, he argued, would be revealed once a structure was laid bare and the parts anatomized and inventoried. He uncovered a parallel skeleton in both poems, a 'logical structure' of parts, subparts, and 'refrain-moral', and he printed the corresponding sections of the poems side by side on facing pages, adding, 'It will be difficult, I believe, for even the most solemn theorist to evade this double-entry evidence of conscious intention, of preconceived "Idea" and architectonic "foreconceit". It is "beauties best, proportion".'[14]

Does the beauty of *The Anniversaries* lie in such a clear, proportional structure? Their reception suggests that perhaps Donne cared more to elude anatomists, in slipping around and beyond the reader's expectations, than for the beauty of a logical frame. His poem reveals physical anatomy to be far from logical or perfectly proportioned. The world's body broods over hidden hollows, unplumbable seas, swelling abscesses, and high peaks—warts and 'pock-holes'. *The Anniversaries* begin and end with a fatal disease.

In his classic work *The Poetry of Meditation*, Louis Martz claimed that the poems adhered to the five-part structure of Ignatian meditation.[15] Yet Donne had just published his anti-Jesuit satire in which Lucifer, alarmed by the rival threat of Ignatius' ambition, sends the 'French-spanish mungrell' to the moon to found a 'Lunatique Church'. Lewalski has argued, on the other hand, for a four-part skeletal frame consistent with the themes of Protestant meditation.[16] Yet Donne's religious mix and 'predicament', as one scholar has argued, 'seems similar to that of the English church at the time, which was its own creation—neither Catholic nor avowedly Lutheran nor completely Calvinist—but rather a combination of elements uniquely English'.[17] By taking the anatomy literally (following what appears to be the poet's lead)—by looking too intently at its parts—earlier theories of organization perhaps have played into Donne's hands. For he tempts the reader to become absorbed in identifying physical parts and to make of his parts what they want. Readers obligingly have responded to the poems' challenge by breaking down and mapping parts. Like those men who 'weau'd out a net, and this net throwne | Vpon

[13] Edward W. Tayler, *Donne's Idea of a Woman: Structure and Meaning in 'The Anniversarie'* (New York: Columbia Universirt Press, 1991), 2.

[14] Ibid. 94, 98.

[15] Louis L. Martz, *The Poetry of Meditation* (New Haven: Yale University Press, 1954), ch. 6.

[16] Lewalski, *Donne's Anniversaries*, esp. ch. 3.

[17] Jill Peláez Baumgaertner, 'Political Play and Theological Uncertainty in the *Anniversaries*', *John Donne Journal*, 13/1–2 (1994), 43.

the Heauens', they have made the heavens of these poems their own. *The Anniversaries* foresee the reader's impulse to 'Meridians, and Parallels' and slip out of a logical grasp just as the natural world they describe tilts and bulges and opens into fathomless vaults, just as its stars list and wobble, sink and swell.

The Anniversaries share with the earlier lyrics, satires, elegies, and epistles a vocabulary of tombs, wombs, rooms, and prisons; carcasses and embalming virtue, quintessence, and tinctures; suns, stars, and circles; souls and names.[18] From the first lines of his first satire, flight and release from small rooms, prisons, and coffins characteristically haunt Donne's imagination. And some of the old bravado of Donne the lyric poet, who leaves yet encompasses a world that rejects him and his love, shapes *The Anniversaries.* But their obtrusive anti-lyrical features announce even the oblique balance of the *Songs and Sonnets* gone askew. Grown more darkly layered through years of disappointment, heavy familial burdens, and ill health—those years in which he wrote the potentially scandalous, unpublished, and little-circulated defence of suicide, *Biathanatos*—Donne's lyric poise demands to be threaded through an even more elaborate formal obstacle course. While in the 'The Canonization' he could deftly expose and camouflage the painful truth of his 'ruin'd fortune' with a joke ('My five gray haires, or ruin'd fortune flout', l. 3), equally distracting but blacker humour in *The Anniversaries* winds around images of fragmentation and ruin that lead to a startling beheaded man. The twinkling dead eye of a bleeding criminal corpse becomes an image for the disturbing energy of these 'most leisurely poetic ruminations': a paradoxical 'motion in corruption' (II. 22) likened to maggots, of 'new creatures' (I. 75) produced on the world's carcass.[19]

The language and behaviour of this speaker suggests, rather than a neat structure of parts, the birth of a new voice in the process of rising to command. As Donne's witness to the reality of how past and present continuously feel, and write, through each other—are apprehended,

[18] Of the *Songs and Sonnets*, think of 'A Feaver' whose woman is 'the worlds soule' and, if she dies, leaves the world 'but thy carkass then'; the released souls as bullets in 'The Dissolution' (as in the Second Anniversary, 182); or the 'she' as prince and state in 'The Sunne Rising'; of taming and fettering grief in 'The Triple Foole'; of phoenixes and suns in 'The Canonization'; and of 'this ragged bony name' and 'my ruinous Anatomie' in 'A Valediction: Of My Name in the Window'. All citations from the *Songs and Sonnets* and elegies refer to John Donne, *The Elegies and The Songs and Sonnets*, ed. Helen Gardner (Oxford: Oxford University Press, 1965).

[19] Marotti, *John Donne, Coterie Poet*, 232.

remembered, and mended together—this pair of poems is his answer to the anatomist's vision of parts:

> . . . for shee rather was two soules,
> Or like to full, on both sides written Rols,
> Where eies might read vpon the outward skin,
> As strong Records for God, as mindes within. (II: 503–6)

The Anniversaries may be two numinous 'Rols' but unroll in a serpentine movement that shoots an oddly joyous poison 'from the liue Serpent' (I. 410).

RESISTING ANATOMY

The length of these poems is part of their extravagance—'that I have said so much'—for which Donne complained of being criticized. The 'so much', however, is aggressive and deliberately digressive, I suggest. *Digressive Voices* begins with *The Anniversaries* because not only does Donne step aside from his ostensible subject, Elizabeth Drury (or 'the Idea of a Woman', as he reportedly said to deflect Jonson's censure), but he makes digressive progress his subject. In addition, Donne's stepping around Elizabeth Drury to address the diseased body politic emphasizes a relation between digression and satire to which we return in the chapters on Dryden. By beginning with a lack or absence, *The Anniversaries* exemplify the way that digressions in the other texts of this book may be used to point to an urgent lack of something or someone, or an absence of connection, that a narrator tries to step around, to cover or fill—in the process, as Browne announces, ranging 'into extraneous things' and joining 'parts of different Subjects' to form a whole text. Donne begins with the earthly absence of Elizabeth Drury, confirmed by a glimpse of her in the heavenly choir (I. 10), which becomes an occasion for the narrator to step into the vacuum. From the first breathless sentence of twenty lines, with two, busy, parenthetical digressive outbursts (I. 3–6, 16–18), the narrator seizes control of the occasion of death and fills in the gap with his own commanding voice. The parentheses act out in miniature the whole project to speak, whose method is to open an occasion and space within a larger occasion.[20] Announcing that the world has been left

[20] For a learned and fascinating discussion of the relation between digression and parentheses in English poetry, see John Lennard, *But I Digress: The Exploitation of Parentheses in English Printed Verse* (Oxford: Clarendon Press, 1991).

'speechless' by Elizabeth Drury's death and is shrinking to nothing, the narrator reverses the momentum and gives birth to a new world, the poems, and his voices, including that of an anatomist, a Mosaic singer, a satiric prophet.

Yet no one fully has accounted for the talkative, witty, argumentative narrator, for his aggressive, even violent, syntax and imagery and rapid shift of mood from wild playfulness to dark visions of human corruption and misogyny.[21] The anatomist in this work seems voyeuristic yet oddly unseeing, instead often irreverent, witty, and figurative. The ascendant soul in *The Second Anniversary* points ecstatically 'Up' but keeps turning back to shake his fist at earth's 'Libellars', 'Courts', and 'spungy slack Diuine'. Most strangely, no one has addressed the grotesque epic simile at the hinge of the diptych, early in *The Second Anniversary*: the twitching, bleeding, beheaded man with a rolling tongue. My remarks about each of the *Anniversaries* lead to and from the man on whose pieces and history the poet has brooded:

> But as a ship which hath stroke saile, doth runne,
> By force of that force which before, it wonne,
> Or as sometimes in a beheaded man,
> Though at those two Red seas, which freely ran,
> One from the Trunke, another from the Head,
> His soule be saild, to her eternall bed,
> His eies will twinckle, and his tongue will roll,
> As though he beckned, and cal'd backe his Soul,
> He graspes his hands, and he puls vp his feet,
> And seemes to reach, and to step forth to meet
> His soule; when all these motions which we saw,
> Are but as Ice, which crackles at a thaw:
> Or as a Lute, which in moist weather, rings
> Her knell alone, by cracking of her strings.
> So strugles this dead world, now shee is gone;
> For there is motion in corruption. (II. 7–22)

Between the two *Anniversaries*, the poet strategically places society's outcast—the lifelike dead. The spectre depicts the passage from life to death to afterlife as a poet's nightmare—to be speechless with a useless tongue, head disconnected from the body. At the beginning of a poem about the soul's ascent to God, the figure seems to mock both life and afterlife, at

[21] Baumgaertner, 'Political Play', notes the shifts of tone as a sign of 'a narrator with many voices—perhaps even a dialogic imagination', a 'hybrid of languages used to simultaneously present and resist ideas' (31–2).

least for those whom deprivation has forced to the margins and who expire in two seas of blood that 'freely ran'—the last dash to liberty. At the centre of *The Anniversaries*, beckoning and grasping, is a seductive figure of 'motion in corruption' which prompts the narrator to explain, 'thou seest me strive for life' (II. 31).

Although hardly an outcast or criminal, Donne had alluded frequently in letters and verse epistles to his low worldly state, fallen from grace and blocked from a civil service post since 1602. His rolling tongue had proved ineffectual. Yet within a sentence from which the reader has no exit for not ten years but twenty-two lines, the poet turns the corpse of personal failure into a rhetorical shudder of life exactly placed at the turn, the *versus*, of *The Anniversaries*. Between 'those two Red seas', I suggest, the speaker escapes out of a past Egypt and assumes the authority to lead us 'up'. The beheaded man at the centre of *The Anniversaries* suggests a sense of a life cut into two parts, and the parts resist even as they invite dissection. As a nightmare of the social outcast and guilty criminal, his career split, like this work, down the middle between heart and head, body and soul, the poet slips free. Against the world's judgemental gaze he turns the otherworldly twinkle of that cold eye.

The image of a ship with furled sails moving eerily on a windless sea by the momentum of a previous gust immediately precedes the beheaded man and his useless tongue. The image reminds us that 'the notion of language animated or inflated by some authentic wind is one of the most persistent *topoi* of Western language theory'.[22] In his discussion of extemporal speaking, Quintilian likens an orator who needs to be filled with the breath or wind of inspiration to a ship that requires wind to sail (10. 7. 22–3) or to a ship's pilot (10. 7. 3). The ship of speech and the beheaded man are followed in Donne's simile by an image less grotesque than that of the man but equally suggestive of isolation, neglect, and impotence, a dark shadow of the Romantics' wind-harp. A lute made for song has been exposed to the elements, so that moisture plays on and cracks 'her strings' which ring 'Her knell alone'; the courtly instrument is gendered female. Once associated with minstrelsy, the lute had become fashionable for aristocratic men and especially women by the mid-sixteenth century. The instrument's soft sounds were considered perfect for women's ears and for private chamber music, such as accompanying the voice and consort playing.[23]

[22] Terence Cave, *The Cornucopian Text. Problems of Writing in the French Renaissance* (Oxford: Clarendon Press 1979), 145.

[23] See Penelope Gouk, *Music, Science, and Natural Magic in Seventeenth-Century England* (New Haven: Yale University Press, 1999), 34, 120.

Where 'An Anatomie of the World' begins with a speechless, nameless 'thou' but ends with the speaker boldly trying 'to emprison' (l. 470) Elizabeth Drury and claiming 'to inuade' (l. 468) the office of sacred poet, 'Of the Progres of the Soule' begins again with speechlessness, images of silenced or broken sound: the silenced, once imprisoned outcast, the singer's cracked vocal chords—depleted wind, castrated, executed speech, and dampened song. An old instrument to please upper-class women lies exposed to the elements. Yet the lifelike twinkle of the beheaded man is a clue or clew, I suggest. Near the end of *The Second Anniversary*, Donne inserts a description of the physical disease of a proud aristocrat. An abscess whose fluid, like poison, the narrator describes twice as 'dangerous' threatens to burst violently and release its contents to 'rise vp' and throttle the courtier (II. 471–88). The speaker imagines instead of another execution an internal attack on the speaking throat of pride and privilege. Society executes criminals; but lower orders, including dependent poets, like repressed humours that begin to fester may suddenly rise up if ignored too long. 'We're scarse our Fathers shadowes cast at noone', says Donne early in these poems (I. 144); but from under the shadow of patriarchs, *The Anniversaries* cast their own distended shadow. The speaker vigorously resists being silenced and rises with moral if not social authority, while his busy voice, perfectly suited for the most responsible and politic service, claims finally to be a masculine, commanding, and public instrument: the brassy trumpet of God (II. 528), not the feminine lute it may have been once.

This chapter argues that the digressive voice of the narrator within these poems resists being silenced by death's blade and also by the pride and distance of the powerful who are figuratively, wittily, throttled at the end. They include surely the woman for whom he composed verse before and after the Drurys—Lucy Russell, Countess of Bedford, the woman who felt that these poems pointedly did not praise her. Donne trumpeted *The Anniversaries* boldly, in publication, to secure not necessarily her attention but that of a male audience: Sir Robert Drury, the King, and, according to a recent reading, James's heir, the popular, newly invested Prince of Wales, namesake of Henry VIII and godson of the virgin queen for whom Elizabeth Drury was named and whose mythological associations with Astraea and the Virgin Mary Donne clearly invokes.[24]

[24] See Baumgaertner, 'Political Play', especially 33–40.

Note that the revolutionary sentiments in *The Second Anniversary*,

> But since all honors from inferiors flow,
> (For they doe giue it; Princes doe but show
> Whom they would have so honord) (ll. 407–9)

echo from an earlier verse epistle, 'To the Countess of Bedford' ('Honour is so sublime perfection'):

> So from low persons doth all honour flow;
> Kings, whom they would have honour'd, to us show,
> And but *direct* our honour, not *bestow*. (ll. 7–9)[25]

When *The Anniversaries* appeared in early spring 1612, Bedford's jealous displeasure at Donne's lavish praise for a girl whom he never knew prompted the poet's hasty obeisance from France, 'To the Countess of Bedford, Begun in France but never Perfected', as well as 'Epitaph on Himself, to the Countess of Bedford', poems where he pictures himself as dead ('Though I be dead, and buried, yet I have | (Living in you,) Court enough in my grave')—yet not quite 'speechless grown' ('Epitaph', l. 8). After several years of writing encomia to Bedford and her female friends who had failed to advance him, this most elaborate celebration of an aristocratic female describes no living woman because, by implication, none deserves the praise. Further, the poet has turned elsewhere for support. While his letters from Paris at the same time to George Garrard and Sir Henry Goodyer castigate himself for having 'descended', 'declined', 'gone down' to print his poems, these are major works designed to announce their poet as a commanding voice suitable for a complex, Jacobean political world—as a Mosaic poet who can fit together all of the world's 'pieces' in song, no longer the private lute for women.

The discursive, digressive voice of Donne's narrator, his 'cozening line' (I. 271), is a literary mode of resistance to the act and vision of both physical dissection and the literary genre of anatomy: to the breakdown and isolation of bodies and subjects into parts. The literary movement of digression—of stepping aside, around, away—is here above all a movement to forestall speechlessness, to step around death. Meanwhile, the speechless Elizabeth Drury who needs his voice becomes a fit vehicle for absorbing, reversing, and transforming feelings of vulnerability, unfulfilled promise, and transcendent visionary capacities into a marketable self. In what follows, I first review the relations among physical

[25] John Donne, *The Satires, Epigrams and Verse Letters*, ed. W. Milgate (Oxford: Oxford University Press, 1967), 101. Citations to the verse epistles and satires are to this edition.

anatomy, the body, and the female in *The First Anniversary* in the context of Donne's complex relation to women who dissolve and 'kill us', and to the Countess of Bedford in particular. I next propose, in the context of Donne's Roman Catholic background, the relation between his deep interest in themes of marginality and the criminal, on the one hand, and the social, religious, and aesthetic politics of anatomy, on the other. His long unpublished treatise on suicide and his two published prose works that immediately preceded *The Anniversaries* appear attempts to approach privately and then distance himself publicly from the history of imprisonment, execution, and martyrdom of his recusant maternal relations; at the same time *The Anniversaries* incorporate Roman Catholic and High Church elements of theology and stylistics. I conclude that the digressive movements of the narrator lead him out of the eerie life-in-death of the images that open both *The First* and *The Second Anniversary* to an image of the explosion of swollen aristocratic pride and an announcement, from commanding moral heights, of a visionary voice that silences anatomists.

The speaker's sharp swerves of tone, from digressive story telling to satire to fantastic hyperbole, parody and defy the anatomist's blade and mode of knowledge by scrutiny of parts, which are equated in *The First Anniversary* with a suffocating, literal-minded, and inexorable feminine rule over the anatomical state. The poet's exaggerated elevation of Elizabeth, on the one hand, and his tales of 'poor' distracted mothers and recital of creation myths, on the other, slip this stealthy 'slow-pac'd starre' (I. 117) around and out from under a female hold: not only on the fallen physical body but on the masculine, poetic promise that struggles between birth and death.

FITTING THE PARTS

The Anniversaries were published early in 1612 while Donne was on the continent as secretary to Sir Robert Drury.[26] When the poet received word of their mixed reception, he wrote to his friend George Garrard,

26 The poems were not composed on the first and second anniversaries of Elizabeth Drury's death early in December 1610. 'An Anatomy of the World' was published by the time Donne left for the continent with the Drurys 'before the middle of November' 1611 ('Some moneths she hath beene dead' (I.39) he says) and *The Second Anniversary* within a few months of the first ('a yeare is runne'). R. C. Bald, *John Donne: A Life* (New York: Oxford University Press, 1970), 244, 246.

and answered a particularly offended readership, 'those Ladies'.[27] He refers to the jealous Lucy Russell, Countess of Bedford, whose patronage he had been courting, and her circle at the Jacobean court: 'If any of those Ladies think that Mistris Drewry was not so, let that Lady make her self fit for all those praises in the book, and it shall be hers'. The challenge around 'fit' is unmistakable from a poet who did not fit into the court world; the crucial word in its meanings of just, right, eligible, or to have a place appears several times in *The Anniversaries*, which seem such a misfit of form to content, whose poet defends his matter as 'fit' for verse and catalogues a misfit world of fragments 'unfit' (II. 73) for the pure like Elizabeth Drury who on earth 'fit' her virtue into us (I. 409–12). Donne scribbled two grovelling apologies to soothe Bedford's vanity including 'To the Countess of Bedford, Begun in France but Never Perfected', in which he genuflects in a parody of the Roman Catholic confession of sin and delicately touches on the economic facts of their relationship.[28] When he writes 'I have to others lent | Your stock, and over prodigally spent | Your treasure' (ll. 11–13), the economic metaphor balances between the witty flattery of describing her beauty and virtue in financial terms of stock and treasure and raising the possibility that he invests elsewhere a stock of flattering words reserved for her because Bedford has not invested enough treasure in him.

The Anniversaries constitute a suspicious fit of long poem to slight or absent subject, but they perform other sleights of hand. The 'Idea of a Woman' is not so much exalted and lamented as controlled. While Donne extols Elizabeth Drury's purity, he excoriates her sex as the source of the corruption he dissects. Eve, the Fall, serpents, and mortality's 'consuming wound' (I. 248): the feminine earth is skewed by the narrator's misogyny which is as unrelenting as Hamlet's in his preoccupation with female corruption, poison, and helpless mothers. According to 'An Anatomie of the World', the Fall saw the painful birth of parts, of dismembering forgetfulness and detail that multiplies like endless children. Direct or indirect references to serpents and poison are particularly prominent—I: 106, 180, 196, 272, 331, 345, 363, 409. The speaker bewails that women give birth constantly and irresponsibly, even 'after fifty', but everything about birth from the womb is 'ruinous' and crippling, although the speaker never loses the chance for wit: 'poore mothers

[27] Donne, *Letters*, 255.

[28] On Donne's knowledge of economics and use of economic terminology in his verse, see Coburn Freer, 'John Donne and Elizabethan Economic Theory', *Criticism*, 38/4 (Fall 1996), 497–520.

crie'—not in tears but cry out—that children are not born 'orderly' unless they come head first, falling on their heads. 'The due birth time' is not observed in natural process (yet the poetic process proceeds 'in due measure', I. 467), and even the world fell out of its cradle and was lamed. But the poet's calibration of the fit of the sexes to each other is hardly a joke. Wombs lead to tombs: mothers lose their children and 'kill' their men. The female is yoked not to fecundity, abundance, and the hopefulness of new birth but vehemently to death and especially to the primary prison of the body.

Under the cover of the barber-surgeons' annual anatomy lesson—a public display of empirical knowledge and order—the poems expose rather than dissect a Medusa's head of the snakes of failure and extinction, of physical and psychological deterioration. Lethargy and depression, loss of memory and vision, speech fallen to groans ('But this is the worst, that thou art speechless grown')—all hiss in turn and threaten to turn the speaker to stone. As his own tombstone, Donne apologetically addresses the angry female in 'Epitaph on Himself, to the Countess of Bedford': 'My fortune and my choice this custome break, | When we are speechlesse grown, to make stones speak' (ll. 7–8).

Between 1608 and 1610, Donne became virtually the laureate of the Countess of Bedford.[29] If the incomparable Lucy felt betrayed in 1612 because her votary would celebrate in print a more exalted model of virtue than herself, her response could not have surprised the poet. Powerful, controversial, and close to Queen Anne, the Countess was by upbringing a Calvinist whose delight and prominence in court masques were notorious, not least when resplendent and 'naked brested' in the costumes of Inigo Jones.[30] She also wrote verses which she showed to Donne and enjoyed the flattery of his intellectual attention. If, as his verse epistles indicate, Donne aspired as well to the role of spiritual adviser, he touched a religious nerve in 1609 and suffered her sharp rebuke, after which their relationship suffered. When Lucy fell dangerously ill in November of 1612, Donne had recently returned from Europe, but another spiritual light was in place at Twickenham—the Calvinist

[29] Bald, *John Donne, A Life*, 172–81, esp. 177.

[30] She acted the Queen of the Amazons in the *Masque of Queenes* and twice Aglaia (Splendor), first in the *Masque of Blacknesse* and again in the *Masque of Beautie*—for the latter, 'In a robe of flame colour, naked brested; her bright hayre loose flowing'. Barbara Lewalski, *Writing Women in Jacobean England* (Cambridge, Mass.: Harvard University Press, 1993), 100–1.

preacher and physician John Burges.[31] Later Donne suspected Burges of turning the Countess against him. In 1614 Donne wrote an elegy on the death from smallpox of Bedford's brother, John Lord Harrington, which he sent to her with a request for financial help. To Donne's acute disappointment, she only sent £30, 'which in good faith she excused with that, which is in both parts true, that her present debts were burdensome, and that I could not doubt of her inclination, upon all future emergent occasions, to assist me', the poet wrote to Goodyer. 'I confess to you, her former fashion towards me, had given a better confidence; and this diminution in her makes me see, that I must use more friends, then I thought I should have needed'.[32]

The Countess's earlier displeasure in 1609 arose over her laureate's 'Elegie upon the Death of Mrs. Bulstrode' ('Death, I recant'). Cecilia Bulstrode had been Bedford's kinswoman and the Queen's lady-in-waiting, also the target of Jonson's vitriolic epigram 'The Court Pucell'. Donne's poem features a gobbling giant Death for whom 'Th'earth's face is but thy table' and macabre, ambivalent passages reflecting on Cecilia's character, for example, lines 39–40, 43–4, 55–7. But the poet had been forced to bow to the Countess's poetic correction: using against him his own divine sonnet X, 'Deathe be not proud', Lucy countered with one of her own. Opening 'Death bee not proudd, thy hand gaue not this blowe', her verse substituted joyful assurance and spiritual elevation for her laureate's depiction of death as 'Nowe wantonly hee spoiles, and eats vs not, | But breaks off friends, and letts vs piecemeale rott'.[33] Her pious lines dwell on the 'endlesse reste' and 'clearer soule' of her friend whose reputation at court was hardly untarnished.[34]

Bedford's poem had ended on a firm 'no' to death: 'The grave no conquest gets, Death hath no sting'. Donne dutifully wrote a new 'Elegie

[31] Without a ministry, he 'was able to make full use of his privileged position at the bedsides of the sick noblemen and ladies he attended'. P. Thomson, 'John Donne and the Countess of Bedford', *MLR* 44 (1949), 333.

[32] Donne, *Letters*, 219.

[33] For Lady Bedford's elegy, see *Variorum: The Anniversaries and the Epicedes and Obsequies*, 235–6. Claude J. Summers, 'Donne's 1609 Sequence of Grief and Comfort', *Studies in Philology*, 89 (1992), 211–31, provides a useful overview of Donne's elegies for Lady Markham and for Cecilia Bulstrode and the Countess's response.

[34] The poem was printed along with Donne's original elegy in the 1635 collected edition as 'Elegy on Mistris Boulstred' and appears in various manuscripts of Donne's work. For a review of its inclusion in the Donne canon and discussion of its authorship, see appendix B, 'The Elegy, "Death bee not proude" ', in *John Donne; The Epithalamions, Anniversaries and Epicedes*, ed. W. Milgate (Oxford: Clarendon Press, 1978), 235–37; and Lewalski, *Writing Women in Jacobean England*, 120–2.

upon the Death of Mrs. Bulstrode', which acknowledged this model of serene confidence, and he added an obeisant apology, 'To the Countess of Bedford' ('T'have written then'). Yet the extravagant cannibalistic death which in Donne's original elegy 'getts twixt soules and bodies such a place | As sin insinuats twixt Iust men and Grace', if banished underground, re-emerges in 1611 with a new sting and conquest in the more comely shape of Elizabeth Drury.

Donne's good friend, the courtier Sir Henry Goodyer, was attached to the Bedford household. In 1610 while visiting Elizabeth Stanley, the Countess of Huntingdon, Goodyer had urged the needy poet to write to Huntingdon. Clearly written for Bedford's eyes as well as Goodyer's are the anxious twists and turns of caution in Donne's letter of response ('that by this occasion . . . I be not traduced'), the poet's quick slight at Huntingdon's intellect ('if these verses be . . . over or under her understanding'), as well as his desire to protect a reputation for sincerity, to maintain 'my integrity to the other Countess [Bedford]', for whom he had reserved 'all the thoughts of womens worthinesse'. For Bedford's eyes and ears, she was the epitome of female worth and Huntingdon was only 'her picture', a copy of the original: 'But because I hope she will not disdain, that I should write well of her Picture, I have obeyed you thus far, as to write [of Huntingdon]'.[35] The imagery of original and copy, however, becomes applied to Elizabeth Drury in 1611: 'Shee that was best, and first originall | Of all faire copies' (I. 227–8). Donne marshals the trope again in 1612 to soothe Bedford at the end of 'To the Countess of Bedford, Begun in France but Never Perfected':

> Next I confesse my'impenitence, for I
> Can scarce repent my first fault, since thereby
> Remote low Spirits, which shall ne'r read you,
> May in lesse lessons finde enough to doe,
> By studying copies, not Originals,
> *Desunt caetera.* (ll. 21–6)

[35] Donne, *Letters*, 104. 'But because I hope she [the Countess of Huntington] will not disdain that I should write well of her picture, I have obeyed you thus far as to write; but entreat you your friendship, that by this occasion of versifying I be not traduced, nor esteemed light in that tribe and that house where I have lived. If those reasons which moved you to bid me write be not constant in you still, or if you meant not that I should write verses; or if these verses be too bad, or too good, over or under her understanding, and not fit, I pray receive them as a companion and supplement of this letter to you; and as such a token as I use to send, which use, because I wish rather they should serve (except you wish otherwise) I send no other', 104–5.

The well-worn compliment carried diminished force. The intense physical discomfort of 'but's and 'or if's in the earlier letter to Goodyer emphasizes the convoluted humiliation of being a learned male poet whose future advancement is bound by worldly female demands and their domestic detail. These women expected constant attention to feed their appetite for flattery and required a sensitivity alert to their competitive jealousies. To Goodyer he is concerned if 'these verses' to Huntingdon 'not fit'. But the unstated, more pressing question might be where does the poet fit? Only a year later, he writes yet another encomium of a woman, *The Anniversaries*, which looks like an exercise in misfit; and he reverses the politics of proportion to suit himself.

The female's control over the immediately absorbing and demanding world of the live body, and the dead body as the male surgeon's territory of privileged gaze, meet in *The First Anniversary*'s fit of form, an anatomy, to obstreperous content that includes mothers and children, ever new stars, and wandering planets and poets.[36] The authoritative, empirical gaze of the anatomist over the dead and outcast, and the gaze of 'wise, and good lookers on' such as discreet courtiers who judge by reputation ('(Since most men be such as most think they be)' I. 334–5) are returned by the beheaded man's uncanny, twinkling eye and are transcended in *The Second Anniversary*. In the dead soul's 'growen all Ey', Donne creates a model for the poet's godlike imaginative liberty for being no part of any body, but overlooking all.

In 'An Anatomie of the World' the myopic scrutiny of parts characteristic of anatomies—and of feminine vanity—is attracted to yet frustrated by the allure of surfaces. Anatomists and mothers, according to *The Anniversaries*, cannot see souls or wholes; the dead and poets do, eschew-

[36] The poem's conjunction of the medical and the female recalls the home where Donne lived for eight years from the age of 4 until he entered Oxford. Within six months of the death of Donne's father, his mother married the Roman Catholic but wealthy and esteemed physician Dr John Syminges, President of the Royal College of Physicians. A widower with only one son still in his care, he offered a comfortable home for Elizabeth Donne and her six children as well as protection for the recusancy of Elizabeth and her relatives. In the view of one scholar, it was an understandable 'marriage of convenience', and Mrs. Donne 'had a utilitarian outlook on marriage if anyone had, for she married another man soon after the death of Syminges'. See Baird W. Whitlock, 'John Syminges, a Poet's Step-Father', *Notes and Queries*, 199 (1954), 424. In the poet's last year of childhood at home, the family moved close to St Bartholomew's Hospital; and while 'he had seen death at work in his own family, he now saw it working wholesale at the hospital. If he had seen doctors at meetings and fireside conversations, here he saw them at their daily tasks'. Whitlock, 'The Heredity and Childhood of John Donne', *Notes and Queries*, 204 (1959), 352.

ing 'matters of fact' as 'vnconcerning things'.[37] The soul of the dead does not reveal gaping absences but fills them instantly, remembers, in a rush of fulfilment and being filled. The dead's and the poet's anti-anatomical vision of proportion goes beyond geometry's pedantic circles, cubes, and squares to a politically subversive one of states, like Elizabeth's 'euen made' complexion, of 'euen constitution' which cannot be broken down because all parts are equal, where 'all good things being met, no one presumes | To gouerne, or to triumph on the rest' (II. 128–30). The dead's and the poet's way to look, to know, and to fit is instantaneous, intuitive, and self-fulfilling like God's; 'the object, and the wit' are the same. Closed is the endlessly frustrating distance between surgeon and body, between past and present, or between a petitioner at court and the inner mysteries of the body politic.

THE FIRST ANNIVERSARY

The Anniversaries resist easy entrance or exit. Imprisonment and mystery separate the poet not only from Elizabeth Drury (I. 469–70) but from the reader as well. Most contrary about these poems on a young girl's death is their manipulative energy and delight—an energy which blows through and around the skeletal or devotional anatomy that has proved

[37] Recall Donne's response to the criticism that the length and weight of the poems appeared unwieldy on the shoulders of his slight ostensible subject. He had answered George Garrard that, unacquainted with Elizabeth Drury, he did not feel 'bound . . . to have spoken just truth' (*Letters*, 255); he repeats these sentiments to Goodyer: 'it became me to say, not what I was sure was just truth, but the best that I could conceive' (*Letters*, 75). That is, his never having known or even seen Elizabeth Drury freed him from 'just truth' to write 'the best'—that difference between chronicle and verse he alludes to at the end of 'An Anatomie of the World'.

Many years later, in March 1625, Donne uses almost the same language to contrast the inhibiting pressure of fact to the possibilities of poetry in a letter to Sir Robert Ker which accompanied 'An Hymne to the Saynts and To the Marquesse Hamilton': 'I presume you rather trye what you can doe in mee then what I can doe in verse; you knewe my vttermost when it was at best. And even then I did best when I had least Truth for my subiect. In this present case there is so much Truth as it defeates all Poetry. Call, therefore this Paper by what name you will' (*Variorum: The Anniversaries and the Epicedes and Obsequies*, 219). His equation of the imaginative work of poetry as 'the best' he can say, as opposed to 'just truths', lies behind 'To the Countesse of Salisbury, August 1614' where he raises, and defends himself against, the charge of meaningless superlatives. He likens the poet's glorifying the beauties of his patrons to Adam as he would have responded if God had unfolded his creation day by day; each day he 'might have said the best that he could say | And not be chid for praising yesterday' (ll. 45–6).

such a battleground for critics. As one student of *The Anniversaries* has noted, 'someone feels empowered, but not everyone'.[38]

Donne teases, thwarts, and masters the reader. In an early sermon he likens the space of life between birth and death to the cart-ride of a prisoner to the executioner's block, and the poet leads us blindfolded in 'An Anatomie' towards an execution.[39] The poem opens with a tortuous, breathless sentence which winds over twenty lines, is interrupted twice by substantial parenthetical matter followed closely by three other extended sentences (of eighteen, sixteen, and thirteen lines) all before line 90. No one is allowed a word in edgewise ('Let no man say', I. 63). The first sentence is a model of frustration, humiliation, and exclusion, of being at another's beck and call. The poet creates a parenthetical club ('all assumed unto this dignity', I. 81).

The first two lines in particular announce that the poems' indirect style will halt, confuse, distract, and diffuse forward progress at almost every

[38] Corthell, 'The Obscure Object of Desire', 127. That Donne's encomium of Elizabeth Drury bears a whiff of triumphant appropriation—even out from under the nose of her father—is suggested first by contemporaries. Even the commendatory poem to *The First Anniversary*, 'To the Praise of the Dead, and the Anatomy', opens with a shuffling of bodies behind Donne's: 'Wel dy'de the world, that we might liue to see | This world of wit, in his Anatomee'. Not only the world but Elizabeth is well dead. One of the elegies on Donne which appear at the end of the 1633 edition of his collected poems comments in its first lines on Elizabeth Drury's good luck: 'There that blest maid to die, who now should grieve? | After thy sorrow, 'twere her losse to liue'.

After musing on the spectacle of such extraordinary life in death ('how can I consent the world is dead | While this Muse lives?'), the author of 'To the Praise of the Dead' hints at an indecorous contest that Donne's poem initiates between its merely 'wel-borne' accomplishment and the memory of the 'thrise noble maid'. He addresses her who acquiesced to die with such feminine grace,

> [thou] couldst not have found nor sought
> A fitter time to yeeld to thy sad Fate,
> Then whiles this spirit lives; that can relate
> Thy worth so well to our last nephews eyne,
> That they shall wonder both at his, and thine:
> Admired match! where strives in mutuall grace
> The cunning Pencill, and the comely face: (ll. 12–18)

Hardly a fair match, the 'cunning Pencill' easily dominates the face.

[39] See the sermon preached upon Easter Day on Psalm 89: 48, 28 Mar. 1619. *John Donne's Sermons on the Psalms and Gospels, with a Selection of Prayers and Meditations*, ed. Evelyn M. Simpson (Berkeley and Los Angeles: University of California Press, 1963), 29. Donne's Roman Catholic grandfather and court entertainer and poet, John Heywood, had been led from The Tower to his execution, then pardoned by Henry VIII at the last minute as a jest. See Dennis Flynn, *John Donne and the Ancient Catholic Nobility* (Bloomington: Indiana University Press, 1995), 27–8.

turn. Clauses beginning with interrogatives such as 'when', 'which', 'whom', and 'who' back into each other to emphasize a dense, confusing world of mysterious referents and information which the poet controls. And he controls when to share it; the main clause of the first sentence does not appear until line 11. The speaker never names Elizabeth Drury, for with the world all else has lost a name, but refers to her as 'that rich soul', 'the Queen'. Most startlingly, after two lines of 'when', 'who', and 'which', he leaves us hanging in mid-sentence to digress. In a long parenthetical roadblock of two complete sentences, he introduces another obstacle course: as if in a whispered aside, he mentions the exclusive body of souls whose members he imagines and presides over—those capable of reading the poem. The immobile, trapped quality of that dull lodger, the 'inmate soul', is emphasized by the arms of the parenthesis and the full stop. Those with an inmate soul go nowhere; they who have rich souls 'follow worthiness' like members of an Elizabethan royal progress.

Elizabeth Drury's absence becomes not only palpable but threatening. Immediately in the first line after the luxurious promise of 'that rich soule' and 'Heauen', she is 'gone'. And to prove it Donne makes sure we briefly glimpse her singing in heaven, 'a part' of that song, not this one. The first seventy lines insist not only that she is gone ('But long shee'ath beene away, long, long, yet none | Offers to tell vs who it is that's gone'; 'Though shee which did inanimate and fill | The world, be gone'); they also make clear that the speaker is filling up the space. In those initial lines he takes control by creating expectation and anticipation (the child waiting at the font, the prince 'expected long'), by perplexing us with a frenzy of diagnoses, explanations, orders, and directions, by reducing the reader to a state like the nameless waiting child.

Donne calls us from languishing to succouring, from joy to mourning, health to lethargy, finally from death and putrefaction to 'a kind of world remaining still'. Lines 39–42 continue his style of mystification. He immediately qualifies 'Some moneths she hath beene dead' by a distracting parenthetical phrase that toys with blasphemy by comparing her death to Christ's ('but being dead, | Measures of times are all determined'); and he confuses further the sense of 'Some months' by the 'But long' and repeated 'long'. Then she is not dead but absent, 'away'; then suddenly we need to be told who is 'gone'.

Filling her absence is Donne's poem, and he describes the birth of his idea. The poet's invention is making a 'new world' (I. 76) with 'new creatures'—a long poem ('the forme our practise is')—out of the old and dead, a carcass, a ghost, and a glimmer of remembered connections.[40] The twilight state that looks backwards and forwards represented by the unknown quantity of Elizabeth Drury permits a form of spontaneous combustion and regeneration. Here is the first thaw of *The Anniversaries*, the poet and his speaker breaking into open sea.

He disguises his excitement by allowing the suggestion that his poem is like maggots and worms. But listen to the explosion of 'free' at the end of line 75, though hedged by commas, and its close juxtaposition with 'Creates' followed by the similar configuration of 'be' and 'Produced': 'Which, from the carcass of the old world, free, | Creates a new world; and new creatures be | Produced:' (ll. 75–7). The release from death into movement and production is tremendous, and this miraculous production specifically contrasts with precarious fallen female fecundity.[41] It belongs with those first days of creation *ex nihilo*, before even the sun began to be boxed (recall the frame within a frame of 'Before the sunne, the which fram'd Daies, was fram'd'). The emphasis on liberation is felt especially in the description of the 'free-borne Sunne'. If mothers say that the 'right' and 'orderly' birth is head first, straightforward, the poet is creating this offspring with its head hidden and protected, deliberately not right or orderly—but free.

Donne performs his anatomy by telling stories. The fictional audience is the new poetic world Donne has created, a child being warned against the dangers of adulthood: 'This new world may be safer, being told | The dangers and diseases of the old' (I. 87–8). The storyteller rebels against a horror of shrinkage in body and mind—'And as our bodies, so our minds are cramped'—and of depression with its thoughts of suicide ('Of nothing he made us, and we strive too, | To bring ourselves to nothing back'). The older speaker looks back to earlier and better times nostalgic for what felt like the 'spacious and large' body of youth and for control of 'a fair kingdom, and large realm' of possibility. *The First Anniversary* repeatedly

[40] 'Old world', 'new world', and 'new creatures' resonate of colonial enterprise, not least for Donne who in his search for a post abroad, having failed with Ireland and Venice, had attempted in 1609 to acquire the secretaryship of the Virginia Company. 'An Anatomie' was published towards the end of 1611, the year when *The Tempest* was first performed, and one may hear an echo of that play's 'brave new world' and magic.

[41] This same vocabulary produces a completely different effect in a stanza from an early verse epistle to Bedford ('Madam, You have refin'd me, and to worthyest things'):

> Out from your chariot, morning breaks at night,
> And falsifies both computations so;
> Since a new world doth rise here from your light,
> We your new creatures, by new reckonings goe.
> This showes that you from nature lothly stray,
> That suffer not an artificiall day. (ll. 19–24)

retraces the Fall acted out in the disappointment of a human life—how the world (and Donne) changed from that poignant, expectant child 'kept from the font, until' (I: 33–8) to a hoary corpse on the gallows, from the red-cheeked 'new born earth' to a weary ghost whose colouring has faded.

Not logically but by analogy the speaker shifts from man's to the world's frame. Again, he tells stories about births and careless mothers—of the world falling out of 'her' cradle and turning 'her' brains, of springs and summers like 'sonnes of women after fifty', as if the fault lay with the women who had children. Most wonderful is his myth of 'wise nature' that invents Elizabeth Drury as a giant magnet to hold the world together—the world of his poem. All other hope of rational order has crumbled, and 'every sort of men', not only the poet, 'Did in their voyage in this worlds Sea stray'. The speaker throws the pieces at us, 'Tis all in pieces, all cohaerence gone', emphasizing that no orderly anatomy is possible. But these myths and stories distract the reader from another tale being told.

Painful injustice and feelings of wandering like a lost planet become a humorous story of shrunken mankind, eccentrically looping stars, and weary suns. Not only Elizabeth Drury's but Donne's absence is projected onto the world as gaping hollows. Disproportioned and diseased, authority dangerously refuses to look inward at its own poisoned parts; hence, references to civil disturbances, wars, and political dissolution run like a scarlet thread through the two poems (I. 43–62, 165, 214–15, 262, 304, 322, 418–22; II. 136–40, 331, 359–75, 407–12, 474–82). As Donne says, 'they confesse much in the world, amisse, | Who dare not trust a dead mans eye with that, | Which they from God, and Angels cover not' (II. 110–12). And the dead man's eye, the twinkling of the beheaded man, is Donne's. The emasculating experiences of exclusion from the centre of power, of effacement and isolation from an impenetrable structure of political favourites, are all projected onto the landscape of female anatomy in *The First Anniversary* where gaping spaces and disproportion speak of disorder at the highest levels.

The present king and father has forgotten one of his worthy sons who has petitioned repeatedly for notice and forgiveness. The mythical phoenix (I. 217) rises like a subliminal suggestion of the poet's own independent, mysterious, self-re-creation out of his own ashes. To be a phoenix is a necessity in a world where rewards are withheld and the subject forgotten; and the associations of the fabulously long-lived bird of the sun with gods and kingship continue the story begun in I. 26 and 113–14 about masculine freedom of movement.

Man may stray in his voyage, but the planets also are reeling in 'their various and perplexed course'. As Manley notes, 'perplexed' can mean either 'involuted, infolded, tangled' or 'confusing to the observer; but they are not mutually exclusive'.[42] The heavens rather than exhibiting perfect spherical movement show an eccentric, wandering course, not 'One inche direct', which is attributed to heavenly violence. Stars appear and vanish in inexplicable upheaval like earthquakes or wars. Man's scheme to order them, characterized by such verbs as 'enforce', 'teares', 'empayld', and 'fetter', sounds like detention of a political prisoner. The description of the sun's course and of the attempts to chart and 'fetter' it becomes expansive and emotional. The speaker's imaginative sympathy suddenly opens to the plight of the 'free-borne' sun. He is the hero of a fairy tale whose goats and crabs control and frighten him:

They haue empayld within a Zodiake
The free-borne Sunne, and keepe twelue signes awake
To watch his steps; the Goat and Crabbe controule,
And fright him backe, who els to eyther Pole,
(Did not these Tropiques fetter him) might runne:
For his course is not round; nor can the Sunne
Perfit a Circle, or maintaine his way
One inche direct; but where he rose to day
He comes no more, but with a cousening line,
Steales by that point, and so is Serpentine:
And seeming weary with his reeling thus,
He meanes to sleepe, being now falne nearer vs. (I. 263–74)

The stealthy, serpentine, cozening course of the sun is also the speaker's in this twilit poem.[43] Donne reclaims the day, the phallic, male sun, as

[42] *Donne, The Anniversaries*, ed. Manley, 147–8.

[43] Serpents have a special tie to this poet. The Donne family seal long had been a sheaf of snakes, the crest on their coat of arms. After his ordination in 1615 Donne had a new seal made, a device of Christ crucified to an anchor; and he meditated on the significance of the serpent and the change of seal in verses to George Herbert:

A Sheafe of Snakes used heretofore to be
My Seal, The Crest of our poore Family.
Adopted in Gods Family, and so
Our old Coat lost, unto new armes I go. . . .
Yet may I, with this, my first Serpents hold,
God gives new blessings, and yet leaves the old;
The Serpent, may, as wise, my pattern be;
My poison, as he feeds on dust, that's me.
And as he rounds the Earth to murder sure,
My death he is, but on the Crosse, my cure.

(*The Poems of John Donne*, ed. Herbert J. C. Grierson, vol. i (Oxford: Oxford University Press, 1912), 399.

'free-borne' and serpentine. In contrast to Elizabeth Drury's queenly, direct, and virginal progress to heaven in the opening lines is the sun's snaky, elusive movement; as a relation of the 'slow-pac'd starre' that 'had stolne away' in I. 117, the sun steals past an expected rendezvous.

The poet redeems what he elsewhere calls his 'planetary and erratique fortune' as the liberated privilege and honest exactness of indirection.[44] He shows impatience with didactic minds that reduce the heavenly to earthly proportions—'Loth to goe vp the hill, or labor thus | To goe to heauen, we make heauen come to vs'—because they have no conception of or capacity for a free-born, winding, uphill progress toward self-refinement. When the speaker of the 'Anatomie' says that the stars are 'diversely content' to abide by men's inferior idea of order, the condescension is the poet's. In this poem the reader labours to come to Donne.

The speaker's free-born arrogance assumes authority over the notions of 'fit' and 'proportion' in the second half of *The First Anniversary.* The poet suggests that his poem may look like a misfit to some 'lookers on', but the anatomists and judges of the world do not know anything: 'Beauty's best, proportion'—not John Donne— 'is dead'.[45] The credentials for talking about aesthetics in this world now come from an experience of social and political injustice:

> . . . but yet confess, in this
> The world's proportion disfigured is,
> That those two legs whereon it doth rely,
> Reward and punishment are bent awry. (I. 301–4)

The seeming disproportion of this poem to its occasion appears to reflect what proportion looks like to the eye of one disfigured by personal injustice.

The speaker's preoccupation with the opened eyes of this new vision of proportion and fit continues through *The First Anniversary.* Poisoned actions and moral deformity disqualify a man from judging correctly about fitness. The poet points to those complacent critics of appearance ('Since most men be such as most thinke they bee') such as worldly courtiers, ironically called 'wise, and good lookers on'. Incapable of

[44] See the letter to Sir Henry Goodyer, Sept. 1608, in *Letters*, 48–52, 52.

[45] Puttenham devotes the second book of *The Arte of English Poesie* to 'Proportion Poetical', opening the first chapter of that book, 'It is said by such as professe the Mathematicall sciences, that all things stand by proportion, and that without it nothing could stand to be good or beautiful'. *The Arte of English Poesie: A Facsimile Reproduction* (Kent State, Oh.: Kent State University Press, 1970), 78.

examining the disease of their own poisoned fountains, they look at surfaces—at indiscretion—as the worst sin: 'For good, and well, must in our actions meete: | Wicked is not much worse then indiscreet' (I.337–8).

The language of poisoned fountains and indiscretion echoes the double-edged courtiership of the two darkest verse epistles to the Countess of Bedford of 1610.[46] In 'Honour is so sublime perfection', the last epistle Donne addressed to her before he wrote *The First Anniversary*, the truth of the interdependence of the politically high and low lurks with 'low persons' like the poet. By likening himself and the low, the exaggeratedly humbled 'despis'd dung' (l. 12), to those dangerous and violent 'fires' of Etna 'from th'earths low vaults in Sicil Isle' (l. 18), the poet hints at his own explosive potential.

The crescendo of references to the female sex, serpents, and poison, as well as to fitness and proportion, reaches a bizarre pitch towards the end of *The First Anniversary* where Elizabeth Drury is likened to a serpent, her virtue to a serpent's poison, and the serpent's sting to her physical presence:

> But as some Serpents poison hurteth not,
> Except it be from the liue Serpent shot,
> So doth her vertue need her here, to fit
> That vnto us; she working more than it. (I. 409–12)

As Milgate notes, 'None of the medical writers to whom Donne refers by name mentions this point, and it has not been exactly paralleled elsewhere'.[47]

These lines complete a passage which begins at I. 377 about the lack of correspondence between earth and heaven. While the accumulated references to 'influence' and 'working' carry political overtones, their immediate context is astrology, alchemy, and Paracelsian medical theory, which held that individuals may be filled with the virtuous influence of the stars. This theory of cure lay behind the widespread belief in the royal power to heal by touch the so-called king's evil, or scrofula. The failure of Elizabeth Drury's influence signifies a heretical breakdown of communication—an unbridgeable distance—between heavenly powers and those earthly princes most presumed to draw on them. And that breakdown is

[46] And of the verse epistle 'To the Countesse of Huntingdon' ('Man to Gods image, *Eve*, to mans was made'), where Donne says of his flatteries, 'So my ill reaching you might there grow good, | But I remaine a poyson'd fountaine still; | But not your beauty, vertue, knowledge, blood | Are more above all flattery, than my will' (ll. 53–6).

[47] Donne, *The Epithalamions, Anniversaries, and Epicedes*, ed. Milgate, 150–1.

demonstrated, in turn, by the failure of communication between prince and subject which the poet's history records; a lack of correspondence between virtue and political reward becomes translated into a lack of receptivity between heaven and earth, 'For heauen giues little, and the earth takes lesse' (I. 397). Under the cover of witty satire on the world's decay and a digression on various kinds of 'influence', the lack of attention Donne has received becomes translated into intimations of a much larger failure of sensitivity to receive and transmit influence: the king has lost his touch with heaven, his divine ability to heal.

That the referent for 'her' in I. 455 ('And you her creatures, whom she workes vpon') is Elizabeth Drury and not the midwife death of the line preceding only becomes clear after several lines. The verb 'workes' appears to continue the argument begun at 402 and 412. But why does Elizabeth Drury blur for a moment into death, and why is she pictured as a 'working' and deadly serpent? Why the grotesque simile which the smooth speaker makes easy to miss, his care to explain that the poison (and virtue) hurts when from 'the liue Serpent shot'? Why the quick contrast from 'shot' to 'So doth her vertue' and the hard, mechanical, yet sexual quality of 'fit' emphasized by enjambment and terse rhyme? Yet 'Shee, shee is dead' has emphasized how death, corruption, and the body—more than virtue—is feminine. Donne almost says, 'She, she [woman, woman] is death'. By displacing onto the 'old world' of the Fall the disproportion and disfigurement of disappointment and loss, he claims the opposite—a perfectly round form—not for the idea of a woman but for the idea of his poem. *The Anniversaries* end on the image of a completed poetic circle, a cover for their more discursive and radical self-assertion.

The implication of our glimpse of Elizabeth Drury as a serpent is that there is only one kind of influence that works now, and it is female, painful, and deadly. The whole problem of fit and influence belongs to the anatomical world of parts. The offensive image derides a functional mentality which can only see influence and virtue as working parts within a hierarchy of parts, the mentality to which Elizabeth Drury would have become subject, like the poet, had she lived—or to which she already had ('Who being solicited to any Act, / Still heard God pleading his safe precontract', II. 459–60).

In contrast to the anatomical and feminine is the vision in *The Second Anniversary* of 'The sight of God, in fulnesse'. Just as law and history are forgettable because they consist of pieces, while seamless songs are memorable, so forgetting is a dismembering and being forgotten is like being dismembered. The digressive 'incomprehensibleness' (I. 469) of *The Anniversaries* reproduces the honest 'full' complexity of experience and argues for the sanctity of remembering and being remembered in full. *The First Anniversary*'s anatomy ends at the incomprehensibleness that cannot be anatomized.

In poems and letters, Donne speaks of 'mixed souls' which 'contain | Mixture of things, they know not what' ('The Ecstasy', ll. 35, 33–4). He is eloquent about his contrary moods and the difficulty of self-diagnosis. In a letter to Goodyer he distinguishes between the physician's ability to recognize diseases of the body with some certainty and the mind's quandary of being simultaneously its own physician and patient: 'Of our bodies infirmities, though our knowledge be partly *ab extrinseco*, from the opinion of the Physitian, and that the subject and matter be flexible, and various; . . . yet their rules are certain, and if the matter be rightly applyed to the rule, our knowledge thereof is also certain. But, of the diseases of the minde, there is no *Criterium*, no Canon, no rule; for, our own taste and apprehension and interpretation should be the Judge, and that is the disease it self'.[48] He likens his changeable moods and contradictory behaviour to hysteria, in the Renaissance called 'the mother' because considered the female disease of a wandering, empty womb or hyster.[49] Transported with 'jollity and love of company, I hang leads at my heels', he writes, 'when sadness dejects me . . . I kindle squibs about me again and flie into sportfulnesse . . . and I find ever after all, that I am like an exorcist, which had long laboured about one which at last appears to have the Mother, that I still mistake my disease'. In his work on dreams and on wit, Freud described how the psyche releases disturbing material deviously to avoid its own censorship, through indirection, reversal, nonsense, a shift to a viewpoint off centre—what he calls 'a displacement of the psychic accent'.[50] Reversal is the strategy, the drama, and the accomplishment of these poems of self-recovery. The wandering womb, the 'strict grave' of *The First Anniversary* of loss and absence, is filled in the second with a thrill of triumph and not without vengeance.

Wesley Milgate calls *The Anniversaries* 'companion poems'. For although Donne opens *The Second Anniversary* with a vision of a long

[48] Donne, *Letters*, 70–1.

[49] See, for example, Coppélia Kahn's discussion of 'the mother' in 'The Absent Mother in *King Lear*', in Margaret W. Fergusson, Maureen Quilligan, and Nancy J. Vickers (eds.), *Rewriting the Renaissance; The Discourses of Sexual Difference in Early Modern Europe* (Chicago: University of Chicago Press, 1986), 33–49.

[50] Sigmund Freud, *The Interpretation of Dreams* (*Die Traumdeutung*), Standard edn., vols. iv–v (London: Hogarth Press, 1955), ch. vi, sect. B, 306–8.

lineage of Elizabeth Drury's progeny, which emphasizes the linear, *annus* half of 'anniversary'—one more and one more—yet these two poems turn to make an uneasy union like the feminine and masculine halves of one whole. They are the imaginative progeny of Donne who becomes divided into two imaginary women whose chaste union has engendered them: Elizabeth Drury as virgin father and the poet's chaste muse as mother. The pair of *Anniversaries* suggests the roundness, the *versus*, of 'anniversary' and the Copernican earth's inexorable if serpentine revolution and return. The second anniversary, then, is not the second of many; it compliments yet corrects, it turns around the first, and the beheaded man's shocking twitch seems to anticipate the satisfaction. Donne's 'long-short Progresse' imagines a release from the compulsion to repeat and remember.[51]

'An Anatomie of the World' draws on the classical commonplace of the satirist as physician who diagnoses the ills of the body politic; Donne's poem transforms satire's deliberate obscurity into a high English literary and polemical genre.[52] Having established the poet's associations of anatomy with the female and with oppressive authority, with claustrophobic scrutiny and blindness to what is there—the dismembering not remembering of the dead—I turn to important political connections between medical and literary anatomies that bear on Donne's work in 1611.

ANATOMY, PRISON, AND POLEMIC

Anatomies in Donne's time were performed on the executed bodies of those judged to be the criminal, anarchic elements of society. The supply of cadavers for the annual lecture on anatomy at Surgeons Hall came from the gallows. Moreover, the surgeon's operation represented a frightening anarchy of deformation and melancholy and finally a bewildering sense of loss, if the anatomy manual of Andreas Vesalius, the founder of modern medical anatomy, is an indication.[53] *De Humani Corporis Fabrica* (1543) is a book whose text and progressively grotesque

[51] See Clark, 'The Plot of Donne's "*Anniversaries*" ', 74.

[52] See Mary Claire Randolph, 'The Medical Concept in English Renaissance Satiric Theory: Its Possible Relationships and Implications', *Studies in Philology*, 38 (1941), 125–57.

[53] See Jonathan Sawday, *The Body Emblazoned: Dissection and the Human Body in Renaissance Culture* (London: Routledge, 1995), 56 and Chapter 4; and Devon L. Hodges, *Renaissance Fictions of Anatomy* (Amherst: University of Massechusetts Press, 1985), 5–6.

illustrations reveal how the manipulation necessary to ruin surfaces in order to get to the depths of the body only exposes more incoherence.[54] After cutting, dissecting, flaying, tearing, and ripping, the anatomist is left with an alien and threatening monster, exactly as Donne's anatomy lays bare: 'Thou knowst how vgly a monster this world is: | And learnst thus much by our Anatomee, | That here is nothing to enamor thee' (I. 326–8).

Patricia Parker has explored the conflation of scientific discovery, spying, and the prurient, pornographic gaze in early modern texts.[55] Her work emphasizes the textbook anatomy's quality of tease and voyeurism whereby each surface folded back and opened up reveals another equally unsatisfying, impenetrable, and mysterious veil to be lifted. Ultimately, according to Parker, the need to penetrate hidden and protected spaces in order to expose and control, the belief that truth can be arrested and broken down like a victim of spying or torture, reflects back the pain of a secret lack within the viewer. His or her self-fragmentation repeats itself, and the inner gap widens with each attempt to see further in an urgency to strip away and expose new mysteries. Donne clearly plays on the reader's fear of a gaping emptiness—he teases our expectation of lurid anatomical detail by tossing us instead a mix of whales, elephants, and pygmies, the world falling out of its cradle, and empty wombs, vacuums, and vaults.

'Worst malefactors', writes Donne in 'Upon Thomas Coryats *Crudities*', 'Doe publique good, cut in Anatomies', although as he observes at the end of 'Love's Exchange', 'Rack't carcasses make ill anatomies'.[56] The superiority of the anatomist is not only his claim to a body of factual scientific knowledge over a tissue of religious ignorance and mystery, or even the superiority of the living over the dead, but that of society's privileged and powerful over the criminal, marginal elements.

An outsider wanting to come in was the young Donne at Lincoln's Inn in the 1590s. In the early satires, which were already full of prisons and

[54] Hodges, *Renaissance Fictions of Anatomy*, 18.

[55] See, for example, 'Fantasies of "Race" and "Gender": Africa, *Othello*, and Bringing to Light', in Margo Hendricks and Patricia Parker (eds.), *Women, 'Race', and Writing in the Early Modern Period*, (London and New York, 1994) 84–100.

[56] One 16th-century medical writer recommends the body of a man hanged, strangled, or drowned but never that of one who has died of wounds or a disease. Another advises against not only the carcasses of men who died of wounds and disease but those who died of hanging, torture, and beheading: 'the best body for dissection is that of one dead by drowning'. D. C. Allen, 'John Donne's Knowledge of Renaissance Medicine', *JEGP* 42 (1943), 329.

tombs, he had pondered the dangerous labyrinth ahead of choosing wisely a religion and a course of advancement when kings were 'Hangmen to Fate'. In Donne's 'Satyre 3' the man who will succeed up the high hill of Truth 'about must, and about must goe; | And what th'hill's suddennes resists, winne so' (ll. 81–2). In a world of resistant, deceptive surfaces, roundabout offers the way forward and in. But Donne was still outside as his fortieth birthday approached in the autumn of 1611.

His experience of imprisonment by his father-in-law in February 1602, and especially his background of Roman Catholicism and of excluded, persecuted relations, gave to prisons and execution a personal and political pressure.[57] Donne alludes to this family history in the two prose works, about suicide and about martyrdom, of the years immediately preceding *The Anniversaries.* 'I have beene ever kept awake in a meditation of Martyrdome', he says in the 'Advertisement to the Reader' before *Pseudo-Martyr,* 'by being derived from such a stocke and race as, I beleeve, no family . . . hath endured and suffered more' for their faith[58]; and in the preface to *Biathanatos* he admits that he was kept awake in a similar meditation of unlocking 'my prison', the body, not least 'because I had my first breeding and conversation with men of a suppressed and afflicted Religion, accustomed to the despite of death and hungry of an imagin'd Martyrdome'.[59] His 'stocke and race' included not only Sir Thomas More but a maternal grandfather and uncle Heywood both imprisoned for popery and Donne's brother Henry, who had died of infection in plague-ridden Newgate for harbouring a Roman Catholic priest subsequently hanged, drawn, and quartered.

In his long, learned treatise on suicide, Donne had performed a roundabout examination of his own 'sickely inclination' to the subject. And in his preface he anatomizes the condemnation of 'these severe men', his judges, who find self-murder scandalous; he exposes their hidden guilt and fear of what they might discover about themselves. Noting that 'disorderly long haire' contained virtue, strength, and sanctification in Samson and Samuel, this defender of disorderly treatises and lives puts 'stiffe wickednesse' on the dissecting table: 'they shall pardon this opinion, that their severity proceeds from a self-guiltines, and give me leave to apply that of Ennodius, That it is the nature of stiffe wickednesse, to

57 For a recent study of Donne's Roman Catholic background and his danger of being persecuted, see Flynn, *John Donne and the Ancient Catholic Nobility.*

58 *John Donne, Selected Prose,* selected by Evelyn Simpson, ed. Helen Gardner and Timothy Healy (Oxford: Clarendon Press, 1967), 46.

59 Ibid. 26.

thinke that of others, which themselves deserve, and it is all the comfort which the guilty have, not to find any innocent'.[60] Guilty and innocent, scandal and punishment, a plea to 'the malitious prejudged man' for tolerance—Donne appears to ask for relief of sentence. The 'multiplicity of not necessary citations' in *Biathanatos*, which the writer acknowledges may appear as 'ostentation, or digression', is necessary to heap the full weight of authority on his scales.[61] In 1608 and 1609 when the poet applied for secretaryships abroad, James I made it clear that the circumstances of Donne's marriage seven years earlier effectively disqualified him for consideration.[62]

Donne's first published work immediately preceded *The Anniversaries*. Composed as a bid for royal favour, *Pseudo-Martyr* (1610) reverses the private argument for suicide from *Biathanatos* to make it politically useful: now claiming the authority of his persecuted ancestry to draw the narrow line between suicide and a martyr's death, he neatly argues support for James I's Oath of Allegiance and attacks the Jesuits for urging disobedience and martyrdom on English Roman Catholics. And he attacks the Jesuits again in his Latin satire which was translated immediately into English, *Ignatius his Conclave* (1611). In print, Donne formally distances himself from his maternal family's heritage of Roman Catholicism—in particular, from his notorious maternal uncle, the jailed and banished Jesuit priest Jasper Heywood. He steps forward for notice as a loyal defender of Protestant monarchy.

Singularly loose and encyclopedic while promising a methodical approach, the Renaissance literary anatomy extended an invitation to preaching and politics, extravagant wit and virulent satire.[63] It ranged in style and subject matter from Lyly's *Euphues: The Anatomy of Wyt* (1578) to William Cowper's 300-page *The Anatomie of a Christian Man* (1611).

[60] Evelyn Simpson, *A Study of the Prose Works of John Donne*, 2nd edn. (Oxford: Clarendon Press, 1948), 169.

[61] Preface to *Biathanatos* as cited ibid.: 'If therefore in multiplicity of not necessary citations there appeare vanity, or ostentation, or digression my honesty must make my excuse and compensation, who acknowledge as *Pliny* doth, [*That to chuse rather to be taken in a theft, then to give every man his due, is obnoxii animi, et infelicis ingenii.*]. I did it rather because scholastique and artificiall men use this way of instructing; and I made account that I was to deal with such, because I presume that naturall men are at least enough inclinable of themselves to this doctrine'.

[62] Bald, *John Donne: A Life*, 161–2.

[63] Lewalski, *Donne's Anniversaries* (228), emphasizes the anatomy's analytic, dissecting point and relation to satire, while Frye (*Anatomy of Criticism*, 312–13) and Devon Hodges (*Renaissance Fictions of Anatomy*, 17) are more impressed by its potential for encyclopedic extravagance and extroversion.

But when Puritan and Presbyterian controversialists adopted the educational and rhetorical programme of French reformer Peter Ramus who had died in the St Bartholomew's Day Massacre of Huguenots in 1572, Ramus' theories of logic and rhetoric mixed with church reform, and the anatomy came to assume an ostentatiously Protestant, methodical, and homiletic guise.[64] Suspicious of Roman and university eloquence, tracts such as *The anathomie of Sinne, Briefly discovering the braunches thereof, with a short method how to detest and avoid it* (1604) had begun to proliferate.

According to Ramist rhetoric, figures of thought and speech do not enhance but dilute clarity of expression and reveal a desire to deceive the listening ear. 'When with delectation or some other motion thy chief purpose is to deceave the auditor', says Ramus, 'then thou shall put some thing away which doth appartaine to thy matter, as definitions, divisions and transitions, and set in there places thinges appartaining nothing to the matter as digressiones from the purpose and long tarrying upon the matter'.[65] When Thomas Nashe in his *Anatomie of Absurditie* (1589) defended the extemporal and rhetorical flare of university wits against their critics who 'seeme learned to none but to Idiots', he singled out Puritan Phillip Stubbes and his popular treatise *The Anatomie of Abuses: Containing a Discoverie, or Briefe Summarie of Such Notable Vices and Imperfections, as now raigne in many Christian Countreyes of the World: but (especiallie) in a verie famous ILANDE called AILGNA: . . .* (1583). Nashe can barely restrain himself: 'I . . . hasten to other mens furie, who make the Presse the dunghill whether they carry all the muck of their mellancholicke imaginations, pretending forsooth to anatomize abuses and stubbe up sin by the rootes'.[66] In the 1590s his flyting, improvisa-

[64] Pierre de la Ramée, better known by his Latinized academic name of Petrus, or Peter, Ramus, was a 16th-century French educational reformer who proposed the separation of rhetoric from dialectic and who opposed both scholastic logic and the classical conception of rhetoric. He converted to Protestantism in 1561; his death in the St Bartholomew's Day massacre probably secured the association of Ramism and Protestantism. The major work on Ramus and chiefly responsible for clarifying his importance in the Renaissance is Walter J. Ong, SJ, *Ramus, Method, and the Decay of Dialogue* (Cambridge, Mass.: Harvard University Press, 1958). See also, for example, James J. Murphy, 'Introduction', Peter Ramus, *Arguments in Rhetoric against Quintilian*, trans. Carole Newlands, ed. James J. Murphy (De Kalb: University of Northern Illinois Press, 1983) and Murphy's introduction to *Peter Ramus's Attack on Cicero*, a translation of the *Brutinae Quaestiones*, trans. Carole Newlands (Davis, Calif.: Hermagoras Press, 1992).

[65] John S. Chamberlin, *Increase and Multiply* (Chapel Hill: University of North Carolina Press, 1996), 79.

[66] Thomas Nashe, *The Anatomie of Absurditie*, in *The Works of Thomas Nashe*, ed. Ronald B. McKerrow, I. 3–49 (Oxford: Basil Blackwell, 1958), 19–21.

tional prose took on Ramist scholar Gabriel Harvey. And within this hectic debate Richard Hooker composed his sonorous defence of Elizabethan Anglicanism and the divine rationality of God's natural law. *Of the Laws of Ecclesiastical Polity* was 'a long tarrying upon the matter' designed to transcend all Ramist itemizing in a synthesis and memorial of past ecclesiastical wisdom, confident in the pattern of its, and of God's, greater whole.[67]

The poet of another 'long tarrying upon the matter', *The Anniversaries*, had 'survayed and digested the whole body of Divinity, controverted between ours and the Romane Church' by 1610.[68] And in 1611 while not directly concerned with theological or linguistic debates, Donne's studied use of indirection—of what he calls elsewhere 'such voyages, such peregrinations to fetch remote and precious metaphors, such extensions, such spreadings . . . such third heavens of hyperboles'[69]—as well as his dominating, eccentric speaker align him against the aesthetics of the most militant Protestantism.

By writing a long, digressive, and obscure work that begins with and rejects anatomy, Donne would have taunted obliquely the Calvinist Countess of Bedford, not only by his praise of another woman but by subverting a Puritan aesthetic.[70] Later from his Anglican pulpit Donne would ridicule Puritan preachers as 'Rhapsoders, and Common placers and Method-mongers'.[71] But 'An Anatomy of the World' already complicates and eludes the rhetoric of reduction and topical procedures identified with Puritan and antipapal tracts, as would Burton's *The*

[67] See Geoffrey Hill's suggestive 'Keeping to the Middle Way: The "Accurate Musicke" in Burton's Anatomizing of Worldly Corruptions', *TLS*, 23 Dec. 1994, 3–6, which considers the relations among Burton, Hooker, Nashe, and Donne as placed against the political, religious, and rhetorical pressures of both Ramism and the Puritanism, for example, of Foxe's *Actes and Monumentes* (1563).

[68] From Donne's preface to *Pseudo-Martyr*, quoted in Donne, *Selected Prose*, 50.

[69] From John Donne, *Devotions upon Emergent Occasions*, ed. Anthony Raspa (New York: Oxford University Press, 1987), the opening of Expostulation XIX.

[70] Frye, *Anatomy of Criticism*, 312–13, considered Boethius' *Consolation*, for example, with its dialogue, its verse interludes, and its pervading tone of contemplative irony, 'a pure anatomy'. Frye first used the term 'anatomy' in association with Menippean satire to describe an 'extroverted and intellectual' category useful for thinking about otherwise such digressive and inclusive prose fictions as Joyce's *Ulysses*. He emphasized the form's disorderly conduct, its history of baffling critics.

[71] *Sermons* I. vi. 167–70, quoted in Chamberlin, *Increase and Multiply*, 91. In *Essays on Divinity* he attacks also Christian cabalists such as Pico della Mirandola and Johann Reuchlin as 'the Anatomists of words', who with 'a Theologicall Alchimy to draw soveraigne tinctures and spirits from plain and grosse literall matter, observe in every variety [of names] some great mystick significance', Chamberlin, *Increase and Multiply*, 105.

Anatomy of Melancholy in 1621.[72] The poet's obscurity and verbal extravagance bear little resemblance to the godly 'homely stile' recommended by Thomas Vicarie 'Esquire, and Sergeant Chirurgion': the envoi to *A Treasure for English men, conteyning the Anatomie of mans bodie* (1587) boasts 'for rules in Rhetoricke have we none. | Our heads do lack that filed phrase, | Whereon fine wits delight to gaze'.[73] Donne will remind his readers that parts of speech outlast body parts (I: 435–8), and their surfaces are even more deceptive than those of bodies.

To call his poems anniversaries, Donne must recall the oldest ecclesiastical and specifically Roman Catholic meaning of the word. The *OED* cites the definition of anniversaries in Blount's *Law Dictionary* (1691) as 'those days, wherein the Martyrdoms or Deaths of Saints were celebrated yearly in the Church; or the days whereon, at every years end, Men were wont to pray for the Souls of their deceased Friends, according to the continued custom of Roman Catholicks'. By his 'Progresse' in *The Second Anniversary* 'Up to' the ancient patriarchs and his large view from 'the watch-towere' of 'all', where details drop away and the whole pattern is revealed, Donne not only associates himself with a figurative ecclesiastical rhetoric (as the basis of Scripture and preaching) in the high tradition of Augustine through Hooker, but he leaves behind the 'stiff' sectarian and philosophic controversialists (II. 280–1) as he castigated 'stiffe wickednesse' in *Biathanatos*.[74]

Donne's show of itemizing knowledge in *The Anniversaries* ('when thou know'st this') plays to the prurient voyeurism of those scientists of zeal, the 'authors, too stiffe to recant'. If it is by a 'short method' that they 'discover and confute', 'plainly show', and 'detest and avoid', Donne detests at great length. And the description in *The Second Anniversary* of direct heavenly knowing only emphasizes the frustrated peeking, spying, and eavesdropping of the anatomizing and gossiping court scavengers whom he transcends: 'Thou shalt not peepe through lattices of eies, | Nor heare through Laberinths of eares, nor learne | By circuit, or collections to discerne' (II. 296–8). Behind its traditional philosophic and religious

[72] Antipapal anatomies included *The Anatomie of Popish Tyrannie* by Thomas Bell (London: John Harrison etc., 1603) and Robert Pricket's *Times Anotomie, Containing The poore mans plaint, Brittons trouble, and her triumph, The Popes pride, Romes treasons, and her destruction* (London: George Eld, 1606).

[73] Thomas Vicary, *The English-mans treasure: with the true anatomie of mans bodie . . . Whereunto are annexed many secrets appertayning to Chirurgerie, with . . . remedies for all diseases . . . with emplasters . . . potions and drinkes approved in phisicke. Also the rare treasure of the English bathes,* (London: G. Robinson for J. Perin, 1587).

[74] Chamberlin, *Increase and Multiply*, see the discussion of Augustine, 28.

associations with the mind, a watchtower rises as a lookout on the approach of danger from below.

THE RISE OF THE ANTIPODES

The revolution of a year and of the spirit is dramatized in these poems as well as another revolution. In an image which anticipates the sounding of Marvell's meadows and the upending of Antipodes in *Upon Appleton House*, Donne drops a plumb line until directions reverse: 'And men, to sound depths, so much line untie, | As one might iustly think, that there would rise | At end thereof, one of th' Antipodes' (I. 292–4). What was down comes up, what was falling will rise. And the voice of *The Second Anniversary* rises. Donne turns the problem of parts and 'fit' inside out: he fits Elizabeth Drury to himself in an ecstatic vision of fullness and freedom from constraint, of being instead of 'nothing' an original and a sovereign 'all'.

If *The First Anniversary* ends on 'incomprehensibleness', the second opens on 'everlastingness'. The vision of the poet spans two poles: from a breaking down into parts and incoherence to a rising up to wholeness; from lethargy as death and forgetfulness to lethargy as 'alacrity'; from a call to remember and know to a call to forget and think; from imprisoning and fettering to expansion and liberty; from crying mothers and miscarriages to virginal, figurative mothers such as 'the blessed Mother-maid', more exalted for goodness than motherhood, sickness's 'true mother, Age' (II. 178), and the 'Immortal Maid', Elizabeth Drury, who 'would'st refuse / The name of mother' (II. 33–4) but becomes a father to generations of poetic progeny.

The signs of male control in *The Second Anniversary* are distinct. One masculine triumph, in which Elizabeth Drury gracefully concurs, is that death has changed character and gender. A midwife in the first poem (I. 454), death has become a tactful male servant, a lowly groom and usher with a taper. Instead of a fearful womb, there is a peaceful room. The heavenly company consists of not only Christ but the patriarchs, the prophets, the apostles, and the martyrs, to whom the poet adds last, 'Up to those Virgins'. They are lesser lights, however; the 'almost' of 'who thought that almost | They made ioyntenants with the Holy Ghost' (II. 353–4) sounds like a backhanded compliment. As 'almost' joint tenants, they perhaps suffer from comparison with those 'ioynt tenants of the world' in *The First Anniversary*, man and the sun (I. 114).

The First Anniversary's feminine threat of gaping absences and wandering, non-fitting parts is answered by *The Second Anniversary*'s phallic version of serpentine power like Moses's brazen serpent on the rod (Numbers 21: 9). The poems enact a descent and resurrection from worm to prince and prophet. The hoped-for future trajectory of this poet ('To advance these thoughts') is the 'speed undistinguished' of poetic thought which threads impermeable mysteries on a backbone incapable of being broken down. And 'though all do know, that quantities | Are made of lines, and lines from points arise, | None can these lines or quantities unjoint'—including these poetic lines.

In *The First Anniversary*, mothers 'cry', the world falls out of its cradle and becomes maimed, and 'we are not men'. But with its injunction to forget after the catharsis of the beheaded man, *The Second Anniversary* assumes a mood of confidence free from both mothers and anatomists. The prospect of being above one's past, even if momentarily, produces one of the poems' simplest lyrical lines: 'And unto thee, | Let thine owne times as an old story be' (II. 49–50). *The Anniversaries* have been full of old stories. The sound of 'an old story' seems a wish for distance, one tentatively managed by the poet's physical remove from England and temporary security of employment. Perhaps his travel with the Drurys has given him a 'watch-towere', and the poem's speaker is also telling himself to 'get' there. The speaker talks about forgetting the world, but he is haunted by bitterness and continuously excites himself with repeated exhortations such as 'Think that', 'Up to', and 'She who' that gather momentum to a pitch. The last 200 lines of the poem write themselves in these cries. Repeatedly what begins as a mood of meditation ends in agitation. The exclusive institutions of power intrude on his meditations and result in such dissonant, worldly images as 'Shee to whose person Paradise adhear'd, | As Courts to Princes' (II. 77–8). The speaker's claim of distant scorn for and superiority to his own times is a pose, not poise, from which his resentment of and engagement with those times continues, as in the angry satire of II. 325–38, which begins in infection ('Canst thou choose out, free from infection, | That wil nor give thee theirs, nor drinke in thine?') and ends in poison ('The poyson' is gone through all, poysons affect | Chiefly the cheefest parts, but some effect | In Nailes, and Haires, yea excrements, will show').

In *The Second Anniversary* the speaker fills exclusive places ('All will not serve') and describes being filled and self-sufficient:

> All will not serve; Onely who have enjoyd
> The sight of God, in fulnesse, can thinke it;
> For it is both the object, and the wit.
> This is essentiall joye, where neither hee
> Can suffer Diminution, nor wee;
> Tis such a full, and such a filling good; (II. 440–5)

This joyful fullness climaxes, however, in a quiet revenge, as if the beheaded man had risen from the dead. At the end of *The Anniversaries* the speaker addresses his soul but also, indirectly, the proud titled courtier who ignores the lower orders that need his attention; and the poet does not decapitate but strangles his figure of pride. The 'joyful casual violence' of laughter is not so casual but includes the bursting of the poet's accumulated anger; 'the dangerous rest', or residue from the abscess that rises with strangling force, fleetingly resembles social revolt:

> If thy Prince will his subjects to call thee
> My Lord, and this doe swell thee, thou art than,
> By being a greater, growne to be lesse Man.
> When no Physician of Redresse can speake,
> A joyfull casuall violence may breake
> A dangerous Apostem in thy brest;
> And whilst thou joy'st in this, the dangerous rest,
> The bag may rise up, and so strangle thee.
> What aye was casuall, may ever bee. (II. 474–82)

The word 'casuall' litters the page five times in thirteen lines like a taunt, hardly casual or accidental. The curiously high emotion of the passage and climactic strangling call attention to themselves through a dizzying repetition, thirteen times, of the word 'joy' and variants like 'joyful', 'joyest', 'joys', and 'joy's'. The last reference to 'casuall', 'All casuall joye doth loud and plainly say' (II. 485), boasts how casual may lead to casualty. And the final 'joy' (and *The Anniversaries*' final reference to 'part') occurs in the last long sentence that snakes syntactically over fourteen lines (II. 495–510). Beginning 'In this fresh joy, tis no small part, that shee', the sentence contains also the poems' final and crucial parenthetical comment whose distinction between moral and worldly elevation clinches the critique on undeserving privilege and social degree that have become now—echoing line 480—'the rest': 'Shee, in whose goodnesse, he that names degree, | Doth injure her; (Tis losse to be cald best, | There where the stuffe is not such as the rest)' (II. 498–500). The line that begins

'There where' and is clogged with 'stuffe' and 'not such' relegates those that name degree to an aurally low end.

From the lonely note of a lute with cracking strings, the poet builds to brassier sounds of victory. *The Second Anniversary* describes a release of authority and energy—of the interior 'great prince' of 'The Exstasie' (l. 68) which otherwise 'in prison lies'. Donne blows his own horn at the end of *The Anniversaries* to announce a private exodus and 'progress'. As the child of I. 33 'kept from the font, until', the speaker prepares for that prince to step forward, 'expected long, come to fulfil | The ceremonies' of naming him—poet, prophet, lawgiver.

THAW, FLOODS, AND REVERSAL

A theme of Donne's verse epistle 'To the Countess of Huntingdon', which opens 'Man to Gods image, Eve, to mans was made', is that great spirits (and, by implication, great poets, too) must remain largely invisible. They are forced to pass through this world in a 'low' and feminine habit of subservience to worldly matters. The poet's slander of Eve's sex for the first five stanzas of the poem shifts when 'we might feare that vertue, since she fell | So low as woman, should be neare her end' (ll. 19–20); suddenly the Countess is wrenched into heaven as a figure for virtue whose ethereal purity was forced to assume gross, apprehensible veils on earth—the 'low names' of woman, wife, and mother. Similarly, 'for allay unto so pure a mind' Elizabeth Drury 'took the weaker sex'. Clearly in and around 1610–12, the female provides the poet with a model for the fate of having one's virtue cloaked by subservience, for being unrecognizable by the world, only by God. Yet, paradoxically, from the low, all honours 'flow'; and the low rise with startling speed in *The Second Anniversary*.

The publication of *The Anniversaries* early in 1612 coincided with the ten-year anniversary of the discovery in February 1602 of the poet's secret marriage that had proved a death to his hopes of advancement. In March 1602, as a dead man released from the prison to which his new father-in-law had sent him, Donne had appealed to Sir Thomas Egerton to be reinstated as secretary, 'The sicknes of which I dyed ys, that I begonne in your Lordships house this love. Wher I shal be buried I know not'.[75] On this ten-year anniversary, Donne was absent from his wife, now pregnant with their eighth child (stillborn in January of 1612). According to Walton she had 'profest an unwillingness to allow him any absence from her; saying,

[75] Bald, *John Donne: A Life*, 138.

her divining soul boded her some ill in his absence; and therefore, desired him not to leave her'.[76] Donne's letter of farewell to Goodyer in November 1611 does not sound as though it was written by a man with a three-year licence to travel abroad, but like the last words of the condemned: 'I am near the execution of that purpose for France. . . . It is ill to look back, or give over in a course; but worse never to set out. I speake to you at this time of departing, as I should do at my last upon my death-bed'.[77]

In the poet's letter to Egerton, the financial, social, and emotional risks his wife had assumed with the separation from her family become translated into a representation of his own situation as one of sickness and death. In 1611, rather than his pregnant wife, again Donne is the one at risk. But the distantly tragic figure of Elizabeth Drury who would 'refuse | The name of Mother', who is absent and escaped from womanly 'infirmities' as he will be when he leaves for the continent, becomes a consummate feminine vehicle for translating feelings of weakness to strength. As Ronald Corthell observed, 'Elizabeth Drury died a pubescent virgin, and that, Donne says, is all to the good'.[78] Unaccusing, uncontrolling, Elizabeth Drury allows the poet to confess obliquely personal regrets and frustrations associated with 'th'infirmities which waite upone | Woman' ('A Funerall Elegie', ll. 77–8). Milgate observed of Elizabeth Drury that 'there is nothing specifically womanly about what she represents in the poem', and Janel Mueller also finds that Donne's 'trajectories of hyperbole often take us a great distance from any recognizable female presence'.[79] Instead this single girl is troublingly reminiscent of the poet's own story of ruptures, unfulfilled promise, and blank pages; in 'A Funerall Elegie', one might catch a glimpse of Donne himself at 14:

> He which not knowing her sad History,
> Should come to reade the booke of destiny,
> How faire and chast, humble and high shee'ad beene,
> Much promis'd, much perform'd, at not fifteene,
> And measuring future things by things before,
> Should turne the leafe to reade, and read no more,
> Would thinke that eyther destiny mistooke,
> Or that some leafes were torne out of the booke. (ll. 83–90)

[76] Bald, *John Donne: A Life*, 242.

[77] Quoted in Maureen Sabine, *Feminine Engendered Faith. The Poetry of John Donne and Richard Crashaw* (Basingstoke: Macmillan, 1992), 97.

[78] Corthell, 'The Obscure Object of Desire', 135.

[79] Janel Mueller, 'Women among the Metaphysicals: A Case, Mostly, of Being Donne for', in Arthur F. Marotti (ed.), *Critical Essays on John Donne*, (New York: Maxwell Macmillan International, 1994), 44.

By allowing Donne the useful rhetorical and emotional stance of virginal superiority over worldly things and, at the same time, of world-worn satirist and Jeremiah for her sake ('no things be | So like as Courts'), as well as a way of remembering and memorializing his own youthful promise and weakness, Elizabeth Drury becomes the blank page filled with this poem that announces achievement and resurrection.[80] Donne turns overlooked into overlooking.

The Anniversaries propose a public, masculine, and religiously hybrid self-definition that breaks through a personal impasse of servility in which the poet felt 'rather a sicknesse and disease of the world than any part of it'. Sounding like a Hamlet to his Horatio, Donne writes in 1608 to Goodyer, 'I would fain do something; but that I cannot tell what, is no wonder. For to chuse, is to do: but to be no part of any body, is to be nothing'.[81] 'He's nothing now', he says of 'man' (I. 171). The boast that Donne achieves is to make something of himself by making so much out of nothing. He fills a vacancy by creating the post—'this great Office boldly to invade'. In a symbolic order which has interested Laura Mulvey, Gayle Margharita, and Sarah Beckwith among feminist critics interested in the male gaze, where for men the silent female form 'speaks castration and nothing else', Elizabeth Drury as literally nothing becomes everything. She becomes a 'bearer of meaning, not maker of meaning' that presses back against those killing wombs.[82] Being 'nothing', a cipher, has always been a conflicted and fertile conceit in Donne's verse; one thinks of 'A Nocturnal upon St. Lucy's Day'. In his correspondence the wordplay it inspires becomes twisted almost a turn too many: 'Though I know you have many worthy friends of all rankes, yet I adde something, since I which am of none, would fain be your friend too. There is some of the honour and some of the degrees of a Creation, to make a friendship of nothing'.[83] On the corpse of the body he loved in his lyrics, Donne breeds a new life which he deviously likens to maggots and worms that are bred by and devour their prince and state (II. 117–18). He makes a mysterious poem, a new heroic body of which he has privileged knowledge and whose secrets he will only gradually, digressively reveal.

80 Yameng Liu, 'The Making of Elizabeth Drury: The Voice of God in "An Anatomy of the World" ', *John Donne Journal*, 8 (1989),:89–102, makes a similar point about the triumph of Donne's godlike creation *ex nihilo*.

81 *Letters*, 50–1

82 Laura Mulvey, 'Visual Pleasure and Narrative Cinema', *Screen*, 16/3 (1975), 7.

83 *Letters*, 65. Quoted in Bald, *John Donne: A Life*, 231.

This nothing resembles not only silent and dead Elizabeth Drury but also himself—the 40-year-old father of seven without a profession, who had referred repeatedly in his letters from Mitcham of 1608–10 to his house as a 'hospital', 'prison', or 'dungeon', his sickbed as 'imprisonment', his soul as walled up, and himself dead to the world. That Elizabeth Drury's absence, her death, might turn the world upside down is a strategic way to portray a miraculous moment of 'thaw' and revolution in his frozen, skewed state of personal affairs. In 1611 Donne acquired a male patron—a reversal in more than one way.

Not only the poet but the patron of *The Anniversaries* needed employment in 1611. Most likely Donne wrote 'A Funerall Elegie' before *The Anniversaries* as a bid for patronage, which was accepted. He became contracted to Sir Robert Drury, three years his junior, to accompany him and Lady Drury on the continent. Drury's distinguished father, Sir William, had been favoured to entertain Queen Elizabeth one night at Hawstead and had served as a soldier and commander against the Spanish in the Netherlands and in France; Sir William's death received mention by Camden in his *Annales*.[84] Yet despite wealth and name, despite knighthood before he was 17, and half a dozen campaigns in the Low Countries, Sir Robert lacked a prestigious state post. Although a Gentleman of the Privy Chamber, he had a reputation for being hot-tempered, domineering, without intellectual interests, and generally unfit for diplomacy. He had tried, in the words of a contemptuous Earl of Northampton, by 'all the Meanes and Mediators he can work for this Employment which his Hart affects', to secure the ambassadorship to Spain in 1609—'to make proof of those Partes which he conceives to rust for want of a right use to be made of them'.[85] Viewed from the heights of favoured nobility, Sir Robert's labouring ambition to demonstrate his 'Partes' was a mild amusement. Sir Francis Cottington in Madrid wrote, 'I pray let me know . . . who shall here relieve me: The general Voyce is that Sir Robert Drury shall come hither, but I can hardly believe it'.[86] Drury's petitions indeed failed.

Like Donne, Sir Robert had repeatedly sought employment overseas. Early in their careers coincidentally both men had sailed from Plymouth on 3 June 1596 on the expedition against Cadiz under Essex. They probably shared a number of acquaintances at court.[87] The 'restless' and,

[84] R. C. Bald, *Donne and the Drurys* (Cambridge: Cambridge University Press, 1959), 9–17.

[85] Ibid. 67.

[86] Ibid.

[87] Most likely Sir Robert knew both Goodyer and Sir Henry Wooten through his attendance at court; in addition, Donne's brother-in-law, William Lyly, who had worked for Sir Edward Stafford, ambassador to Paris and uncle to Sir Robert. Lyly had resided at Hawstead and enjoyed the friendship and patronage of the Drurys until his death in 1603.

according to Bald, 'naturally energetic' but less than subtle-tongued Sir Robert must have seen the advantages to urging his suit in acquiring the services of Donne's learning and languages.[88] But Donne did not create an occasion to repolish the lustre of his patron's name; Drury appears only on the title pages, and in contrast to the omnipresence of Lord and Lady Fairfax in Marvell's *Upon Appleton House* Sir Robert figures not at all.

A hint that the state of lament and spiritual loss occasioned by Elizabeth Drury's absence bears a paradoxically hopeful relation to reversing the material lack of place for Donne (and perhaps for his patron) is audible in the second unusually long sentence of the poem (I. 43–62). The eighteen lines that begin 'When as in states doubtful of future heirs' introduce *The Anniversaries*' first of many political analogies: a vacuum of authority opens and widens at the fatal sickness of a monarch who has no successor, and it threatens to collapse a state whose nobility are unwilling to admit their impending loss. Simultaneously 'a general thaw' spreads, a loosening of the glue of orderly human connection. Drury had just lost his second child, Elizabeth 'that Queen', and has no other heir. Yet an unexpected loss leads not to frozen grief but to a thaw—a dissolution but also a thaw in the sense of sudden freedom from constriction, of spring's hopeful melting of winter ice and its associations of warming, loosening, rebirth, and movement. A thaw opens *The Second Anniversary*, too: the movements of the beheaded man are like 'Ice, which crackles at a thaw'. Then a 'new Deluge, and of Lethe flood, | Hath drown'd us all'. Other images of loosening and flooding include Donne and his lover who are now 'both fluid, chang'd since yesterday' like river waters which flow always new ('So flowes her face, and thine eies', II. 390–6). Death becomes the unbinding of a pack—or its bursting, for the proud noble who succumbs to the floodwaters of his moral abscess.

These poems, I propose, while written in autumn and winter, burst like an unexpected thaw in a frozen period of isolation, ill health, and lack of professional progress, a thaw which releases enormous energy and movement 'packed up in two yards of skin'. The physical escape and new perspective offered by the open field of Drury's financial support, fellowship, and the trip abroad, and the blank page provided by Elizabeth Drury's death for writing about loss and injustice on a variety of levels and in a variety of voices, have contributed to that thaw. In a deluge that upends the world of the poem, the poet transposes the wrong state of

[88] Bald, *Donne and the Drurys*, 67.

affairs out of himself and onto the lost world in a combustion of satire, myth, and humour and without the fear that 'our weakness was discovered | In that confession'.

CONCLUSION

One explanation of the ostentatious length of *The Anniversaries* has been that Donne 'wrote more because he felt poor'. As Maureen Sabine observed, 'in some respects, the harder he made it for himself and his readers the better. For the financial return from this poetic commission ... depended on his capacity to spin out the lines'.[89] But perhaps he wrote more because he felt rich. While reminiscent and resonant of the conflicted epistles to the Countess of Bedford, *The Anniversaries* speak from quite another position of authority and autonomy. The poet is not a frustrated suitor of female patronage but engaged to a rich male patron; and the woman about whom he writes is not a powerful court personality bartering favours but a deceased 14-year-old girl whom he never met.

Out of this reversal *The Anniversaries* subtly erupt, fusing the strands of two stories of loss in a deceptive, digressive plot. The revolution is executed and concealed within those bounds of fall and rise, praiser and praised, which had haunted Donne's language and life since his Roman Catholic childhood. The occasion of these poems may be the anniversary of the tragic death of Sir Robert's daughter; but the symbolic arc of past descent 'represented' and future ascent 'contemplated' announced in the carefully worded titles suggests the consuming personal drama for the poet of failed opportunities and talents and his determination, and new hope, to rise with Drury.

Marotti characterized the work of the complimentary verse epistle as that of a vatic utterance or prayer for 'keeping open a channel of communication' and creating 'favorable circumstances for continued transactions between speaker and addressee'.[90] He observes that Donne used the epistle's occasion to go beyond the expected communication in 'repeated metapoetic digressions' which 'had the contradictory effect of both confirming the patronage relationship in which he was involved and undermining it. By scrutinizing the conditions and conventions of

[89] Sabine, *Feminine Engendered Faith*, 81.
[90] Marotti, *John Donne, Coterie Poet*, 228.

praise, Donne wittily resisted performing the encomiastic act directly'.[91] The deliberate resistance shaping his difficult rhythms, startling diction, and 'metapoetic digressions' characterizes more than Donne's verse epistles. The *Songs and Sonnets* are defiantly spacious microcosms that claim to be 'an everywhere'. Empson's 'space man' is always drawing attention to his anxiety to make space, to be able to leap through and over bounds of form while acknowledging them, and the space man enjoys a large arena in *The Anniversaries.*[92] If he creates 'a symbolic mode', as Barbara Lewalski has suggested, he does so by creating the expectations in order to overturn them.

The pressures of the speaker's brooding lament and anger on physical and psychical imprisonment, on depletion and loss, and on freedom and power—similarly audible in Donne's letters and verse epistles—and of irresistible, competitive ambition propel the inordinate length of *The Anniversaries.* The tension of balancing revelation with concealment also contributes to the knotty, digressive resistance of these poems. The poet displaces his spectres onto 'thou', a mortally 'sick world'; and assuming the authority of Elizabeth Drury's imagined perspective he gains freedom of movement, energy, and playfulness, and never more so than when stating the worst—'There is no health'.[93] As demonstrated by the footwork of pronouns 'I', 'thee', 'we', 'thy', 'Her', 'us', 'thou', 'thy', for example, in one short passage, I. 59–62 (especially 'Her death hath taught us dearly, that thou art | Corrupt and mortal'), Donne slips freely back and forth among identities, the parts of his anatomy, 'partaker, and a part'. He uses the public occasion of mourning for unfulfilled promise to send an elaborate private challenge for recognition to a new world, even if one well lost.

[91] Ibid.

[92] William Empson, 'Donne the Space Man', in *William Empson: Essays on Renaissance Literature*, ed. John Haffenden, vol. I (Cambridge: Cambrige University Press, 1993), 78–128.

[93] 'for our condition and state in this [religion], is as infirm as in our bodies; where Physitians consider only two degrees; sickness, and neutrality; for there is no health in us'. Donne, *Selected Prose*, 139 (?1609).

PART II

Sounding Interior Gardens at Mid-Century

2
Marvell's Watery Maze at Nun Appleton

Parts I and III, whose voices strategically defend, allure, and attack, enclose this Part of contemplative or interior gardens, as 'without' encloses 'within' at Marvell's Nun Appleton, the visible world the invisible in Browne's 1658 volume, or Milton's Paradise the promise of a 'paradise within'. The writers in Chapters 2–4 draw on rich traditions of mythic, pastoral, and biblical gardens to wander and to reflect on digressive movement as the play of the mind or the psyche. The abundance characteristic of these garden homes of and for the mind is bounded inevitably by an encroaching wilderness of trial that the digressive narrators attempt to hold beyond the walls or hedgerows; they inevitably confront within them death's spectre. Marvell, Browne, and Milton represent, at their times of writing, political sympathies ranging from ambiguous to royalist to republican, and they work as a family tutor, a country physician, and (Milton, for a decade) as civil servant. From a country-house poem circulated in manuscript to a published yet obscure personal essay to the epic triumph of a career, each imagined garden or plantation cultivates branching thought and rhetorical flowers; each speaker sounds and examines interior spaces and the nature of reflection by collecting together, to remember and connect, a landscape of voices past and present.

The narrative structure of *Upon Appleton House* has long invited and as long resisted explanation. The poem opens with promise of sobriety, its tetrameter couplets display the epigrammatic concision we associate with Marvell, and its sculpted stanzas seem balanced and self-contained. Yet the bounds and walls and close-fitting spaces of the house at Nun Appleton fail to hold the narrator as he wanders beyond their confines, over meadow and wood, through fantasy and apostrophe, into ventriloquized moods and prophetic strains. The lyric miniaturist promises control, yet his poem slips from the containment of an English country house into a dark landscape which seems at once portraiture of the estate, of the spirit, and of the deepest recesses of the self.

Rosalie Colie's masterly reading began by admitting what appeared to her the unresolvable problem of form, the frank and wilful irregularity of *Upon Appleton House.*[1] Later scholarship struggled unevenly with the poem's pressure toward dispersal and multiplicity,[2] its seeming disregard for, even subversion of, the usual signs of formal coherence,[3] while recent critical work has reflected increased theoretical sophistication and ease with narrative disjunction and fragmentation. John Rogers, Barbara Estrin, and Lynn Enterline have reopened the poem and reimagined its

[1] ' "Upon Appleton House" is frankly irregular. It flaunts its own seams, points to its own joinery, publicizes its own gaps'. Rosalie L. Colie, *'My Ecchoing Song': Andrew Marvell's Poetry of Criticism* (Princeton: Princeton University Press, 1970), 181.

[2] Kathleen Hunt Dolan, 'Readers of Upon Appleton House have found it difficult to discern any unity in the poem' (Lee Erickson, 'Marvell's "*Upon Appleton House*" and the Fairfax Family', *English Literary Renaissance*, 9 (1979), 158); a more recent article begins, 'Andrew Marvell's *Upon Appleton House* is a poem difficult to apprehend as a whole, elusive in its parts and particulars' (Derek Hirst and Steven Zwicker, 'High Summer at Nun Appleton, 1651: Andrew Marvell and Lord Fairfax's Occasions', *Historical Journal*, 36/2 (1993), 247–69). Perceptions of the unifying design of the poem, a hermetic key, have ranged from 'a map of the contours of the imagining mind' or 'a sequence of dramatic poems, skillfully divided', to a circular structure built on a pattern of concentric circles, and a 'hexagon' of pastorals, its own 'Bee-Like Cell'. See Isabel MacCaffrey, 'The Scope of Imagination in "Upon Appleton House" ', in K. Friedenreich (ed.), *Tercentenary Essays in Honor of Andrew Marvell* (Hamden, Conn.: Archon Books, 1977), 224–44; D. C. Allen, 'Upon Appleton House', in *Image and Meaning: Metaphoric Traditions in Renaissance Poetry* (Baltimore: Johns Hopkins University Press, 1968), 187–225; Maren-Sofie Røstvig, '*In ordine de ruota*: Circular Structure in "The Unfortunate Lover" and Upon Appleton House', in Friedenreich (ed.), *Tercentenary Essays in Honor of Andrew Marvell*, 245–67; T. Katharine Sheldahl Thomason, 'Marvell, his Bee-Like Cell: The Pastoral Hexagon of "*Upon Appleton House*" ', *Genre*, 16 (1983), 39–56.

[3] G. R. Hibbard, who first isolated the genre of the 17th-century country house poem, located its final stage in Marvell's puzzling poem which he refused to address beyond the first ten stanzas, 'after which it then grows into something new and different'. G. R. Hibbard, 'The Country House Poem of the Seventeenth Century', *Journal of the Warburg and Courtauld Institutes*, 19 (1956), 169. A later scholar of the genre was troubled by the poem's 'deformation of the language of praise into idiosyncratic meditations' (William A. McClung, *The Country House in English Renaissance Poetry* (Berkeley and Los Angeles: University of California Press, 1977), 147). Colie noted the debt of its 'tentativeness' to Montaigne's *Essais* but concluded that *Upon Appleton House* most resembles that forest of forms, a 'sylva' or miscellany, a mixed genre in the tradition of Donne's *Anniversaries* and Burton's *The Anatomy of Melancholy*. John Wallace reads the poem's literary echoes, inordinate length, and international landscape as that of a Christian epic answering D'Avenant's *Gondibert* and its famous Preface. Colie, '*My Ecchoing Song*', 183, 277–94; John Wallace, *Destiny his Choice: The Loyalism of Andrew Marvell* (London: Cambridge University Press, 1968), 232–57. Some critics have even tried to smooth over the poem's structural and psychological oddities by thematizing its regularity. For example, 'The "sober frame" of the first line is the sign that the *vita sobria* or temperance is to exercise a control over the action' (Wallace, *Destiny his Choice*, 244).

structure with fresh readings of historical and psychoanalytic complexity.[4] One scholar has uncovered a late sixteenth-century map of Nun Appleton crossed by the river's serpentine line and finds that Marvell's poem provides 'an entirely plausible account of a sinuous yet circular walk through the Fairfax estate'.[5]

Upon Appleton House is indeed exact and detailed in its allusions to Fairfacian property and history; yet the celebration of the house is darkened, not only by the civil turmoil from which the General has withdrawn but by the absence of exactly those compliments to patrons traditional in country-house poems—the display of abundant blessings, gifts, and tributes. At Nun Appleton no cheerful brows glow in firelight, no groaning board suggests feasting, no stewards or tenants populate the scene. Instead bloody Thestylis serves up a baby rail, and abundance figures in the number and density of the estate's orphaned creatures and sinister domains of garden, meadow, and flood.

The narrator's progress through the poem not only swerves from the anticipated path of country-house discourse; it strays in ways synonymous with transgression and moral deviation. A generic deviant, the poem raises the spectre of disorder and deviance at many levels: personal, familial, national, sexual, spiritual. As a subordinate yet intrusive presence among his employers, the tutor pulls at various threads of their story but appears to have no history himself. He is neither a Fairfax nor of a military line, neither child nor parent, not a tree or a bird despite his wishful woodland masque—perhaps neither male nor female but an amphibian of doubtful nature. And through his peculiar 'survey' (l. 81) and his movements 'betwixt', we encounter a series of silent, sacrificial

[4] See John Rogers, *The Matter of Revolution: Science, Poetry, and Politics in the Age of Milton* (Ithaca, NY: Cornell University Press, 1996), ch. 2–3. Barbara Estrin, *Laura: Uncovering Gender and Genre in Wyatt, Donne, and Marvell* (Durham, NC: Duke Univesity Press, 1994), 'A-Mazing and A-Musing', 278–303, offers a provocative reading of the experimental 'formlessness' of Marvell's narrator, while Lynn Enterline, *The Tears of Narcissus: Melancholia and Masculinity in Early Modern Writing* (Stanford, Calif.: Stanford University Press, 1995), has probed Marvell's lyric poise as a containment like melancholy's narcissism of explosive vacillation between psychological and physical pain and psychological and aesthetic pleasure. The poet's characteristic entanglement of pain and pleasures, and of aggression and sadness, she notes, is 'comparable to the alterations that interested Freud in melancholia' and which led him to propose a connection between narcissism's 'wound' in the ego and melancholy's pleasurable indulgence in narcissistic pain. On Marvell's work as reflection on the problem of how 'things greater are in less contain'd', see Donald M. Friedman, 'Rude Heaps and Decent Order', in Warren Chernaik and Martin Dzelzainis (eds.), *Marvell and Liberty* (Houndmills: Macmillan Press, 1999), 123–44.

[5] Timothy Raylor, ' "Paradice's Only Map": A Plan of Nun Appleton', *Notes and Queries* (June 1997), 186–7.

victims. The grounds surveyed become depths to be plumbed; and a mariner's line (ll. 381–2) sounds an underworld of digression, drowning, and the translation of youth.[6]

Beginning with the digression into the nunnery, *Upon Appleton House* celebrates yet oddly highlights the skirmish of parents, suitors, and rivals around the youthful Isabel and Maria. We are not allowed to forget, by contrast, Maria's 'studious Hours', her languages, and her wisdom cultivated in the halcyon days before her translation into a bride; nor can we forget how Isabel was tempted generations earlier into spiritual retreat. And behind the impulse to retreat from or postpone the demands of heterosexual reproduction hovers the child's tutor, the narrator whose intellectual fertility Lord Fairfax employs to extend the family fame in lines of verse. Some of the poem's alarm which collects around children may be anger and sadness that belongs to the tutor, a progenitor whose personal lines do not go forward but inward and back to the past. He mocks his erotic play and sterility on 'Velvet Moss' in the woods, and his sensual sanctuary pointedly recalls the lesbian cloister. Yet the caricature and tortured self-mockery also distract attention from the poem's interest in arrested adolescence, in virginity, and in alternative modes of reproduction, such as poetry.

Marvell's speaker moves cautiously between two female heirs who preside over the Fairfax property and whose destinies of marriage and pedigree have become as fixed as those boiled fruits of the cloister. In suspension between past and future, between the cloister's blooming flower and Nun Appleton's 'sacred Bud', the poem's depths and disjunctures not only reveal the plan of an estate and a family's history, but they trace the lines of Marvell's powerful moves into the tutor's, and not Lord Fairfax's, longing and loss.[7] In the irregularities of the estate's divisions, the speaker attempts to map himself in the story of the Fairfax family, one

[6] Throughout this chapter, references to the line numbers of Marvell's poems refer to the text in *The Poems and Letters of Andrew Marvell*, ed. H. M. Margoliouth, 3rd edn., rev. Pierre Legouis with collaboration of E. E. Duncan-Jones (Oxford: Clarendon Press, 1971). Nigel Smith's magnificent new edition of *The Poems of Andrew Marvell* (London: Pearson, Longman, 2003) appeared after this text went to press.

[7] The tutor proposes to 'survey' (p. 81) the property; and his ambition might suggest the instruments and mathematics of a 17th-century survey which was designed to 'reveal the true order of the landscape' and discern absolute boundaries of 'a higher order' than otherwise visible, as distinct from 'the lived local experiences of and attachment to the land'. But while the tutor wittily praises the 'holy mathematics' of the house and envisions the Yorkshire property as 'paradise's map', his perspective is not disinterested. See Crystal Bartolovich, 'Spatial Stories: The Surveyor and the Politics of Transition', in Alvin Vos (ed.), *Place and Displacement in the Renaissance*, Medieval and Renaissance Texts and Studies 132 (Binghamton, NY: Medieval and Renaissance Texts and Studies, 1995), 274, 279.

whose fragments, persons, and episodes have driven him to sound the very bottom of the self:

> To see Men through this Meadow Dive,
> We wonder how they rise alive.
> As, under Water, none does know
> Whether he fall through it or go.
> But, as the Mariners that sound,
> And show upon their Lead the Ground,
> They bring up Flow'rs so to be seen,
> And prove they've at the Bottom been. (st. 48)

The scene is the meadows before the flood, yet already we are at sea. At the centre of this great poem the speaker dives 'within' where the rhetorical 'Flow'rs' of poetry now testify to human depth.

Drowning as an image for chaotic dissolution, whether of the self or the state, haunts other poems by Marvell, such as 'The Unfortunate Lover' and 'The First Anniversary of the Government under O.C'. In *Upon Appleton House* under the pressure, and temptation, of the threat of dissolution, the tutor moves between the confines of the house and the danger of an emotional flood. Unravelling a thread which begins in the nunnery with Isabel, the narrator meanders on the estate and simultaneously dives through history, memory, and the psyche—almost drowning yet always finding ground to dive further 'within'. This maelstrom, like the close-lacing circles of the woodbines, draws more tightly the loops of the narrator's progress until he ends in a tunnel, a thread of light, which leads between two stocks of the wood. The narrator's ground disappears in the flood, but he appears to find a footing in the 'passable' wood. The ground narrows, however, to a last thread of a lane (621) onto which he asks to be staked—the sacrifice, or monster, at the centre of the labyrinth. He has reached his antipodes, touched bottom. Then on the hook of a 'But' ('But, where the Floods did lately drown, | There at the Ev'ning stake me down', ll. 623–4) the speaker becomes his own angler and catches himself. The antipodes have turned. The thread of light becomes a line by which he rises to the surface and lands, for this tutor's imagination needs to be staked down finally like a storm-tossed boat.

Into a flood of sensation and memory he had descended like a plummet and almost drowned. Now those depths are contained behind the snaky mirror of the river.[8] The slick and blinding glitter, like the dazzling surface of Marvell's poetry, closes over and seals what has happened

[8] In the river's surface, 'the metaphorical turns literal and the literal explodes again into the metaphorical'. Enterline, *The Tears of Narcissus*, 181.

below. The poem opens up dizzying depths yet returns us to land. 'Things greater' are 'in less contain'd' by Marvell's line.

The speaker's leisurely survey, while a linear progress that maps one Yorkshire estate, becomes also a series of dives into another landscape, a psychological interior which includes the Yorkshire of Marvell's childhood. Apocalyptic images of flood and ark in *Upon Appleton House*, when read together with the storm-tossed, wandering ships elsewhere in his work, suggest the poet's exploration in the early 1650s of the nation's but also of his own fantasy, which he protectively satirizes in the mock-heroic of William Fairfax: the desire to be rescued from exterior but also interior chaos by a bold manly arm. Such a force appears in the 'lusty Mate' who with clear eye and calm mind wrests the helm from his addled steersman and saves the drowning ship of state in 'The First Anniversary' (ll. 265–78). These two poems of the 1650s to Marvell's commanding patrons feature threatened fathers and shadowy accusing sons, the danger of falling trees and drowning seas. Marvell's great celebration of Cromwell nearly drowns, awash with the floods in the speaker's head. And Marvell's 'lusty Mate' at the helm stands in sharp contrast to all of the poet's painfully landlocked and self-enclosed gardeners, mowers, and complaining nymphs who retreat from loss and hopeless desire. The mate points back to Marvell's youth in the port and military fortress of Hull—origins recalled and mocked years later by Samuel Parker in *A Reproof to the Rehearsal Transprosed* (1673). Parker deplores Marvell's low language which he attributes to 'your first unhappy Education Among Boat-Swains and Cabin-Boys'; and he attacks the poet's impertinence to instruct royalty 'and as if you were the Skipper of the State talk to them of nothing but Sea-marks, and Buoys, and Rocks, and Sands, and Charts, and Compasses, etc'.[9] The world of the sea would seem to have no place at Nun Appleton, but surely it does.

Before we enter those meadows and woods, I will show that by 1655 Marvell can allow the celebration of his new patron, Oliver Cromwell, to digress into vivid, even melodramatic images of drowning and grief, of loss and a vacuum of authority, because those fears will be answered and contained by the apocalyptic figure of a strong leader who is Cromwell, the angelic and 'lusty' steersman. By contrast, the earlier poem to Lord

[9] Samuel Parker, *A Reproof to the Rehearsal Transprosed in A Discourse to its Author* (London: James Collins, 1673), 227, 481. I am grateful to Derek Hirst for directing me to Parker's *Reproof.* See Derek Hirst, 'Samuel Parker, Andrew Marvell, and Political Culture, 1667–73', in Derek Hirst and Richard Strier, (eds.), *Writing and Political Engagement in Seventeenth-Century England* (Cambridge: Cambridge University Press, 1999), 145–64.

Fairfax demands that the lone 'I' save himself and contain the flood-waters, because no strong leader exists; yet his charge of blooming youth, whether his own or that of 'the young Maria', will be sacrificed. Paradox, nostalgia, and self-mockery must do the work of government in *Upon Appleton House*; abruptly the waters withdraw and shrink beneath the dazzling surface of a river whose serpentine line through the estate looks like the poetic progress from which we emerge. The virtuosic, labyrinthine structure and variety enfold criticism as well as compliment. The poem's brilliance, if a celebration, is also a foil for impoverishment.

LOST SHIP IN LIMBO

Thomas Fairfax, who almost single-handedly created the New Model army, first joined his cavalry with that of Cromwell in 1643 in Hull, the city of Marvell's youth. Cromwell was then an inexperienced colonel, although older than Fairfax. Sir Thomas in the footsteps of his military father had trained in the Netherlands with Horace Vere, the father of the future Lady Fairfax, and by 1642 had led a company of dragoons in the King's Scottish campaign. Worshipped by his soldiers, the young Fairfax was described by one military historian as 'the only Parliamentarian commander who was Rupert's equal in dash and drive'.[10] But where 'An Horatian Ode' tells us that Cromwell left his gardens and domestic comforts to answer history's call to duty as 'the Wars and Fortunes Son', *Upon Appleton House* ponders Fairfax's decision in 1650 to reverse Cromwell's direction—to leave history and the millennium for retired self-scrutiny and domestic economy. The poem appropriately begins 'Within'; but the Fairfax household with its head drawn into a shell appears bowed to the active masculine force which the terseness of 'An Horatian Ode' observes as Cromwell's signature.

Marvell's longest panegyric to Cromwell, 'On the First Anniversary', opens unusually for a celebration—with a drowning:

> Like the vain Curlings of the Watry maze,
> Which in smooth streams a sinking Weight does raise;
> So Man, declining alwayes, disappears
> In the weak Circles of increasing Years;
> And his short Tumults of themselves Compose,
> While flowing Time above his Head does close. (ll. 1–6)

[10] Brigadier Peter Young and Richard Holmes, *The English Civil War: A Military History of the Three Civil Wars, 1642-1651* (London: Eyre Methuen, 1974), 99.

The poem later veers into an extended digression on the coaching accident which in 1655 had endangered Cromwell's life. The tension between gravity's pull to end time, characterized as 'a sinking Weight' of 'Man, declining alwayes', and life's stubborn impulse to escape from necessity, characterized by a digression which steals and opens up time, lies behind Marvell's image later at line 157 of history as a ship unable to land ('Hence landing Nature to new Seas is tost'). This image appears as well in 'A Dialogue between the Soul and Body', where the Soul laments itself as a ship wandering in a forced exile of life ('And ready oft the Port to gain, | Am shipwrackt into Health again', ll. 29–30). From the image of history as a storm-tossed ship, 'The First Anniversary' returns to the initial spectre of drowning in the speaker's relation of the coaching accident.[11]

As Royalist pamphlets thrilled to exclaim, the charioteer of state who would manage three kingdoms could not control his own horses. The 'Angelique' (l. 126) Lord Protector could not protect himself, and the poem's hysterical praise wraps itself around, and overcompensates for, accusations of his frailty. Within the digression, storms twice rock the wandering ship of history in passages which emphasize drowning as the inevitable and welcome end to physical chaos. First, at lines 211–14, shipwreck is a horrible personal assault—we hear the shrieks of passengers to 'deaf Seas and ruthless Tempests' and watch the 'plundering Streams' of ocean ripping apart shipboards. The second reference is the epic simile of the lusty mate who 'with more careful Eye' spies the stars, rights the steering, and saves his chaotic vessel and exhausted passengers from the ocean floor (ll. 265–78). Marvell consistently characterizes Cromwell's vigour and power as superhuman, whether the image be 'three-fork'd Lightning' in 'An Horatian Ode' or the 'Sun-like' angel at the opening of 'The First Anniversary'. Now this strong masculine figure focuses and calms the disorganizing power of natural turbulence reflected in 'whirling', 'Giddy' minds. Specifically a drowning man's pull must be countered by an intensely upward, angelic force such as Cromwell's—and not only in 'The First Anniversary' but deep in Nun Appleton. 'Give me but Wings', exclaims the narrator in the woods (l. 565). If the Lord Protector

[11] It was not a simple fall. Known for his fondness for horses, Cromwell had received a gift of six grey Frieslands from the Count of Oldenburg and wanted to try out the team. He drove the coach into Hyde Park: 'First Oliver tumbled down and was then jerked along with his foot caught in the reins for some distance, only saved when the Protectoral shoe fell off and released him. Furthermore the presence of the devoted Thurloe on the expedition nearly proved fatal to his master; he too fell out and the pistol he carried in his pocket went off, narrowly missing Oliver'. See Antonia Fraser, *Cromwell, our Chief of Men* (London: Weidenfeld and Nicolson, 1973), 512.

temporarily drops out of sight like the sun, he will rise smiling; and not only does he not drown, but he commands the ocean with monstrous ships which frighten wave and wind. The nightmare of storm-tossed seas which threatens this poem is magically tamed and harnessed by Cromwell to intimidate England's neighbours and enemies: hurricanes are his cannon, and thunder their shot.[12]

The digressive interlude of about sixty lines in which the Lord Protector falls, dies, and rises is the distended opposite of 'thy sudden Fall', and the digression exerts a power of delay and suspended, repeated scrutiny diametrically opposed to Cromwell's own contractive force. The image of Cromwell as Noah is particularly confusing: Marvell raises the spectre of Noah's drunkenness, and so of Ham's gaze, in order to clear Cromwell of the charge of personal ambition. He 'only didst for others plant the Vine | Of liberty, not drunken with its Wine' himself (ll. 287–8). But the poet does not drop the story of Noah; he proclaims the impossibility of 'sober Liberty' for the disruptive sects, a raging 'Chammish issue' who 'such as to their Parents Tents do press, | May shew their own, not see his Nakedness' (ll. 291–2). Marvell's insistence on the self-exposure of the voyeur who presses to the parent's tent reflects on his poem's speaker; but the self-exposure of voyeurism also recalls the furtive narrator of *Upon Appleton House*, who gazes on a distinguished although hardly drunken father in retirement and invokes the 'first Carpenter' and godly steersman in the woods (l. 485) before turning our gaze on himself.

The anniversary tribute, like the poem to Fairfax, blends panegyric with digressive, ambiguous passages not easily accounted for within the aims of celebration. Finally Cromwell becomes 'the Angel of our Commonweal' troubling the waters to make them heal; but surely it is the poet who is troubling these waters to make them heal, and they are as much personal as political deeps. Cromwell and Fairfax trigger private floods and digressions in the poet who is both Ham and Shem. Marvell curiously distends his poems to cover up and to expose these godly parents but also himself in a pattern like reverberation of ever-widening, but not weakening, circles around 'a sinking Weight', a drowning man.

The numerical centre of 'The First Anniversary' is a halting, startling line within the passage on the accident: 'Thou Cromwell falling, not a stupid Tree' (l. 201). And while the next line completes the meaning, the

[12] On 'The Unfortunate Lover', see, for example, Terri Clerico, 'The "Amphibium" Poet: Phallic Identity in Marvell', *Criticism*, 34/4 (1992), 539–61; and Enterline, *The Tears of Narcissus*, ch. 3, 'The Mirror and the Snake: The Case of Marvell's "Unfortunate Lover"', 146–88.

initial dumb power of a falling tree deep in the middle of remembrance and celebration threatens like a perpetually sinking weight in a stream. For 'falling' attracts to itself and focuses all of the references to 'fall' which collect in the first half of the digression (ll. 163, 175, 190, 201, 206) before the joyous sunrise of Cromwell 'triumphant'. In that imagined moment of helplessness as the Lord Protector loses power to protect, the poet takes control—he seizes the force Cromwell loses, and he gains time and space to fill. In response to the hopeless 'Curlings' of one 'Watry maze' (l. 1), he creates a maze of his own. The threatened loss of a protector, a vacuum of authority to be filled by the rushing waters of chaos, propels this poet to wind imaginatively around the vacuum in order to camouflage yet point to a spectre of vacancy—and perhaps not only in 1655. On 23 January, 1641 Marvell, aged 19, while hardly a child was left an 'Orphan of the Hurricane' when his father, the Reverend Andrew Marvell, drowned in the Humber in a storm—the barrow-boat 'sand-warp't', a drunken steersman suspected. That year the poet left Cambridge abruptly and afterwards travelled on the continent, most likely as a child's tutor.[13] The itinerant tutor of *Upon Appleton House* appears to have landed; yet he circles around anger, eros, and loss in a peculiar vortex, one which draws him down like a lost ship in limbo.

ADRIFT 'WITHIN' CHILDHOOD

Marvell imagines Appleton House with an open door, but the door stands open as if to ease the narrator's exit. The poor hover outside, but they never enter; and 'Furniture of Friends' reduces guests to the wooden tropes of a genre that has become rigid like life at Nun Appleton, except for the tutor's discreet excursions. Who would find enticing such words of invitation as 'sober', 'hew', 'Work', and 'pain', or enjoy the tension between 'contain'd' and 'unconstrain'd' (ll. 43–4)? Forced to choose between 'spread' or 'dead', the narrator wanders for almost a hundred stanzas. And he unravels a thread that leads from the first child and virgin of the poem, its delectable Isabel Thwaites, to the labyrinth in the wood. In the Presbyterian house, disconcerted sweating walls dilate to fit

[13] See John Kenyon, 'Andrew Marvell: Life and Times', in R. L. Brett (ed.), *Andrew Marvell: Essays on the Tercentenary of his Death* (Oxford: Oxford University Press, 1979), 6–7. See also *The Complete Works in Verse and Prose of Andrew Marvell*, ed. Revd Alexander B. Grosart, 4 vols. (London: Robson and Sons, 1872–5), vol. i, 'Memorial Introduction', p. xxxi.

the master, and sexual coupling presses against the coffin's sobriety; but the cloister and the poem relax their contours around Isabel.[14] Through a digression which follows the Yorkshire Proserpina into the 'gloomy' underworld of the convent, *Upon Appleton House* opens to hectic light and fragrance, a flush of warmth and embracing arms. The sensuous cloister opens its gates to Isabel while it closes them against the world, and it opens the poet's psyche in a way that makes possible the whole poem.[15]

The poem's first words, 'Within this sober Frame', and those of the nun's subtle speech, 'Within this holy leisure', are interesting twins: and in stanza 13 we begin the poem again but on a deeper note. After the initial stanzas of stooping, bending, and bowing, which emphasize that here the poet will 'not remain', it is the nun's delicious voice of seduction which sucks us in. The soft luxury and inviting pleasure of the word 'leisure' sets off a rapid chain reaction of verbs barring trespass but also exit, which echo later in the wood—'restrain', 'hedge', 'inclose', and 'shuts'—until the stanza 'locks' its 'Gates' and harsher 'Grates'.

Isabel is the first flower of youth in the poem. And Marvell emphasizes the miracle and delight of her bloom by locating it near, and in contrast to, the 'gloomy' cloister. Yet compared to the sobriety of the House, the Roman Catholic gloom seems to cast a softer shadow. Once guaranteed privacy the nunnery feeds the senses with oriental perfumes, lamplight, and with appreciation for beauty, ornament, and those 'Pasts' for 'curious tasts'. While feasting is not a prominent feature of life at the Fairfaxes, the nuns seem to enjoy their food: what is more, the Cistercian sisters are handling, touching, and embracing; they love sweets, warmth, and beauty. And after the tense control and hints of the grave represented by a house that competes with beasts' dens to fit the body exactly, Isabel appears like a welcome flush of life. Her fairness is not of dwarfish or measured confines but 'beyond Measure' (l. 91), true to nature's artless abundance. The hungry nun excited to inspiration by such wealth and loveliness translates Isabel as she speaks: in fairy-tale chemistry she

[14] Patricia Parker has written extensively on figures of 'dilation' in Shakespeare, their relation to the female anatomy and the unfolding of secrets and to inflation of language. See most recently her *Shakespeare from the Margins: Language, Culture, Context* (Chicago: University of Chicago Press, 1996), chs. 6 and 7.

[15] About the Cistercian nuns Judith Haber observed, 'Within the bounds of their enclosure everything that is excluded comes back', and the same might be said of other bounds in this poem. Judith Haber, *Pastoral and the Poetics of Self-Contradiction: Theocritus to Marvell* (Cambridge: Cambridge of University Press, 1994), 129.

transforms that beauty under summer suns, boils it into a perverse glowing 'Order' to disguise the fact that she wants to eat the girl like a candy.

Along with other sacrificed young in the poem (the baby rail, the heron's 'eldest'), Isabel reminds us of Marvell's keen and repeated interest in the breathless poise of a childhood soon to be extinguished. The poet's characteristic tension between precision and nostalgia holds in relation not only child with adult but also victim with saviour, childlike repose with the sexual bed and sacrificial altar. For example, Isabel is swept from one enchanted and ambiguous altar to another ('that blest Bed'), and Mary Fairfax is prepared for the sacrificial knife of matrimony. In a memorable moment of the 'Horatian Ode', Charles I pillows his royal head childlike on a public bed that suggests not only personal but sexual humiliation before bloody hands.[16] Marvell's Restoration satire 'The Last Instructions to a Painter' suddenly modulates from furious disgust to hushed reverence for the magic of pubescent Archibald Douglas—his chaste denial of heterosexuality and his embrace of a fiery self-consummation and dissolution in a sacrificial but erotic bed.

Violence mixed with eroticism in Marvell's work ruptures the delicately poised moment between the bud of childhood and the flower of maturity, but it lurks disturbingly within such female children as little T.C. whose strong will to tame alarms her adult observer and belies the 'simplicity' of 'golden daies'. Mary Fairfax, too, disciplines her surroundings, but the breathless attention she commands reflects her own arrested moment of safety in the study of languages, her brief, timeless poise suspended from the demands of sexuality and family. Critics have long noted Marvell's ambivalence about the aggression of sexuality and noted the violence he associates with the self-assertion of birth—aggression and violence which the poet often displaces onto females and nature.[17] John Rogers, for example, situates Marvell's 'unique poetics of passive agency' and vegetable sexuality in relation to pacific, millenarian discourses of the period.[18] Yet while he illuminates Marvell's vision of the virgin Mary,

[16] Rogers, *The Matter of Revolution*, 74, rightly draws attention to the similarity between Charles's posture in 'An Horation Ode' and the 'severed bud' of Mary Fairfax's virginity.

[17] In the 1970s Jim Swan published a number of psychoanalytic essays on Marvell and aggression including, ' "Caesarian Section": The Destruction of Enclosing Bodies in Marvell's "Horatian Ode" ', *Psychocultural Review*, 9 (1977), 1–8, ' "Betwixt Two Labyrinths": Andrew Marvell's Rational Amphibian', *Texas Studies in Language and Literature*, 17 (1975), 551–72, and 'At Play in the Garden of Ambivalence: Andrew Marvell and the Green World', *Criticism*, 17 (1975), 295–307. More recently, see Clerico, 'The "Amphibium" poet', Estrin, *Laura*, Enterline, *The Tears of Narcissus*, and Rogers, *The Matter of Revolution*.

[18] Rogers, 'Marvell and the Action of Virginity', in *The Matter of Revolution*, 70–102.

he hints at but does not pursue connections among the feminine Roman Catholic enclave, the nuns' cult of abstinence from heterosexual reproduction, and the seductions of language.

The poet and the 'Suttle' nun are both vulnerable to dismissal as sterile makers of images. They are linked by their ambiguous relations to language and theft, children and money, and by their distance from the patriarchal, heterosexual family and its demands for blood and pedigree. Once we join the narrator on his extended detour into the nunnery, we enter a key to the poem's seductive design of self-scrutiny and self-exposure. Like a persuasive poet the nun weaves a spell of rich plenty but to disguise poverty and sterility, enchantment and theft. When her rhetorical fabrication is exposed and destroyed by the literal-minded William Fairfax, she and the nuns shrink from supernatural witches to outcast 'Gipsies' who have lost a stolen child (l. 268). The nuns have lost a source of wealth and also their reproductive line, for those phallic needles and thread were ready to multiply Isabel's image 'Through ev'ry Shrine' (l. 134).[19]

From the Gunpowder to the Popish Plots, anti-Catholic polemic invoked Egypt and the East, along with Rome, as the home of dark papist devils and their rhetorical wiles. Sixteenth-century documents also link Egypt with gypsies (reflecting the etymology of gypsy) who were believed to steal children and sell them for labour abroad.[20] Roman Catholics,

[19] See Estrin, *Laura*, 288.

[20] 'The Spanish word gitano, like the English "Gypsy", comes from "Egyptian", the most persistent tag, which first turned up in popular Byzantine poetry. The designation was taken up by Gypsies identifying themselves to local authorities, perhaps in the belief that it was better to come from somewhere than from nowhere, and preferably somewhere incontestably exotic (particularly useful for fortune-tellers)'. Isabel Fonseca, *Bury me Standing: The Gypsies and their Journey* (New York: Knopf, 1996), 237. The *OED* cites Shakespeare's allusion to the connection between gypsy and Egypt in *Antony and Cleopatra*, IV. xii. 28. See also Fonseca, *Bury me Standing*, 72, 89, 236–7. According to the *OED*, the verb kidnap originally referred to the feared gypsy practice: 'to steal or carry off (children and others) in order to provide servants or labourers for the American plantations'. Kidnap appears during the Restoration in several publications about English rogues, which include dictionaries of gypsy slang. See, for example, Richard Head's *The Canting Academy, or, the Devils Cabinet Opened: Wherein is shewn the Mysterious and Villanous Practices of that wicked Crew, commonly known by the Names of Hectors, Trapanners, Gilts, &, to Which is Added a Compleat Canting-Dictionary, both of old Words, and Such as are now most in use . . .* (London: F. Leach etc., 1673), 40–1; and the references to kidnap in *The Life and Death of the English Rogue, or, his Last Legacy to the World . . .: to which is added an alphabetical canting dictionary, English before the canting* (London: Charles Passinger etc., 1679). See also Thomas Dekker, 'English Villanies, Eight Severall Times Prest to Death by the Printers . . . And because a companie of rogues, cunning canting Gypsies, and all the scumme of our nation fight here under their owne tottered colours: at the end is a canting dictionarie, to teach their language; with canting songs' (London: E.P. etc., 1648).

especially Jesuits, and gypsies were alike characterized as aliens skilled in wheedling talk and disguise.[21] Indeed, what society could be further from the sober establishment of Lord and Lady Fairfax, yet these 'glad Parents' will sell or allow 'Fate' to 'translate' their child (l. 747), who must supply 'the Line' (l. 738). The early modern usage of 'translation'—a word that literally means to convey, transfer, or transport property and language from place to place—carries associations with theft and counterfeit.[22] Patron and poet seem to be obscurely implicated as they shuffle counters of children and words for purposes of gain. Meanwhile, orphaned at 19 and magician of tongues, the childless poet reads family futures in the lines of a landscape instead of a palm.

To William Fairfax the nuns are a den of thieves. But when he steals Isabel back the poem allows the reader to wonder whether he simply continues the theft begun by the lesbian sisters, since Isabel remains silent as to where she feels she belongs.[23] The poet, too, is said to have been stolen once by Jesuits, lured from his Cambridge studies into Roman Catholicism about the time that his mother died and his father, a respected Puritan clergyman of no property, remarried into wealth (1638–9). According to Thomas Cooke's eighteenth-century account, Marvell's 'Genius beyond his Years', like Isabel's beauty and wealth, attracted the Order's interest to gain him as 'a great Instrument towards carrying on their Cause. They used all the Arguments they could to seduce him away'.[24] Once a prized youthful genius whose abilities in Latin and languages at Cambridge elicited puns on his name, Marvell now tutors youth and speaks most intimately for the young and the mute.

[21] See, for example, British Museum, *Catalogue of Prints and Drawings in the British Museum, Political and Personal Satires Division I: Political and Personal Satires*, i: *1320–April 11, 1689* (London: The Trustees, 1870). Alison Shell, *Catholicism, Controversy, and the English Literary Imagination, 1558-1660* (Cambridge: Cambridge University Press, 1999), 25, notes that anti-Catholic propaganda drew on the Book of Revelation for apocalyptic images. The Pope was identified with Antichrist and with the scarlet Whore of Babylon, another Eastern image.

[22] Coincidentally, Lord Fairfax was nicknamed 'Black Tom' Fairfax for his dark hair and eyes and swarthy complexion, although certainly no gypsy. See, for example, M. A. Gibb, *The Lord General: A Life of Thomas Fairfax* (London: L. Drummond Ltd., 1938), 4. On the early modern associations of 'translate' with the conveyance and transfer of material property, see Parker, *Shakespeare from the Margins*, 137–43, 149–84.

[23] James Holstun makes a similar point in ' "Will you Rent our Ancient Love Asunder?" Lesbian Elegy in Donne, Marvell, and Milton', *ELH* 54 (1987), 850. He notes that William Fairfax 'competes with the nuns on their own economic level'; see 849–50.

[24] Hilton Kelliher (ed.), *Andrew Marvell, Poet and Politician 1621-78: An Exhibition to Commemorate the Tercentenary of his Death.* (London: British Museum, 1978), 25.

If a stolen child presides over Marvell's meditation on and for the Fairfaxes, the historical Isabel Thwaites who was an orphan and a ward of the king silently presides over this family.[25] Sir Thomas Fairfax (1521–1600), the great-grandfather of Marvell's patron, was the second son of Sir William who had married Isabel; and valiant Sir William 'whose offspring fierce I Shall fight through all the universe', whose eldest son had been a lunatic and died without issue, mysteriously revised his will to disinherit this second son 'of an estate better than two thousand pounds per annum'. The principal family residence and all of the property over which Sir William had control fell to a younger son,[26] while Sir Thomas inherited Denton along with Nun Appleton and other properties from his mother Isabel.[27] By the 1640s these Fairfaxes of Denton, Nun Appleton, Bilborough, and Newton Kyme had prospered like Jacob to become the most prominent of three Yorkshire branches and one of the two younger 'cadet lines' to shed Roman Catholicism.[28]

Yet until the late sixteenth century, a Roman Catholic, Sir William Fairfax of Walton and Gilling, still headed the family. Modest additions to his house at Gilling included a heraldic frieze in the Great Chamber and genealogical windows, the forerunners of a whole series of genealogical and archaeological studies fostered by the Fairfaxes 'to hymn the

[25] See also Brian Patton, 'Preserving Property: History, Genealogy, and Inheritance in "Upon Appleton House" ', *Renaissance Quarterly*, 49/4 (Winter 1996), 824–39, for another discussion of the Fairfax family's concerns with genealogy and property.

[26] George W. Johnson (ed.), *The Fairfax Correspondence: Memoirs of the Reign of Charles the First*, vol. i (London: R. Bentley, 1848), pp. xvi–xix.

[27] She had inherited them from her brother John. And Isabel and John's grandfather John Thwaites, who had married 'a great heiress', was the heir of his mother Alice Thwaites. See *Letters and Papers, Foreign and Domestic of the Reign of Henry VIII*, 2nd edn. (London: HM Stationery Office, 1862–1920), 968; 'The Victoria History of the Counties of England: *A History of Yorkshire, North Riding*', William Page (ed.), 2 vols. (London: A. Constable, 1914), ii. 400–1; and James Raine and John William Clay (eds.), *Testamenta Eboracensia; or Wills Registered at York* . . ., vol. iv, Surtees Society (London: J. B. Nichols, 1869), 10 n. See the entry for 20 Jan. 1562 in *Calendar of State Papers, Domestic Series, of the Reigns of Edward VI, Mary, Elizabeth, 1547-1580*, ed. Robert Lemon (London: Longman, Brown, Green, Longman and Roberts, 1856), i. 193, which states, 'Geo., Earl of Shrewsbury, to same [Sir William Cecill]. Shews that the application of Thos. Fairfax to be put into full possession of the manor of Nun-Apleton is not founded on facts'.

[28] My information about Roman Catholicism in the Fairfax families of Yorkshire is drawn from Hugh Aveling's article in two parts, 'The Catholic Recusancy of the Yorkshire Fairfaxes', Part 1 in *Recusant History* (then entitled *Biographical Studies 1534–1829*, 3/2 (1955): 69–114, and Part 2 in *Recusant History*, 4/2 (Apr. 1957), 61–101. See also Aveling, *Northern Catholics: The Catholic Recusants of the North Riding of Yorkshire* (London: Geoffrey Chapman, 1966), and *The Catholic Recusants of the West Riding of Yorkshire 1558–1790*, Proceedings of the Leeds Philosophical and Literary Society, Literary and Historical Section 10/6 (Leeds: Leeds Philosophical and Literary Society, 1963).

nobility, and, equally important, the industrial and commercial vigor of their family and class'.[29] The antiquarian Roger Dodsworth was later employed by the first Baron Fairfax of Denton and continued on pension from the Lord General.[30] The editor of the Fairfax correspondence has not missed the Fairfaxes' extraordinary attention to family record and their hunger for pedigree, perhaps not unlike the nuns' interest in preservative syrups:

> it may be remarked, that the care with which the family records of the Fairfaxes were preserved is almost without a parallel. In no other collection are there to be discovered such a mass of letters and documents, public and private; pedigrees, not only of the different branches of their own family, but of all the families with whom they were connected by intermarriage; seals, mottoes, arms, and the varied paraphernalia of heraldic honours.[31]

The 'glad Youth' who captures Isabel for the 'great Race' reappears as the 'glad Parents' at the end of the poem as they prepare to send Maria into marriage—as it happened, to acquire what they would have believed was rightfully theirs, the estates of George Villiers, second Duke of Buckingham. Fairfax and Cromwell had jointly assumed possession of those confiscated estates, Cromwell holding the larger share; and early in the 1650s they simultaneously began to court the exiled Duke as a son-in-law.[32]

[29] Aveling, 'The Catholic Recusancy of the Yorkshire Fairfaxes: Part 1', 69–114. See 85.

[30] Together they produced 160 volumes of transcriptions of various Yorkshire and family records later given to the Bodleian Library at Oxford. Charles Fairfax compiled his own 'Analecta Fairfaxiana' (manuscript), featuring pedigrees of all the different branches of the Fairfax family. In 17th-century England, antiquarianism often encouraged or cohabited with a deep suspicion of iconoclastic enthusiasm. Margaret Aston, 'English Ruins and English History: The Dissolution and the Sense of the Past', *Journal of the Warburg and Courtauld Institutes*, 36 (1973), 231–55; see 236. Antiquarianism cultivated regret over the Dissolution's wholesale sacking of historical monuments and documents, shock at the ruthlessness of the idea of such total erasure and its vigorous enactment, and nostalgia for England's monastic culture of contemplation. The Dissolution, according to Margaret Aston, 'was the first time that it had seemed possible to wipe out for ever a whole department of religious life. . . . And the architectural fossils which remained as testimonies to the royal guillotining of the monastic past fostered a growing nostalgia for what had been swept off in this break' (Ibid. 231–2).

[31] Johnson (ed.), *The Fairfax Correspondence*, p. lviii.

[32] The day after Fairfax resigned his commission, Cromwell assumed the post. And these former comrades of the saddle continued to compete off the field. Fairfax had only one daughter, Mary; Cromwell had two married and two still marriageable daughters. On 23 June 1653, Theodorus writes from London to Lord Conway that, 'I hear the Duke of Buckingham is now at Calais, ready to come over, Lord Fairfax, whose sole daughter and heir he is to marry, having made his peace, and way for his safe return'. *Calendar of State Papers, Domestic Series, 1652–1653*, ed. Mary Anne Everett Green (London: Longman & Co., 1878), 436. Only a few weeks later, on 4 July, the Venetian Secretary in England, Lorenzo

Sir Thomas was related to Buckingham's Roman Catholic mother, Katherine Manners of Roos, heiress of the sixth Earl of Rutland.[33] But Lord Fairfax's great-grandfather, so oddly omitted from Sir William's will, had been excluded from acquiring any property of the Lords Roos. In the courtship of George Villiers for their 'little Moll', Lord and Lady Fairfax thus faced the temptingly honorable possibility of renewing and solidifying the ties among Fairfax, Villiers, and Manners and simultaneously securing Buckingham's estate of Helmesly in Yorkshire and of York House in the Strand. According to Brian Fairfax, Lord Fairfax's cousin, Sir Thomas

> lived [in the 1650s] in York-house, where every chamber was adorned with the arms of Villiers and Manners, lions and peacocks. He was descended from the same ancestors, earls of Rutland—Sir Guy Fairfax his two sons having married two of the daughters of the earl of Rutland which my lord took frequent occasion to remember.[34]

Sir Thomas had need for 'frequent occasion to remember' his noble descent. In the balance of Mary's marriage, which took place in 1657, lay the chance for Lord Fairfax to continue the pattern established by his own alliance of tightening existing relations between families to a thick wood which locks out embarrassment, such as poverty-stricken recusant relations, and which locks in wealth, not unlike the cloister gate.

Fairfax had not only trained with his wife's father Sir Horace in the Netherlands but was related to the Veres through his mother Mary

Paulucci, writes in his report of Cromwell, 'He becomes increasingly presumptuous and authoritative though it is possible that the policy attributed to him may be only a device of his enemies to render him universally unpopular. On the other hand he seeks all possible means to captivate the goodwill of both great and small. Possibly with a view to the better establishment of his supremacy, it is understood that he has recalled the Duke of Buckingham, the eldest son of the late prime favourite. Report says that he wants to arrange a match between the duke and one of his two marriageable daughters, so as to gain the good will of the aristocracy, though between him and them mutual distrust will be eternal, their affections being all centered in the late monarchy'. *Calendar of State Papers and Manuscripts, Relating to English Affairs, Existing in the Archives and Collections of Venice, and in Other Libraries of Northern Italy*, xxix: *1653–1654*, ed. Allen B. Hinds (London: HM Stationery Office, 1929), 94. See also the letter from Col. Herbert Price to Sir Edward Nicholas, *Correspondence of Sir Edward Nicholas* (London: The Camden Society, 1886–1654), N.S. 50, 261–2.

[33] The mother and aunt of Sir William who had married Isabel Thwaites were sisters of Lord Manners of Roos. See Clements R. Markham, *A Life of the Great Lord Fairfax* (London: Macmillan and Co., 1870), 39.

[34] Brian Fairfax, *Memoirs of the Life of George Villiers, Second Duke of Buckingham*, 3–10 of the introduction to *The Rehearsal* by George Villiers, ed. Edward Arber (London: Constable and Co., 1927), 6.

Sheffield, daughter of the first Earl of Mulgrave. Sir Horace Vere had been twice heir presumptive to the earldom of Oxford, the most ancient in England; and Fairfax's grandfather had settled the entail of his property on a male heir out of fear that his grandson would dissipate the estate in an attempt to satisfy his proud Vere in-laws.[35] Marvell's poem notes the crucial absence of a male heir (ll. 727–8), a lack or vacuum which Fairfax must transform into wealth. The marriage of Fairfax's daughter to Buckingham would extend the estates Lord Fairfax had inherited in trust from the first Baron Fairfax, despite breaking the entail on the male. And by acquiring as a son-in-law the ward of Charles I, Lord Fairfax would assume the place of the guardian whose death weighed so heavily on his conscience. The 'sober frame' indeed swells to bursting with great hopes. The Fairfaxes' dynastic pretensions and the ambitions of 'starry Vere' and her more ancient and distinguished family constellation seem to come under carefully obscured satiric fire in this poem, beginning with the portrait of the nuns' acquisitive desire to preserve and consume. Whether Isabel in the cloister, the chained narrator between the two woods, or Mary Fairfax walking her map of Paradise without a mate, a child or childlike sacrificial figure hovers in the poem as an enchanted, contested property.

Isabel's story may recall a more recent piece of unsightly Fairfax history. A stolen heir and an intercepted Roman Catholic past must have had direct personal resonance for this general whose 'first operation', in the words of one historian, was the removal in 1642 of a 12-year-old relation from the child's mother, a convicted recusant, and the immediate dispatch of the boy to a Puritan schoolmaster. Equally 'small honour' was in that storm as in Sir William's charge on the cloister walls (l. 233).[36]

[35] About the entail see the introduction to Johnson (ed.), *The Fairfax Correspondence*, vol. i, for the first Baron's fears of his grandson's dissipating the estate in order to satisfy the Veres' ambitions.

[36] A family race for baronetcies and peerages was launched in the 1620s between Lord Fairfax's grandfather, Protestant Sir Thomas Fairfax of Denton, and Sir Thomas Fairfax of Gilling, heir of the Catholic branch, who was a Protestant but whose wife was a convicted recusant. Denton managed to storm the Privy Council and bought a Scots peerage by 1627 for £1,500 to become the first Baron of Cameron. The patent for peerage of Sir Thomas of Gilling, much to his frustration, was not issued until 1629 when he was granted the Irish Viscountcy of Emley. Amidst this competition the heir of Sir Thomas of Gilling returned from studies abroad a Roman Catholic liable to conviction. 'The future of the estate and so much accumulated by the patient labour and ambition of generations seemed to be at stake' (Aveling, 'The Catholic Recusancy of the Yorkshire Fairfaxes: Part 1', 93), and Sir Thomas of Gilling ordered his son out of Yorkshire. This future second Viscount of Emley married a Catholic, and when their first child, William, was born (1630) the child's grandfather created a trust to hold the Fairfax estates between his own death and the coming-of-age of his

While still at school, the stolen 15-year-old married 'a gentleman's daughter in the towne there',[37] subsequently left school, produced three children in as many years, and died penniless at the age of 18.[38] And it was Thomas Lord Fairfax, Marvell's patron of scrupulous conscience, who retained under his protection the child's Roman Catholic relations.[39] If we keep in mind this family crisis only resolved in 1651 and the ongoing association, if discreet, of Lord Fairfax with popish relatives (necessarily demanded by his genealogical and antiquarian research), the repressive, sentinel function of the militant garden assumes a more complex, ironic weight.

Appleton House aspires to the order of a 'Bee-like' monastic cell; yet the poet suggests a disorder behind monasticism. The cloister offers Isabel a seductive but corrupted self-image: the girl is a pattern for the sisters, for the saints, and even for the virgin herself. And a flattering voice which offers a sanctified self-image may be tempting Lord Fairfax. We should remember that Anne Vere, Lady Fairfax, became a notorious female voice when she twice interrupted the King's trial by irreverent calls to the judges from the balcony. Almost fired on, she had to be forcibly removed. Of this 'Vere of the fighting Veres', Clarendon wrote,

> She was of a very noble extraction, one of the daughters and heirs of Horace lord Vere of Tilbury; who, having been bred in Holland, had not that reverence for the church of England, as she ought to have had, and so had unhappily concurred in her husband's entering into rebellion, never imagining what misery it would bring upon the kingdom; and now abhorred the work in hand as much as any

grandson; and he stipulated that the future third Viscount be raised a Protestant. But the father, though 'the most heavily fined recusant in the county', refused to release his son, and not until after the father's death in 1641 was the young third Viscount removed. By then the Long Parliament was in session, strong anti-Catholic sentiment ruled, and the king had left London and arrived in York on 19 March 1642. The Puritan Master of the London Court of Wards hastened to nominate four Protestant guardians headed by Ferdinando, Lord Fairfax of Denton; but it was Ferdinando's son Thomas who negotiated with the mother 'to demand her son forward' and arranged for his swift deportation. Two letters from Thomas Fairfax written from York in March 1642 to his father Ferdinando describe his negotiations with Lady Alethea Fairfax 'to demand her son forward' and preparations for his abduction. Aveling, 'The Catholic Recusancy of the Yorkshire Fairfaxes: Part 2', 77.

[37] 'Isaac Barrow', in John Aubrey, *'Brief Lives', chiefly of Contemporaries, set down by John Aubrey, between the Years 1669 & 1696*, ed. Andrew Clark, 2 vols. (Oxford: Clarendon Press, 1898), i. 88–9.

[38] According to Aubrey's life of Isaac Barrow, while yet a schoolboy himself Barrow had been appointed tutor to William Viscount Fairfax, a 'ward to the lord viscount Say and Seale', Master of the Court of Wards. 'But my Lord Say was so cruel to him that he would not allow anything that 'tis thought he dyed for want'.

[39] Aveling, 'The Catholic Recusancy of the Yorkshire Fairfaxes: Part 2', 81–4.

body could do, and did all she could to hinder her husband from acting any part in it. Nor did he ever sit in that bloody court, though out of the stupidity of his soul he was throughout overwitted by Cromwell, and made a property to bring that to pass which could very hardly have been otherwise effected.[40]

Clarendon's Fairfax, who like Isabel was 'made a property' of tougher spirits, resembles the eclipsed commander addressed in Marvell's poem. A staunch, even zealous Presbyterian who detested Cromwell, Lady Fairfax was an acknowledged presence behind her husband's resignation and exerted influence on his decision not to invade Scotland.[41] In Fairfax's desire to weed ambition and till conscience, Marvell allows the hint of a spiritualized and feminized substitute for the more virile act of taking control of the country.[42]

Stanza 44 which begins, 'And yet there walks one on the Sod | Who, had it pleased him and God', might be read as a flattering and consoling inner voice for the Lord General as he paces among his floral troops. Yet the poem offers its own dazzling mirror for Fairfax, like the river where 'all things gaze themselves, and doubt | If they be in it or without' (ll. 637–8). Himself subtle as the nun, Marvell ventriloquizes the voice of a temptation not to literal sainthood but to the belief that an example of conscience 'Shall draw Heav'n nearer, raise us higher'. Marvell's poem may take Lady Fairfax to task among those who try to redirect history's masculine course. For if there were escape from history in the cloister, the General's garden guards against masculine assertion; the stiff flowers which stand watch have replaced his raised sword of command. No nesting and hatching young fill this space, as they appear elsewhere on the estate. Only the female sentinel bee buzzes like a version of the inhospitable abbess.

At the age of 38 Lord Fairfax had no male heir. And from the childless tutor and orphaned son, one may hear a hint of unflattering portraiture in the General's preference for 'five imaginary Forts' to real ones or to the five senses, and in the reference to 'half-dry Trenches' and 'spann'd | Pow'r'. The fantasy of retreat requires intense physical restraint. We might expect Marvell of all poets to celebrate the purity and fulfilment of

[40] Edward Hyde, Earl of Clarendon, *The History of the Rebellion and Civil Wars in England*, vol. v (Oxford: Clarendon Press; repr. Boston: Wells and Lilly, 1827), 2399–400.

[41] See Hirst and Zwicker, 'High Summer', esp. 255, 260–2, who hear in the 'cannon lungs' of the cloister a hint of Lady Fairfax's famous outburst at the trial of Charles I. See also Johnson (ed.), *The Fairfax Correspondence*, i. 311.

[42] For a recent discussion of Marvell's feminization of Lord Fairfax, see, for example, Rogers, *The Matter of Revolution*, 91–5.

the mind's microcosm, the advantages of introspection in a green shade, yet the shadow of castration and impotence around Fairfax almost overwhelms the celebration of this lord's contemplative bent. Marvell makes no direct reference to Lord Fairfax's considerable literary interests and learning. In John Aubrey's eyes, for example, the great Lord Fairfax was a 'lover of learning' who single-handedly preserved the Bodleian Library from devastation by his troops when Oxford surrendered in 1646.[43] Nor does Marvell mention his patron's relation to the famed translator of Tasso, great-uncle Edward Fairfax, and, in a poem about retirement with unmistakable gestures to epic, this omission is puzzling. Yet the 'half-dry Trenches' and stiff poetic flowers may accommodate Marvell's need to judge, although over the head of his patron, Fairfax's penitential versifying as a reflection of the flowers' stiff military creator.

> For he did, with his utmost Skill,
> Ambition weed, but Conscience till.
> Conscience, that Heaven-nursed Plant
> Which most our Earthly Gardens want.
> A prickling leaf it bears, and such
> As that which shrinks at ev'ry touch;
> But Flowrs eternal, and divine,
> That in the Crowns of Saints do shine. (ll 353–60)

The distance in stanza 45 between 'did' in the first line and 'weed' and 'till' in the second, separated by the slightly condescending 'with his utmost Skill', delivers 'weed' and 'till' finally deflated. And the other weak verbs—'want' meaning to lack, 'bears', and 'shrinks' combine in a sense of void, or shrinking from life: at whose threatened 'touch' does Lord Fairfax shrink? We are ready for 'Flowrs' to be a verb and to lift the limp passage.[44] Not only is it not a verb, but the language with which Marvell describes the flowers of this conscience plant, the vocabulary of saints and divinely shining crowns, comes tainted with Roman Catholic associations (as does the fifth stanza's 'Shall hither come in Pilgrimage, | These sacred Places to adore, | By Vere and Fairfax trod before'). Reference to heavenly 'Crowns of Gold' and saints occurs, for example, in stanzas 15–18, which climax in the nun's vision of Isabel's sainthood, 'I see the Angels in a Crown/On you the Lillies show'ring down: | And round about you Glory breaks, | That something more than humane speaks' (ll. 141–4). The sisters' inversion of the value of action with the value of ornament

[43] Aubrey, '*Brief Lives*', i. 250–1.

[44] Rogers understands the effeminizing quality of Marvell's conscience plant as a revision of Milton's haemony, *The Matter of Revolution*, 94.

('But what the Linnen can't receive | They in their Lives do interweave') is mirrored in Fairfax's substitution of his garden for the field of action. By smoothly conflating the voice of the nun and that of the narrator, Marvell has managed to cast a shadow of the sterility of the cloister's feminine world onto his military patron and also onto his speaker—and perhaps a shade of witchery from abbess to 'Governess'. He leaves them encamped in the garden and descends to the sadness of meadows.

In Marvell's Mower poems, meadows are a solitary world of displaced feelings, of withered hopes and grief which cannot be plumbed; the mower is mown by his own sorrow. Simultaneously sympathetic and clumsy, Damon is also an uncomfortable voice of the poet 'hamstring'd' like the frogs who 'can dance no more'. The mower's world does not extend beyond his meadows: 'I am the Mower Damon, known | Through all the Meadows I have mown'. The repetitive sounds of 'am', 'Mower', 'Damon', 'known', 'mown' emphasize how he remains caught as if within the bounds of his name. Michael Long has called the mower for whom there is no ease 'the greatest of Marvell's childlike, displaced people'.[45] Similarly childlike and circumscribed by her isolation, the 'Nymph complaining' is thrown into ever more intense withdrawal by provocation from without the strictly drawn lines of her emotional and imaginary world represented by a garden. Marvell translates feelings of helplessness, displacement, and isolation into uncanny yet childlike sounds of pain and accusation which he speaks through Damon, the outsider of pastoral, whom he can complexly mock, and through a figure as unlike himself as the girl with a pet fawn. These lonely child-adults, like the 'Orphan of the Hurricane' of 'The Unfortunate Lover', are relations of the wandering narrator of *Upon Appleton House*, an androgynous child at sea.

The meadows onto which are opened dykes and 'Cataracts' might remind us of 'Holland, that scarce deserves the name of Land'—and not only in seventeenth-century Dutch landscape painting. In the Low Countries, meadows which had once been seas easily became seas again. Traditionally, the Netherlands were the first stop in a seventeenth-century Englishman's continental tour, as they were for Evelyn in 1641 and probably for Marvell in 1642.[46] As a place of fighting and floodings,

[45] Michael Long, *Marvell, Nabokov: Childhood and Arcadia* (Oxford: Clarendon Press, 1984), 62.

[46] John Evelyn, only five months the poet's elder, lost his father in December 1640, just weeks before Marvell lost his, and by July 1641 had sailed for the continent where he first landed in Flanders (he returned to England, however, before continuing on to France and Italy). See *The Diary of John Evelyn*, ed. E. S. De Beer, vol. ii (Oxford: Clarendon Press, 1955), beginning with the entry for 15 Oct. 1640.

where attention is paid to high and low ground, the Netherlands also figured prominently in the military past of the Veres and Fairfaxes.[47] Holland, presided over by its natural citizen, Anne Vere, floats into view in *Upon Appleton House* as a fluid landscape of military parents and martial childhoods. For the opening of dykes in the poem appears to open other floodgates as well related to the 'double Sluice' (l. 45) in 'Eyes and Tears', where tears 'Like wat'ry lines and Plummets fall' and 'better measure all' than sight (ll. 5–8). Sorrows of loss threaten like a nightmare of drowning from which the speaker is driven to save himself.

The obscure voices of Nun Appleton which draw the narrator are those of mourning—of rails, doves, and nightingales. Human tears appear in the cloister but are called floods of pleasure (ll. 111–14), while the sisters make balms 'for the griv'd' and Isabel weeps instead of speaks; nor do we sound the bottom of those tears. Isabel and the birds appear to share the speaker's ambivalence about where to hide safely in the world and about marriage and fertility.

The twinning of military action and flooded sanctuaries would have begun for the poet not at Nun Appleton but in that other Yorkshire fortification and Marvell's childhood home, the city of Hull. Three years after his birth in Winestead-in-Holderness, Marvell's father was appointed Lecturer at Holy Trinity Church in Hull and Master of God's House, an almshouse commonly called the Hull Charterhouse. Marvell satirizes the Netherlands in 'The Character of Holland', yet the city where he spent his fourth to thirteenth year resembled a Dutch military landscape in miniature. A fortification of dykes and floods built at the mouth of the river Hull, the city of Kingston-upon-Hull was flanked on the east by the Hull and on the south by the great Humber where the Reverend Andrew Marvell drowned, and which opens into the North Sea. A moat ran around the base of the city walls from the Hull to the Humber, and banks had been raised against overflowing rivers at spring tides. A

[47] From the Netherlands, the brothers Horace and Francis Vere had invented modern British military science and produced several generations of their country's finest soldiers. Not only had Thomas Lord Fairfax trained with Sir Horace Vere, General of the English forces in the Low Countries; his father and particularly grandfather Fairfax had made their careers under Sir Horace's older and more famous brother Francis. Lord Fairfax's wife was born and raised there. Her father's heroic but unsuccessful defence of Breda (1624–5) for the Dutch Stadholder against the siege of the great Spanish general Ambrosio Spinola later won him the peerage of Tilbury; and the turning event in that struggle which lasted almost a year was Spinola's opening the dykes to cause impassable floods. He had drowned the meadows. Clements R. Markham, *'The Fighting Veres'* (Boston: Houghton Mifflin and Company, 1888), 427.

bustling merchant city and port, Hull was also 'the strongest fortress in the Kingdom', a military garrison, and 'the pivot upon which the defence of the north of England hinged'.[48] For young Marvell, the sight of drilling militia, including children, must have been commonplace.[49]

The Marvells lived in the Master's residence; and what had been a Carthusian priory until its dissolution stood a few yards west and housed the wealthy Alureds or Aldreds, the family of the woman who became Marvell's stepmother in 1638.[50] Through the Alureds the poet was related distantly by marriage to Lord Fairfax.[51] When the Earl of Newcastle led Royalist forces in a siege of Hull on 2 September 1643, not quite nine months after the death of the Revd Marvell, Ferdinando Fairfax, Sir Thomas's father, decided to flood the country beyond the city walls and on 14 September cut the dyke which held back the Humber, swamping Newcastle's works. In the process, Fairfax was forced to demolish the buildings of the Charterhouse and former priory in order to construct the 'Charter House Fort' on the banks of the Hull. On the site of Marvell's childhood home grew a fort. The levelling of the Dissolution was repeated by the wars' levelling of childhood relics. And in *Upon Appleton House* the opening of the dykes sends Marvell's childlike tutor to the bottom of the sea in the wood—where he translates pain of abandon-

[48] Kenyon, 'Andrew Marvell', 2.

[49] In a letter of 1660 to the Mayor of Hull, the poet recalls not only military exercises but 'those blessed days when the youth of your own town were trained for your militia, and did methought become their arms much better than any soldiers that I have seen there since'. *The Poems and Letters of Andrew Marvell*, 2. Interestingly, the vision of besieged childhood in *Upon Appleton House* whereby 'We ordnance plant and powder sow' by 1660 becomes 'those blessed days'.

[50] According to Markham, *A Life of the Great Lord Fairfax*, 101, the Alureds, originally of Suffolk, bought the Charterhouse at Hull in the time of Henry VIII.

[51] Henry Alured, Lucy's father, was the grandson of Thomas Alured and Eleanor Constable, of the same family as Sir William Constable of Flamborough who had married Sir Thomas Fairfax's aunt Dorothy Fairfax, and who had negotiated the marriage of his nephew to Anne Vere. In addition, Colonel John Alured, a nephew of Marvell's stepmother, served under Sir Thomas Fairfax in the civil wars, while John's brother Matthew also fought on the side of the Parliament. John Alured, Fairfax's fellow Yorkshireman in arms and public affairs, was thus in the perfect position to introduce and support his cousin Marvell's candidacy for employment with the distinguished General. John Alured, Lord Fairfax, and Sir William Constable, who was Fairfax's uncle and related as well to the Alureds, fought as soldiers together; and when Sir Thomas rode into London in February 1645 to receive from Parliament their newly voted appointment of him as Commander-in-Chief of the army, he entered accompanied by these two relations. Both Constable and Colonel Alured were among the commissioners of the High Court which judged the King, and both signed the king's death warrant. See Pauline Burdon, 'Marvell and his Kindred: The Family Network in the Later Years: The Alureds', *Notes and Queries*, 229 (Sept. 1984), 379–85. See also Young and Holmes, *The English Civil War*, 99.

ment and his longing for saving arms into images of self-exposure and dissolution, a confusion of sensuality, punishment, and self-mockery.

RESURRECTION IN THE WOOD

Upon Appleton House circles about anger and loss at the betrayal of childhood which is gendered feminine and at the failure of a male guardian. If he is the referent of 'one, as long since prophecy'd, | His Horse through conquer'd Britain ride', Lord Fairfax has refused to ride through Scotland, has refused prophecy. In one historian's judgement, 'The suddenness of his eclipse was the most remarkable incident of his life—more remarkable than the piled-up glory of his breathless triumphs'.[52] And to an 'Orphan of the Hurricane', this general's retreat and refusal to fill the vacuum created by the loss of the King is comparable to abdicating control of a ship in a storm and retiring bewitched to prayer.

Rather than present Fairfax as a loving, protective father along the lines of the portrait of Cromwell with his daughter Eliza in 'A Poem upon the Death of O.C'. (1658), Marvell shows a figure unable to stop thinking about war in his tense garden. There is no dilation on the affectionate Fairfax, no playing with Maria in his 'mighty Arms', the muscles carefully slackened—there are no mighty arms. In their absence, the nun's arm curves in an illicit night-long embrace of 'Chrystal pure with Cotton warm' (l. 192); her imagination vitrifies Isabel as a jewel.[53] The guardian who flexes human and martial arms will be the Lord Protector; the wishes and emotion which arms represent will be aroused by the figure of Cromwell, twenty-two years the poet's senior and the father of seven surviving children and numerous grandchildren. The younger 'Black Tom' Fairfax brings out a harder yet more feminized Marvell whose playful military vocabulary suggests the lowered tone of his patron's once brilliant career—for example, the nun's luxurious martial fantasy of Isabel and a fellow nun 'as chaste in Bed, | As Pearls together billeted' (ll. 189–90).

[52] Robert Bell (ed.), *Memorials of the Civil War, Comprising the Correspondence of the Fairfax Family with the Most Distinguished Personages Engaged in That Memorable Contest*, vol. ii (London: R. Bentley, 1849), 87.

[53] One might note that, later, Maria Fairfax, 'yet more Pure', makes the 'Chrystal Mirrour' (l. 636) of the snaky river, Nun Appleton's 'little' Egyptian 'Nile', more 'Chrystal-pure' (ll. 694–5), just as Isabel, the 'Chrystal pure', was to purify those gypsy nuns of Rome, of Eastern luxury.

This eclipsed general, neither a natural nor an angelic force, cannot hold together the world of the poem or of the poet, as Cromwell will do in 1655. In *Upon Appleton House*, neither Fairfax nor Cromwell but an ambivalent, orphaned child 'betwixt' performs that function. Anger haunted by longing lies behind the poet's insinuating himself in such curious self-display in the wood's lane between Fairfax and his wife. As the poem carefully observes from its fifth stanza, Vere and Fairfax, Fairfax and Vere are named always together, grown to the muffled darkness of wood. The coffin-like fit of Nun Appleton House—the family's unease with empty space and the suggestion of a void that transgressive thoughts might fill—reappears as the wooden fortress of Fairfax and Vere 'Linked in so thick' as if locked.[54] The narrator's drowning circles of descent close in on him at the bottom of the estate between the two woods that seem as one trunk, two pedigrees, two labyrinths suggesting tortuous complication, hidden entrance and exit, a minotaur which devours youth and Ariadne's thread. And there is a loose thread: 'closely wedged | As if the night within were hedged', the woods are separated by 'a long and equal thread' of an opening where the narrator places himself like the proffered sacrifice. The two woods guard an opening over whose mysteries of transgression, imprisonment, and sacrifice he is the humiliated lord. Is he a divisive figure or one who needs protection? Is he 'their Lord'—an accusation of self-sacrifice as self-abandon? Charles I was the moment's most omnipresent Christ-figure, and Charles's martyrdom lay close to the heart of this couple's decision that Fairfax resign his command. Deep in the woods of their landscape and their past, between even such close stocks as Fairfax and Vere, is a hidden opening where they guard a secret figure; and at the bottom of the poet's dive is his own secret figure fixed at the edge of the water, like a newly emerged amphibian.

The narrator's propulsion to dive inward to sound memory and feeling is triggered by an impulse at Nun Appleton as strong as a military manœuvre to preserve 'Nature's finest parts'. The preservative drive is a

[54] Markham, *A Life of the Great Lord Fairfax*, 22; Johnson, (ed.), *The Faifax Correspondence*, i, pp. cvii–cvix. In a postscript to the 'Analecta Fairfaxana', Charles Fairfax records the interview with his father, the first Baron, shortly before his death, in which he prophesies that his grandson, soon to be the great Parliamentary General, will bring disaster on the house. According to family history, the first Baron of Denton despaired of his grandson's ability to protect and enlarge his inheritance: 'Such is Tom's pride', he is reported to have said, 'led much by his wife, that he, not contented to live in our rank, will destroy his house', (p. cviii). Charles was commanded to relay this prophetic warning, if he saw the danger of its coming true, to his nephew Sir Thomas, and he duly records that he carried out this unpleasant duty when Lord Fairfax cut off the entail for the settlement of the estate on the male heir.

seductive voice which lurks behind a 'black-bag' and a holy mask and whose associations with death are caricatured in the speech of the nun ('that which perished while we pull, | Is thus preservèd clear and full', ll. 175–6), in the pastes and crystallized fruits and portraits sewn in linen. Marvell's speaker moves sinuously to avoid becoming a fly in crystal (l. 678); yet in self-irony he finally pins himself down, an unattractive, drowned specimen imprisoned 'within' and burlesqued with the help of the nuns. Marvell summons his sturdy opposite, William Fairfax, to expose the nuns who 'though in prison yet enchant', but perhaps covertly to expose himself. 'An art by which you finelier cheat' might refer as well to Marvell who allures and enchants and crystallizes a world from within the prison of his unconventional self.

Not only Isabel Thwaites but Mary Fairfax reminds us of what happens on this estate to youthful genius. The poem concludes with this girl who would be 13 in July 1651. While a tender flower, Mary has been taught to walk a disciplinary inspection tour like her father; of military fibre, she has weathered skirmishes of temptation. Raised around battlefields, Mary Fairfax early followed her father between military camps: her 'domestic heaven' required, for example, at the age of 5 that she ride in a retreat from Leeds for over twenty hours until, after 'frequent swoonings', she had to be left behind with a nurse in a precarious state.[55] But the narrator hints that all of her studiousness, her capacity like his for languages and ventriloquy, and her disciplined Fairfax strength will not save her from the priest's sacrificial knife.[56] Compared with Isabel's summer suns and innocence, Maria of the civil wars seems coolly steeled against menace; but she, too, is being sucked towards an ambiguous altar.

To suspend the freedom of her poise, the poem imagines time and nature charmed to stillness by an image of 'betwixt'. The 'modest halcyon' flying between day and night against the last light on the horizon suggests calmed grief and an extended moment of vision before complete darkness descends. In Marvell's stanza the bird's quality of being betwixt charms, but it will be devoured: as the nun wants to eat Isabel, the darkening air follows and sucks the kingfisher's blue colour. In Ovid's

[55] Sir Thomas Fairfax, *Short Memorials of Thomas Lord Fairfax, Written by Himself*, ed. Brian Fairfax (London: Ri. Chiswell etc. 1699), 56.

[56] Robert Cummings, 'The Forest Sequence in Marvell's "Upon Appleton House": The Imaginative Contexts of a Poetic Episode', *Huntington Library Quarterly*, 47 (1984), 179–210, describes the violence of the primitive Druidic rites which Marvell recalls in stanza 93. Cummings reprints the frontispiece to 'the most considerable work on Celtic religion before modern times, Schedius' *De Diis Germanis* (Amsterdam 1648)', which 'shows a Druid standing in a grove of mutilated bodies'. See 296–7.

Metamorphoses, Alcyon foresees her husband's shipwreck and drowning before she finds his body washed ashore. While the couple reunite as kingfishers, the halcyon's mythological relation to death at sea and transfiguration, and its desire to nest on peaceful waters, hint that perhaps a drowning and resurrection have happened in this uneasy nest.[57]

I began with questions about the poem's narrative coherence. I would like to conclude that, while the narrative seems to follow the contours of the Fairfax estate, the poem's deepest and most coherent landscape seems to extend not in a linear fashion but in a vertical dive whose lifeline is not genealogical but poetic and psychological. Behind the celebration of lineal descent, the poem contains a chaotic plummet, a descent which sounds 'within'. The Marvellian line plumbs; yet finally the poet can reverse gravity with a mocking twang of an angler's line as if nothing had happened.

In response to the vacuum created when the 'Israelites' cut down the Stuart patriarch, the Fairfaxes have chosen to cultivate and preserve their own line, and Marvell's poem would appear to celebrate their past and future greatness. Yet the narrator repeatedly draws attention to the ritualistic, primitive way that parents and elders sacrifice youth to promote and immortalize themselves. The poet addresses a distinguished patron, but the absence of protective authority haunts and disturbs the landscapes within and without. While Lord Fairfax appears briefly in the opening stanzas and in the garden scene, he hardly commands our attention. He is dwarfed instead by a host of striking feminine figures who are either predators or prey: Isabel Thwaites and the lesbian nuns; the garden's sentinel bee ('She runs you through, nor asks the word', l. 320) and the rail 'Whose yet unfeathered quills her fail'; sinister 'Bloody Thestylis' and the women who pitch hay, sweat, and dance; in the woods the nightingale who sings 'the trials of her voice' and another bird who listens darkly motionless as if 'she were with lime-twigs knit'; near the river the studious young Maria; and finally the grotesque and vain 'fond sex'. Curiously, we do not see Lady Fairfax in the poem, but the narrator reminds us of the stern 'Governess', and we feel the cool eyes of 'starry Vere' high and unapproachable above the tutor's head.

That household creature, the tutor, presents himself as more feminine than the aggressive females he sees, to whom at the end he slyly adds the 'Governess'. He rhymes the family name of Lady Fairfax with 'severe'

[57] In Book 11 of the *Metamorphoses*, Ovid tells how Alcyon first dreamed of her husband's shipwreck, then found the drowned Ceyx washed up on shore; afterwards the tragic pair were reunited, transformed into kingfishers which nest on a peaceful sea.

(stanza 91) two stanzas before the priest 'shall cut the sacred bud', so that we hear a disquieting association of 'severe' with the verb 'sever'. The fearful female adult finally culminates in the nuns' living counterparts, the grotesque women who wear a 'black-bag' or mask and are addressed with Juvenalian fury in stanza 92. Without warning, the narrator attacks the sex most obsessed with preserving the appearance of the youth they have lost, and the smoothest face in the poem, to the point of blank invisibility high among the stars of the Veres' coat of arms, is 'Vera the Nymph'.[58]

The narrator also suggests something of his own face behind a mask. At Lord Fairfax's feet, Marvell lays a personal labyrinth. The poem is his pedigree which like the snake of the River Wharfe enfolds reflections of himself and of his patron: glimpses of family heroism and self-deception; of a drowning abyss of grass and a desert of negligence; of the tilling of conscience and the reaping of youth; of gypsies and tawny mowers, Levellers and the militant voice of vanity and zeal. 'Yet your own face shall at you grin', he taunts the women, and perhaps his own looks wearily back. As he contemplates with Lord Fairfax difficult and delicate issues of retirement, Marvell may begin to imagine and prepare for the opposite—a forward move out of the shadows cast in 'An Horatian Ode' (l. 3).

The Reverend Andrew Marvell's body was never recovered, but his son rises from the depths. The wood vanishes as abruptly, as dreamlike, as the nunnery. We wonder again what we saw. In a blurred transition of vision dazzled by the sun's reflection in the river, he rises to the surface and lands on the riverbank like a fish transformed into a lazy angler. From there we are asked to move not 'within' but more starkly 'in' under the tortoise shell frame of the opening stanzas, as the salmon-fishers retreat under the shells of their canoes. The House has become indeed a shell. The 'contains' of line 765 ('Your lesser world contains the same') recalls the meaning of restraint or control of the verb in stanza 6: Nun Appleton House strains to contain not exuberant strength and abundance, not lush beauty or greatness, but its own gulfs and precipices. The snug domesticity of 'lap' is challenged by the superior, strategic, perspective of its flat rhyme word, 'map'. The salmon-fishers, with their appearance of having plumbed the world to the Antipodes, carrying the depths on their heads, bear a reminder of the poem's other, interior, map. Their dark mystery suggests Marvell's underwater accomplishment and authority.

[58] 'Upon the Hill and Grove at Bilbrough', l. 43.

3
'Lights Framed like Nets' in Sir Thomas Browne's Garden

> Norwich is a place, I understand, which is very much addicted to the flowery part.
>
> (Letter of John Evelyn to Thomas Browne, 28 Jan. 1660)[1]

During the Interregnum when the presence of the English army was felt at home and abroad, the garden of England seemed to many under siege, as Andrew Marvell laments in *Upon Appleton House*:

> Unhappy! shall we never more
> That sweet *Militia* restore,
> When Gardens only had their Towrs,
> And all the Garrisons were Flowrs. (ll. 329–32)

In the 1650s writers as distinct as Marvell, Izaak Walton, Sir Thomas Browne, and virtuoso and diarist John Evelyn contemplated the country's violent political upheavals and institutional uncertainty from the covert, underground perspective of a garden retreat or horticultural study. As late as January 1660, in his first letter to the Norwich physician, Evelyn described his project for an *Elysium Britannicum*, a 'noble, princely, and universall Elysium' of gardens in which a philosophical 'society of the *Paradisi Cultores*, persons of ancient simplicity, paradisean and hortulian saints', might pursue vulgar errors 'whilst brutish and ambitious persons seeke themselves in the ruines of our miserable yet dearest country'.[2] Browne's *The Garden of Cyrus* (1658), perhaps more than Marvell's estate poem of militarized flowers and descending darkness, appears to offer a safe, leisurely retreat from contemporary guns and politics into natural abundance, into esoteric numerology and hermeticism exceeding Fairfax's interest in such studies to which Marvell's stanzas on 'Natures mystick book' (l. 584) allude, and into the great

[1] Sir Thomas Browne, *The Works of Sir Thomas Browne*, ed. Geoffrey Keynes, 4 vols. (Chicago: University of Chicago Press, 1964), iv. 273–4.

[2] Ibid. 275.

cultural wealth of Sir Thomas Browne's library. Yet Browne's Norfolk garden appears in a volume that begins underground, 'In the deep discovery of the Subterranean world' (137), with a discourse on human burial and funeral practices, beginning with crematory fires, and *Hydriotaphia, or Urne-Buriall* ends deep within the speaker's darkness lit only by the fire of 'an invisible Sun within us' (169).[3] *The Garden of Cyrus* puts the sun's fire back in the sky in the first sentence and ends wrestling with wakefulness at midnight when 'the Huntsmen are up in America' and the possibility exists that at some hour 'sleep it self' may end. Like Marvell's Yorkshire meadows, Browne's garden suggests the moral primacy of a world whose dimensions extend below and above a visible surface level, and scholars early perceived the diptych of Browne's texts on burial and gardens as two dichotomous yet twinned halves of one movement of vision that distinguishes yet connects body and spirit, darkness and light, time and space.[4] Marvell's and Browne's garden texts observe intricate networks of life hidden in shadow invisible to those who read, and like Marvell's mowers who attack, surfaces. While readers have long acknowledged the political and psychological subtlety and complexity of Marvell's poem, many have hesitated to consider Browne's Interregnum prose *Garden* as a similarly ambiguous subterfuge of natural and literary delights, one from which the speaker politically protests, tests, and excludes.[5] Yet through the aggressive intellectual range, the

[3] All citations to *Religio Medici, Hydriotaphia*, and *The Garden of Cyrus* will be to *The Works of Sir Thomas Browne*, ed. Geoffrey Keynes, 4 vols. (Chicago: University of Chicago Press, 1964), vol. i, and are included parenthetically by page number in the body of the text. Citations to other texts by Browne will be to this edition and will be included by volume and page number in the footnotes.

[4] On the 1658 volume as a whole, see, for example, Jonathan F. S. Post, 'Motives for Metaphor: *Urne-Buriall* and *The Garden of Cyrus*', ch. 7 in his *Sir Thomas Browne* (Boston: Twayne Publishers, 1987), 120–46; and Frank L. Huntley, 'Sir Thomas Browne: The Relationship of *Urn Burial* and *The Garden of Cyrus*', in Stanley E. Fish (ed.), *Seventeenth-Century Prose: Modern Essays in Criticism* (New York: Oxford University Press, 1971), 424–39.

[5] Previous studies of *The Garden of Cyrus* other than those in the previous note include Frank D. Walters, 'A Strategy for Writing the *Impossibilium: Aporia* in Sir Thomas Browne's *The Garden of Cyrus*', *Prose Studies*, 18/1, (Apr. 1995), 19–35; Janet E. Halley, 'Sir Thomas Browne's *The Garden of Cyrus* and the Real Character', *English Literary Renaissance*, 15/1 (1985), 100–21; C. A. Patrides, ' "The Best Part of Nothing": Sir Thomas Browne and the Strategy of Indirection', in C. A. Patrides (ed.), *Approaches to Sir Thomas Browne: The Ann Arbor Tercentenary Lectures and Essays* (Columbia: University of Missouri Press, 1982), 31–48; Frank L. Huntley, '*The Garden of Cyrus* as Prophecy', in Patrides (ed.), *Approaches to Sir Thomas Brown*, 132–42; Margaret Ash Heideman, '*Hydriotaphia* and *The Garden of Cyrus*: A Paradox and a Cosmic Vision', *University of Toronto Quarterly*, 19 (1949), 235–46; and Joan Bennett, 'The Garden of Cyrus', ch. viii in *Sir Thomas Browne* (Cambridge: Cambridge University Press, 1962).

conjectural byways that celebrate digression, and the figurative plenitude of Browne's garden, the writer claims access to levels of perception—to a visible but also an invisible universe—unavailable to those disdainful of ornament, tropical meanings, and sacred music.

In the first sentence of *The Garden of Cyrus*, at the intersection of his paired texts, each five chapters—like two mirror-image Roman numeral fives joined at their base forming a quincunx—Browne alludes to the creation of the sun and moon in Genesis and in Roman mythology. His reference to Apollo reminds us that the classical sun-god united the healing arts of medicine and of lyric or poetry, and was the god of prophecy, and that Browne writes as a physician whose profession is to heal and preserve life in all of life's fragments and broken bodies. Browne writes also as an antiquarian and a collector who preserves life by collecting and linking together fragments of artefacts, knowledge, and friends.[6] The sun of life in 1658 would suggest naturally Christ and perhaps also England's monarch, both the executed Charles and his resurrection through a son whose presence was still withdrawn from Englishmen, some of whom waited wearily. Speaking of the cross of intersection in nature, an image whose source Browne finds in Plato's *Timaeus* and thence, through Justin Martyr, in Christ's initial in Greek (*X*), the Christian cross, and the mix of natures represented by Christ, the doctor notes, 'Physicians are not without the use of this decussation in several operations, in ligatures and union of dissolved continuities' (189). The 'dissolved continuities' of broken bodies and lives for English Royalists in the 1650s were not hard to find, and Browne's texts suggest that a collection of human and cultural fragments, buried in exile, prepares for and awaits their resurrection. Buried in his survey of funeral customs and of the human response to loss and extinction, woven into his ode to the quincunx, and driving the pressure of Browne's immense learning that overflows the text into the margins, is a protest against the enormity of death and dissolution, of all ends, including those wrought by the civil wars.

Browne's stylistic and mental habits of connection and mixture—his crossing of literary allusion with natural knowledge, his crossing of

[6] Marjorie Swann has written perceptively about Browne the collector in her consideration of *Urne-Buriall* in the context of other antiquarian works whose 'textualizing of a collection of objects . . . is, first and foremost, a social act; the antiquarian collector/author creates social networks through the circulation of artifacts, metamorphosing groups of physical objects into collections of men'. Marjorie Swann, *Curiosities and Texts: The Culture of Collecting in Early Modern England* (Philadelphia: University of Pennsylvania Press, 2001), ch. 3, 133.

ornate diction, syntax, and digressions with exact and detailed observation of the natural world—perform the fertile decussation, or crossing of lines like an X, whose network design as quincunxes is his subject. Moreover, crossing in this text means infinite reaching, connection, and inclusion, as demonstrated by the illustrative diagram of a honeycomb-like network of quincunxes that introduces Browne's text, reproduced from two sixteenth-century Latin treatises on agriculture.[7] The quincunx, in the words of Jeremiah Finch, 'was used by the Romans to denote an arrangement of five trees in the form of a rectangle, four occupying the corners, one the centre, like the cinque-point of a die, so that a massing of quincunxes produces long rows of trees with the effect of latticework'.[8] The diagram that serves as Browne's frontispiece also resembles a network of stick figures. Small circles, like bodies, sprout four diagonal lines, two reaching up in a V like arms and two stretching down in an inverted *Λ* like legs. The ends of the lines connect to other circles above, below, and to the side, so that what was an arm for one becomes the leg of the circle above and vice versa. The network or lattice of lines encloses rhomboids of space, while suggesting infinite relation and expansion in all directions. At the end of *Hydriotaphia*, the geometry is less optimistic: 'Circles and right lines limit and close all bodies, and the mortall right-lined circle must conclude and shut up all' (166), he writes, referring to the Greek *theta* (θ), the initial of *thanatos*. The quincunx, however, as the 'central decussation' and 'mystical decussation' at the connection of the principles represented by the divine circle's perfection and the right line dividing that perfection into death and life, opens up closure and limits, as Browne explains in the next to last paragraph of chapter iv (220).

Its expansive latticework of connecting lines and protected spaces links the quincunx to Browne's love of digression.[9] Decades ago William Dunn noted of Browne's *The Garden of Cyrus*, 'we get at the heart of the book by

[7] Jeremiah Finch has studied Browne's extensive borrowings from Giovanni Baptiste Della Porta, *Villæ Io. Baptistæ Portæ, Neapolitani Libri XII* (Frankfurt, 1592) and Benoit Court or Benedic. Curtius, *Hortorum Libri Triginta Autore Benedicto Curtio Symphoriano* (Lyon, 1560). See Jeremiah Finch, 'Sir Thomas Browne and the Quincunx', *Studies in Philology*, 37 (1940), 742–7.

[8] Finch, 'Sir Thomas Browne', 274.

[9] In what he calls Browne's 'fimbriated discourse', C. A. Patrides finds that the doctor does not 'provide digressions from his nominal subject: he provided a nominal subject for his digressions', far exceeding the precedent for digressiveness that Browne notes in the margins of his dedicatory epistle, offered by Hippocrates' digressions on tonsillitis and sexual intercourse. Patrides, 'The Best Part of Nothing', 38–9. An earlier 20th-century student of Browne admits that his 'writings are often little more than patchworks of digression'. See Egon Stephen Merton, *Science and Imagination in Sir Thomas Browne* (New York: Columbia University Press, 1949), 5.

way of two digressions. The lozenge figure is only the rough rind of his thought; so too are the statistics of quinary arrangement'.[10] Browne's digressions inspired by meditation on the quincunx lead him through the crossing of intersecting lines in nature and in thought to his deepest concerns: the generation and branching of life and the relation of shadow to light and to vision. He buries digressions on these subjects deep in his text, in chapters iii and iv, protectively wrapped like a seed's 'little nebbe or fructifying principle', 'the seminall nebbe' (348) that nature carefully shrouds and that becomes the subject of his excited excursion. Browne created in the shadow of political opposition a dazzling yet obscure garden for the intellectual 'excursions' in print and 'wide liberty' that he claims in the preface to *The Garden of Cyrus.* In particular, his quincunx, like the 'labyrinths' (l. 622) of Nun Appleton, suggests networks that urgently remember and connect personal and cultural fragments, names and literary voices past and present, in a sonorous, learned vision—one where centuries and continents, languages, animals, and vegetables intersect. Yet Browne's garden retreat and quincunx are not only defensive but subtly armed and aggressive in their celebration of expansive yet hidden byways that lead to 'collaterall truths' (320).

In 1658 'this handsome Oeconomy' (381) of quincunx textures and text challenged a crucial Reformation claim to the simple accessibility of the Word and particularly to the book of nature presumed accessible to even the illiterate. In his now classic study of the relations among science, medicine, and politics in the first half of the seventeenth century, Charles Webster called Oxford gardener Ralph Austen's *The Spirituall Use of an Orchard: Held forth in divers Similitudes between Naturall and Spirituall Fruit-trees* (1653), published with Austen's treatise on planting fruit orchards, 'in some respects, the puritan counterpart of Sir Thomas Browne's *Garden of Cyrus*'.[11] In his dedicatory epistle to the Revd Dr Langley, Master of Pembroke College, Austen returns repeatedly to the 'plaine' writing of nature's book whose instructions for spiritual life 'teacheth us so plainely', are 'most plaine', and 'plaine to every man's eye', even to the illiterate:

The Apostle Paul tells us . . . that the invisible things of God (his Attributes) are clearly seene by, and through his Creatures: It is our duty (therefore) to study the

[10] William P. Dunn, *Sir Thomas Browne: A Study in Religious Philosophy* (Minneapolis: University of Minnesota Press, 1950), 134–5.

[11] Charles Webster draws the quoted parallel between Austen's and Browne's texts in *The Great Instauration: Science, Medicine and Reform 1626–1660* (New York: Holmes and Meier Publishers, 1975), 508.

Book of his Works, together with the Book of his Word, of them we may learne many profitable Lessons. . . . The Garden of Fruit-trees is a Volume full of good Notions: some Instructions lye obvious, and plaine to every mans eye, an illiterate man may here read distinctly.[12]

In 'A Preface to the Reader', Austen reiterates, 'The World is a great Library, and Fruit-trees are some of the Bookes wherein we may read & see plainly the Attributes of God . . . they have a Voyce, and speake plainely to us, and teach us many good lessons'. All of nature's 'dumb companions' have 'a teaching voice' because nature speaks 'to the mynde, and Conscience' through likeness, resemblance, and similitude 'of many high and great Mysteries in the Word of God', and 'teaching by SIMILITUDES is the most plaine way of Teaching'.[13]

In contrast to Austen's vision of nature's plain speaking and instruction, Browne's 'Conjugall or wedding number' five (380) and network of the quincunx, which emphasize the crossing of the sexes and lines of life, reflect less a clearly graduated, vertical hierarchy of God's creatures, leading man up a spiritual ladder, than a climactic vision as through a lattice of connections, a web of dark and light lines that represent the fertile, shadowy processes of human and divine creation. Together with the 'Library' of nature, we hear Thomas Browne read and conjoin the texts and voices of Homer, Thucydides, Plato, Aristotle, Xenophon, Euclid, Virgil, Ovid, and Plutarch; and instead of moral lessons, the intersecting threads of Browne's wandering syntax and text weave together remembered fragments of books and observations of nature as a reflection and replication of the highest and deepest operations in the visible and invisible world. Moreover, the connecting lines of the quincunx become a representation of Browne's moral, aesthetic, epistemological, and political passion to digress in order to seek 'collaterall truths, though at some distance from their principals', as he explains to Nicholas Bacon in the dedicatory epistle to *The Garden of Cyrus*. But exactly what is collateral and what is principal truth becomes a devious question raised by 'this handsome Oeconomy' about the relations between aesthetic pleasure and natural order in a divinely figurative universe.

[12] Ralph Austen, *A Treatise of Fruit-Trees, Shewing the Manner of Grafting, Setting, Pruning, and Ordering of Them in All Respects . . . Together with the Spiritual Use of an Orchard: Held forth in divers Similitudes between Naturall & Spirituall Fruit-Trees: according to Scripture & Experience* (Oxford: Thomas Robinson, 1653). See 'The Epistle Dedicatory' to *The Spiritual Use of an Orchard.*

[13] Austen, *The Spiritual Use of an Orchard*, 'A Preface to the Reader'.

In what follows I suggest that the orderly domestic and healing, sacred but sensuous and infinitely elaborate world of this Interregnum literary garden of networks expands in the face of what Browne refers to as death's 'brutall terminations' (157) and particularly of the arts of war which use the quincunx to organize not patterns of flowers but patterns of fighting men and tools of death, as Browne illustrates in chapter ii. Moreover this elegant garden text and the quincunx take shape in contrast to millenary, even eschatological, enthusiasm at mid-century for progressive horticultural and economic schemes, such as those promoted by Samuel Hartlib and his circle, to reclaim wastelands and advance national industry, fruitfulness, and economic self-sufficiency.

Browne's fiftieth year, 1655, marked the uneasy midpoint of the fifth and middle decade of a century in which England had seen two civil wars, a regicide, and an experiment in republican government. The year of fives of Browne's half-century marked as well the first anniversary of Cromwell's appointment as Lord Protector, celebrated by Marvell's 'On the First Anniversary of the Government under His Highness the Lord Protector', a moment whose instabilities seem reflected in the poet's restless, strident lines of alternately heroic tones and anxiety about mortal decline. From Marvell's troubled opening image of a curling 'Watry maze' through which man sinks, drowning in 'the weak circles of increasing years', the poem swerves from an encomium of Cromwell as '(Sun-like)' into a central, extended digression on Cromwell's near-death in a coach accident, before reviving the Puritan Protector as a militant rising planet that alarms Europe's sleepy princes—'Up from the other world his flame he darts, | And princes (shining through their windows) starts' (ll. 345–6)—and finally as the healing angel of Bethesda. Three years later, Dr Browne published a pair of tracts whose healing sun at their centre, shining through windows, is not busily military but sensual and aggressively mystical, from the Song of Solomon—'behold . . . he looketh forth at the windows, shewing himself through the lattice' (2: 9). Marvell had written of England's Protector, 'He secrecy with number hath enchased'. But with the 'Conjugall' number five—'the character of Generation' (381) in cabalistic writing—and the quincunx to challenge even Marvell's craft of tetrameter couplets, the Norwich doctor enchased number and secrecy in *The Garden of Cyrus.*

In an uncertain and militant time, in his garden not of Eden but of Persian Cyrus whose name means sun, Thomas Browne uncovers the five-pointed quincunx and two related images of profound vision with which this chapter concludes: the blissful scriptural lattice of Solomon and a darker, pagan tableau, the fabulously enchased Achilles' shield which in the face of death preserves a brilliant vision of all of life's movements.[14] Homer's Hephaestus cannot save Thetis' son; but he hammers a vast emblem that commemorates vicissitude and the savage fertility of the human round.[15] Through artful, imaginatively fertile networks commemorated in texts—of quincunx, lattice, and emblazoned shield—Browne suggests images of texts as labyrinthine, embroidered texture expressive of intricate connections between art and nature and among human, natural, and spiritual realms. Celebrated student of Oxford and of the great continental medical schools and their botanic gardens—Montpellier, Padua, and Leiden—Browne joined classical and biblical scholarship to interests in antiquities, history, astronomy, travel, geography, and languages, together with his commitment to empirical study, 'confirmable by sense and ocular Observation' (386), centred in the physical and natural sciences. He created an eclectic intellectual, aesthetic, and political vision of the ornamental complexity and interconnected properties of life whose surprising detail and unsolved mysteries oppose a one-dimensional, literal-minded, and profit-seeking mentality.

'VULGAR' READERS

When Dr Browne turned 50 in 1655, he was famous throughout England and Europe for *Religio Medici* (1643, authorized edition), which had spawned numerous translations and other 'Religios', and for his multi-volume correction of popular superstition and 'vulgar errors' of factual belief, *Pseudodoxia Epidemica* (1646).[16] Although not knighted until 1671, he was celebrated earlier for vast learning and great wit (as Pepys noted in his *Diary*, 27 January 1664),[17] and for religious and philosophical tolerance in an age of

[14] 'Cyrus took his name of the ancient Cyrus, as he, they say, had his from the sun, which, in the Persian language, is called Cyrus'. Plutarch, *Plutarch's Lives. The Translation Called Dryden's*, ed. A. H. Clough, 5 vols. (Boston: Little, Brown and Company, 1859), vol. v, 'Artaxerxes', 421.

[15] For a discussion of the emblematic significance of Achilles' shield and the shield as ekphrasis, see James A. W. Heffernan, *Museum of Words; The Poetics of Ekphrasis from Homer to Ashbery*: (Chicago University of Chicago Press, 1993), esp. 10–14.

[16] For a discussion of the influence and critical heritage of Browne's *Religio Medici*, see Daniela Havenstein, *Democratizing Sir Thomas Browne: Religio Medici and its Imitations* (Oxford: Oxford University Press, 1999). See also James N. Wise, *Sir Thomas Browne's Religio Medici and Two Seventeenth-Century Critics* (Columbia: University of Missouri Press, 1973).

[17] 'Up and to the office; and at noon to the Coffee-house, where I sat with Sir G Asckue and Sir William Petty, who in discourse is methinks one of the most rational men that ever

militant partisanship and zeal. In May 1658 appeared *Hydriotaphia* and *The Garden of Cyrus*, Browne's last published work in a lifetime that extended almost another quarter-century, in which he continued to practise medicine and write on a wide range of subjects, as the posthumously published letters, verse, and miscellaneous tracts, and the ever-expanding editions of *Pseudodoxia Epidemica* (1658, 1669, 1672), testify.

Browne's politically disengaged persona—the bookish medical doctor busy with his large practice and household in Norwich, with his collections of physical curiosities and his garden—has allowed us to forget that he chose to emerge into print from the obscurity of his professional and private intellectual pursuits only during the years of England's civil wars and Interregnum. If the militant times for print and politics drove Milton, Browne's contemporary only younger by three years, into an extended prose career just when he had announced to the world his poetic voice; if civil violence propelled the much younger Marvell to produce but retain safely in manuscript his greatest body of lyric; the times appeared to prompt Dr Browne to write and to publish texts at a level of rhetorical and figurative complexity that he never attempted again.

Unlike his writing from the 1640s, Browne's 1658 volume generated little contemporary comment;[18] and the treatises have maintained a reputation as antiquarian and obscure—as, at times, sublime if eccentric prose. Coleridge wrote to Sara Hutchinson on 10 March 1804 about his pleasure in Browne, 'a quiet and sublime Enthusiast with a strong tinge of the Fantast', and urged her to read the final paragraphs of *The Garden of Cyrus* 'as a fair specimen of his manner':[19]

> Quincunxes in Heaven above, Quincunxes in Earth below, & Quincunxes in the water beneath the Earth; Quincunxes in Deity, Quincunxes in the mind of man; Quincunxes in bones, in optic nerves, in Roots of Trees, in leaves, in petals, in every thing! In short just turn to the last Leaf of this volume, & read out aloud to yourself the 7 last Paragraphs of Chapter V . . . Think you, my dear Sara! That there ever was such a reason given before for going to bed at midnight, to wit, that

I heard speak with a tongue . . . (saying that in all his life these three books were the most esteemed and generally cried up for wit in the world – Religion Medici, Osborne's Advice to a Son, and Hudibras)'. Samuel Pepys, *The Diary of Samuel Pepys*, ed. R. C. Latham and W. Matthews (London: Harper Collins, 1995), v. 27, entry for 27 Jan. 1664.

[18] See Geoffrey Keynes, *Bibliography of Sir Thomas Browne, kt. M. D.*, 2nd edn. (Oxford: Oxford University Press, 1968), esp. pp. 183–202.

[19] Samuel Taylor Coleridge, *Coleridge on the Seventeenth Century*, ed. Roberta Florence Brinkley (Durham, NC: Duke University Press, 1955), 448.

if we did not, we should be acting the part of our ANTIPODES!! And then, 'The Huntsmen are up in America'—what Life, what Fancy![20]

Coleridge's ecstatic exclamations are now familiar history in the critical reception of Browne, and the final chapter of *Hydriotaphia* that proclaims with Ecclesiastes the vanity of all monuments has become itself a literary monument. Yet few today share Coleridge's excitement or could join Samuel Johnson in his enthusiastic praise of Browne's 'exuberance of knowledge, and plenitude of ideas', that 'sometimes obstruct the tendency of his reasoning'. Few students would pursue Browne with Johnson's pleasure through 'collateral considerations' and 'mazes, in themselves flowery and pleasing'.[21] Browne's enormous learning and digressiveness, his style that Johnson characterized as a 'tissue of many languages', and the wealth of detail and allusions can make his writing seem utterly impenetrable.[22] But what can we expect from one who in the final chapter of *Hydriotaphia* praises the protection of obscurity and privacy, who invokes the 'superior ingredient and obscured part of ourselves' (305), and who in the letter of dedication to *Hydriotaphia*, which opens the 1658 volume, urges the necessity for patching together a self and goodness in bad, barren days?

'Tis opportune to look back upon old times, and contemplate our Forefathers. Great examples grow thin, and to be fetched from the passed world. Simplicity flies away, and iniquity comes at long strides upon us. We have enough to do to make up our selves from present and passed times, and the whole stage of things scarce serveth for our instruction. A compleat peece of vertue must be made up from the Centos of all ages. (132)

According to the *OED*, 'cento' in the seventeenth century could mean either a patched garment, a piece of patchwork, or 'a composition formed by joining scraps from other authors'—a fabric, in all the senses of that word, constructed from pieces. 'Knowledge is made by oblivion', wrote Browne in 'To the Reader' before *Pseudodoxia Epidemica* (1646), 'and to purchase a clear and warrantable body of Truth, we must forget and part

[20] Ibid. 449.

[21] Samuel Johnson, *The Life of Sir Thomas Browne*, in Sir Thomas Browne, *The Major Works*, ed. C. A. Patrides (New York: Penguin, 1977), 507. Johnson edited the second edition of Browne's *Christian Morals* (1756) for which he composed his *Life* of Browne, prefixed to that edition. According to Keynes (*Bibliography*, i. 242), the 'last separate edition of *Christian Morals*', with Johnson's *Life*, was published in 1927 by Cambridge University Press, edited by Sir Sydney Roberts.

[22] 'His style is, indeed, a tissue of many languages; a mixture of heterogeneous words, brought together from distant regions, with terms originally appropriated to one art, and drawn by violence into the service of another'. Johnson, *Life of Sir Thomas Browne* (1977), 508.

with much we know'.[23] But Mary Baine Campbell has noted that Browne's correction of vulgar errors, 'an anecdotal and copious (but not systematic) register . . . redolent with wonder but in the mode of irony and nostalgia', seems oddly to memorialize more than obliterate.[24] By 1658, as if responding to a sense of life foreshortened by the lightening speed of change that Marvell celebrates in 1655, Browne's wakeful speaker evokes a shortness of time, a lateness and degeneracy in history, and a desire to observe and preserve: 'we were very unwilling they should die again' (132); ''Tis time to observe Occurrences, and let nothing remarkable escape us' (132); 'We are coldly drawn unto discourses of Antiquities, who have scarce time before us to comprehend new things, or make out learned Novelties' (132); 'Great examples grow thin, and to be fetched from the passed world' (132); 'in this latter Scene of time' (166), ''Tis too late to be ambitious. The great mutations of the world are acted' (166), 'We whose generations are ordained in this setting part of time' and 'being necessitated to eye the remaining particle of futurity' (166). Both the burial urns with their ornaments and other fragments of humanity in *Hydriotaphia* and the quincunx of *The Garden of Cyrus* become figures for a text as a space that holds, preserves, and mingles fragments and voices, a form that reflects natural and accidental labyrinths of interconnection and the 'obscure method' of providence. These texts and the textures he invokes, urgently commemorative and expressive of continuities, also reflect and connect the writer's large circle of past and present acquaintance through books and daily life, including an extensive network of Royalist gentry and the best families of Norfolk, such as the Bacons, the Le Groses, the Townshends, the L'Estranges, and the Pastons.[25]

[23] Browne, *Works*, ii. 3.

[24] Mary Baine Campbell, *Wonder and Science: Imagining Worlds in Early Modern Europe* (Ithaca, NY: Cornell University Press, 1999), 86.

[25] *Hydriotaphia* is dedicated to Thomas, son of Sir Charles Le Gros whose family extended back to the 12th century. In a passage of the dedication on mortality and memory in which the urns sound not 'a joyful noise' like the Psalmist, but rather 'no joyful voices', Browne's speaker connects himself and the family of Le Gros to another major Norfolk family who own the 'noblest pyle among us'. Browne's marginal note explains that the 'pyle' refers to Raynham Hall, 'worthily possessed by that true Gentleman Sir Horatio Townshend, my honored Friend'. The mother of Sir Roger Townshend, Sir Horatio's father, who had begun the construction of the new house at Raynham, was the daughter of Sir Nathaniel Bacon, the second son of the Lord Keeper, Sir Nicholas Bacon, who was grandfather of the dedicatee of *Garden of Cyrus*, Nicholas Bacon of Gillingham; Francis Bacon was half-brother to Nathanial and to the grandfather of Nicholas, so Browne's marginal note links these three important Norfolk families. Browne was also a friend of Sir Robert Paston of Oxnead (who would introduce Evelyn and Browne), and of the

Scholars such as Michael Wilding, Jonathan F. S. Post, Frank Huntley, Aschah Guibbory, and Michael Stanford have begun to challenge the philosophical and detached persona Browne perfected with his 1658 volume.[26] Daniela Havenstein, James Wise, and others have reminded us that the learned Browne who claimed 'to affect all harmony' and who 'delighted not in controversy', according to John Whitefoot, was nonetheless attacked for Laudian tendencies and softness toward Catholics by his vigorous early critic, the Scottish doctor Alexander Ross.[27] Ross also accused Browne of dodging controversy and for emphasizing, with his fondness for the image of a labyrinth, the unnecessary

L'Estranges of Hunstanton, probably the family in longest 'continuous possession of their estates'. R. W. Ketton-Cremer, *Norfolk in the Civil War: A Portrait of a Society in Conflict* (Hamden, Conn.: Archon Books, 1969), 40. Sir Hamon, their head in the early 17th century, harboured Royalists escaped from capture after the siege of Colchester and also wrote an eighty-five-page unpublished commentary on Dr Browne's *Pseudodoxia Epidemica.* The letter of dedication to *The Garden of Cyrus,* which immediately followed the letter to Sir Thomas Le Gros in the first edition, was addressed to Nicholas Bacon, Esq., of Gillingham, fourth son of the Lord Keeper's son Nicholas. Towards the end of the letter, in a marginal note added to 'And being a flourishing branch of that Noble Family, unto which we owe so much observance', Browne names his dedicatee's eldest brother who had died in 1649, 'Of the most worthy Sr. Edmund Bacon, Prime Baronet, my true and noble Friend'. Sir Edmund had been the brother of Lady Drury who had employed Joseph Hall as rector of Hawstead and religious tutor to their daughter Elizabeth, later subject of Donne's *Anniversaries*; Hall had also travelled with Sir Edmund on the continent early in the century. So old friends and old virtues pass down through old families, and Browne's marriage into a large Norfolk family in 1641, that of Dorothy Mileham, granddaughter of John Hobart, helped to connect him to most of the important families in Norfolk. See *The Works of Sir Thomas Browne,* ed. Geoffrey Keynes, vol. iv, p. viii.

[26] Michael Wilding has criticized the intellectual elitism and political conservatism of *Religio Medici*; Post, 'Motives for Metaphor', has argued that the subterranean world of Browne's burial urns figures the underground world—the obscure life in death—of the Anglican and Royalist community during the Interregnum, while to Frank Huntley, '*The Garden of Cyrus* as Prophecy', *The Garden of Cyrus* assumes the Old Testament prophetic mode, adopted by Puritan 'saints' and republicans, to prophesy instead a resurrection of the ancient order of monarchy. Aschah Guibbory has revealed the politics of Browne's wide-ranging study of burial rites and beliefs about an afterlife in light of the Puritan ban on Anglican sacraments, including the rites for burial. Michael Wilding, *Dragon's Teeth: Literature in the English Revolution* (Oxford: Clarendon Press, 1987), ch. 4, 89–113; and Aschah Guibbory, ' "A Rationall of Old Rites"; Sir Thomas Browne's *Urn Buriall* and the Conflict over Ceremony', *Yearbook of English Studies,* 21 (1991), 229–41; Michael Stanford, 'The Terrible Thresholds: Sir Thomas Browne on Sex and Death', *English Literary Renaissance* 18, (1988), 413–23.

[27] See Alexander Ross, *Medicus Medicatus* (London: James Young etc., 1645) and *Arcana Microcosmi* (London: Tho. Newcomb etc., 1651). For other contemporary responses, see Keynes, *Bibliography.* Another Scot and author of *Religio Stoici* (1663), Sir George Mackenzie chastised Browne along with Walter Charleton for their learned 'university' styles that embroidered discourse 'with Latin and Greek termes' and for 'thinking, like these who are charmers, that the charme loses its energie, if the words be not used in Latine'. Havenstein, *Democratizing Sir Thomas Browne,* 31–2.

difficulty of knowing what is true. And to a pirated edition of the Latin translation of *Religio Medici* by Browne's friend John Merryweather, which appeared in Paris in 1644, was appended a preface, as Merryweather wrote to Browne, 'by some papist . . . in which making use of, and wresting some passages in your book, he endeavor'd to shew, that nothing but custom and education kept you from their church'.[28] Browne was also attacked for atheism: '*Religio Medici* though th' wor[l]d Atheism call' is the first line of 'On Doctor Browne. *His Religio Medici and Vulgar Errors*', published in *Poesis Rediviva* (1656) by John Collop, MD, a Roman Catholic who defended Browne against his attackers. 'More zeal and charity Brown in twelve sheets shows, | Then twelve past ages writ, or th' present knows', continues Collop:

> Though gut-inspired zelots bark at him,
> He hath more knowledge then their Sanedrim.
> Or the Scotch pedant a worm in every book,
> To maim the words and make the sence mistook.[29]

Collop elides Browne's enemies—Ross, 'the Scotch pedant', and the zealous sectarians—as beastly and ignorant.

Browne's published and unpublished writings reflect his anticipation of and impatience with the experience of critical attack and of being misread. Witness the cautiously self-deprecating preface to the authorized edition of *Religio Medici*, written to forestall, with no success, Sir Kenelm Digby's published response to an earlier pirated edition.[30] Browne claims that his immature 'private exercise', in which are 'many things delivered Rhetorically' or 'meerely Tropicall', was not designed for 'the rigid test of reason'. By 1646 Browne had published his encomium to the faculty of reason, his survey and correction of vulgar errors; and although he treated such politically neutral subjects as beavers, badgers, and Unicorns, a text of that year whose first book of eleven chapters concerns the deluded and self-deluding ignorance of 'the multitude' and 'Democraticall enemies of truth', while English families and neighbours were killing each other over their perceptions of truth and error, is clearly political, although a contempt for, or frustration with, 'the blockish vulgar', 'the Common sort', 'the mad multitude' also characterized

[28] Wise, *Thomas Browne's Religio Medici*, 51.
[29] Keynes, *Bibliography*, 181–2.
[30] On Digby's response, see Wise, *Thomas Browne's Religio Medici*, 57–121.

Browne's political opposite, Milton.[31] Not surprisingly, the preface to *Pseudodoxia Epidemica*, in which he identifies his audience as the 'ingenious English gentry', is as embattled as was England in that year, which saw the collapse of most Royalist strongholds and the King's surrender to the Scots:

we are often constrained to stand alone against the strength of opinion; and to meet the Goliah and Giant of Authority with contemptible pebbles, and feeble arguments, drawn from the scrip and slender stock of our selves. Nor have we indeed scarce named any Author whose Name we doe not honour; and if detraction could invite us, discretion surely would contain us from any derogatory intention, where highest Pens and friendliest eloquence must fail in commendation.

And therefore also we cannot but hope the equitable considerations and candour of reasonable mindes. We cannot expect the frown of Theologie herein; nor can they which behold the present state of things, and controversie of points so long received in Divinity, condemn our sober enquiries in the doubtfull appertinancies of Arts, and Receptaries of Philosophy. Surely Philologers and Criticall Discourses, who look beyond the shell and obvious exteriours of things, will not be angry with our narrower explorations. . . .

Lastly, We are not Magisteriall in opinions, nor have we Dictatorlike obtruded our conceptions; . . . And we shall so farre encourage contradiction, as to promise no disturbance, or reoppose any Penne, that shall Fallaciously refute us; that shall only lay hold of our lapses, single out Digressions, Corollaries, or Ornamental conceptions, to evidence his own in as indifferent truth.[32]

Browne asks for the 'candour of reasonable mindes' instead of the 'frown of Theologie', especially for those 'who look beyond the shell and obvious exteriours of things'. The writer promises not to be, like some, 'Magisteriall' or 'Dictatorlike' and shows experience of critics who 'only lay hold of our lapses, single out Digressions, Corollaries, or Ornamental conceptions'. The *OED* notes that one seventeenth-century meaning of 'corollary', and surely Browne's here, is 'Something additional or beyond the ordinary measure, a surplus, a supernumerary'. In 1658 Browne will assume the right to 'erre by great example' (176), that is, Hippocrates, in 'excursions' again beyond the ordinary. Those 'Digressions, Corollaries, or Ornamental conceptions' become central to his representation of the deepest order.

[31] The quoted phrases are from *Eikonoklastes* in John Milton, The *Complete Prose Works of John Milton*, ed. Don M. Wolfe et al., 8 vols. (New Haven: Yale University Press, 1953–82), iii, 339, 345.

[32] Browne, *Works*, ii. 5–6.

In the third chapter of *Pseudodoxia Epidemica* on 'the erroneous disposition of the people', Browne again complains about readers who cannot comprehend figurative language or the pleasures of literary ornament. The inability of people 'to wield the intellectual arms of reason' means they are led rather by example and event and, in understanding Scripture, are confined 'unto the literal sense of the Text; from whence have ensued the gross and duller sort of Heresies'. Unable to attain the 'second intention of words, they are fain to omit their Superconsequencies, Coherencies, Figures, or Tropologies. . . . therefore also things invisible, but unto intellectual discernments, to humour the grossness of their comprehensions, have been degraded from their proper forms'. Sounding like Milton's *Eikonoklastes* castigating the 'image-doting rabble', Browne continues, 'so likewise being unprovided, or unsufficient for higher speculations, they will always betake themselves unto sensible representations, and can hardly be restrained the dullness of Idolatry'.[33] Browne makes no secret of his intellectual politics—or snobbery—in his distinction of 'things invisible, but unto intellectual discernments' and his distaste for 'the gross and duller sort of heresies' associated with 'the grossness' of literal-minded heads. As Marjorie Swann has noted, '*Pseudodoxia Epidemica* . . . clearly establishes Browne's allegiance with the landed gentry and his disdain for the plebeian rabble which he dismissed in *Religio Medici* as "those vulgar heads, that rudely stare about". '[34]

In the dedicatory letter to *The Garden of Cyrus*, 'To my worthy and honored friend Nicholas Bacon of Gillingham Esq', Browne laments the rarity of good readers in 'this ill-judging age', the impossibility of increasing 'the number of Scholars beyond the temper of these times':

> *Nullum sine venia placuisse eloquium* is more sensibly understood by Writers, then by Readers; nor well apprehended by either, till works have hanged out like Apelles his Pictures; wherein even common eyes will finde something for emendation.
>
> To wish all Readers of your abilities, were unreasonably to multiply the number of Scholars beyond the temper of these times. (177)[35]

[33] Browne, *Works*, ii. 26–7.

[34] Swann, *Curiosities and Texts*, 122.

[35] Browne translates the Latin phrase in his marginal notes, 'Eloquence has never been accepted without a measure of condonement', according to the edition, Sir Thomas Browne, *The Major Works*, ed. Patrides, 321.

Publication means hanging 'out' works for critical 'common eyes'. In a posthumously published Latin tract entitled 'Amico Opus Arduum Meditanti', or 'To a Friend Intending a Difficult Work', Browne warns with appropriate medical imagery of shameless attacks on one's literary 'tumours' and even 'warts' by 'pedants', and about being misread, especially by literal-minded readers 'intent on the sense':

> You know how wanton is the literary tribe, how eager for contest, that not for nothing surely you may fear shameless attacks from all sides. . . . Most pedants are censorious, satirical even, unsparing not merely of tumours, but even of warts. Mockers abound, if you fall short in achievement; if you exceed, envy beyond limit.
>
> Some will strain at words but judge the matter lightly; others (and this is the heart of the matter) intent on the sense will pass dryshod over words and phrases. . . . Variety of wits, discord of studies, parties, heresies, divide the fates of the noblest productions; and you may fail to please them all, unless you are wise beyond Wisdom.[36]

As in *Pseudodoxia*, Browne reveals particular impatience, '(and this is the heart of the matter)', with readers who never get their feet wet but 'pass dryshod over words and phrases'. The ranks of pedants, mockers, envious persons, and partisan wits require a writer to be wise but obscure, like Solomon and God.

The arcane mystery and complexity of his 1658 volume begins with the titles, one an original construction from two Greek roots—*ὑδξία* meaning water-vessel and *ταφφή* meaning burial—and the other Browne's only published title in English but with a tease of obscurity, until one has finished chapter i, whether the title refers to Cyrus the Great (d. 529 BC) or the Younger Cyrus (d. 401 BC). Browne's obscurity constitutes a retreat from but also critique of a bleak moment of cultural 'grosseness', when 'iniquity comes at long strides upon us' and 'A compleat peece of vertue must be made up from the *Centos* of all ages' (132), as his work exhaustively attempts by creating a living fabric of elaborate patchwork, each allusive thread and voice a nerve. Indeed reminiscent of Milton's passion in *Areopagitica* for the life of books is Browne's encouragement in 'To a Friend Intending a Difficult Work' that 'the books you have to disclose are no common ones, nay they are living things'.[37] *Hydriotaphia* and *The*

[36] From 'To a Friend Intending a Difficult Work', English translation of 'Amico Opus Arduum Meditanti', in Browne, *Works*, iii. 153.

[37] *Ibid.* The parallel between a book and that which preserves and contains life, the burning and burying of bodies and of texts, becomes a radical theme in Milton's argument in

Garden of Cyrus fold multiple voices into a personal network of Norfolk acquaintances and of writers and thinkers past and present—Browne's mind moves easily to thread classical and biblical with medieval and Renaissance names—as they construct a veil of complexity against ignorant and unfriendly readers.

The Greek roots of 'hydriotaphia' suggest a water-vessel become a burial urn. A baked earthen container for the element that quenches fire and thirst and that generates the fourth element, air, in the breath of Browne's words, may hold the remains of life that proves easily combustible, especially in combustible times. Against the pressure of silent dissolution, the stop of life's pulse, Browne pulls out the musical stops of his language, notably in the final chapter of *Hydriotaphia*, whose powerful rhythms denote invisible life in the muffled dark of the moment—life-in-death. In the year the Puritans sacked Norwich Cathedral and destroyed its 'fayre and large butt playne organ',[38] Browne published the authorized *Religio Medici* where he observed, 'Whatsoever is harmonically composed, delights in harmony',

> which makes me much distrust the symmetry of those heads which declaime against all Church musicke. . . . I will not say with Plato, the Soule is an Harmony, but harmonicall, and hath its neerest sympathy unto musicke: thus some, whose temper of body agrees, and humours the constitution of their soules, are borne Poets, though indeed all are naturally inclined unto Rhythme. (84).

In *Hydriotaphia* sound and rhythm are signs of life's pulse otherwise invisible in darkness and despair. Browne's texts explore the possibility that the rhythmic and figurative operations of language that point to interconnected levels of meaning parallel the deepest working of the sensuous and the spiritual universe.

1643, from the other side of the political fence: that the government's suppression of books by a refusal to licence their publication would be a deathblow of oppression comparable to the Inquisition's book-burning and that both were as bad as or worse than killing a man: 'Many a man lives a burden to the Earth; but a good Booke is the pretious life-blood of a master spirit, imbalm'd and treasur'd up on purpose to a life beyond life. . . . We should be wary, therefore, what persecution we raise against the living labours of publick men, how we spill that season'd life of man preserv'd and stor'd up in Books' (John Milton, *Complete Prose Works of John Milton*, ed. Don M. Wolfe et al., vol. 2, 492–3). Later Coleridge would exclaim of Browne, 'A library was a living world to him and every book a man, absolute flesh and blood!' *Coleridge on the Seventeenth Century*, 439.

[38] Browne, *Repertorium or Some Account of the Tombs and Monuments in the Cathedrall Church of Norwich, 1680*, in *Works*, iii. 140.

THE ORNAMENTAL SHIELD

In the first pages of *The Garden of Cyrus*, Browne traces the etymology of 'Paradise' to a Persian word that signifies an enclosed park, and he notes that the Hebrew word for the garden of Genesis means 'a Field enclosed' and is the same root for garden and 'a Buckler' or shield.[39] He also dilates on the fame of 'our Cyrus' for both military arts and domestic economy in ordering and planting his estate. From the beginning, this tract expresses a constant tension between garden fertility and war, between forces of life's drive to connect, such as learning and friendship, and death's disconnection—or, as the order of the twinned essays suggests, between death and life. After the descent of *Hydriotaphia* from funeral fires to the invisible 'pure flame' of life, the first sentence of *Cyrus* names two kinds of fire, Vulcan, god of destructive fire but also smith to the gods, and Phoebus Apollo, healing and generative god of the sun and the lyre. While Apollo appears to shine on this physician's discourse that observes and delights in the winding growth of herb and sentence, Vulcan the dark artisan reappears when Browne defends his long insistent litany of questions at the close of chapter v, posed 'unto acuter enquirers, nauseating crambe verities and questions over-queried' (225). He castigates 'trite' and 'flat and flexible truths' that bend for the occasion, designed for popular consumption, and compares the elaborateness of his enquiry and garden text to Achilles' shield neither flat nor flexible; yet Homer's narrative about the scenes as they are hammered out on the shield accentuates their fragmentation and indeterminacy and the vulnerability of the figures to treachery and violent death.[40] Containing a microcosm of forged worlds of sound and movement—narratives of wedding festivity and bloody battle, of harvest song and a dirge for the dying year—this fabulous centrepiece of glittering armour was the height of Vulcan's artistry and an

[39] One might recall Milton's walled garden for innocent Adam and Eve in *Paradise Lost.* Marvell's mower objects to the private enclosure of the common fields, that 'enclos'd within the Gardens square | A dead and standing pool of Air' (ll. 5–6). *The Poems and Letters of Andrew Marvell*, ed. H. M. Margoliouth, 3rd edn., vol. i (Oxford: Clarendon Press, 1971), 43.For an account of the resonance of English enclosure politics on the biblical poetics of the 17th century, see Christopher Hill, 'The Wilderness, the Garden, and the Hedge', in his *The English Bible and the Seventeenth-Century Revolution* (London: Allen Lane, 1993), 126–53. On the literary tradition of the enclosed garden, see for example Stanley Stewart, *The Enclosed Garden: The Tradition and the Image in Seventeenth-Century Poetry* (Madison: University of Wisconsin Press, 1966).

[40] See Heffernan, *Museum of Words*, 17.

ambiguous symbol of protection, forged to honour the doomed Achilles whom no god could shield 'from pain and death, | that day his grim destiny comes' (*Iliad* 18: 542–3, trans. Robert Fagles). Although no shield either from pain and death in 1658, elaborate and heroic, visionary armour is needed still because 'Truth' for the English Royalist community, whether in Norfolk or in the exile of Paris and Antwerp, is a shadowy 'Labyrinth' not easily traced (226). The superficial probing of 'discursive enquiry and rationall conjecture', of reasonable religion, may only 'leave handsome gashes and flesh-wounds', but wisdom needs more serious, complicated armour forged by sharpest 'sense and ocular Observation' to deal 'mortal or dispatching blows unto errour' (226).

Of known Royalist sympathies, Browne lived in a county predominantly Puritan and famous for the diversity of sects that had collected there from the sixteenth century onwards, thanks to East Anglia's proximity to Holland and distance from the civil and ecclesiastical centre of London. Dutch and Flemish refugees including many weavers had fled to the region to escape Spanish persecution.[41] By 1655 Norwich was the second largest city in England and capital of the nation's textile trade. Evelyn's first letter to Browne, from which my epigraph is taken, alludes to the fact that the Dutch settlers in Norwich brought besides skills in weaving their knowledge of engineering and gardening; they helped to rescue the 'light, free-draining soil of East Anglia' from the Wash, and instituted in 1631 the first florists' feasts in England.[42]

Friend and physician to Bishop Joseph Hall, formerly Dean of Worcester and Bishop of Exeter, Browne had witnessed with him the destruction of Norwich Cathedral in April 1643 by Puritan zealots, which Hall describes in his memoir in a horrified passage beginning, 'what clattering of glasses! what beating down of walls! what tearing up of

[41] See Frank Livingstone Huntley, *Bishop Joseph Hall 1574–1656* (Cambridge: D. S. Brewer, 1979), 136. There were Adamites, Anabaptists, Antisabbatarians, Antitrinitarians, Arminians, Brownists, not to mention Valentinians and Socinians, Ranters and Seekers, Soul-Sleepers and Millenaries, and French Huguenots. See also Ketton-Cremer, *Norfolk in the Civil War*, 17. Little of Browne's correspondence before 1660 survives, and one biographer has speculated that as a doctor allowed unusual freedom of travel despite his personal politics, who rode throughout the county to visit patients and must have carried news to and corresponded with a wide circle of acquaintances, he was careful to see that his letters were immediately burnt. After the Restoration, writing to his son Edward, for example, Browne expressed horror and sadness at 'the Abominable murther of King Charles the first'. See his letters to Edward Browne, 31 Jan. 1661 and 4 Jan. 1662 in *Works*, iv. 5 and 16.

[42] Anna Pavord, *The Tulip: The Story of a Flower That has Made Men Mad* (New York: Bloomsbury, 1999), 102.

monuments! what pulling down of seats! What wresting out of irons and brass from the windows and graves!'[43] In 1680, two years before his death, Browne composed *Repertorium or Some Account of the Tombs and Monuments in the Cathedrall Church of Norwich*, in which he commemorates Hall as 'a person of singular humillity, patience, and pietie' whose 'works are his best monument', bows to 'my learned and faythfull old friend Mr John Whitefoot' who preached at Hall's funeral and would deliver Browne's funeral oration, and, remembering across thirty-seven years 'the late confusion', 'the late tumultuous time', 'the Rebellious times', gives a few measured glimpses of the violence. The cathedral's organ 'was pulled downe, broken, sould, & made away'. Browne recalls '5 or 6 copes belonging to the church, which though they looked somewhat old were richly embroydered. These were formally carryed into the market place, some blowing the organ pipes before them, and were cast into a fire provided for that purpose, with showting and Rejoyceing'.[44] Three years after the destruction of the cathedral appeared *Vox Populi, or The Peoples Cry against the Clergy, Containing the Rise, Progress, and Ruine of Norwich Remonstrance*, written 'when only ten of Norwich's parish churches still held Anglican services' and accusing eight of the ministers of 'conspiring with the Mayor to suppress freedom of worship'.[45] In immediate response came *Vox Norwici: or, The Cry of Norwich, Vindicating their Ministers . . . from the foule and false aspersions and slanders, which are unchristianly throwne upon them in a lying and scurrilous Libell, lately come forth, . . . Vox Norwici* defends the Anglican ministers from aspersions against their character and preaching and was signed by fifteen members of the Anglican congregation of St Peter Mancroft, Browne's signature third from the top in the far left of three columns.[46]

On 24 November, 1655, a month after Browne's fiftieth birthday, Cromwell issued a proclamation to take effect 1 January 1656 that

[43] Huntley, *Bishop Joseph Hall*, 138.

[44] Browne, *Works of Sir Thomas Browne*, iii, 140–1. Browne's strong words in *Hydriotaphia* against those who rob tombs of their treasure, 'For which the most barbarous Expilators found the most civill Rhetorick' (152), could recall the Puritan desecrators of church and personal property and artefacts of Royalist families. In response to the fury behind the startling sentence that stands alone as a paragraph, 'To be knav'd out of our graves, to have our sculs made drinking-bowls, and our bones turned into Pipes, to delight and sport our Enemies, are Tragicall abominations, escaped in burning Burials' (155), one wants to ask: who are the 'we' of 'our' and who are 'our Enemies'? The personal desecration of 'our' bodies or our church's relics or our texts all seems possible and conflated here.

[45] Huntley, *Bishop Joseph Hall*, 139.

[46] See Keynes, *Bibliography*, 177. For Browne's signature, see *Vox Norwici* (London: William Franckling, 1646), 15.

forbade, in Evelyn's words, 'all ministers of the Church of England from Preaching, or Teach any Scholes' or from administering sacraments on pain of imprisonment or exile. Later in September 1656 when Joseph Hall died, Whitefoot's funeral sermon referred to Hall's being 'muzzled' from the 'Enjoyment' of his ecclesiastical appointments and represented the sequestered Hall to Anglicans as a reminder of their unjust treatment at the hands of Puritan authorities. On 30 December Evelyn travelled to London to hear 'preached the funeral Sermon of Preaching, this being the last day, after which Cromwells Proclamation was to take place . . . so this was the mournfullest day that in my life I had seene'. Two years later, Evelyn describes the disruption by government soldiers of a surreptitious Anglican service held in London on Christmas Day 1657. The soldiers 'held their muskets against us as we came up to receive the Sacred Elements, as if they would have shot us at the Altar', arrested and examined all present, carrying some off to prison, some 'to the Martial'. Evelyn was questioned 'why contrarie to an Ordinance made that none should any longer observe the superstitious time of the Nativity . . . I durst offend, & particularly be at Common prayers, which they told me was but the Masse in English', and then with 'frivolous & insnaring questions, with much threatning . . . with much pitty of my Ignorance, they dismiss'd me'.[47] In May of the following year, the month when Browne's *Hydriotaphia* and *The Garden of Cyrus* were published, Evelyn lamented, 'There was now a Collection for Persecuted & sequestered Ministers of the Ch: of England, whereof dive[r]s in Prison: The Church now in Dens & Caves of the Earth'.

[47] 'Mr. Gunning preaching in Excester Chapell on 7: Micha 2. Sermon Ended, as he was giving us the holy Sacrament, The Chapell was surrounded with Souldiers: All the Communicants and Assembly surpriz'd & kept Prisoners by them, some in the house, others carried away: It fell to my share to be confined to a roome in the house, where yet were permitted to Dine with the master of it, the Countesse of Dorset, Lady Hatton & some others of quality who invited me: In the afternoone came Collonel Whaly, Goffe & others from Whitehall to examine us one by one, & some they committed to the Martial, some to Prison, some Committed: When I came before them they tooke my name & aboad, examind me, why contrarie to an Ordinance made that none should any longer observe the superstitious time of the Nativity . . . I durst offend, & particularly be at Common prayers, which they told me was but the Masse in English, & particularly pray for Charles stuard, for which we had no Scripture: I told them we did not pray for Cha: Steward but for all Christian Kings, Princes & Governors: The[y] replied, in so doing we praied for the K. of Spaine too, who was their Enemie, & a Papist, with other frivolous & insnaring questions, with much threatning, & finding no colour to detaine me longer, with much pitty of my Ignorance, they dismiss'd me'. *The Diary of John Evelyn*, ed. E. S. De Beer, 6 vols. (Oxford: Clarendon Press, 1955), iii. 203–4.

Browne's 1658 volume that begins under the earth's surface and examines the shadowy quality of all certainty and the shapes of light revealed by shadow, occurs at a historical moment when English Anglicans were muffled in shadowy 'Dens & Caves', and when a sensitivity to the figurative shadows of textual ornament had been replaced by reading for political typology and prophecy. Moreover, the pointed retreat and enclosure of Browne's settings—burial urns and gardens—that persist apart from the more transient world of muskets and conquest, and his sonorous and sensuous imaginative expansiveness within their constraints, appear in a decade characterized by the increasing activity and imperialism of the English army led by the Puritan Lord Protector. English forces had defeated the Dutch in 1654, occupied Jamaica in 1655, entered into war against Spain between 1656 and 1658 and a treaty of alliance with France against Spain in 1657. At home, England's taxpayers had been paying monthly assessments since 1645 to finance the army's costs; 'these receipts provided the largest single component of England's revenue in this period and the vast majority of the money used to support the professional armies deployed in England, Ireland, Scotland, Jamaica, and Dunkirk'.[48] After a Royalist rising led by Col. Penruddock in March 1655, the country was divided into military districts, each governed by a major-general with between 1,000 and 1,500 men at his disposal. The system was financed by the decimation tax, which took 10 per cent of the property of all Royalists and lasted until February 1657, the month Cromwell had been petitioned to accept but rejected finally the title of king. The Second Protectorate was installed in June 1657.

With the country ruled by a military general and supporting the presence and cost of an expensive and continuously active army, Browne plays with his choice of 'our magnified Cyrus' for the title of his garden discourse. He does not commemorate the famous and popular Cyrus the Elder, founder of the Persian Empire, celebrated as a tolerant and ideal monarch who liberated the Jews from captivity and cultivated the hanging Gardens of Babylon. Browne raises expectations of this conquering Cyrus whose military achievements and reputation as a liberator would resemble the official image of Cromwell as God's instrument to liberate England and Europe from the tyranny of kings and who in 1655 had readmitted Jews to England. Browne chooses instead the more shadowy Cyrus the Younger, described by Plutarch as 'a man of great spirit, an

[48] James Scott Wheeler, *The Making of a World Power: War and the Military Revolution in Seventeenth-Century England* (Stroud: Sutton, 1999), 194.

excellent warrior, and a lover of his friends', who barely lived twenty years and, as the second son of Darius II, did not inherit the throne. After being imprisoned on false charges of conspiracy by his elder brother, Cyrus was freed but forced to remain in exile as governor of Lydia, the chief Persian territory in the western Empire, the province most closely connected to Greek history and most influenced by and influential in Greece. He died at the great battle of Cunaxa, near Babylon, in 401 BC, after a long march with 10,000 mercenary Greek soldiers from his home in Sardis to challenge his brother's crown, and was memorialized as a great ruler and generous friend by the Greek historian Xenophon, one of the mercenaries who fought beside Cyrus and who negotiated the troops' dangerous western retreat after Cyrus' death.

Xenophon's account of the campaign and long western journey home, what Browne calls 'that memorable work, and almost miraculous retrait' (180), is entitled *Anabasis*, meaning 'journey up-country or inland', a title that curiously refers only to the events of the first of seven books: Cyrus and his army's march east 'from the coast of Asia Minor to the Tigris-Euphrates river valley' where he dies in battle.[49] In the first book, the Greek eulogizes the fallen Cyrus the Younger as an ideal leader of remarkable warmth and delight in social connections, whose good estate planning enabled him to give generous gifts of food and wine (1. 9. 27). He recalls that 'all agree that he showed himself preeminent in his attentions to all the friends that he made and found devoted to him . . . surely he of all men distributed gifts most generously among his friends, with an eye to the tastes of each one . . . the fact that he outdid his friends in the greatness of the benefits he conferred is nothing surprising . . . but that he surpassed them in solicitude and in eagerness to do favours, this in my opinion is more admirable'.[50] Xenophon praises Cyrus as a leader loved by his followers ('Hence, as I at least conclude from what comes to my ears, no man, Greek or barbarian, has ever been loved by a greater number of people').[51]

Xenophon turns to the quincunx in *Oeconomicus*, a treatise on the management of country households and estates that he composed while in rural retreat in Scillus, probably banished from Athens in part as punishment for

[49] Xenophon, *Anabasis*, with trans. by Carleton L. Brownson, rev. John Dillery (Cambridge, Mass.: Harvard University Press, 1998), 1, 8.

[50] Ibid. 1. 9. 20–4 (in the Greek text), 133–5. Xenophon also composed *Cyropaedia* on the education and career of an ideal ruler, a modified, idealized account of Cyrus the Great, which draws substantially on Xenophon's knowledge and admiration of the Younger.

[51] Xenophon, *Anabasis*, 1. 9. 28, 135.

his participation in Cyrus' expedition.[52] In the work's imagined dialogue between Socrates and Critobulus, Socrates recounts a visit of Spartan leader Lysander to the Younger Cyrus in his garden 'paradise' at Sardis. Lysander praised the regularity and straightness of the planting 'and the multitude of the sweet scents that clung round them as they walked' (4. 21), astounded to learn that the governor who stood before him in beautiful perfumed robes and elaborate jewels had measured, arranged, and even planted his fields.[53] Socrates notes, 'if Cyrus had only lived, it seems that he would have proved an excellent ruler', and Brown describes him as 'naturally a King, though fatally prevented by the harmlesse chance of post-geniture: Not only a Lord of Gardens, but a manuall planter thereof: disposing his trees like his armies in regular ordination' (181). Note the conjunction of 'naturally a king' with the garden's fragrant figure of natural plenitude and order, where royalty is characterized by its affinity with disciplined high spirit and manual labour but also with the elaborate, fertile beauty of naturally divine rule represented by the quincunx. Like a young beloved bridegroom but without a bride, this princely friend to his friends, who desires to serve and please others, and his fertile, orderly beauty and associations with sensuous pleasure might recall not Cromwell but the young exiled Charles II.

The Garden of Cyrus suggests not only a retreat from military action and a military regime comparable to the retirement of the household of Lord Fairfax in Marvell's *Upon Appleton House* but also an aggressive counter-move to retreat. Above the 'drums and tramplings of three conquests' and at a time of Puritan restriction on Anglican ritual and the aesthetics of figurative representation, Browne expands into an intellectual space of learned play and vision, crosses centuries, continents, and languages through the ancient and biblical *topos* of an enclosed garden of wisdom and delight.

COLLATERAL PROFITS

In the concluding paragraph of 'A Digression Concerning Blackness', book 6, chapter xii of *Pseudodoxia Epidemica*, he justifies his long excursion by employing the adjectives 'collaterall' and 'capital' that by mid-century carried economic resonance along with other meanings:

52 Jo-Marie Claasen, *Displaced Persons: The Literature of Exile from Cicero to Boethius* (Madison: University of Wisconsin Press, 1999), 49.

53 Xenophon, *Memorabilia and Oeconomicus*, trans. E. C. Marchant, Loeb Classical Library (Cambridge, Mass.: Harvard University Press, 1979), 397–9.

'Thus have we at last drawn our conjectures unto a period . . . although in this long journey we miss the intended end, yet are there many things of truth disclosed by the way; and the collaterall verity may unto reasonable speculations some what requite the capital indiscovery'.[54] The word 'collateral' was capable of meaning side by side, parallel and accompanying, as well as lying aside from the main subject or subordinate. In the sixteenth and seventeenth centuries, 'collateral' also appears modifying such terms involving property transactions as warranty, bond, and assurance. The elegant truths that lie alongside the main subject—although deemed subordinate by most eyes—carry for Browne a large value of assurance or warranty that makes up for the wealth or profit which was the apparent goal but not reached. We might hear playfulness but also sarcasm and even lofty disdain in the careful understatement of 'reasonable' and 'some what requite' of his defence of digression, a defence repeated as a search for 'collaterall truths' in *The Garden*'s letter of dedication to Bacon, which celebrates 'invention' and the unconfined 'Imagination': 'Beside, such Discourses allow excursions, and venially admit of collaterall truths, though at some distance from their principals' (175–6).

Browne's narrative voice assumes the leisure and privilege to digress and connect his subject to 'collaterall truths'. The speaker is almost coy in his reluctance to omit an association and piece of information. To name nouns or proper names is to set off, yet require the control of, a reverberating network of associations and pieces of detail to fit in an endlessly self-generating mosaic. Frequently the doctor names what he professes to omit and produces a long list of related fragments of learning from various sources. The overriding virtuosic impulse seems to be to link proper names and nouns through delight in theme and variation, in the association of sounds and meaning, and through delight in collection. The sixth paragraph in chapter ii of *Cyrus*, for example, is concerned not to omit and links 'nets' to 'networks' to 'Retiarie' to 'Reticulum Jecoris', links 'rushey labyrinths' to 'gnatnets' to 'nosegaynets':

That the networks and nets of antiquity were little different in the form from ours at present, is confirmable from the nets in the hands of the Retiarie gladiators, the proper combatants with the secutores. To omit the ancient Conopeion or gnatnet of the Aegyptians, the inventors of that Artifice: the rushey labyrinths of *Theocritus*; the nosegaynets, which hung from the head under the nostrils of Princes; and that uneasie metaphor of *Reticulum Jecoris*, which some expound the lobe, we the caule

[54] Browne, *Works* ii. 480–1.

above the liver. As for that famous network of *Vulcan*, which inclosed *Mars* and *Venus*, and caused that unextinguishable laugh in heaven; since the gods themselves could not discern it, we shall not prie into it; Although why Vulcan bound them, *Neptune* loosed them, and *Apollo* should first discover them, might afford no vulgar mythologie. Heralds have not omitted this order or imitation thereof. (187).

The networks of which Browne writes are there to catch and hold the pieces of his thought, including echoes of 'that unextinguishable laugh in heaven'. The next paragraph which links the quincunx to memory, 'The same is not forgot by Lapidaries', continues the fertile pattern of 'not's, each 'not' a verbal *X* or cross, although they lead in the middle of the paragraph to an exception to nature's rule of the omnipresent quincunx: 'But this is no law unto the woof of the neat *Retiarie* Spider, which seems to weave without transversion . . . beyond the common art of Textury' (188). The next paragraphs retrieve the thread from the spider, however, and spin out additional natural and mythic examples of decussation. Yet the associative network represented by a playful pun on 'nettle'—the spider's uncommon art of textury 'may still nettle *Minerva* the Goddesse of that mystery' (188)—recalls the warring world, the constant rivalry whether of Minerva and Arachne or Ajax and Achilles or Puritan and Anglican.

In another outburst of 'not's that hold, connect, and include like a net, chapter v opens with protestations that the speaker cannot 'enlarge' on what he then 'cannot omit' and documents at length:

To enlarge this contemplation unto all the mysteries and secrets, accomodable unto this number, were inexcusable Pythagorisme, yet cannot omit the ancient conceit of five surnamed the number of justice, . . . Nor can we omit how agreeable unto this number an handsome division is made in Trees and Plants. . . . Not to omit the Quintuple Section of a Cone. . . . He that forgets not how Antiquity named this the Conjugall or wedding number, and made it the Embleme of the most remarkable conjunction, will conceive it duely appliable unto this handsome Oeconomy. (221–2)

The 'cannot omit' and the connection between 'handsome division' and 'most remarkable conjunction' are more important to the construction of 'this handsome Oeconomy'—this text—than what Browne calls earlier, in *Pseudodoxia Epidemica*, the 'intended end' missed for the sake of 'many things of truth disclosed by the way'. The branching quincunx that connects so 'many things of truth . . . by the way', and Browne uninterested to spell out what they are, turns a learned garden tract into a quietly radical text.

In the millenary 1650s, many were occupied in reading nature's book to advance knowledge of God's world and to build a fruitful and productive English economy—to transform England's fallen garden into a new

Eden. For example, Walter Blith, ex-trooper of Cromwell's New Model Army, published *The English Improver Improved or the Survey of Husbandry Surveyed* (1652) with a banner across the title page that unfurls 'Vive La Republick'. The author promises 'to make the poor rich and the rich richer, and all to live of the labour of their owne hands'.[55] Indeed Browne's *The Garden of Cyrus* appeared towards the end of a decade when science, religion, and nationalism had joined hands in a ferment of interest in and publications on horticultural and agricultural theory and design.[56] 'Francis Bacon's empirical method of experiment, discussion and communication was seen as the way to hasten' Christ's Second Coming by creating national prosperity.[57] Samuel Hartlib, 'a half-English, half German Pole', who after 1646 until the Restoration drew his pension from Parliament, promoted a nationalistic movement 'towards large economical agrarian units laid out for maximum production with only slight regard for visual charm' and issued numerous tracts on husbandry, such as *The Reformed Husband-Man* (1651) and *The Reformed Spirituall Husband-Man* (1652).[58] In *A Discoverie for Division or Setting out of Lands to the Best Form* (1653), Hartlib popularized 'austere and rigorous' geometrical gardens and utilitarian estate plans, in which the manor house sits imperiously at the centre of a circle divided into four quadrants beyond which extend a large single farm divided into great quadrants of corn lands and meadows, with no village or commons, everything 'laid out for the profit of a single family'.[59] Hartlib had become a conduit for exchange of ideas and correspondence about English gardening, among other subjects, and his circle which had brought together learned men such as John Dury, Frederick Clodius, Benjamin Worsley, Robert Boyle, and Moravian educationalist Johann Amos Comenius included as well gardening enthusiasts Ralph Austen, John Beale, and John Evelyn.

Austen, the Oxford gardener introduced at the beginning of this essay, who trusted the 'plaine' writing of nature's book, praised the work of Hartlib and Blith in the dedicatory epistle to 'my much Honoured

[55] See Timothy Mowl, 'New Science, Old Order: The Gardens of the Great Rebellion', *Journal of Garden History*, 13 (1993), 22. I am grateful to John Shanahan for this source.

[56] As Andrea Finkelstein has noted, 'The tide of agricultural manuals produced in the first half of the seventeenth century swelled to incredible proportions in the second'. Andrea Finkelstein, *Harmony and the Balance: An Intellectual History of Seventeenth-Century English Economic Thought* (Ann Arbor: University of Michigan Press, 2000), 121.

[57] Mowl, ' New Science, Old Order', 21. [58] Ibid. 20. [59] Ibid. 21.

Friend, Samuel Hartlib' of *A Treatise on Fruit-Trees, Showing the Manner of Grafting, Setting, Pruning, and Ordering of Them in All Respects*, the principal tract to which he appended *The Spiritual Use of an Orchard.* Austen's volume advocates a national movement to plant fruit trees that would transform barren wastelands, increase England's productivity for home and foreign markets, and employ the poor. Herefordshire clergyman John Beale in *Herefordshire Orchards A Pattern for All England: Written in an Epistolary Address to Samuel Hartlib Esq.* (1657) urged the economic benefits for England of the production of crabapple cider that could compete with the best wines of Europe.[60] Adolphus Speed's *Adam out of Eden* (1658) argued for 'more efficient domestic production' and use of lands at home, including a scheme for rabbit-breeding.[61]

A utilitarian, nationalistic, and eschatological fervour characterizes many of these tracts. 'Are not these the times of the Gospell prophesied of Esay 49.19, 20. When the Wast and desolate places shall be inhabited', declares Austen.[62] He compares England well planted with fruit trees to the promised land of the Israelites:

> An eminent person once said of this Nation, that it is a very Garden of delights, and a Well that cannot be exhausted: What then would it be, did it abound with goodly Fruit-trees, and other Profits, where now are barren Wasts: Might it not then be called another Canaan, flowing with Milke and hony, of which it is recorded that there were Fruit-trees in abundance. Nehem.9.25.[63]

The common identification of Cromwell's 'Saints' with the Israelites underlines the importance to Austen's passage of the previous verse in Nehemiah as well, which remembers how the children of Israel 'went in and possessed the land' while God subdued the Canaanites for his chosen people 'and gavest them into their hands, with their kings, and the people

[60] See Mayling Stubbs, 'John Beale, Philosophical Gardener of Herefordshire. Part I. Prelude to the Royal Society (1608–1663)', *Annals of Science* 39 (1982), 479.

[61] See Peter Harrison, *The Bible, Protestantism, and the Rise of Natural Science* (Cambridge: Cambridge University Press, 1998) 246. Adolphus Speed, *Adam out of Eden, or, An abstract of divers excellent experiments touching the advancement of Husbandry. Shewing, Among very many other things, an Aprovement of Ground by Rabbiss [sic], from 200 l. annual Rent, to 2000 l. yearly profit, all charges deducted* (London: Henry Brome, 1658). Harrison dates this tract as 1659. The title page of the Thomason copy, however, bears the annotation 'Octob:'; and the 9 in the imprint date is crossed out and replaced with an '8'.

[62] Austen, 'To the Worshipfull Samuel Hartlib Esquire, My much Honoured Friend', Epistle Dedicatory prefixed to *A Treatise on Fruit-Trees* (1653).

[63] Austen, 'To the Worshipfull Samuel Hartlib Esquire, My much Honoured Friend', Epistle Dedicatory prefixed to *A Treatise on Fruit-Trees* (1653).

of the land, that they might do with them as they would'. Austen's exhortation to 'labour diligently for all necessary, and usefull things, within our own Nation' is a different side of the Parliamentary army's conquest of land and king.

For Austen the happy conjunction of profit and pleasure ensures the success of any art, and the cultivation of fruit trees joins both perfectly hand in hand: 'This Art is a full store-House, out of which may be brought both Meat, Drink, and Mony, it is a rich Myne, without bounds or bottom, out of which we may dig Profits and Pleasures great, and many, and worthy the study, and labour of the most wise and Learned'. Finally, 'Now therefore seing there is so much profit, and advantage to be received from this imployment of Planting Fruit-trees, both in Temporall, and Spirituall respects, Let us set about it, and labour in it. ... That thereby the Glory of God, and Publique Profit (together with our own advantages) may be promoted'.[64]

The national wasteland Browne intends to cultivate, however, is that of 'bye and barren Themes', to make the old new for the intellectual entertainment of a community of readers that begins with his friend Sir Nicholas Bacon. His detractors, Browne suggests, are those who think they know the truth or are envious of high learning and playful, imaginative invention: 'of old things we write something new, If truth may receive addition, or envy will have any thing new'. Browne's fertile quincunx, that might recall rather the ornaments of Caroline formal gardens than Hartlib's quadrants, exists at a critical remove from the contemporary millenary horticultural schemes for England's economic improvement.[65] When Browne defends his tract of unconfined imagination that 'venially' admits of 'collaterall truths', the slyly playful adverb 'venially', akin to the Latin *venus*, meaning charm, loveliness, and love, aligns digressions and Browne's garden with captivating aesthetic pleasure rather than the handshaking union of pleasure and profits that Austen urges. Browne's deepest scientific interests have been described as the study of biology and physiology and specifically the nature of sexual reproduction—generation, including the possibility of spontaneous generation, being the 'most

[64] Austen, *A Treatise of Fruit-Trees*, 'To the Reader'.

[65] Roy Strong once included quincunxes along with 'bosquets ... étoiles, wildernesses, cascades and grottos' as characteristic of the French-influenced 'Baroque' garden in England. Timothy Mowl, however, finds those elements present in the much earlier formal gardening style of the Caroline period, as exemplified by the three-part formal garden at Wilton created by Inigo Jones and Isaac de Caus and completed in 1638. See Roy Strong, *The Renaissance Garden in England* (London: Thames and Hudson, 1979), 221, cited in Mowl, 'New Science, Old Order', 16–17 and 31.

ubiquitous topic in his writings'.[66] Hartlib advocated 'scientific exploration of "the true causes of fertility" ' to improve agricultural yield, while Browne's quincuncial economy becomes an elaborate image for the natural yet asexual generation and fertility of intellectual life, of memory and aesthetic pleasure, and for the economies of association and friendship.[67]

READING THROUGH THE LATTICE

The inexorability of death and oblivion, specifically the single-minded force of military movement and its parallel in dogmatic literal reading that together raze surfaces and ornament, constitute a blind, linear, ahistorical movement against which Browne densely elaborates his twin texts of innumerable voices and detail. He complicates the opposition of dark and light into a shadowy texture of experience, a text as a lattice-like window onto the invisible world, vision of which is available only to those who can look deeply and read figuratively. Browne recommends that the complexities of God's Word and of nature's book be approached through attentive 'ocular Observation' which *The Garden of Cyrus* recommends at every turn while hinting that 'signal discerners' are few and far between. Such looking he links with the pleasures of elegance or of seeing what most eyes miss ('elegantly observable', 192; 'elegantly conspicuous', 204): 'Now although this elegant ordination of vegetables, hath found coincidence or imitation in sundry works of Art . . . though overlooked by all, was elegantly observable, in severall works of nature' (192). 'The same is observably effected . . . discoverable also in long Pepper, and elegantly in the *Julus* of *Calamus Aromaticus*' (193); 'The like so often occurreth to the curiosity of observers'; 'he that from hence can discover in what position the two first leaves did arise, is no ordinary observator' (195, 196); 'wherein a watchfull eye may also discover the puncticular Originals of Periwincles and Gnats' (199); 'which cannot escape the eyes of signal discerners' (202). Browne even makes the quincunx an order 'gratefull unto the eye' because of the physical organization of the organs of sight and the laws of vision (218–19); and the blue and green colours of sky and earth, 'above and below the sight', are

66 Merton, *Science and Imagination*, 12.

67 The Renaissance interest in encyclopaedic gardens as re-creations of Eden's plenty and order resulted in the creation of 'the six most famous botanical gardens in Europe—Padua, Leyden, Montpellier, Oxford, Paris, and Uppsala—. . . in the sixteenth and seventeenth centuries'. Harrison, *The Bible, Protestantism, and the Rise of Natural Science*, 238.

designed by nature to be easy on and protect the eye and help us see below and above surfaces (217).[68] His lattice for looking deeply recalls the 'perspective windows' or grids that appear in numerous sixteenth-century drawings, through which draftsmen look at and draw a landscape or, for example in a drawing by Dürer dated 1527, a reclining nude. For *perspectiva*, a Latin noun meaning the science of sight or optics, is related to the Latin verb *perspicere* that means 'to look through, look closely into'.[69]

In chapter ii when Browne dilates on decussation, or the cross of intersection, he recalls the windows in the Temple of Solomon that were 'termed *fenestrae reticulatae*, or lights framed like nets. And agreeable unto the Greek expression concerning Christ in the Canticles, looking through the nets, which ours hath rendered, he looketh forth at the windows, shewing himselfe through the lattesse; that is, partly seen and unseen, according to the visible and invisible side of his nature' (187). Browne conflates New and Old Testaments, apostolic fishnets, and a window lattice of Solomon's Temple into a celebration of the profound intersection of invisible and visible, spiritual and natural, realms of knowledge. The protected rectangles created by the lines of the quincunx become enclosed but fertile gardens of order. Moreover, the experience of looking through one world into another, the deepest vision, becomes an image for reading not only nature's and God's book but Browne's. In contrast, when men like Hartlib, Austen, and Beale argued the joint economic and spiritual usefulness of horticulture in Protestant devotion, they drew on the tradition of the enclosed garden 'based on the allegorization of the Song of Songs' as an emblematic space for solitude and meditation pledged to Christ, which became mixed with an enthusiasm for formal gardens and the trope of the national garden of England.[70]

The Song of Songs had become a central expression of the relation of divine to profane love and of the senses to spiritual life in medieval and

[68] Close vision sees both exactly what is there and what is there figuratively speaking: 'He that would exactly disceren the shop of a Bees mouth, need observing eyes, and good augmenting glasses; wherein is discoverable one of the neatest peeces in nature, and must have a more piercing eye than mine; who finds out the shape of buls heads, in the guts of Drones pressed out behinde, according to the experiment of *Gomesius*; wherin notwithstanding there seemeth somewhat which might incline a pliant fancy to credulity of similitude' (206–3).

[69] See the *OED* for 'perspection' and 'perspective'; see also James Elkins, *The Poetics of Perspective* (Ithaca, NY: Cornell University Press, 1994), 49–52.

[70] Stewart, *The Enclosed Garden*, p. xiv and ch. 1. For the Protestant association of Christ with gardens, see William Prynne, 'A Christian Paradise', in *Mount-Orgueil* (1641), 126:

Renaissance biblical commentary. Its multiple levels of meaning elaborated in Roman Catholic exegesis included the literal, historic sense along with a fertile allegorical life as the dialogue between Christ and his bride the Church or individual soul.[71] With the Reformation, the Song's popularity as a text for commentary and sermon, and for prose and verse paraphrase, proved almost 'a preoccupation'.[72] Seventeenth-century writing, richly referential of songs and gardens, wilderness and love, recalls the Song repeatedly—not only *Paradise Lost* but Herbert's 'Paradise', for example, or Quarles's *Emblemes*, Vaughan's 'Regeneration', and Marvell's 'The Garden'.[73] But while Protestant biblical commentators generally insisted on a single and literal meaning of Scripture, they tended to adopt a rigid allegorical and moralistic reading of Canticles and reject both the historic reference to Solomon and the literal, carnal sense—the troubling kisses and thighs—that had inspired a mystical, sacramental spirituality for the Catholic 'mystery-oriented' tradition.[74]

> Christ, here on earth did Gardens highly grace.
> Resorting oft unto them, in which place
> He was betray'd, entomb'd, rais'd up, and then
> First there appear'd to Mary Magdalen.
> Each Garden then we see, should still present
> Christ to our sight, minds, thoughts, with sweete Content.

Quoted in Stewart, *The Enclosed Garden*, 116. For an introduction to the life and work of John Beale, see Stubbs, 'John Beale, Philosophical Gardener of Herefordshire'.

For 17th-century natural philosophers, Solomon was associated with a perfect knowledge of nature believed to have been lost with the Fall; the 'legendary books of King Solomon' to which Browne refers in *Religio Medici* I. 24, were considered part of the recordings of a lost oral tradition of 'scriptural science'. See Harrison, *The Bible, Protestantism, and the Rise of Natural Science* 137. 'I have heard some with deepe sighs lament the lost lines of Cicero; others with as many groanes deplore the combustion of the Library of Alexandria; for my own part, I thinke there be too many in the world, and could with patience behold the urne and ashes of the Vatican, could I with a few others behold the perished leaves of Soloman'. *Religio Medici*, I. 24 (35).

[71] See George L. Scheper, 'Reformation Attitudes toward Allegory and the Song of Songs', *PMLA* 89 (1974), 551–62. Medieval hermeneutics and allegorical reading, based on belief in a direct relationship between God's invisible and visible kingdoms, according to Romans 1: 20, traced the lines of eternal meaning made accessible by God to skilled readers through the visible world, including natural bounty and man-made creations. See Harrison, *The Bible, Protestantism, and the Rise of Natural Science*, 11–63.

[72] Scheper, 'Reformation Attitudes', 556.

[73] In the preface to book II of *The Reason of Church Government* (1641), Milton notes, 'the Scripture also affords us a divine pastoral Drama in the Song of Salomon, consisting of two persons and a double Chorus, as Origen rightly judges'. Milton, *Complete Prose Works*, i. 815. See also Stewart, *The Enclosed Garden*, esp. ch. 1.

[74] For Protestant spokesmen the sense of the Song was rationalized as an account of the divine love of Christ for the human soul, which served as a model for the domestic hierarchical relation of husband and wife. Scheper, 'Reformation Attitudes', 558.

During the 1640s and 1650s an exception to the Protestant reluctance to read Canticles literally were Ranters such as Abiezer Coppe and Laurence Clarkson who rejected the allegorical conventions that discouraged sexual readings and instead 'placed the underlying carnal sense of the biblical verses at the centre of their delicate balance between flesh and spirit'.[75] The Ranters invoked the Song of Songs to argue for the holiness of lust and unlimited sexual acts 'as long as they are done "in light and love" '.[76] As a commentary on Isaiah 42: 16, 'I will make darkness light before them', Clarkson's *A Single Eye* (1650) claims that what are traditionally termed dark acts of the devil become acts of light and purity as long as one's imagination is pure and spiritual. Abiezer Coppe appropriated as his own the language of Canticles, for example, to describe his ascending spiritual 'fiery chariots' of sexual experience:

> And then again, by wanton kisses, kissing hath been confounded; and externall kisses, have been made the fiery chariots, to mount me swiftly into the bosom of him whom my soul loves, . . . Where I have been, where I have been, where I have been, hug'd, imbrac't, and kist with the kisses of his mouth, whose loves are better then wine.[77]

Moreover, according to Noam Flinker, the 'motif of secrecy' in Coppe's writing concerning God's meaning, and Coppe's occupation of biblical texts without citations of book, chapter, and verse, argued 'that language itself is part of the old way which is to be abandoned. . . . Since the aim is to move from sign to signified, there is a point in the text that words and language itself must be abandoned as mere signs'.[78] The Ranters radical politics, explicated through their use of biblical texts, including the Song of Songs, and themes of light and darkness, and their desire to overturn traditional uses of language and reasoned discourse constitute yet another competing appropriation, contemporary with that of Browne's quincunx and of Hartlib and his horticultural reformers, of the rich intersection of biblical gardens, religious vision, and the books of God and nature.

I return finally to Austen's *A Treatise on Fruit-Trees . . . Together with the Spiritual Use of an Orchard: in divers Similitudes between Naturall and*

[75] Noam Flinker, *The Song of Songs in English Renaissance Literature: Kisses of their Mouths* (Cambridge: D.S. Brewer, 2000), 139.

[76] Ibid. 132.

[77] Cited ibid. 133. See also Nigel Smith (ed.), *A Collection of Ranter Writings from the 17th Century* (London: Junction Books, 1983), 51.

[78] Flinker, *The Song of Songs*, 126. On Coppe's use of Song of Songs and transformation of biblical language, see also Clement Hawes, *Mania and Literary Style: The Rhetoric of Enthusiasm from the Ranters to Christopher Smart* (Cambridge: Cambridge University Press, 1996), esp. 70–2.

Spirituall Fruit-trees, according to Scripture and Experience in order to emphasize the political conjunction of science and aesthetics of Browne's text. Like Browne, Austen invokes the Song of Songs, as well as Romans 1: 20 on the relationship of God's visible and invisible kingdoms. Crowning the title page of the first edition are two clasped hands of Profits and Pleasures; below circling the illustrative plate of a walled garden is a band containing verses from the Song of Solomon: 'A Garden inclosed is my sister my spouse: thy plants are an orchard of pomegrants, with pleasant fruits' (4: 12–13).[79] The 'first Humane Argument' in Austen's text, 'of the dignity and value of Fruit-trees, and the art of planting', is the example set by ancient kings and princes, and at the head of his list appears Cyrus, King of Persia.[80] *The Spiritual Use of an Orchard* lists observations in nature followed by their uses for moral instruction; for 'Fruit-trees are a TEXT from which may be raysed many profitable Doctrines, and Conclusions, which may be proved by Scripture, and Experience'.[81] The Oxford gardener reads in nature's book twenty different similitudes that would 'shadow forth' corresponding moral and spiritual truths for man.[82]

But unlike Austen and others who wrote about gardens in the 1650s, Browne is not interested in a nationalistic vision of industry and fruitfulness, of the union of profit and pleasure. His stems and seeds are not pages in a moral lesson book nor part of a progressive agricultural scheme but a rich source of natural patterns of growth and connection that only assume figurative force because nature is 'Artificiall'. Austen urges, 'as Windowes are to a house, so are Similitudes to a Discourse: they both let in light'. The

[79] On the title page of *The Spiritual Use of an Orchard* appears among other scriptural verses Canticles 2: 3, 'Like the Apple-tree among the Trees of the Forrest; so is my beloved among the Sonnes. I sate downe under his shadow with great delight, and his fruit was sweet to my taste'. In both his 'Dedicatory Epistle' and 'A Preface to the Reader' before *The Spiritual Use*, Austen quotes Romans 1: 20; in the former he describes God's creatures as 'the Book of his Workes' to be read along with 'the Book of his Word'; in the latter he calls Nature's creatures 'Bookes' to be studied, which shadow forth the divine world.

[80] Austen, *A Treatise on Fruit-Trees*, 20.

[81] Austen, *The Spiritual Use of an Orchard*, 'A Preface to the Reader'.

[82] A beautiful fruit growing on a wild, ungrafted tree proves sour to taste, which shadows forth that there are 'many men in the world, being eminent in Learning, Gifts, and Parts, who can performe many workes . . . yet these very fruits, to the taste of the Husbandman, are very bitter . . . because they are from ungrafted Trees, such as are wild and Corrupt by Nature, the Principles from which they proceed is Corrupt'. The 'Use' of this observation is 'Let none content themselves with outward performances in the worship of God though never so faire, and unreprovable, to the eye of men, but looke to the Principles . . . and examine whether they be steames from the Divine Nature. . . '. Ibid. 4.

lattice and figures that Browne imagines, however, evoke light criss-crossed by laths that frame hidden depth.[83] Browne's garden is neither a herbal nor a horticultural experiment nor an attempt to rally England to economic and spiritual health but resembles a lover's ecstatic *blazon*: a personal, closely observed account of a mysterious and various order of beauty, not created and imposed by man on, in order to master, nature but seen to exist in infinite complexity within the natural world. Browne's Cyrus proves to be not a conqueror but a generous and beautiful exiled prince who inspires love and the orderly profusion of delight.

Following the descriptions of quincunxes in nature, in art, in the human body, and in animals comes the climactic discussion at the end of chapter 4 of the relationship between light and shadow and especially of the illuminating and protective role of shadow, which makes this text the shield and lattice and fabulous labyrinth it is, yet flagrantly mystical, provocatively unreformed:

> Light that makes things seen, makes some things invisible: were it not for darknesse and the shadow of the earth, the noblest part of the Creation had remained unseen, and the Stars in heaven as invisible as on the fourth day, when they were created above the Horizon, with the Sun, or there was not eye to behold them. The greatest mystery of Religion is expressed by adumbration, and in the noblest part of Jewish Types, we finde the Cherubims shadowing the Mercy-seat: Life it self is but the shadow of death, and souls departed but the shadows of the living: All things fall under this name. The Sunne it self is but the dark *simulachrum*, and light but the shadow of God. (218)

Shade and shadow not only are 'the greatest mystery of Religion' and make 'the noblest part of the Creation' visible but play an important protective role in nature, parallel to the protection that writing in shadow offers to dissident points of view. Trees' dense branches and leaves help them protect, preserve, and 'cherish' themselves: 'Nor are only dark and green colors, but shades and shadows contrived through the great Volume of nature, and trees ordained not only to protect and shadow others, but by their shades and shadowing parts, to preserve and cherish themselves' (217). Earlier the speaker makes a similar observation about the 'triangular foliations' in pinecones 'orderly shadowing and protecting the winged seeds below them' (195). Light and dark 'alternately rule the seminal state of things', and deep in the shadows, inside the invisible world of the tiniest seed, Browne locates the seminal principle of life from which vast productions come, as if from nothing—including *The Garden*

[83] Austen, *The Spiritual Use of an Orchard*, 'A Preface to the Reader'.

of Cyrus from an apparently 'bye and barren' theme yet 'best fitted for invention' (175). Browne's intense imaginative interest in the invisible drama of asexual generation—'beside the open and visible Testicles of plants, the seminall powers lie in great part invisible' (197); 'The Aequivocall production of things under undiscerned principles, makes a large part of generation' (198)—colours his almost wistful description of nature's careful swaddling of the 'generative particle' of seeds, more safely protected than human infants can ever be: 'But Seeds themselves', he writes, 'do lie in perpetual shades, either under the leaf, or shut up in coverings; and such as lye barest, have their husks, skins, and pulps about them, wherein the nebbe and generative particle lyeth moist and secured from the injury of Ayre and Sunne' (218).[84] Access to the spiritual world's unseen seminal principles comes through careful, close seeing and reading of nature's (and Browne's) book: an intellectual and religious, an aesthetic and political, position that opposes a one-dimensional, literal world of reading and writing associated with zealous Protestant suspicion of rhetorical arts or of imagery not capable of being translated directly into moral lessons.

Amid a variety of horticultural pamphlets that urged diligence and design to turn England into a perfect 'Garden of delights' as Ralph Austen imagined, Thomas Browne composed his meditation on garden geometry that begins deep underground in the ashes of burial urns. He answers the funeral pyres of *Hydriotaphia* not with Eden but with the sun-lit ornamental form of an ancient, Eastern prince, the sun of natural kingship and the soul's shining Spouse; he answers, too, with the fiery breath of Vulcan's forge whose art created a brilliant, immortal world of light and shadow in the inexorable face of death. Instead of the reformed horticultural geometry, the quadrants advocated by Hartlib and other writers, a confident, rigid order imposed on nature to produce more for a new England, Browne celebrates aesthetic order, 'this handsome Oeconomy' of the five-pointed quincunx, as an ancient, seminal figure of connection within nature, visible to those who know how to look and read closely nature's figurative book. Browne forges the interconnected

[84] Peter Harrison has noted that the medieval and Renaissance 'garden derived much of its power as a symbol or literal recreation of Paradise on account of the widespread belief that plants reproduced asexually', unsullied by sexual reproduction. As Browne writes in *Pseudodoxia*, 'the natural way of Plants, who having no distinction of sex, and the power of the species contained in every individuum', is to 'beget and propagate themselves without commixtion' (*Works*, ii. 195–6). See Harrison, *The Bible, Protestantism, and the Rise of Natural Science*, 238.

order of natural, imaginative, and spiritual life into a protective shield of complexity impervious to militant bad readers and reformers of states, nature, and texts.

EXILE AND EXTRAVAGANT ORDER

The Garden of Cyrus creates figures of design and texture—the quincunx, the lattice, the Homeric shield—which suggest that the medical son of Thomas Browne, mercer, cultivates a rich parallel among gardens, texts, and other fabrics or fabrications whose elegant crossed lights and shadows suggest worlds of depth and high pleasures. Extending the Psalmist's 'Elegant expression . . . Thou hast curiously embroydered me, thou hast wrought me up after the finest way of texture, and as it were with a Needle' (204), Browne the physician probes all creation as intricate texture, including the complex and invisible 'inward parts of man'. The writer's complex syntax and figurative language that honour nature's forms of quincunx and labyrinth dismiss those who misread and attack finely wrought surfaces, whether the embroideries of Norwich Cathedral or the fabric of the natural world.

Three days before Browne's *Hydriotaphia* and *The Garden* entered the Stationers' Register, John Evelyn observed in his diary for 6 March 1658, 'This had ben the severest Winter, that man alive had knowne in England: The Crowes feete were frozen to their prey: Ilands of Ice inclosed both fish & foule frozen, & some persons in their boates'. Against the cold shadow of death over the two and a half years following his fiftieth birthday in October 1655, Thomas Browne produced an outburst of writing on mortality. Evelyn's chill included the loss of two sons in two months; Browne had lost children throughout the 1650s, an infant in 1651 and again in 1652, then newborn twins in 1656. Also in 1656, the year in which workmen unearthed the funeral urns in Old Walsingham that prompted the composition of *Hydriotaphia*, Browne mourned the loss of Sir Charles Le Gros, father of the dedicatee of *Hydriotaphia*, and a former schoolmate from Pembroke College, at one time Browne's patient; Bishop Joseph Hall whom Browne had known for over a decade and attended in his last days; and Robert Loveday, aged 35, whom Browne nursed through consumption and at whose death he wrote to Norfolk Royalist Sir John Pettus 'A Letter to a Friend, upon Occasion of the Death of his Intimate Friend', published after Browne's death. The repetition of 'friend' in the title and the warmth of 'Intimate

Friend' characterize Browne's emphasis and eloquence not least in the late 1650s in letters of dedication, in personal correspondence, and particularly in *Hydriotaphia* and *The Garden of Cyrus* on themes of friendship and human connection.

Browne's 1658 volume, and *The Garden of Cyrus* in particular, are radical texts for a dark time. They are radical in their protest against personal and cultural fragmentation, radical in their labyrinthine vision, their rhetorical elegance, and their learning, and Browne is provocatively both learned and mystical, as the full title suggests: *The Garden of Cyrus, or The Quincunciall, Lozenge, or Network Plantations of the Antients, Artificially, Naturally, and Mystically Considered.* Browne reclaims for himself and his community a voice and sweep of vision distinct from that of Puritan and sectarian visionaries, one in which the artful, the natural, and the spiritual are embraced equally. From the first paragraph when the writer describes God's 'vegetable creation' as 'the first ornamental Scene of nature', he celebrates the primary order of ornament, including rhetorical flowers. The accompanying illustrative plate of the quincunx bears a quotation from Quintilian's *Institutio Oratoria*, out of the eighth book devoted to verbal ornament, that translates, 'What fairer sight is there than rows of trees planted in echelon [*quincunce*] which present straight lines to the eye from whatever angle they be viewed?' (8. 3. 9).[85] The passage occurs in a section where Quintilian defends rhetorical ornament against charges of effeminacy and argues for the equal virtue and usefulness of rhetorical and garden beauty. Browne notes that Cicero, 'the most elegant of the Latines', famous for his copious grand style and amplifications, recalls Xenophon's story of Cyrus in order to praise its 'copious eloquence' on agriculture and to argue that nothing was 'more befitting royalty than zeal in husbandry' (17. 59, the Loeb translation). Browne's marginal note reminds us that Cicero's comment on Xenophon and the quincunx occurs in his last years writing *De Senectute* ('On old age') in rural retreat and exile from Rome dominated by Caesar. Cyrus, Xenophon, and Cicero—and the writer of *The Garden of Cyrus*—are in country retreat from a political regime and take solace in husbandry and copious writing. Cicero had just lost not twin sons like Browne but his adored only daughter and composed *De Senectute* among other works in a grief-stricken frenzy of composition. With Quintilian and Cicero, Browne joins the rhetorical and natural in a celebration of

[85] Quintilian, *Institutio Oratoria, Books VII–IX*, trans. H. E. Butler (Cambridge, Mass.: Harvard University Press, 1996), 215.

elegancy, privacy, mystery, and extravagant interconnectivity that exists beyond the ken of his community's captors, in opposition to death's silences and to the intellectual and spiritual modes of England's Interregnum government. 'In Garden Delights 'tis not easie to hold a Mediocrity', he writes to Nicholas Bacon, the dedicatee of *Cyrus.*

4
Eve's 'Grateful Digressions' and the Birth of Reflection

Over the course of an epic that ends in human expulsion from a place of much talk, and in the creation of an interior, silent Paradise of conscience and self-knowledge, Milton distinguishes the movement of digression from transgression. The figure of stepping aside comes to represent a movement away from the potentially insatiable, consuming appetite to be godlike in knowledge and a diversion instead into self-contained and self-containing pleasure and relationship. Milton reveals the pressure of appetite—for knowledge, for power, for praise—to be a Satanic, linear, self-isolating pressure to consume until one consumes oneself. As did Donne, Marvell, and Browne, Milton creates in his epic a narrative voice whose tension resides in the urgency of being of such digressive complexity and mystery that the voice refuses easy consumption, eludes death.

The narrator of *Upon Appleton House* addresses his sense of lost direction in a nation at war but also within the Fairfax family and himself, their sharp-eyed tutor. Through an apparently leisurely outdoor survey, he plumbs the meaning of the poem's first word, 'within'. In a different militarized, abundant, and provocative patriarchal garden, Milton's Eve confuses exterior for interior life: she mistakes not only a reflection or image for the act of reflective thought, but also other voices for her own.[1] Milton's epic traces how her earliest pleasure of 'unexperienc't thought' (IV. 457) while hovering above her reflection in the lake, and the sufficiency of her reflection's 'answering looks | Of sympathie and love' (IV. 464–65), become exchanged first for playful, self-reflexive moments

[1] The more obvious figure from Marvell's poem with whom to compare Eve is Mary Fairfax. Donald Friedman, 'The Lady in the Garden: On the Literary Genetics of Milton's Eve', *Milton Studies*, 35 (1997), 114–33, has surveyed the literary tradition of the female in the garden, specifically the females in the 17th-century country-house or estate poem, and considered how Milton's Eve in her 'happy rural seat' reflects and transforms her predecessors in this 'mini-genre'.

with Adam and then again for a seductive, Satanic appetite: less for reflection and 'answering looks' than for a godlike superior perspective of absolute knowledge.[2] From the safety of 'Grateful digressions' with Adam—their stepping aside from the pressure to do and know more—Eve makes the startling Satanic swerve of transgression to overstep the bounds of answering looks, which are ultimately her own. Eve falls to discover a new private experience of reflection, not on an image but on her self.[3]

Satan's self-serving but magnificent oratory to his followers in heaven and hell and his eloquence from the serpent's mouth, reminiscent of 'som Orator renound | In Athens or free Rome' (IX. 670–1), exemplify rhetorical persuasion as diabolic. Such classical skills and devices including *digressio* must be fallen and suspect in this poem, hence the epic speaker's repeated requests for divine aid and sanction for his song. At a historical moment when the English word 'digression' could signify transgression and in a story full of digressions about primal transgression, Milton's narrator uses the word 'digression' only once, in VIII. 55, to refer to the innocent 'Grateful digressions' of speech and touch that Adam would 'intermix', to Eve's great pleasure we are told, when they talked. His digressions, his narrative mixtures that included 'conjugal Caresses' (VIII. 56), moved the couple aside from the burden of the unanswered questions about the garden and their exterior world, cleared

[2] All citations to *Paradise Lost* are to *The Works of John Milton*, ed. Frank Allen Patterson et al., 18 vols. (New York: Columbia University Press, 1931–8), vol. ii, parts 1–2, and are included parenthetically by book and line numbers in my text. Citations to other poems by Milton are to the texts in *Complete Poems and Major Prose*, ed. Merritt Y. Hughes (New York: Macmillan, 1957).

[3] The commentary on Eve and her reflection is voluminous, beginning with Stanley Fish, *Surprised by Sin: The Reader in 'Paradise Lost'* (New York: St Martin's Press, 1967), 216–32; Lee A. Jacobus, *Sudden Apprehension: Aspects of Knowledge in 'Paradise Lost'* (The Hague: Mouton, 1976), 21–44; Patricia Parker, 'Eve, Evening, and the Labor of Reading in *Paradise Lost*', *English Literary Renaissance*, 9 (1979), 319–42; Parker, 'Coming Second: Woman's Place', in *Literary Fat Ladies* (New York: Methuen, 1987), esp. 191–201; Mary Nyquist, 'The Genesis of Gendered Subjectivity in the Divorce Tracts and in *Paradise Lost*', in Mary Nyquist and Margaret Ferguson (eds.), *Re-membering Milton*, (New York: Methuen, 1987), 99–127; Diane Kelsey McColley, *Milton's Eve* (Urbana: University of Illinois Press, 1983), 74–89; Christine Froula, 'When Eve Reads Milton', *Critical Inquiry*, 10 (1983), 321–47; and, for its associations with gazing more broadly in the poem, Regina Schwartz, 'Through the Optic Glass: Voyeurism and *Paradise Lost*', in Valeria Finucci and Regina Schwartz (eds.), *Desire in the Renaissance; Psychoanalysis and Literature*, (Princeton: Princeton University Press, 1994), 146–66, also the editors' 'Introduction: Worlds Within and Without'. For an example of more recent analysis, see, 'The Figure in the Pool: Milton's Epistemology of Nature', in Diana B. Altegoer, *Reckoning Words: Baconian Science and the Construction of Truth in English Renaissance Culture* (Madison: Fairleigh Dickinson University Press, 2000), 137–65.

an invisible inner space not unlike the visible walkways kept clear in their daily work, and turned each in reflection toward the other and their interior existence of shared affection and pleasure. 'Grateful digressions' dissolved the pressure to know more, left disorderly mystery tolerable.

Milton's Eve, tempted by an apparent reduction of all divine mystery to a literal fruit—a reduction of mystery to consumption that is death—deliberately bypasses 'Grateful digressions' that swerve like God away from ends. Instead she falls for the temptation to reach straight for an end—an end to ignorance. By the end of the poem, her mind's inner eyes and ears preside over not an elevated view of earth from above but instead a fallen yet sacred interior place where the self exists in reflection in the sense of clearest self-perception and deepest thought with an inner ear open to God. The discovery of that space of thought happens in struggle with her consumption of the world through the eye but especially through the ear—that ever open, although deeply convoluted, entrance to the brain. The deepest reflection and knowledge will become an experience of hearing one's self and God as sound, not of seeing an image. In contrast, Adam receives his 'fill' of knowledge (XII. 558) from Michael as talk and a panorama of images.

Although Eve appears to understand herself subordinate to Adam in wisdom, God tells Eve that she is Adam's 'image' (IV. 472), and that Adam longs to look on her in the way that she had gazed delighted at her reflection. She reflects Adam back to himself; hence, he calls Eve, 'Best Image of my self and dearer half' (V. 95). God to Adam calls her 'Thy likeness . . . thy other self' (VIII. 450). As God's creation she is an image and reflection of her creator as well, and the poem refers repeatedly to the couple as in Uriel's words 'God's latest Image' (IV. 567). God announces within Raphael's narrative, 'Let us make now Man in our image, Man | In our similitude', referring to Adam and Eve, 'and let them rule' the other forms of earthly life (VII. 519–20). God has many images, including 'the radiant image of his Glory' (III. 63), the Son. To Adam, and to Satan briefly, the pleasure Eve gives is also, paradoxically, that of something different from themselves: a transfixing experience of the goodness, grace, and sufficiency of innocent beauty that, as an image of heavenly beauty, requires and reaches for nothing more. In her intense, complex relationship to images—being an image for so much—and in her relationship to reflection in the root sense of flexing, bending, turning light and pleasure back (although 'back I turnd', she remembers, deflected from the first sight of Adam to find her 'watry' image), mankind's first mother gives painful birth to a place of suspension within the self where one turns or flexes back into self-reflection and insight, a private home of thought and conscience, unassailable by external voices or images.

In Milton's age of new scientific interest in the behaviour of light and sound waves and the physical processes of reflection and refraction of light, the verb 'to reflect' and the noun and adjective 'reflection' and 'reflective' carried a range of meanings. Generally the words pointed either to the literal physical reflection of light, colour, or heat—the sense in which Milton uses the word 'reflection' in the poem (III. 428, VII. 367)—or to a figurative turning back of other kinds: for example, to reflect disgrace or discredit back on a person, or to experience the mind's eye and vision as a reflection of spiritual light. 'Shine inward', calls the narrator to the holy Light that he invokes in book III, 'and the mind through all her powers | Irradiate, there plant eyes' (III. 52–3), eyes to receive and send back the light. The speaker's words, that begin in dark with 'thoughts, that voluntarie move | Harmonious numbers' (III. 37–8), become a reflection of sacred light.

Beginning in shallow reflection suspended over the image of her face and the sky, Eve's small internal life of thought will be invaded and shaped through her ear first by God's, then by Adam's, and then by Satan's voice that will mimic and alter God's commands. A night-time dream landscape will separate her temporarily from Adam, as Satan's voice reaches into her mind, and later will become indistinguishable from her thought. She loses her way without but especially within—in her fall plunges through the reflecting pool's surface, as it were, to a solitary new interior place where she begins to see herself more deeply, hear her own thought, and speak with a voice that reflects the fallen experience of solitary reflection as interior vision. Adam is associated by the narrator specifically with reasoned thought: first with 'contemplation' (IV. 297, V. 511), which etymologically (*con* + *templum*) means to survey, behold, observe in an open place, and then with 'speculation' whose Latin roots also link its movement with surveying but with spying too, seeing from on high as from a *specula* or watchtower. Both words with their senses of surveying a visible field carry connotations of authority and observation, of control, through knowledge. Hence, Adam, 'formd', according to the narrator, for contemplation and control of Eve through his reason, is elated that Raphael promises him step-by-step ascent to a godlike perspective through contemplation of the hierarchical scale of created things; hence, Adam climbs with Michael to the top of Paradise's highest hill and later descends from 'this top | Of Speculation' (XII. 588–9) where he has learned 'his fill', been filled up with the future.

Hence, Satan who has lowered himself into the body of the serpent yet craves the heights of godhead tells Eve that eating the forbidden fruit altered him. 'Sated', he resembles Adam from a week earlier, 'in Heav'n' (VIII. 210) from speculation, although Adam experienced an insatiable appetite for Raphael's words.

> I spar'd not, for such pleasure till that hour
> At Feed or Fountain never had I found.
> Sated at length, ere long I might perceave
> Strange alteration in me, to degree
> Of Reason in my inward Powers, and Speech
> Wanted not long, . . .
> Thenceforth to Speculations high or deep
> I turnd my thoughts, and with capacious mind
> Considerd all things visible in Heav'n,
> Or Earth, or Middle, all things fair and good. (IX. 596–605)

Unlike speculation or even contemplation, the processes of reflection, I propose, are associated specifically with Eve; from being an image that reflects back others, she falls through images in withdrawing her attention inward. Her reflection becomes a bending back, as the etymology suggests, but to turn eyes and also ears onto one's self to hear one's inner voice. Another, though obscure, meaning of 'to reflect', in the seventeenth century, according to the *OED*, was 'to bring back from anger or estrangement, to appease', which Eve accomplishes through her voice of desperate self-reflection: she wins Adam back from his anger.

THE EAR'S LABYRINTH

Interest in the role of the ear's structure in intercepting and interpreting sound for the brain has been called 'essentially a 17th-century development': in Milton's lifetime, acoustical theories and theories about music, as well as comparisons of audible and visual reflection, were being developed and discussed by experimental scientists from Bacon to Hooke and Newton.[4] Early modern perceptions of hearing linked music and

[4] Penelope Gouk, 'The Role of Acoustics and Music Theory in the Scientific Work of Robert Hooke', *Annals of Science*, 37 (1980), 595; see also Gouk, 'Some English Theories of Hearing in the Seventeenth Century: Before and after Descartes', in Charles Burnett, Michael Fend, and Penelope Gouk (eds.), *The Second Sense: Studies in Hearing and Musical Judgement from Antiquity to the Seventeenth Century* (London: Warburg Institute, University of London, 1991), 95–113; and Gouk, *Music, Science and Natural Magic in Seventeenth-Century England* (New Haven: Yale University Press, 1999).

rhetorical eloquence in their primary appeal to the ear and, through the ear, to the stirring and ordering of both the passions and the mind. Control of another's ear was control of his or her thought and body. 'For the eare', writes George Puttenham in 1589,

> is properly but an instrument of conveyance for the minde, to apprehend the sence by the sound. And our speech is made melodious or harmonicall, not onely by strayned tunes, as those of Musick, but also by choice of smoothe words: . . . to say truly, what els is man but his minde? which, whosoever have skil to compasse, and make yeelding and flexible, what may not he commaund the body to perfourme? He therefore that hath vanquished the minde of man, hath made the greatest and most glorious conquest. But the minde is not assailable unlesse it be by sensible approaches, whereof the audible is of greatest force for instruction or discipline.[5]

Puttenham's ideas about the close connection between hearing, thought, and will are echoed in anatomist Helkiah Crooke's *Mikrokosmographia* (1615), the earliest English account of hearing from an anatomical perspective. Crooke notes that Aristotle called the ear '*Sensum disciplinæ*, because it was created for the understanding of Arts and Sciences'.[6] We learn things through hearing more easily than through reading, he observes, because 'a voyce doth more affect us by reason of his inflexion and insinuation into our Sense, whereas reading is onely a dumbe Actor'.[7] Things heard, stated Crooke, make a deeper impression on our minds than things seen, a view that again essentially echoes Aristotle: 'seeing, regarded as a supply for the primary wants of life, and its direct effects, is the superior sense; but for developing intelligence, and in its indirect consequences, hearing takes the precedence'.[8] *Paradise Lost* stages a drama about hearing and knowledge in which the ear becomes internalized in silent reflection—reflection through which the eyes and ears are turned outside-in—and an original voice of penitence, a new *sound* of new knowledge, emerges. Helkiah Crooke had identified already the physical connections between the ear and the tongue, which I come to below.

Phoebus Apollo touches the 'trembling ears' of the narrator of 'Lycidas' (77) with exhortations to a life of poetry and fame, but elsewhere

[5] George Puttenham, *The Arte of English Poesie: A Facsimile Reproduction*, introd. Baxter Hathaway (Kent State, Oh.: Kent State University Press, 1970), iii. xix. 207.

[6] Helkiah Crooke, *Mikrokosmographia: A Description of the body of man. Together with the controuersies thereto belonging. Collected and translated out of all the best authors of anatomy, especially out of Gasper Bauhinus and Andreas Laurentius* (London: William Jaggard, 1615), 573.

[7] Ibid. 698.

[8] Aristotle, *De Sensu et Sensili* (1. 437a406).

Milton draws attention to ears as more dangerously passive and permeable, subject to enchantment, labyrinthine entrances to the will and, indirectly, to the mouth that sings and eats. Perhaps his most startling image of ears enslaved appears in a passage he added to the penultimate sentence of the second edition of *Eikonoklastes* (1650), in his frustration at the 'herd' consuming *Eikon Basilike*, who 'inchanted with these popular institutes of Tyranny, subscrib'd with a new device of the Kings Picture at his praiers, hold out both thir eares with such delight and ravishment to be stigmatiz'd and board through in witness of thir own voluntary and beloved baseness'.[9] The people's worship of the king's icon brands them like criminals; their bored ears, ready for chains, carry the stamp of the authority that once clipped Puritans' ears.

Particularly in *Comus* (1632) and *Paradise Lost*, however, Milton dramatizes the dangers of vulnerability to seductive voices through the ear by imagining the vulnerability not of a poet but of an innocent female: the virginal Lady of *Comus* and the married yet unfallen Eve. Each is physically invaded and led through her listening ear by a deceiving voice, initially at night when her eyes are closed or can see little, and each becomes in danger of profound transformation and loss of self by being tempted to taste, an eating that would translate the metaphoric and passive ingestion of false words through the ear into active, literal consumption of death through the mouth. The Lady of *Comus* dramatizes the delicacy and vulnerability of the ear, as well as the poet's sharp sense of the physical invasion possible first through the ears and then through the mouth that eats and can pollute the self's integrity. Comus is transfixed at first by the sound of the lost Lady's song, but his voice in response is the deceptive lyrical prelude to the poisonous cup he holds at her lips with the offer, 'Be wise, and taste.—' (l. 813). Similarly Satan tries to 'reach' into sleeping Eve through her ear to the 'Organs of her Fancy' (IV. 801–2); the winged figure in her dream then held the forbidden fruit 'Even to my mouth' (V. 83), she reports, and tempted her to taste. In both cases, eating would translate the metaphoric and passive ingestion of false words through the ear into literal consumption of evil, even death, through the mouth. Earlier Satan had 'infus'd | Bad influence into th' unwarie brest' (IV. 694–5) of half-sleeping Beelzebub through the ear. To possess the sleeping serpent's 'brutal sense | In heart and head', he enters its mouth whereby disguised he can speak to Eve's waking ear. *Paradise Lost* keeps us constantly aware of the competition between heavenly and

[9] John Milton, *The Complete Prose Works of John Milton*, ed. Don M. Wolfe et al. 8 vols. (New Haven: Yale University Press, 1953–82), iii. 203.

hellish speakers for human ears and mouths, a contest that happens within the context of a blind narrator's reception of his song brought 'nightly to my Ear' (IX. 47) and his seduction of our ear. Flattering and commanding voices have both personal and political stories to tell.[10]

The ear that stays open day and night becomes the crucial battleground in this poem. That 'men can be "led by the ear" had become a favorite topos among humanist writers on rhetoric by the end of the sixteenth century', Quentin Skinner notes.[11] Lucian's account of the ancient Gauls' representation of Hercules as both strong and exceptionally eloquent, drawing followers by fetters attached at one end to Hercules' tongue and at the other to his listeners' ears, was well known.[12] Helkiah Crooke, however, held a more cheerful view of the ear's relation to the tongue. His detailed anatomical discussion of the ears makes clear that the instrument of hearing is not the external but the internal ear, whose second cavity or Labyrinth is full of 'Meanders' 'like a Connyburrough'; the 'cavities or holes, saith *Aquapendens*, are so innumerable and intricated one with another, that it may well be called a Labyrinth. For their number they are rather to be admired then numbred, neither can a man finde any order in them'.[13] He divides the inner ear into the Labyrinth and the *Cochlea* or the 'Snaile-shell'.[14] In two consecutive sections of his treatise, Crooke connects the ears, through the labyrinthine inner ear, to the mouth and throat; he connects hearing and speaking through anatomical 'sympathy' or 'communion'. He names two inner, physical

[10] On the political landscape of *Paradise Lost*, see, for example, Mary Ann Radzinowicz, 'The Politics of *Paradise Lost*', in Kevin Sharpe and Steven N. Zwicker, *Politics of Discourse: The Literature and History of Seventeenth-Century England* (Berkeley and Los Angeles: University of California Press, 1987), 204–229; Stephen M. Buhler, 'Kingly States: The Politics in *Paradise Lost*', *Milton Studies*, 28 (1992), 49–68; Steven Zwicker, 'The Politics of Pleasure: *Annus Mirabilis*, *The Last Instructions*, *Paradise Lost*', in his *Lines of Authority: Politics and English Literary Culture, 1649–1689* (Ithaca, NY: Cornell University Press, 1993), 90–129, esp. 119–29; David Quint, *Epic and Empire: Politics and Generic Form from Virgil to Milton* (Princeton: Princeton University Press, 1993); David Armitage, Armand Himy, and Quentin Skinner (eds.), *Milton and Republicanism* (Cambridge: Cambridge University Press, 1995); Charles Cantalupo, 'By Art Is Created That Great . . . State': Milton's *Paradise Lost* and Hobbes's *Leviathan*', in Margo Swiss and David A. Kent (eds.), *Heirs of Fame* (Lewisburg, Pa: Bucknell University Press, 1995), 184–207; Martin J. Evans, *Milton's Imperial Epic: 'Paradise Lost' and the Discourse of Colonialism* (Ithaca, NY: Cornell University Press, 1996).

[11] Quentin Skinner, 'Thomas Hobbes on the Proper Signification of Liberty', *Transactions of the Royal Historical Society*, 40 (1990), 137. See also Skinner, *Reason and Rhetoric in the Philosophy of Hobbes* (Cambridge: Cambridge University Press, 1996), 92–3.

[12] Skinner, 'Thomas Hobbes', 137. On the importance of the Gallic Hercules for Renaissance perceptions of rhetoric, with reference to allusions to the fable in texts and iconography, see Wayne Rebhorn, *The Emperor of Men's Minds: Literature and the Renaissance Discourse of Rhetoric* (Ithaca, NY: Cornell University Press, 1995), 66–74.

[13] Crooke, *Mikrokosmographia*, 573, 604.

[14] Ibid. 604.

connections: a large branch of the auditory nerve goes into the ear and carries sounds thence to the brain, while a lesser branch runs to the ears and the tongue; secondly, 'a gristly Canale like a water-pipe' connects the inner ear to the mouth and palate, allowing air to run between.

The best learning, stresses Crooke, takes place through a pleasurable mix of talk and hearing; only live discourse provides a memorable aural and intellectual feast. Hearing is easier than reading, and we are 'more recreated' by hearing than reading because 'there is a kinde of society in narration and acting, which is very agreeable to the nature of man':

> we have opportunity to demaund a reason of some doubts from him which speaketh to us; . . . books cannot digresse from their discourse for the better explication of a thing, as those may which teach by their voice. For in changing of words and mutuall conference, many pleasant passages are brought in by accident. . . . And by these sauces, as it were, of discourse, is the Hearing more sumptuously feasted.[15]

Milton's narrator similarly describes Eve's preference for a feast of discourse with Adam, when she could 'demaund a reason of some doubts'—just as she aired a question in book IV—rather than listening while Raphael and Adam converse. Talking with her, Adam would bring in 'pleasant passages . . . by accident'; he 'would intermix | Grateful digressions, and solve high dispute | With conjugal Caresses' (VIII. 54–6). Adam will use the metaphor of eating for hearing as he listens to, feasts on, Raphael's words after their literal feasting, and Adam's vocabulary in Book VIII prepares for Eve's ear being feasted by Satan in book IX to make her 'taste', feed herself to death, unlike the Lady in *Comus*.

In one of his first speeches Milton's God creates, with the verb 'to place', an invisible place within fallen man, home to a heavenly interior voice. This place suggests the need for a figurative inner ear sharper than Crooke's labyrinth, whose hearing brings the light of understanding, whose deafness brings inner darkness:

> . . . I will place within them as a guide
> My Umpire Conscience, whom if they will hear,
> Light after light well us'd they shall attain,
> And to the end persisting, safe arrive.
> This my long sufferance and my day of grace
> They who neglect and scorn, shall never taste;
> But hard be hard'nd, blind be blinded more,
> That they may stumble on, and deeper fall. (III. 194–201)

[15] Ibid. 698.

The off-rhymes—'my day of grace' and 'shall never taste' (III. 198–9), then 'blind be blinded more' and 'stumble on, and deeper fall' (III. 200–1)—emphasize how the elevation of other senses seems to depend on this most subtle inner ear.

Joel Fineman drew attention to the peculiarly Renaissance and rhetorical concatenation of ears, eyes, and mouth or voice: to Renaissance representations of the ear as a mazelike 'instrument of delay and deferral' and 'momentous suspense' and to the period's sensitivity to the relations through textuality of the consumption of language, sexuality, and ideology.[16] In 'Shakespeare's Ear', he recalls the following lines on 'Hearing' by Elizabethan poet Sir John Davies from his long philosophical poem on the soul, *Nosce Teipsum* (1599). Where Crooke represents the inner ear's labyrinth as nature's way to convey more sharply refined sound to the brain, Davies's 'Wickets of the Soule' serve a different function: they diffuse and temper sound. The poet's description recalls the mix of euphoric dawdling and self-bewilderment of Ovid's Daedalus in the midst of his creation, reviewed in this volume's Introduction. Davies's 'labyrinth' anticipates the competition between ears and another, a more protected, interior space for listening and talk in *Paradise Lost*:

> These Wickets of the Soule are plac'd on hie,
> Because all sounds do lightly mount aloft;
> And that they may not pierce too violently,
> They are delayed with turnes, and windings oft.
>
> For should the voice directly strike the braine,
> It would astonish and confuse it much;
> Therefore these plaits and folds the sound restraine,
> That it the Organ may more gently touch.
>
> As Streames, which with their winding banks do play,
> Stopt by their Creeks, run softly through the plaine,
> So in the Eares labyrinth the voyce doth stray,
> And doth with easie motion touch the braine.
>
> It is the slowest yet the daintiest Sense.[17]

As will Satan, Davies imagines the fastidious, delicate ear as a gateway to the soul but one in whose winding passages the voice strays, slows, and softens so far that the effect of words appears to be exquisitely tempered. The ear's labyrinth is designed to suspend the potentially shocking force

[16] Joel Fineman, 'Shakespeare's Ear', *Representations*, 28 (Fall 1989), 6–13.

[17] Sir John Davies, *The Poems of Sir John Davies*, ed. Robert Krueger (Oxford: Clarendon Press, 1975), 38.

of words to the brain yet retain their subtle, persuasive pressure. Robert Erickson, in his persuasive reading of Satan as 'a perverse, demonic seventeenth-century anatomist', seems correct in calling his invasion of Eve's body 'a protracted rape', although the anatomist is not allowed to touch Eve's body.[18] Milton's sensitivity to the physically invasive pressure of aural persuasion understands the insidious danger that the listening ear's labyrinth may conduct a voice's words so easily to the brain that the divine, not anatomical, inner ear and voice, which exist to balance the outer, are never engaged, like home watchdogs that sleep through the crime. The invading voice seems to belong to, easily merge with, the invaded.

To 'justifie the wayes of God to men', Milton must justify what appears to fallen eyes as God's highly indirect, labyrinthine ways to bring his universe to fulfilment—a divine plan that appears to lurch forward and backward, winding with interminable waiting through dark detours of human misery. As Adam and Eve questioned what seemed the mysterious waste of too many stars and too much fruit rotting on the vine, men have wondered about the excess and waste of pain in such a plan. As examples on a small scale of God's natural order that characteristically absorbs diversions, *Paradise Lost* includes the mazes and branching of vegetation and streams in Paradise, the intricate angelic songs and labyrinth dances in heaven (V. 618–27), along with the leisurely pleasures and delays of digression exemplified in miniature by the 'Grateful digressions' of unfallen Adam and Eve. Forms of heavenly abundance and variety, including excess and digressions, are here characteristic of divine creativity and harmony, and they contrast with the imprisoning rigidity, the hellish mazes, of the transgressor's unrepentant, impatient mind and of emotions like hate fixed in an unswerving line of revenge.

The text's own unhurried expansiveness, such as Milton's time-looping and time-stopping 'Grateful digressions' into the worlds of epic similes, into personal addresses by the narrator and autobiographical recollections by various speakers, and into prophecy emphasize the experience of reflection and relation. The digressions diffuse the seduction of finality, curb that most dangerous appetite—including the reader's—for the end, for death. Here amplification functions not only as an exercise in classical *copia*, to be rejected ultimately along with all epic grandeur, but as an experience of the delay and seeming frustration of divine progress through digression. The poet's complex and suspended

[18] Robert A. Erickson, *The Language of the Heart, 1600–1750* (Philadelphia: University of Pennsylvania Press, 1997), ch. 3, 89–90, 94.

harmonies mimic the mysterious, divine mode of intermixture and, to fallen perception, of delay and digression to effect human salvation. Characterized by winding indirection, copious detail, and suspension of ends, God's plan becomes impossible to subvert. From a divine perspective there is no hurry and no end.

From the late seventeenth and eighteenth centuries onward, readers have observed the parallels between the teasing, testing, almost unlimited invitation to consume and worship extended by Adam and Eve's creator and by the creator of this poem's bewildering abundance that also invites a huge appetite and grateful praise. In what follows, I first highlight how a number of early readers' responses to the poem and the poet's voice, their impatience with Milton's digressions and aggressive displays of learning, first drew attention to the fact that Adam and Eve's peculiar experience of the pressures of abundance resembles the reader's experience inside this heavenly poem. Richardson noted that 'a Reader of Milton must be Always upon Duty; he is Surrounded with Sense, it rises in every Line'.[19] And the poem, like the garden, imposes its anxieties along with its demands of grateful orisons; Milton expresses gratitude for its bounty in the invocations, and he likewise expects the 'fit audience' (VII. 31) to enjoy and consume. 'Eate freely with glad heart' (VIII. 322), God invites Adam who with Eve is 'fit' though few, 'fear here no dearth'; and the poem overflows with evidence of its creator's exuberance and delight—the beauties of aural sensation at every turn and wandering streams of syntax. Milton ensures that we consume his poem with our ears as well as with eyes and mouth.

The tease of human and divine abundance and multiplicity becomes most provocative in the garden where I centre this chapter. Among the sprawling vines, overripe fruit, and clouds of fragrance occur a clash and modulation between visible and invisible, exterior and interior worlds. I follow the digressive progress of an obtrusive question that appears in book IV, Eve's to Adam about the stars that shine unseen all night to no one's delight, eyes that receive no answering look. The question winds like a meandering underground stream in Paradise—through Eve's dream, Raphael's visit, and the Fall—to emerge as Eve's new and penitent voice at X. 914–36. For all of her visible ornament, Eve evolves through secrecy, through dreams and silences, and through gaps that she creates and fills. She was originally what Adam and Paradise lacked, the conspicuous absence; and her creation to complete him required Adam to lose a

[19] Jonathan Richardson, father and son, *Explanatory Notes and Remarks on Milton's 'Paradise Lost'* (London: Jame, John, and Paul Knapton, 1734), p. cxliv.

rib. From a trance he had witnessed her fashioning; then afterwards 'She disappeerd, and left me dark' (VIII. 478). Not long lost, she reappears and Adam sees 'my Self | Before me'—his demand for a bodily self-reflection and complement in contrast to Eve's delight with a watery image. But she threatened to disappear again, and he retrieved her. The narration twists back and forth: between Adam who feels hollow then complete, then weakened within by 'the charm of Beauties powerful glance' (VIII. 533), between Eve lost to and then found by Adam, then lost again and found by herself. Milton describes a convoluted, halting progress: a rib is lost, Paradise lost, all to create not more exterior worlds but an invisible, interior home to human depth, the paradise of reflection. And Eve's trail of alternating revelation and secrecy, of fullness and depletion, reflects the pointedly agonistic, digressive movement of the poem.

For Milton creates the garden as an anachronism that he will leave behind. Thirty years beyond the pastoral elegy which announced his graduation from a lyric apprenticeship, and with almost twenty years of polemical prose behind him, Milton reclaimed copious fertility and gardens from the Stuart Restoration only to expose again the anachronism of pastoral and claim the wilderness of invisible, interior growth as his home. The passionate writer of *The Readie and Easie Way* had addressed a nation that in his eyes did not know how to wait and labour patiently to bring the promise of liberty to fruition but instead was treading backwards away from self-knowledge and responsibility to an infantile state of bondage that required less work and thought. Indeed the importance of waiting for fruition of poetic and prophetic promise had long been a crucial theme of Milton's work. Now the fruit of Eve's mazy story is the long-awaited birth not of her first child but more importantly of an interior domestic space for thought—a home for the inner ear and inner voice of experience. The seductive illusion of perfect vision and visibility, of Eve's elaborate, ornamental exterior that made her seem to Adam as 'in her self compleat' (VIII. 548) as she had felt first in reflection, will be plumbed through the ear to dramatize Milton's late aesthetics of the heroic labour and sound of self-knowledge.

'NONE EVER WISHED IT LONGER THAN IT IS'

'What an Expansion of Facts from a Small Seed of History! What Worlds are Invented!'[20] Not only Jonathan Richardson in his edition of *Paradise*

[20] Ibid., p. clix.

Lost (1734) but the theory and practice of epic from antiquity up to the Renaissance associated sublimity with expansive imagination and copious invention, a long, convoluted narrative design and sweeping historical perspectives, 'elaborate formulaic figures', extended similes—and frequent digression.[21] Digression and *copia* inhere in the nature of epic as Milton shows us while he nods his debt to the models and authorities whom he had surpassed. From Homer to Ovid and Virgil, from the Bible to Dante, Ariosto, Tasso, and Spenser—the critical literature has followed where the poet pointed.[22] Scholarship has traced his copious reading and detailed the sources of the epic traditions on which he drew for the long narrations by Raphael and Michael.[23] Yet this chapter's interest in Miltonic digression begins in the observation that the poet simultan-

[21] Recent work on Milton's reformation of epic includes Catherine Gimelli Martin, *The Ruins of Allegory: 'Paradise Lost' and the Metamorphosis of Epic Convention* (Durham, NC: Duke University Press, 1998), and Patrick J. Cook, *Milton, Spenser and the Epic Tradition* (Brookfield, Vt.: Scolar Press, 1996). For Renaissance critical theory about epic, see Bernard Weinberg, *A History of Literary Criticism in the Italian Renaissance*, 2 vols. (Chicago: University of Chicago Press, 1963); see also Mindele Anne Treip, *Allegorical Poetics and the Epic: The Renaissance Tradition to 'Paradise Lost'* (Lexington: University of Kentucky Press, 1994). On Milton's epic style, see Christopher Ricks, *Milton's Grand Style* (Oxford: Clarendon Press, 1963); F. T. Prince. 'Milton's Blank Verse: The Diction' and 'Milton's Blank Verse: The Prosody', in *The Italian Element in Milton's Verse*, rev. edn. (Oxford: Clarendon Press, 1962); Lindsay Waters, 'Milton, Tasso, and the Renaissance Grand Style and its Effect on the Reader', *Stanford Italian Review*, 2 (1981), 81–92. See also Francis C. Blessington, *'Paradise Lost' and the Classical Epic* (Boston: Routledge & Kegan Paul, 1979); Barbara Kiefer Lewalski, *'Paradise Lost' and the Rhetoric of Literary Forms* (Princeton: Princeton University Press, 1985); Joan Webber, '*Paradise Lost*', in *Milton and his Epic Tradition* (Seattle: University of Washington Press, 1979), 103–63; Richard J. DuRocher, *Milton and Ovid* (Ithaca, NY: Cornell University Press, 1985).

[22] Besides the sources noted above, see also D. M. Rosenberg, *Oaten Reeds and Trumpets: Pastoral and Epic in Virgil, Spenser, and Milton* (Lewisburg, Pa.: Bucknell University Press, 1981); Jason P. Rosenblatt, *Torah and Law in 'Paradise Lost'* (Princeton: Princeton University Press, 1994); Davis P. Harding, *The Club of Hercules: Studies in the Classical Background of 'Paradise Lost'*, Illinois Studies in Language and Literature: University of Illinois Press 50 (Urbana: University of Illinois Press, 1962); William M. Porter, *Reading the Classics and 'Paradise Lost'* (Lincoln: University of Nebraska Press, 1993); Mary Ann Radzinowicz, *Milton's Epics and the Book of Psalms* (Princeton: Princeton University Press, 1989); Stella P. Revard, *The War in Heaven: 'Paradise Lost' and the Tradition of Satan's Rebellion* (Ithaca, NY: Cornell University Press 1980), and her 'The Heroic Context of Book IX of *Paradise Lost*', *JEGP* 87 (1988), 329–41; John M. Steadman, *Milton's Biblical and Classical Imagery* (Pittsburgh: Duquesne University Press, 1984).

[23] Anna K. Nardo, 'Academic Interludes in *Paradise Lost*', *Milton Studies*, 27 (1991): 209–41; Ann Coiro, ' "To Repair the Ruins of our First Parents": "Of Education" and Fallen Adam', 28 (1988), 133–47; Michael Allen, 'Divine Instruction: *Of Education* and the Pedagogy of Raphael, Michael, and the Father', *Milton Quarterly*, 26 (1992), 113–21; Regina M. Schwartz, *Remembering and Repeating: Biblical Creation in 'Paradise Lost'* (1988; rep. Chicago: University of Chicago Press, 1993).

eously sounds the depths of epic and writes himself through and out of epic's fabular abundance as he writes Adam and Eve out of Paradise.

Paradise Lost is a spectacular exercise in amplification: the poet's learning, languages, and rhetorical skills enabled him to extend and suspend the story of Genesis 1–3 for over 10,000 lines of blank verse, to prepare yet delay his reader through nine books to witness man's fall. Milton's masterful blank verse sentence capable of being suspended unresolved over many lines resembles the long suspended sentence of God's law whose full meaning is withheld until the last. Particularly the suspended worlds of Milton's epic similes, those leisurely digressions characterized by one critic as 'faerie' or 'twilight' zones of poetry 'in and for itself', have provoked interest since Milton's earliest readers.[24] Alert to the poem's habits of omniscience, of a Janus-eyed suspension, scholars such as Christopher Ricks have examined the 'variously divisible' openness of Milton's expansive Latinate diction and 'syntactical fluidity', while H. R. MacCallum has remarked on the 'loops in time' of Michael's narrative, a phrase descriptive also of the whole poem's digressive, redundant narrative, characteristic of what John Tanner calls Milton's 'economy of abundance'.[25] He who in *Paradise Regained* will dismiss classical learning as 'false, or little else but dreams, | Conjectures, fancies', and affirm that 'many books, | Wise men have said are wearisome' (IV. 291–2, 321–2), in *Paradise Lost* signals easy familiarity with and mastery of the classics at almost every line. He digresses in and beyond the footsteps of their digressions, prompting Richardson's assessment that 'he is an Ancient', and we 'read Homer and Virgil in reading Him'.[26]

Other eighteenth-century readers of *Paradise Lost* could not respond with Richardson's unqualified delight in the poem's wandering, self-conscious grandeur, its displays of erudition, the perpetually demanding detail and hidden mysteries of its *copia*. With a command of classical

[24] James Whaler's work on Milton's epic similes ('The Miltonic Simile', *PMLA* 46 (1931) 1034–74) has been extended by numerous scholars, including Christopher Ricks *Milton's Grand Style*; Fish, *Surprised by Sin*; Geoffrey Hartman, 'Milton's Counterplot', *ELH* 25 (1958), 1–12; Anne D. Ferry, *Milton's Epic Voice: The Narrator in 'Paradise Lost'* (Cambridge, Mass.: Harvard University Press, 1963); Michael Murrin, 'The Language of Milton's Heaven', *Modern Philology*, 74 (1977), 350–65; Patricia Parker, *Inescapable Romance: Studies in the Poetics of a Mode* (Princeton: Princeton University Press, 1979), 'Milton', 114–58.

[25] Ricks, *Milton's Grand Style*; H. R. MacCallum, 'Milton and Sacred History: Books XI and XII of *Paradise Lost*', in Millar MacLure and F. W. Watt (eds.), *Essays in English Literature from the Renaissance to the Victorian Age*, (Toronto: University of Toronto Press, 1964), 166; John S. Tanner, *Anxiety in Eden: A Kierkegaardian Reading of 'Paradise Lost'* (New York: Oxford University Press, 1992), 45.

[26] Richardson, *Explanatory Notes and Remarks on Milton's 'Paradise Lost'*, p. cxlviii.

rhetoric and stylistics, they were outspoken about Milton's indulgence not only in digression but also in an aggressive mystery distinct from sublimity. Addison cites the poet's 'Complaint for his Blindness, his Panegyrick on Marriage, his Reflections on Adam and Eve's going naked, of the Angels eating, and several other Passages' as 'too many digressions', although too beautiful to omit.[27] Johnson similarly granted Milton his seductive 'superfluities'—the personal 'short digressions at the beginning of the third, seventh, and ninth books'.[28] But Addison and others were more impatient with the ostentation of Milton's digressions of learning. By contrast with Homer and Virgil's 'indirect and concealed Manner . . . Milton seems ambitious of letting us know, by his Excursions on Free-Will and Predestination, and his many Glances upon History, Astronomy, Geography, and the like, as well as by the Terms and Phrases he sometimes makes Use of, that he was acquainted with the whole Circle of Arts and Sciences'.[29] Addison's deflation of such 'ambitious' display momentarily lifts the mantle of sublimity from the polemicist who dwells at the centre of this abundance. Despite his stern commands of self-knowledge, temperance, and patience, a competitive, combative poet spins a web of anticipation and echo into which readers are led to wander—hardly an example of Michael's advised moderation (XI. 553).

Joseph Trapp (1715) found inexcusable 'those luxurious Comparisons that deviate from the Subject'. His concern about the 'luxurious' in this Protestant epic, like the doubts of Adam and Eve about their 'too luxuriant' world, identifies a tension built into the poem, and the garden, between the advocation of limitation and proportion and, in the words of another critic, Milton's 'revelling in the luxuriant and unrestrained'.[30] When Johnson wrote 'reality was a scene too narrow for his mind', when he sensed the pressure of the poet's insatiable 'appetite for greatness' and an imagination which demands 'unrestrained indulgence', he touched on a restlessness that the poem simultaneously acts out and condemns. *Paradise Lost* begins in hell with mental restlessness, with the restless thoughts of those perplexed and roving 'advent'rous Bands'. An impatience with physical and mental bounds and for self-authorship and

[27] Joseph Addison, *Spectator*, 297 (1712), quoted in John T. Shawcross (ed.), *Milton: The Critical Heritage* (New York: Barnes & Noble, 1970), 167.

[28] Samuel Johnson, 'Milton', in *Lives of the Poets* (1779), reprinted in part in James Thorpe (ed.), *Milton Criticism: Selections from Four Centuries* (London: Routledge & Kegan Paul, 1951), 75.

[29] Shawcross (ed.), *Milton: The Critical Heritage*, 168.

[30] Marjorie Hope Nicolson, *The Breaking of the Circle* (New York: Columbia University Press, 1960), 186.

revenge drives Satan into and out of hell, Adam and Eve to fall, the narrator to wander through the universe—but also God to proliferate his image, to delight in new reflections, new worlds. Like Eve over her reflection, God hung over the waters of the deep until he saw a new world in himself.

'None ever wished it longer than it is', concluded Johnson wearily. 'We read Milton for instruction, retire harassed and overburdened, and look elsewhere for recreation; we desert our master and seek for companions'—as Adam and Eve seek each other's company against the pressure of God's challenging abundance and mystery.[31] Long the student in preparation, Milton became the master, or taskmaster, with a vengeance. What provokes rebellion against this master is that while he always reminds the reader of the learning which allows him, although blind, a godlike vision as from the 'top | Of Speculation' (XII. 588–9) to see in all directions, he tells a story whose moral comes down to knowing only 'That which before us lies in daily life' (VIII. 193). Raphael similarly seems to tantalize Adam and Eve by alternating the rich imaginative food of extended flights over vistas of heavenly war and earthly creation with abrupt warnings that 'Knowledge is as food, and needs no less | Her Temperance over Appetite'—in the next breath proceeding, 'Know, then . . .'. (VII. 126–31)

But he who knows all can dismiss all. And at the end of Milton's long, lingering farewell to the epic imagination and its babel of voices, this dismissal has occurred in the subtlest split second of modulation, of feet shifting direction, of haste blurred by delay and a flutter of mood—a changing of the guard. For a moment it is possible to wonder whether Adam and Eve or the copious, demanding garden are being banished. The final lines hold in their cautious balance, like those holding hands and slow steps, the tension and ambivalence of both possibilities.[32] Addison would have preferred to omit the last two lines which 'fall very much below the foregoing Passage, and renew in the Mind of the Reader that Anguish which was pretty well laid by that Consideration'.[33] Yet behind the mixed 'Anguish' and nostalgia at displacement, the apprehension yet expectancy at a new start, occurs a quiet separation of mythic *copia* from a private, new voice of digression. The mystery of self-possession becomes interiorized as the sound of 'wandring steps and slow'.[34]

[31] Samuel Johnson, *Lives of the English Poets*, ed. George Birkbeck Hill and Harold S. Scott, 3 vols. (Oxford: Clarendon Press, 1905), vol. i, 'Milton', 183–4.

[32] Parker, *Inescapable Romance*, 158.

[33] Addison, *Spectator*, 369, quoted in Shawcross (ed.), *Milton: The Critical Heritage*, 218.

[34] See *Patricia* Parker, 'Eve, Evening, and the Labor of Reading in *Paradise Lost*', 336.

PARADISE AND THE PRESSURE TO CONSUME

Michael urges on Adam after the fall 'The rule of not too much, by temperance taught | In what thou eatst and drinkst' (XI. 531–2). But the problem of containing 'too much' begins with God's garden where abundance is less a temptation to dissipate than a struggle to focus, as readers have struggled amidst the poetic wealth. When we enter the garden in book IV, we view its creation and containment through Satan's eyes as a strategic offence of war. Paradise represents a divine countermove designed to bring good obliquely out of evil at a safe remove from heaven's precincts. The sensuous abundance and the exhibit of undiminished, unlimited creativity of God's earthly garden not only compensate for God's loss of a third of his angels but represent a new idea, a third party, that complicates the dichotomy of heaven and hell. Angelic troops surround Paradise and reinforce its forbidding wall because the glorious abundance within, especially 'innocent frail man' (IV. 11), has been created in a context of conflict. His being creates a new balance, but as the contested prize Adam and Eve must maintain, each alone as well as together in their marriage, a protected interior space within which to guard their balance and free will.

This novel inner space of man's free will, like the earth suspended between heaven and hell, is hotly contested, but all space is in this universe. When God fills Chaos, for example, the 'Anarch old' shows alarm that his 'Frontiers' have been 'encroacht on' (II. 1001) by a large hell for the rebels and a new world for man. Satan, however, a constricted prisoner of his own hell of hate and pride, makes us most sensitive to a curious connection that God establishes between his authority and his power to fill empty space; after the creation of Paradise which seems to leave no unfilled space within its 'narrow limits' (IV. 384), Satan realizes that man's ear and stomach are signs of a much more subtle interior space to fill.[35] That interior space created for conscience and self-knowledge represents human freedom as a balance that Satan's frenzied, solitary pride will invade and corrupt.

[35] On the importance of the ear for Milton, see, for example, Donald M. Friedman, '*Comus* and the Truth of the Ear', in Claude J. Summers and Ted-Larry Pebworth (eds.), *'The Muses Common-weale': Poetry and Politics in the Seventeenth Century* (Columbia: University of Missouri Press, 1988), 119–34; Joseph F. Loewenstein, *Responsive Readings: Versions of Echo in Pastoral, Epic, and the Jonsonian Masque* (New Haven: Yale University Press, 1984); and Angus Fletcher, *The Transcendental Masque: An Essay on Milton's 'Comus'* (Ithaca, NY: Cornell University Press, 1971), 166.

Images of a fruitful space within, yet in between, hold each other in *Paradise Lost* like nested Chinese boxes: the frail, new world suspended between heaven and hell that claim and patrol it; within Eden and in Satan's eyes the 'narrow room' (IV. 207) of Paradise; within Paradise the protected sanctum of the blissful bower; within the bower Adam and Eve 'Imparadis't in one anothers arms'—and within Eve, the delicate sanctum of inner balance in her ear and in the womb which will bring forth multitudes and ultimately the Son. The heroic, self-creative tasks of Adam and Eve, for which God provides no model, become to plumb their own depths and to possess that inner stand from which to listen and speak. From Satan's internal hell and the birth of Sin in dizzy mental pain so unlike God's painless invention and multiplicity, *Paradise Lost*, like *Upon Appleton House*, begins and ends at 'within'.

This 'frail world', both the visible earth and the invisible space of free will, 'This pendant world' (II. 1051), is a negotiation between fierce absolutes and offers relief from their inexorability.[36] Yet because we enter the garden through Satan's eyes and within the hell of his imprisoned 'fixed mind' of hate, the precarious space mankind occupies feels squeezed from the beginning. The garden is a teasing, mysterious, crowded room—'In narrow room Natures whole wealth, yea more' (IV. 207). Satan's gaze of amazed longing holds the 'more' in suspension at the end of its line. Claustrophobic from mental and physical entrapment, Satan is obsessed with the 'room' he has lost. The space created by his fall has relieved heaven's dangerous congestion; and the new race created to fill, one day, 'our vacant room' in heaven is 'more remov'd, | Least Heav'n surcharg'd with potent multitude' explode again in war (II. 835–7). He sees 'advanc't' into 'our room of bliss' lesser creatures (IV. 359); he mentally addresses Adam and Eve offering them hell's 'room | Not like these narrow limits' (IV. 383–4); in book IX he again recalls the indignity of earthly beings advanced 'into our room' (IX. 148). In this spacious poem with whose narrator we range among heaven, hell, and earth, the protagonists show constant sensitivity whether space is full or empty.

In Raphael's story of creation, the God of infinite dimensions 'And through all numbers absolute, though One', echoes Satan's preoccupations with space, room, and number. Assessing his losses like a military strategist, God finds 'Heav'n yet populous retaines | Number sufficient to possess her Realmes | Though wide, (VII. 146–9). Confirming Satan's fears, Raphael praises the creation of a better race to fill the rebels' 'vacant

[36] Parker, *Inescapable Romance*, 138–49.

room' over time. Meanwhile, every inch of Paradise has been filled; Satan's first vision of the garden as a narrow space struggling to contain its overflowing abundance is never corrected. However infinite in its dimensions and demands on Adam and Eve to consume and prune, from an angelic perspective Paradise shrinks to 'this Rock only' and 'these narrow bounds', in Michael's words (XI. 336, 341), to which God cannot be expected to confine himself.

Even within this confinement, God and Milton push on the boundary between wildness and 'rule or art', between much and too much.[37] *Paradise Lost* is a poem 'suspicious of technology', says William Kerrigan, where 'the overflowing of the useful into the beautiful inheres in the order of nature. It stems from God, and it perplexes Adam and Eve'.[38] But the beautiful overflows into the oppressive. The overreaching 'pamper'd boughs' of Milton's Paradise hide a constant tension between, on the one hand, a mother nature whose profusion invites unchecked indulgence of every sense and, on the other, the orderly habits, hard work, and quiet pleasures and anxieties of the couple set in its midst.

Curiously God extends his divine authority of abundance inward, through the mouth. At the heavenly banquet to celebrate the Son's vice-regency, the angels partake of a groaning board piled with food 'secure | Of surfet where full measure onley bounds | Excess, before th' all bounteous King, who showrd | With copious hand' (V. 638–41). The angels always eat exactly what fills them completely. Added to the 1674 edition of *Paradise Lost*, the preceding lines emphasize that in heaven 'the concept of immoderation is displaced by a perfect food', a heavenly version of Eve's new-born experience of perfect sufficiency in her reflection. God produces endlessly for his creatures, angels and man alike, to eat all they want, to know that they will always be filled, always hunger more, and always be able to eat more.[39] Adam and Eve serve Raphael a splendour of fruits 'which our Nourisher', says Adam, 'from whom | All perfet good unmeasur'd out, descends', has provided 'for food and for

[37] That hair's breadth separating abundance and surfeit tests even sharp-eyed Uriel's judgement: while accustomed to brightness 'beyond expression', the angel pauses over the distinction between 'seems excess' and 'no excess' as he considers the wandering cherub's wish to approach and admire man but fails to perceive Satan in disguise (III. 696–8).

[38] William Kerrigan, *The Sacred Complex: On the Psychogenesis of Paradise Lost* (Cambridge, Mass.: Harvard University Press, 1983),290.

[39] In the 1667 edition, more simply 'They eat, they drink, and with refection sweet Are filled, before the all bounteous king'. See W. Gardner Campbell, 'Paradisal Appetite and Cusan Food in *Paradise Lost*', in Kirstin Pruitt McColgan and Charles W. Durham (eds.), *Arenas of Conflict* (Selinsgrove, Pa.: Susquehanna University Press, 197), 244.

delight' (V. 398–400). God pours out 'unmeasur'd' delight, as the ever-growing garden testifies, but man must be aware of measure in order to organize and enjoy heavenly abundance, whether of food or words. After the Fall, God anticipates revenge on his hellish enemies as a lurid stuffing of mouths shut: Sin and Death will cram disgusting food down their throats and then themselves become crammed into the mouth of hell as the final obstruction and seal. They will

> . . . lick up the draff and filth
> Which mans polluting Sin with taint hath shed
> On what was pure, till cramm'd and gorg'd, nigh burst
> With suckt and glutted offal, at one sling
> Of thy victorious Arm, well-pleasing Son,
> Both Sin, and Death, and yawning Grave at last
> Through Chaos hurld, obstruct the mouth of Hell
> For ever, and seal up his ravenous Jawes. (X. 630–7)

The 'yawning Grave', the 'ravenous Jawes' of hell's mouth: the mouth of nightmare is bottomless, insatiable, when open. God does not eat in this poem of eating, but he externalizes rewards and punishments as endless food—what fills emptiness and satisfies hunger or, in the case of hell, satiates to suffocation.

Adam and Eve experience the authority of plenty in the garden as God's command to 'Eat freely with glad heart', to fear no dearth among ceaseless growth and variety that is both a gift and a reminder of subjection. Man's limited capacity to consume can never match heaven's unlimited capacity to produce. The act of consumption as a substitute for the godly pleasures of creation as self-reflection, and as a substitute for knowledge—with the exception of the fruit of the Tree of Knowledge—is pressed on the couple. Eve's eating of the apple dramatizes the extraordinary pressure of the garden, of God, to claim and fill their space—their external but also internal bounds.

Barbara Lewalski has argued that 'Adam and Eve, like the Garden, have natures capable of a prodigious growth of good things, but which require constant pruning . . . constant direction of overreaching tendencies, constant propping of weaknesses'; yet the two appear almost too busy for self-indulgence.[40] For immortals notably conscious of the demands of time, they worry about waste and haste and untidiness as fruit rots on the

[40] Barbara Kiefer Lewalski, 'Innocence and Experience in Milton's Eden', in Thomas Kranidas (ed.), *New Essays on* 'Paradise Lost' (Berkeley and Los Angeles: University of California Press, 1969), 94.

ground. When Eve's bad dreams cause her to oversleep, they 'haste' late to their work, the word repeated (V. 136, 211); they hurry to discipline disorderly nature whose growth requires daily correction. Later Eve describes the garden as 'Tending to wilde' (IX. 212). Adam and Eve must teach their plants, and exemplify, the proper habits of mutual dependence and support. Yet the pressures of this heavenly excess provoke an equivalent outreach in them but inwardly—an elusive, mental wandering that temporarily separates each from the other.[41] For despite their work of clearing away and binding together, Adam and Eve struggle as well with their own stray ends. The 'wilderness is there, waiting to encroach at the slightest neglect',[42] as Adam's words, though carefully chosen to reassure, nevertheless underscore: 'These paths & Bowers doubt not but our joynt hands | Will keep from Wilderness with ease, as wide | As we need walk' (IX. 244–5). Paradise and wilderness inhabit such close quarters, the line between plenty and surfeit is so fine, only daily labour of restraint maintains the minimum requirement of 'as wide | As we need walk'. And while Adam calls their work 'our delightful task' and 'our pleasant labor', in the same breath he urges 'we must be ris'n' at dawn for overnight the branches begin to 'mock' (IV. 437, 624–8). For such constant vigilance and reformation, their reward is purposefulness in the omnipresent eye of Uriel's 'great Work-Maister' (III. 696)—'my great task-master's eye' of Sonnet VII.

As they ponder the meaning of 'too much' in 'this delicious place | For us too large', the poet frequently reminds us of the expectation of their own fertility (IV. 629, 731; IX. 207–8, 246, 622–4). They require additional hands to prune, mouths to consume, the bounty. The command to be fruitful and multiply is everywhere, wedded love hailed the 'true source | Of human ofspring'—yet the garden sees only a vegetable 'Nurserie'. Before they create offspring Adam and Eve must create their selves, and for Milton's poem this gestation begins with Eve's suspended moment over the pool's sympathetic reflection.

In Eve's first moments she responds to a speech-like sound, the 'murmuring' water that draws her to the lake. Her earliest memory is the pleasure of her gaze at that smooth surface, and her solitary looking holds

[41] On the garden's excess and the tensions of vigilance associated with the work of cultivation, see Stanley Fish, *How Milton Works* (Cambridge, Mass.: Harvard University Press, 2001), ch. 15, esp. 527 ff. Tanner, *Anxiety in Eden*, begins with Milton's 'economy of abundance', 45.

[42] Isabel MacCaffrey, *'Paradise Lost' as 'Myth'* (Cambridge, Mass.: Harvard University Press, 1959), 154.

the possibility of deepening into solitary speculation, the activity of creative thought—into reflection in the deepest sense. Surely we are meant to reflect on, besides Narcissus, Eve's primitive reflection of the Creator when in darkness 'the Spirit of God moved upon the face of the waters' (Genesis 1.2) or Milton's first invocation of that epic Spirit which 'Dove-like satst brooding on the vast Abyss | And mad'st it pregnant' (I. 21–2). As others have noted, when Adam awakes at his creation, by contrast, he looks up at the sky towards the sun whose warmth he felt had 'fed' on and dried his sweat. He stands and experiments with his limbs (VIII. 256) in an interactive, physical relationship with his world and with God whom he questions, with whom he disagrees, and from whom he receives information. Eve sees the sky but in reflection, and the smooth image of her own smiling reflection emphasizes the rippled surface of her first wilful act and its smoothing correction to obedience. But in this case the ripples augur depth. A human Eden with 'all her shows' (VIII. 575), Eve will lose her perfect, if superficial, balance of reflection and deepen by falling in over her head, through an appetite for the closed, complete, sufficient circle of approving eyes rather than for consumption of physical pleasure.[43] She precedes and exposes, by contrast, the superficiality of Narcissus and his end.

Like Eve, Milton's readers have long reflected on her reflection and memory of this moment,[44] but I want to focus on Eve's later nostalgia for the pool when she gazes not in the water 'Pure as th'expanse of Heav'n', but at the heavens themselves (IV. 657). Adam and Eve rest down by the stream after work in 'youthful dalliance as beseems | Fair couple, linkt in happie nuptial League, | Alone as they' (IV. 338–40)—but they are hardly alone. God and the heavenly guards of Paradise, Satan (who also believes he is unseen but who has been recognized), Milton, the reader—we the

[43] It is unclear, for example, whether she eats as well as 'Ministers' at the banquet of fruit which she provides for Adam and Raphael. Minaz Jooma argues that she abstains, 'just as she does not partake of the knowledge transmitted from God through Raphael to Adam that the feast serves to celebrate' ('The Alimentary Structures of Incest in *Paradise Lost*', *ELH* 63 (1996), 37).

[44] For representative examples of attention to this scene and to Milton's allusion to Narcissus, see Parker, 'Eve, Evening, and the Labor of Reading in *Paradise Lost*'; McColley, *Milton's Eve*, 74–89; Richard DuRocher, *Milton and Ovid*; Froula, 'When Eve Reads Milton'; James Earl, 'Eve's Narcissism', *Milton Quarterly*, 19 (1985), 13–16; Kenneth J. Knoespel, 'The Limits of Allegory: Textual Expansion of Narcissus in *Paradise Lost*', *Milton Studies*, 22 (1986), 79–99; John Guillory, 'Milton, Narcissism, Gender: On the Genealogy of Male Self-Esteem', in Christopher Kendrick (ed.), *Critical Essays on John Milton*, (New York: G. K. Hall, 1995), 194–233; William G. Riggs, 'The Temptation of Milton's Eve: "Words, Impregn'd/With Reason" ', *Journal of English and Germanic Philology*, 94/3 (July 1995), 368–71.

great Panopticon all observe the happy couple. Like the disturbing profusion of Paradise, the poem's jungle of voyeurs that includes the reader's eyes becomes a lavish camouflage and signature of one-upmanship of the blind Milton who is as secret as God in his darkness. Yet the poem's anxious universe of spectators and telescopes, of heavenly creatures with multiple eyes, also reminds us how intensely the poet has been watching himself, so consciously prepared, delayed, and waiting with his talent.

The poem's interest in the tension between godlike omniscience and self-concealment is only matched by that of a God who, in Raphael's words, has 'Plac'd Heav'n from Earth so farr' not to be spied on himself, 'that earthly sight, | If it presume, might err in things too high, | And no advantage gaine' (VIII. 119–22). The narrator addresses Him as 'Thee Father' who is a 'Fountain of Light, thy self invisible'; he is 'Thron'd inaccessible', whose veil of clouds yet so dazzles heaven that the seraphim must veil their eyes with their wings (III. 372–82). In our first glimpse of this far-sighted voyeur, God has bent down the telescope of his eye on Adam and Eve and on Satan's flight and announces with weary disgust in four matter-of-fact lines what is going to happen: man will 'easily transgress the sole Command, | . . . so will fall, | Hee and his faithless Progenie: whose fault?' (III. 93–6). With so many knowing ahead the course of events, so many eyes focused on Adam and Eve, how can the two gardeners retain any of God's dignity of mystery—any secrets?

Our expectant gaze has waited almost 3,000 lines to see them. We have wandered patiently in circles with the rebel angels; we have slowly begun to stalk Adam and Eve with Satan 'in wandring flight' across the dangerous abyss, through Chaos up to the sun's radiance, then further up to the bottom stair of heaven before descending to earth. Once in Eden we had to mount a densely wooded hill to the elevated 'enclosure' of Paradise's green world and through perplexing, 'thick entwin'd', forbidding thickets 'overgrown, grottesque and wilde, | Access deni'd'. Closing in, we continued to be led by the narrator's voice through the sensual, thick warmth of this sumptuous garden and were invited to trace its large river divided into four mazy 'wandring' streams.

The first exchanges of Adam and Eve, in contrast to the riot of growth and in contrast to Satan's conflicted, twisting soliloquies, constitute a coolly measured and poised duet. As if performing before an audience (which they are), these inexperienced voices still sound stiffly formal in their echoes of each other: 'Sole partner and sole part of all these joyes, | Dearer thy self then all', begins Adam, and 'O thou for whom | And from whom I was formd flesh of thy flesh, | And without whom am to no end, my Guide | And Head', responds Eve; 'Fair Consort', opens Adam, 'My Author and Disposer', answers Eve; 'Daughter of God and Man, accomplisht Eve', concludes Adam.[45]

Eve's speech at 4.635–58 is formal, obeisant, and balanced, like the 'self-balanced', pendent earth—until the end. Critics have remarked on its '*da capo*' repetition, its 'self-quotation' as an 'echo, a structure (and a mythical allusion) which directs us back to the 'narcissism' of Eve's initial experience'. [46] She draws a circle of a contained world of obedience and contentment with Adam's and with God's will, wherein 'to know no more | Is woman's happiest knowledge and her praise'. Knowing 'more' would be unhappy knowledge because it would upset the tightly constrained balance. Eve details the beauties of a day from the sweet 'breath of morn' down to 'grateful Eevening milde' (the day's wilting heat being another Edenic excess), the night and nightingale, moon and stars—only to turn and repeat this catalogue but with the variation that none of this ('neither breath of Morn . . . | . . . nor rising Sun . . .') is sweet 'without thee'. The lulling sequence comes to rest with a full stop. Yet a song which progresses 'from an expression of union ('[w]ith thee') to an expression of separation ('without thee') . . . seems, in its foregrounding of absence', to take a troubling turn.[47]

Then Eve abruptly opens up the circle she had closed: 'But wherfore all night long shine these, for whom | This glorious sight, when sleep hath shut all eyes?' (III. 657–8) Her question might recall in the stars those friendly eyes of the pool, except instead of two there are many but with no answering looks. Apparently she is neither oblivious in Adam's company of her surroundings nor indifferent to know 'more', nor perhaps does she find the world as balanced as her aria suggests. Paradise is characterized not only by 'more' but by excess. She may ask the question, however, to prompt his answer that she knows will close the circle her question opened; she may want to continue the balancing act of their exchange in which questions are contained by answers. Adam's answer, however, only ties up the question's loose end temporarily. A hundred lines earlier, Satan had quitted his observation of the couple in order to roam Paradise, so it is unlikely that he overheard Eve's question. Yet he

[45] Mary Jo Kietzman, 'The Fall into Conversation with Eve: Discursive Difference in *Paradise Lost*', *Criticism*, 39 1 (Winter 1997), 55–88, suggests that Adam and Eve's inability through conversation to recreate and narrate their deepest experiences contributes to their fall. She suggests that Eve's narration of memories and feelings, more speculative, exploratory, and open to other points of view than Adam's, provides a 'better discursive model for the conversation and the collaborative history that could have made Eden' (57).

[46] Riggs, 'The Temptation of Milton's Eve', 378.

[47] Ibid.

seems to revive and answer it for her that night in the dream that he insinuates, apparently, at her ear.[48] A voice that she thinks is Adam's calls her forth to wander alone in the night because otherwise the moon would shine 'in vain, | If none regard'; then in a subtle, most flattering reversal it urges 'Heav'n wakes with all his eyes, | Whom to behold but thee, Natures desire'. Suddenly Eve is the object of all ravished eyes: her question has been revealed, or transformed, by Satan to be a hidden wish for that friendly gaze of her reflection multiplied. Eve's original experience of contentment and completeness, however, of a circle closed depended on the 'answering looks | Of sympathie' to her eyes of one other pair. We have no reason to believe that she wants 'all' eyes on her, since the crucial experience of complete sympathy, the loving gaze returned, would be dissipated; she can only gaze at one pair of eyes at a time.

In the dream she rises to walk as if to look for Adam, but she rehearses the scene of the Fall. She is still passive and does not pluck the fruit. The 'he' of her dream does the deed, while she only observes and feels the shock of disobedience, the chill that Adam will feel for her. Once she has survived that tremor (crossed that 'black line', as Richardson says), she allows herself to be fed, as if the angelic dream-arm were an extension of the branch that reaches its fruit to her mouth. Straight she goes to the clouds:

> So saying, he drew nigh, and to me held,
> Even to my mouth of that same fruit held part
> Which he had pluckt; the pleasant savorie smell
> So quick'nd appetite, that I, methought,
> Could not but taste. Forthwith up to the Clouds
> With him I flew, . . . (V. 82–6)

Her dream suggests an inverted image of losing her balance as she hangs above the pool: she seems to fall into those multiple answering eyes yet be high above. If the dream is Satan's work, he has altered her original wish for the closed circle of approval into the desire more characteristic of the male eyes in the poem, not hers—to see and know from high above, to control knowledge. Eve is not interested in control or power but in cultivating responsive life that approves of her—Adam's gaze, the flower

[48] Albert Labriola has noted rightly that Satan's temptations of Eve in her dream and later in the garden emphasize her queenship and specifically reproduce language of praise from the cult of Elizabeth I. The narrator reproduces that image of Eve as ravishing queen in his account of her departure from the scene of Raphael's narration, VIII. 59–63. See 'Milton's Eve and the Cult of Elizabeth I', *JEGP* 95/1 (1996), 38–51. See also Riggs, 'The Temptation of Milton's Eve', 378–9; Parker, *Inescapable Romance*, 114–23.

nursery's appreciation of her care—that affirms her self in a circle of sympathy. Through Eve the poet dramatizes the fallen experience, but not hers at this point, of following the tempting inner voices that promise a quick path to godhead. Later Eve will be led to test this fantasy that she can consume all mystery—consume the bounds of subjectivity, which constrain but also protect.

With this innocent female subjectivity, the poet represents the experience of what it must have felt like to want to swallow the world whole and, like the speaker of the invocation to book III, to acquire opened eyes: to be, yet be the subject of, all eyes. Her blind attempt to ingest that heady moment of all-consuming vision reveals her to be a vulnerable subject of others' eyes and voices until invisibly, even from our eyes, she creates her own sound that sees—reflects on darkness—from 'within'. Marvell's tutor similarly falls through a complicated landscape to a climactic, narrow space, hugged by vines, of temptation and self-exposure that only seems secret, like Eve's eating the apple. Within a deceptive landscape, these two subordinates lose themselves to that most secret temptation and illusion of reflective poets: to see all when they open their mouths.[49]

'GRATEFUL DIGRESSIONS'

The word 'digression' appears only once in the poem, modified by 'grateful' which, in the seventeenth century, could mean pleasing or welcome to the mind or senses, full of grace. The context is a fleeting moment. Raphael has just completed for Adam and Eve his narration of the earth's creation and has asked with awkward caution, delaying the 'Aught' and hedging it with 'not', 'if else thou seekst | Aught, not surpassing human measure, say' (VII. 639–40). Listening enrapt Adam craves the angelic sounds to continue, and he asks excitedly a long, abstruse question. As he finishes Eve emerges from her paradoxical invisibility of the beautiful but silent female 'retir'd in sight' since the middle of book V, but only to retire completely from the scene. She recedes through a maze of 'nots' in order to reserve for herself later a greater, more intimate pleasure:

[49] See also Kathleen Kelly, 'Narcissus in *Paradise Lost* and *Upon Appleton House*: Disenchanting the Renaissance Lyric', in David G. Allen and Robert A. White (eds.), *Traditions and Innovations: Essays on British Literature of the Middle Ages and the Renaissance*, (Newark: University of Delaware Press, 1990), 200–13.

Yet went she not as not with such discourse
Delighted, or not capable her eare
Of what was high: such pleasure she reserv'd,
Adam relating, she sole Auditress;
Her Husband the Relater she preferr'd
Before the Angel, and of him to ask
Chose rather; hee, she knew would intermix
Grateful digressions, and solve high dispute
With conjugal Caresses, from his Lip
Not Words alone pleas'd her. O when meet now
Such pairs, in Love and mutual Honour joyn'd? (VIII. 48–58)

Why does she leave at this moment? Why does the epic speaker interrupt the narration with a glimpse of her walking off, and why introduce the reassurance of 'Such pairs' joined in love? Why insert the troubling ambiguity in twisted syntax as to whether anyone sees her go: she stood up with 'grace that won who saw to wish her stay' (VIII. 43)? Who saw? Finally, why does the narrator use this sudden glimpse of Eve to remind us that lips communicate not only with words, that, more than words, spousal kisses can 'solve high dispute'?

Notice the tension between withdrawal and exposure in the narrator's convoluted phrasing of her departure: 'which Eve | Perceaving where she sat retir'd in sight, | With lowliness Majestic from her seat, | And Grace that won who saw to wish her stay, | Rose' (VIII. 40–4). She slowly gathers herself over three lines until the initial strong stress of 'Rose' brings her decision to full height. Suddenly she is gone, and the reader is transported briefly from the heady preoccupations of Adam and Raphael to observe her arrive at her nursery among fruits and flowers. Moreover, after the narrator's explanation of her anticipated pleasures with Adam, and although she has already left, Eve leaves again at line 59; but the image of her departure has been revised now. The narrator recalls Eve's tempting dream voice, 'be henceforth among the Gods | Thy self a Goddess' (V. 77–8), and anticipates the serpent's flattery of goddess and queen in the next book. Here she has become 'Goddess-like', moreover a queen of love whom the narrator alone imagines. We do not know for sure if Adam and Raphael see her:

With Goddess-like demeanour forth she went;
Not unattended, for on her as Queen
A pomp of winning Graces waited still,
And from about her shot Darts of desire
Into all Eyes to wish her still in sight. (VIII. 59–63)

She is waited on 'still' by Graces like those of Venus, though the only mention of graces before occurred when Adam that morning hung over her sleeping form after her bad night 'and beheld | Beautie, which whether waking or asleep | Shot forth peculiar Graces' (V. 13–15). The Graces are shooting desire into 'all Eyes' to make them wish her stay—but are there not only two pairs of eyes? The Graces are shooting desire because, the speaker implies, those eyes do not see her. This second reminder that Eve is leaving, and with the help of the Graces' 'Darts of desire', suggests that 'all Eyes' are not on her—especially, the important eyes of Adam. Almost like the eyes of her reflection, his eyes must usually shine 'with answering looks | Of sympathie and love', but Adam is looking for answers now, not answering looks; and Eve retreats to the flowers for their affirmation of her presence and response to her touch.

In a poem that hails wedded love and 'Domestic sweets' (IV. 760), which troubles to distinguish unfallen sexual bliss from the adulterous adventures of ancient myth and Restoration 'Court Amours' (IV. 767), why 'still' are Venus, her Graces, and 'Darts of desire' evoked? Eve appears poignantly human and vulnerable by comparison. The speaker has taken pains to emphasize both her beauty, lovelier than that of Venus, and her innocent lack of self-consciousness, as he affirms when she is serving Raphael ('no vaile | Shee needed, Vertue-proof, no thought infirme | Alterd her cheek', V. 383–5). She is no proud goddess. For with the 'And' of line 64, which does not follow from the preceding line but returns the reader to where the narrator had left off ('So spake our Sire', VIII. 39), Raphael begins to answer Adam as if the narrator's digression of the last twenty-five lines had been parenthetical.

Remembering how instinctively Eve turned away from Adam at their first encounter and then her recent dream of wandering alone, the reader might feel reasonably alarmed at her disappearance. Amidst Raphael's narration of so many secrets of heaven unfolded, with the scale of good and evil apparently in delicate balance, the narrator opens a space of mystery; he leaves an absence, a blank like the crucial week which disappears between books VIII and IX while Satan marks time by circling the globe. In the midst of this epic when mankind's freedom is threatened occurs an absence of knowledge—a secret. The poem suggestively points to and closes up Eve's thoughts that we never know.

Readers' explanations of why Eve departs have ranged from her boredom and preference for female 'rapport-talk' over male 'report-talk' to the poet's need to allow Adam to speak freely about her with

Raphael.[50] Yet no one has addressed the defensive mist that the narrator raises around her departure: the repeated 'not's and the more acceptable visions we are told that she has chosen and anticipates, introduced by the phrases 'she reserv'd', 'she preferr'd', she 'Chose rather'. The narrator gives her a will and strong preferences. Nor have critics remarked on the fact that her disappearance looms ominously because she repeats this withdrawal with accumulated determination when we see her next. Then, paradoxically, she will not choose exactly those 'grateful digressions' of word and touch for which we are told she would wait in book VIII; she will deny herself and her husband the pleasure of that 'sweet intercourse | Of looks and smiles' which Adam then affectionately invokes (IX. 235–43). In this anxious poem of questions asked, of instruction delivered but information withheld, the protecting arms of Adam and Eve's digressions into conjugal caresses do not push for answers. They contain and hold the absence of resolution, are a balance to mystery. In their circling, protective motion of relation and their suspended freedom ('A nice and suttle happiness' in God's bemused phrase), they constitute a safe model for listening to voices, including one's own, and for the bower of self-possession.[51]

Eve as a submissive listener knows the interior pleasures of suspension within another's voice but also the habits of indirection, retirement, and secret, wandering thought. From her first day she has been talked to, whispered to, urged by mysterious male voices at her ear to follow an invisible or a disguised leader. She first is called to abandon her reflective life by a heavenly voice in order to be found by him whose image she is (but who, she feels, is not hers). She feels no choice ('what could I

[50] Joan F. Gilliland, ' "Grateful Digressions" and Casual Discourse: Eve's Rapport-Talk', in Charles Durham and Kristin McColgan (eds.), *Spokesperson Milton: Voices in Contemporary Criticism* (Selinsgrove, Pa.: Susquehanna University Press, 1994), 249–59; James Grantham Turner, *One Flesh: Paradisal Marriage and Sexual Relations in the Age of Milton* (Oxford: Clarendon Press, 1987), 234; McColley, *Milton's Eve*, 114; Joseph Wittreich, *Feminist Milton* (Ithaca, NY: Cornell University Press, 1987), 92. John Guillory, 'From the Superfluous to the Supernumerary: Reading Gender into *Paradise Lost*', in Elizabeth D. Harvey and Katharine Eisaman Maus (eds.), *Soliciting Interpretation: Literary Theory and Seventeenth-Century English Poetry* (Chicago: University of Chicago Press, 1990), 79–81, attacks the interpretation of Sanford Budick (in *The Dividing Muse* (New Haven: Yale University Press, 1985), 101–2) that Eve leaves in a state of triumph because her question from the evening before has returned to crown this masculine colloquy; 'she apparently departs only to tend her flowers, . . '. (81).

[51] On the multivocality of, the plethora of narrators in, *Paradise Lost* and Milton's exploration of intervention in history through voice, see Elizabeth Sauer, *Barbarous Dissonance and Images of Voice in Milton's Epics* (Montreal: McGill-Queen's University Press, 1996).

doe, | But follow strait, invisibly thus led?'), although when she sees Adam she instinctively ignores the command and turns back. Adam seizes and claims her as a physical part of himself: he saw the proof of their connection.[52] But in Eve's account, the oxymoron of 'gentle' and 'Seisd' and the rapid sequence of verbs convey an effect of having her preference corrected by force: 'with that thy gentle hand | Seisd mine, I yielded, and from that time see | How beauty is excelld by manly grace | And wisdom, which alone is truly fair' (IV. 488–91). Because the 'I' is not repeated before 'see', the verb hangs at the end of its line precariously without agent, as if she had yielded her self in her opinions. Does she mean 'I see' or an imperative?

Adam sees in her 'Part of my Soul', 'My other half', and 'my Self | Before me', but she sees difference, at first a yielding not yet a union. One sex must outshine the other: Adam's 'wisdom . . . alone is truly fair', while her fairness results in the dangerous confusion of wisdom. In retrospect Eve describes her first impulse towards the pool as 'unexperienc't thought', as if she cared what experienced thought was. But her yielding to the call sets a pattern of yielding to the voices of mysterious others and a pattern of Adam's refusal to hear or believe literally what she says, for when he recounts his own creation story to the Archangel he explains Eve's initial rejection of him as natural coy modesty, not repeating the reasons she told him. It will prove as hard to hear as to see one's self. Later when Eve believes she has led and asserted herself, she again will have yielded in confusion, although to violate aggressively not only God's law but her own original experience of self-sufficiency. For when Adam exclaims, 'how hast thou yeelded to transgress | The strict forbiddance, how to violate | The sacred Fruit forbidd'n!' (IX.902–4), she will have imitated as she seized the fruit the masculine gesture of claiming another physical creation as part of one's self. She will have denied her own initial delight in reflection, not possession, mistaken another voice for her own interior speaker, and 'cramm'd and gorg'd' her self, eating like the hell-hounds.

The experience of being led internally through the ear, to wander blind after false voices, is central to this poem and its poet. William Riggs has noted the poem's dramatization of 'the power of language to lead thought'— Milton's old 'association of villainy with false eloquence and his sensitivity to the dangers of self-intoxication'.[53] Recall the narrator

[52] And Milton will repeat 'Her hand he seized', starkly without the 'gentle', when their eyes have been opened after the Fall (IX. 1037).

[53] Riggs, 'The Temptation of Milton's Eve' 376.

and his muses, Eve and the intrusive dream-words of Satan, or Satan's whisper of rebellion to his sleeping companion (V. 673) and his seductive oratory to his followers, Adam's transport dangerously intoxicated and thirsty through Raphael's speech, the reader following Milton's wandering periods from 'Norway foam' to Vallombrosa. Even that 'Universal blanc' (III. 48) with which nature presents the poet's unseeing eyes becomes the recovered 'ancient liberty' of blank verse to withhold and suspend from the ear too easy closure. When Milton describes 'true musical delight' in verse as consisting of 'apt Numbers, fit quantity of Syllables, and the sense variously drawn out from one Verse into another', the 'variously' suggests the poet's liberty of gesturing, and the reader's task of listening, in all directions at once. And Adam and Eve's uncertainty within the garden's echo chamber of whether a voice be external or internal, true or false, can be corrected only by the sounding and the containment of voices within the pleasurable testing movement of their own 'grateful digressions'. The self-abnegation and play of their innocent union guard against the temptation to haste into sterile imitation and self-consumption.

Satan once experiences a similar suspended feeling from a transport of bliss in the garden, although not through discourse. Before the temptation he hungrily gazes on Eve's beauty that momentarily stupefies and suspends him disarmed from evil (IX. 455–66). The grateful transport of pleasure threatens to divert him from his path of destruction: 'Thoughts, whither have ye led me, with what sweet | Compulsion thus transported to forget | What hither brought us, hate, not love' (IX. 473–5). As Gabriel taunts him, the compulsion to escape his pain in forgetful transport drove him to Eden. But he cannot digress so far as to forget his hate, which is a sign of his damnation. Satan's transgression is characterized not by digression but by the inability to digress, by his rigidity of pride and ingrown, incestuous, constricted vision. Satan cannot be led to meander off into the rich beauty of the earth, the New World Eve represents balanced between heaven and hell, because his mission is to destroy that balance.[54] He is bound within 'the hateful siege | Of contraries' (IX. 121–2) where all diversity is narrowed to a suffocating point: 'love or hate, | To me alike' (IV. 69–70). And he infects Eve with this desperation and rigidity in her dream.

Most important, Satan is denied the experience of erotic transport. The earthly counterpart to God's 'secresie although alone, | Best with thy self accompanied' (VIII. 427) is the suspension, even absence, of self repre-

[54] As Kerrigan, *The Sacred Complex*, 290, notes, 'function, the bitter compulsion, rules him'.

sented by Adam and Eve 'Imparadis't in one anothers arms' (IV. 506). That protective, reflexive circle of affection has replicated and replaced the experience of 'answering looks | Of sympathie and love' (IV. 464–5) Eve enjoyed at the pool. *Paradise Lost* envisions unfallen sexual union as a safe, containing form of reflection that produces sufficiency, not hunger. And they are protected from prying eyes symbolically by the nuptial bower of bliss with its expectations of fruitfulness, until Satan's invasion of their privacy. His intrusive presence in that bower, as easily accomplished as his leap into Paradise, enacts a mental and physical violation—'Assaying by his Devilish art to reach | The Organs of her Fancie' (IV. 801–2)—a Miltonic nightmare of anatomical invasion.[55] For Satan has observed that transport and suspension take various forms—for example, that of physical and mental rapture through kissing, talking, and listening, which form their own completeness and contain their own detours; and in solitude that of the wandering or dreaming mind like an 'amaz'd Night-wanderer' (IX. 640). The seduction of the serpent must disguise the fact that the Satanic isolation of feeding on one's self, exemplified by Satan's self-imprisoning malice and by the incestuous triangle of Satan, Sin, and Death, is a sterile imitation of the self-sufficiency and reflexivity embraced by the couple in Paradise. Incest replaces inwardness—feeding replaces the testing, balancing, interior process of Adam and Eve's 'grateful digressions'.

'Then feed on thoughts, that voluntarie move | Harmonious numbers', intones the narrator who nightly wanders in the muses' haunts (III. 37–8). Along with the ear, the mouth of talking, eating, and kissing looms large in this poem about controlling access to 'within' and about the difference between digressions within the bounds of the self and stepping over those bounds. God hides death in delectable food and in the hunger of the ear; Satan will enter the serpent through its mouth. And when Eve plucks the apple, Milton makes us feel a sterile, pathetic isolation about her eating 'without restraint' in the hope to feed both body and mind:

> . . . for Eve
> Intent now wholly on her taste, naught else
> Regarded, such delight till then, as seemd,
> In Fruit she never tasted, whether true
> Or fansied so, through expectation high
> Of knowledg, nor was God-head from her thought.
> Greedily she ingorg'd without restraint,
> And knew not eating Death: (IX. 785–92)

[55] For Satan as anatomist, as mentioned earlier (n. 18), see Erickson, *The Language of the Heart*, 89–146.

The frenzied greed around 'ingorg'd' reflects the restless and self-consuming quality of the act to which Eve has allowed herself to be led. She who from the first was associated with reserve, with reluctance and delay, and with the pleasures of sympathy—Adam with desire to seize his own—now hurries to engorge. To recapture the immediate sufficiency of that gaze in the pool, she turns back upon herself like a snake 'self-rowld' (IX. 183).

Adam's memory of their first meeting emphasizes how hidden Eve's mind remains from his, as in book VIII she remains hidden in absence. Elusive and wayward, she is finally 'led' not by a guiding voice but firmly by his hand to the nuptial bower. Eve, it seems, is meant for retirement—in the shade, in the bower, for Adam's eyes alone. Although she was led once by heavenly command and then by Adam's hand from her delight in solitary retirement, in book IX she attempts to lead herself, first to work away from the distraction of human eyes and touch and then, choosing to follow the snake, toward having perfect vision that dissolves the difference between exterior and interior and needs no other eyes. She is tempted not to be gazed on by multitudes, as Satan begins by offering, as the dream-tempter had, but to gaze above all with eyes 'Op'nd and cleerd' (IX. 708). Satan's temptation to open up her retirement appears to repeat the original scene of her hearing a commanding voice, but the voice does not command now but offers her not only Adam's gaze but visibility to unlimited others not 'shallow to discerne' that becomes translated into an unlimited vision of herself:

> Fairest resemblance of thy Maker faire,
> Thee all things living gaze on, all things thine
> By gift, and thy Celestial Beautie adore
> With ravishment beheld, there best beheld
> Where universally admir'd; but here
> In this enclosure wild, these Beasts among,
> Beholders rude, and shallow to discerne
> Half what in thee is fair, one man except,
> Who sees thee? (and what is one?) who shouldst be seen
> A Goddess among Gods . . . . (IX. 538–47)

Satan's repetitions coil insistently up to and around a subtle parenthesis. That 'one' pair of eyes, which represents the original sufficiency of balance acquired by gazing on her own, becomes an enclosure, a stifling reflection as much as was her 'unexperienc't thought' (IV. 457). She confuses the offer of, the desire for, limitless external visibility, characteristic of Satan's pride but not of Eve, with an offer of perfect vision that plumbs every mystery, turning outside inside, and she attempts to internalize the highest and most far-seeing, most suspended perspective. She takes literally the figure of the forbidden fruit of knowledge because consumption is easy and seems to imply that something is missing inside; she mistakes the metaphoric vehicle for the tenor, an error which Satan delighted reports back to his followers: 'Him by fraud I have seduc'd | From his Creator, and the more to increase | Your wonder, with an Apple' (X. 485–7). After her fall from innocence, she will hear what is missing and fill the gap.

The apple is only a figure for what looks like a quick fix, in contrast to the daily labour of weeding, cultivation, propping, to the need to control exterior but also interior disorder. Raphael warns Adam against the passion of touch for 'An outside' (VIII. 568), Eve's beauty. In her confusion of, and suspension between, outside and inside, face and image, and her rejection of her own visible ornament for Adam's fairer wisdom, Eve becomes Milton's instrument for the transformation, domestication, of sensuous beauty, and not least of language, into an interior space of reflection. After she has eaten the fruit, the poet allows Eve in her confusion to characterize 'Wisdoms way', as will Christ in *Paradise Regained*, as secret and retired; when only minutes earlier she had imagined being the focus of all eyes, she now hopes guiltily, 'And I perhaps am secret' (IX. 809–11). She is a secret to herself.[56]

Renaissance biblical commentary, both Catholic and Protestant, is clear that woman, as Adam says, resembles 'less | His Image who made both', although Satan sees in both Adam and Eve 'Divine resemblance' (IV. 364, 4. 291–2).[57] Created at an extra remove from God to assuage and enrich human solitude, Eve feels the difference and distance of herself from him and the angels, and from Adam. She registers a distinction created by her otherness of feminine softness, her being 'Too much of Ornament'. By virtue of this apparent distance from God, although nearer resembling than Adam the Creator's flowery creation, by virtue of this human solitude of difference, Eve has more room and flexibility—and necessity—to extemporize what it is like to be Eve, to make her own

[56] On the relations between Eve and the female figure of Wisdom from Proverbs, see Theresa M. DiPasquale, '"Heav'n's Last Best Gift": Eve and Wisdom in *Paradise Lost*', *Modern Philology*, 95/1 (1997), 44–67.

[57] See Arnold Williams, *The Common Expositer: An Account of the Commentaries on Genesis, 1527–1633* (Chapel Hill: University of North Carolina Press, 1948), 87, for citations to Benedictus Pererius and David Pareus. See also Turner, *One Flesh*, ch. 3.

mould. The poem's insistent pun on mould points to her progress from earth to idea: to, inside herself, 'there plant eyes' (III. 53) of self-knowledge. But Eve is never more elusive than when she emerges out of her retirement for that brief moment at the opening of book VIII. Her query to Adam from the evening before about the stars has reappeared at that moment with new urgency in Adam's mouth.

Satan's stealing into Paradise by the underground Tigris and surfacing 'involv'd in rising Mist' (IX. 71–4) becomes a figure for the secret, invisible process by which thoughts like Eve's question, once entered the mind, follow a winding, interior map to emerge hidden in mist. Overnight Eve's musing query of two lines has expanded into not only a troubled dream but now Adam's question to Raphael at VIII. 13–38, an indirect criticism of their Father framed by reason and admiration. Despite Adam's logical reasoning, his coupling of wise with 'frugal' reflects the limited mental circles of an earthly labourer (and reader) for whom divine superfluity remains a mystery. Adam's preoccupation is not Eve's, however, is not about unanswered eyes but concerns waste in the universe, all those stars, is of a piece with his reasonable gardener's distress at the messy, dropping gums and blossoms, the litter of overripe fruit. His insistence on economy and 'use', after Raphael's expansive storytelling of heavenly war and creation, only reveals perhaps his unreadiness to appreciate the indirection of Raphael's warning. If 'frugal' be wise, then digressions can no longer be grateful:

> . . . reasoning I oft admire,
> How Nature wise and frugal could commit
> Such disproportions, with superfluous hand
> So many nobler Bodies to create,
> Greater so manifold, to this one use,
> For aught appeers, and on thir Orbs impose
> Such restless revolution day by day
> Repeated . . . . (VIII. 25–32)

'Such disproportions', 'Such restless revolution' daily 'Repeated'—the problem of the dream seems to have revolved in Adam's restless mind since the morning. His words express anxious impatience with what feels like too much, and still expanding, mystery—including the 'addition strange' of Eve's dream.

Apparently no longer safe within their leafy bower of embroidered and mosaic richness, a figure for their own rich mixture, Adam tosses out his anxious words to anchor himself on what seems a safe shore—the impulse of that deceived pilot 'of some small night-foundered skiff' (I. 203). With that question Adam wishes to anchor himself in the daylight to the knowledge and safety Raphael represents, to hold on to the haven of the moment and to delay the night which may bring the invasion of another 'addition strange'. Eve slips away in reflection of her husband's mental separation and absence from her, her invisibility to him. Through his intense delight in the hidden promise of insight in Raphael's words, and desire to feed on them as if they could forestall disaster, Adam lists dangerously in the direction of wanting to consume all knowledge in order to clear up mystery once and for all. He appears to have become unmoored, especially from his other self and haven, Eve, just as she felt unmoored from him in her dream. His unreflective urgency to be fed an answer will be remembered and copied by Eve in her mistaken attempt on her own to resemble him; his taut suspense of absence becomes the urgent absence, the deferral of pleasure, she attempts in book IX.

The narrator's repeated 'to wish her stay', 'to wish her still in sight' echo her own wish to stay and to be seen. And she goes where her presence not only will be noticed but will provoke a response: the flowers 'at her coming sprung' and 'toucht' by her 'gladlier grew'. But for the long moment of the afternoon Adam springs to another's attention and cannot be touched. Eve's retirement signals a crucial separation for Adam and Eve: a shift from the internal circle of balance and protection of mutual bliss in book IV to their growing isolation and imbalance of grim determination and finally self-denial—qualities far removed from the expansive, leisurely indulgence of their affable guest.

Raphael's well-tempered art of delay and suspension, his musing ambivalence and improvisation around the secret and the forbidden, recall not only the digressive epic narrator and the love of secrecy and suspense characteristic of God obscured on 'the secret top' of Sinai, but also the conflicted progress between secrecy and visibility of Eve. Eve's movement of wandering off after Adam's question in book VIII is a reaction to its dark urgency—is her unmooring from her husband's already unmoored figure, an odd consequence of a visit from this angel famous for his ability to secure marriages. And when we see her next, after a week of revolving planets and thoughts, she repeats this movement as a gesture pondered, delayed, and finally chosen. To Adam's impassioned question which began as her apparently more idle one, she proposes an answer: to gain control of the excess if not of the stars then in the garden—to clear more space without and within—they must work alone and depart from exactly the mingling of talk and kisses they most enjoy, a small reflection of the intermixture that God practises in his creation. After all, Raphael's parting words, which Eve said she had overheard like a shadow ('As in a shadie nook I stood behind'), warned against the sway of passion and do not suggest relationship: 'Perfet within, no outward aid require' (VIII. 642). Yet God's word for their transgression will be 'excess' (XI. 111), paradoxically that which they rigorously want to control.

RAPHAEL AND THE HUNGER TO KNOW

Books V–VIII have been described as 'the hinge of the whole epic, a narrative interval in which movement forward is temporarily suspended, and Adam, on the threshold of a decision, is provided with a space for reflection'.[58] But many readers have felt, in the words of Philip Gallagher, 'a vague sense of dissatisfaction with Raphael' and have struggled to rationalize his 'futile office of hopeless admonition'.[59] Why does Milton open up space for reflection and diffuse Raphael's warning through such a relaxed, rambling afternoon of eating and storytelling? Why not a cry of alarm as the narrator repeatedly demands in the long, emotional period that opens book IV: 'O for that warning voice, which he who saw | Th' Apocalyps, heard cry in heaven aloud', continuing 'that now, | While time was, our first-Parents had bin warnd' and so 'scap'd | Haply so scap'd', 'for now | Satan, now'—as if the urgent voice could not pause to breathe. Rather than Raphael's suspension of earthly bounds in an over-rich feast of fables, why not Michael's gentle firmness? The discursive centre of this epic appears not to hold.

What a far cry from the angel of the apocalypse is this seasoned heavenly agent and servant of matrimony, who with six wings alights in a sensual fantasy of feathers, soft colours, and clouds of fragrance, of waist, loins, and thighs. In what James Turner calls 'an astonishing burst of sensuous imagery', Raphael's appearance opens an unexpected interlude

[58] Parker, *Inescapable Romance*, 143.

[59] Philip J. Gallagher, *Milton, the Bible, and Misogyny* (Columbia: University of Missouri Press, 1990), 140–1; for his full discussion of Raphael, see 137–50. More recent studies of Raphael include Corine Abate, 'The Mischief-Making of Raphael upon Adam and Eve in *Paradise Lost*', *English Language Notes* (Mar. 1999), 41–54; and Charles Eric Reeves, ' "Lest Wilfully Transgressing": Raphael's Narration and Knowledge in *Paradise Lost*', *Milton Studies*, 34 (1996), 83–98, who makes a case for two Raphaels, one who foreknows the Fall as announced by God in book III and one who does not, who fully imagines the experience and drama of human freedom.

of diversion after the anxiety of Eve's dream, the haste to work, haste to assemble lunch.[60] In this grateful digression Adam, Eve, and the reader are invited to pause for various refreshments. As this angel of matrimony comes forward even Paradise shimmers and shivers expectantly in the spicy odours of Canticles, of 'Cassia, Nard, and Balme', as the narrator grows more lyrical and sensuous (V. 291–7). Having entered Paradise in book IV, the reader re-enters it with Raphael in a crescendo of 'blissful field', 'Wilderness of sweets', 'Wantond as in her prime', 'plaid at will', 'Virgin Fancies, pouring forth more sweet', 'Wilde above Rule or Art', and 'enormous bliss'.

This heavenly adviser trails the expected classical parallels: the precedent of the conniving god in Hesiod's *Works and Days* when Zeus sends Hermes to give Pandora to mankind; and the correction to that tradition of the descent of Hermes to warn, but to no avail, 'excellent Aigisthos' as described by Zeus at the opening of the *Odyssey*, 1. 28–43.[61] Yet the angel's curious experimentation with his mission on earth, the sense he suggests of feeling his way around forbidden territory, sounds notes of mystery and improvisation familiar by now in this unusual garden to which everyone is new.

As if Raphael were musing about the larger meaning of his mission, he early observes, in the vein of Eve's bemused speculation in book IV, the glimpsed possibility of a reflective, metaphorical congruence between heaven and earth: 'though what if Earth | Be but the shaddow of Heav'n, and things therein | Each to other like' (V. 574–5)? But the import of this suggestive vision is lost on Adam who wants a different kind of answer and becomes increasingly anxious to speak about what most immediately concerns him. After the angel has narrated his story of the war in heaven and thus indirectly 'forewarn'd | Adam by dire example' (VII. 41–2) not to overreach, his listener is shaken with doubts at the incomprehensible eruption of hate and evil in God's presence but moved to focus the angel on more comprehensible, visible, things as 'What neerer might concern' Adam. Adam struggles to comprehend the connection between what he has heard of war in Paradise and the possibility of such a war erupting within himself, between him and God, or between him and Eve. Although in a transport of attention, Adam still listens with what Eve so carefully and self-consciously accused her new self of, 'unexperienc't thought'; but suspended over the image of heaven's rebellion, his gaze into those depths glimpses his own reflected tumult—hence, his moving

[60] Turner, *One Flesh*, 270.

[61] Gallagher, *Milton, the Bible, and Misogyny*, 142–8.

the talk to himself.

Raphael's and Adam's discourse has looped with tantalizing detail and leisure from the most distant yet unsettling heavenly events gradually closer to home. Like the poet, the archangel dramatically ventriloquizes a fabulous cast, wanders into parenthetical notes comparing heaven and earth ('wee have also our Eevning and our Morn', V. 628; 'For Earth hath this variety from Heav'n | Of pleasure situate in Hill and Dale', VII. 640–1; 'nor Hath this Earth | Entrails unlike' heaven's, VI. 516–17), and he wanders into the suspended, seemingly subversive beauty of simile. He will lift into romance Satan's passage north with his followers who suddenly glitter as several kinds of stars, 'an Host | Innumerable as the Starrs of Night, | Or Starrs of Morning, Dew-drops, which the Sun | Impearls on every leaf and every flouer' (V. 745–7). Soon afterwards the firm marching of the Messiah's troops filled with 'Heroic Ardor to advent'rous deeds' is likened to 'the total kind | Of Birds in orderly array on wing' coming to Adam to be named (VI. 73–7), an image which tilts oddly back from the heroic. Besides, Raphael says later that he was not present at the naming of creation.

When Raphael refers to divine amusement at the 'quaint Opinions' of those who attempt to understand God's creation, the archangel's words might also be spoken by the contemptuous creator of this poem to 'them who ought | Rather admire' its ultimately mysterious 'Fabric' (VIII. 71–8). In fact Raphael sounds much like the poet on his epic mission. The speaker's invocations hover behind the angel's tones of 'High matter' and secrets 'Not lawful to reveal' (V. 563–70); the loitering of Adam and his angelic guest around forbidden territory is only exceeded by the poet's, for example in his invocation to book VII. Having been an 'Earthlie Guest' whom Urania led up even to 'the Heav'n of Heav'ns', the poet requests a safe return to earth's 'narrower' bounds. But his warning spectres of presumption, Bellerophon and Orpheus, belong to the 'empty dreame' (VII. 39) of pagan myth, part of the outdated externality of *copia*, which is being corrected by this more primary poem.

Critics have noted that the narrator is quick to stake his claim to the territory of first causes and secret knowledge of origins by correcting mistaken fablers.[62] But in the poet's account of Mulciber, the architect of Pandemonium, the patient correction of 'Men call'd him Mulciber; and how he fell | From Heav'n, they fabl'd, thrown by angry Jove', is

[62] Jonathan H. Collett, 'Milton's Use of Classical Mythology in *Paradise Lost*', *PMLA* 85 (1970), 88–96; Charles Martindale, *John Milton and the Transformation of Ancient Epic* (Totowa, NJ: Barnes & Noble, 1986), 72–8.

suspended through an exquisitely lyrical account of Mulciber's fall. It is a last, lingering look before the heavy judgement of 'Erring' cuts off the lyricism, halting temporarily the momentum of enjambment (I. 740–7). The Son's rejection of classical learning in *Paradise Regained* begins in *Paradise Lost*, yet the process of farewell which keeps memorializing the 'falling Star' of that lush, safe world of the schoolroom is complex and conflicted like Raphael's narration. And in numerous digressions the stories are repeatedly and delicately rendered and diffused into the fabric of the poem. The parallel of talk and listening between Raphael and Adam, on the one hand, and Milton and the reader, on the other, points at once to the prophetic project of the warning visit and of the poem.

Through his suspension, and rebuilding, of tension at the centre, the poet corrects the reader's expectations of what an appropriate warning could be. And who should know better than the writer of the *The Readie and Easie Way to Establish a Free Commonwealth* published in March and April of 1660—the second, enlarged edition only weeks before Charles II stepped triumphantly on English soil. Milton would know the feel of a suspended, precarious balance when history is about to turn, the uncertainty of knowing whether the imperceptible turning has begun.[63] Books V–VIII of *Paradise Lost* restage in a sacred context Milton's recent warning voice as part of a different prophetic task. For his words, like Raphael's, would not alter the immediate course of events, but they would reach beyond the moment to the gradual, interior movements which are the invisible, inward life of moral heroism. Mankind will fall, the Commonwealth will fall; but the prophet's view extends deeper and further.

Linda Gregerson has remarked not only on Raphael's sensual entrance but on the continuation of its lush mood in Adam's mounting lyricism about, even intoxication with, the angel's voice. And as she notes, Raphael and Adam, far from including Eve in this sensuous euphoria, 'are apparently oblivious to her presence for hundreds of lines, as they are to her departure when at last it occurs'.[64] To describe his delight in Raphael's discourse, Adam echoes 'deliberate invocations of erotic love poetry' but also invokes the poem's dangerous language of eating and drinking and their appetites—of bottomless hunger and thirst, of longed for sweetness, of the impossibility of satiation. In his listening Adam feeds on Raphael's words as Eve will feed intoxicated on the apple. Satan

[63] Gallagher, *Milton, the Bible, and Misogyny*, 141–2.

[64] Linda Gregerson, *The Reformation of the Subject* (Cambridge University Press, 1995), 174–6; quoted material from 175.

finds his way into Eve's ear and thoughts, but Raphael had already 'in Adam's ear | So charming left his voice' that Adam waited flattered and transfixed even when the angel had finished.

Empson believed that Eve and Adam would not have transgressed if Raphael had not allowed them to feel almost angels themselves ('For while I sit with thee, I seem in Heav'n', says Adam, VIII. 210).[65] Raphael cautions them to be 'lowlie wise' (VIII. 173) and remember their 'human measure', but then he fills their heads with visions of 'wee' up there, flatters Adam about his resemblance to God and to the angels ('his image faire', and 'Nor less think wee in Heav'n of thee on Earth | Then of our fellow servant' VIII. 221, 224–5); and he holds out the possibility that they will in time 'wingd ascend | Ethereal, as wee' (V. 498–9), and move between heaven and Paradise. As one 'new wak't', Adam thanks him 'who thus largely' (but not completely) 'hast allayd | The thirst I had of knowledge' (VIII. 4–8); he declares, 'For while I sit with thee, I seem in Heav'n, | And sweeter thy discourse is to my eare | Then Fruits of Palm-tree'—than the fruits Eve prepared for lunch. While his hunger for food is soon allayed, 'thy words with Grace Divine | Imbu'd, bring to their sweetness no satietie' (VIII. 210–16). We see first with Adam, not Eve, the dangers of the ear's boundless appetite, unlike the stomach's. By the end of book VI, God's friendly angel had issued the warning about Satan that he was sent to give; at the end of his account of the Creation, at VII. 625–32, he had fulfilled God's request to 'advise' Adam 'of his happie state' (V. 234). Yet Raphael has not yet reminded Adam specifically on what a 'mutable' base rests that 'happie state'. As he prepares Raphael, God's sudden labyrinth of look-alike words creates a brief, confusing echo chamber, or hall of mirrors, of monosyllables. The repetitions of 'free' and 'will' seem to lock man in and difference out yet subtly shift 'will' from a strong verb to a vulnerable noun capable of being modified by not only 'free' but the upsetting polysyllabic 'mutable':

> Happiness in his power left free to will,
> Left to his own free Will, his Will though free,
> Yet mutable; whence warne him to beware
> He swerve not too secure: . . . (V. 235–38)

Here 'swerve' means to turn away from a right path or course of action with a determination distinct from the pleasures of roving. Adam will use the word in warning Eve, 'Firm we subsist, yet possible to swerve' (IX.

[65] William Empson, *Milton's God*, rev. edn. (London: Chatto & Windus, 1965), 147.

359). The slight syntactical confusion in line 238 of whether the 'not' modifies the verb or 'too secure' deepens a sense of impending danger, both meanings allowed to hover; but the blur heightens the mystery God adds to advice that might have been expected to be crystal clear.

The narrator's description of Adam—'now | Led on, yet sinless, with desire to know' (VII. 60–1)—recalls Eve's memory of her curious dream self and anticipates the narrator's epithet for her 'yet sinless' (IX.659) led by the serpent to confront the Tree of Knowledge. Adam begs for more words, more instruction, 'as one whose drouth | Yet scarce allay'd still eyes the current streame, | Whose liquid murmur heard new thirst excites' (VII. 66–69). Adam's yet innocent thirst to be godlike and excitement for the murmuring 'streame' of talk contrasts with the more placid delight aroused by the 'murmuring sound | Of waters' that drew newly awoken Eve to the lake to look 'with unexperienc't thought', not to drink. The diffusive ease of Raphael's manner like that of the poet's is only matched by the single-minded ease with which mankind will fall rapt into the 'liquid murmur' of talk.

Especially confusing is how closely Raphael's conversation reproduces the tempting voice of Eve's dream recounted that morning—'happie though thou art, | Happier thou mayst be, worthier canst not be' (V. 75–6). Raphael almost exactly echoes the dream voice which offered the possibility to be 'Thy self a Goddess, not to Earth confind, | But sometimes in the Air, as wee, sometimes | Ascend to Heav'n, by merit thine' (V. 78–80)—and Adam is tempted. The serpent's taunt in book IX, 'And what are Gods that Man may not become | As they, participating Godlike food' (IX. 716–17), has been prepared for by Raphael's cheerfully sharing mankind's food in exchange for the secrets of heavenly digestion, adding, 'time may come when men | With Angels may participate, and find | No inconvenient Diet' (V. 493–5). Sharing food, sharing knowledge, sharing secrets—but after holding out such a rich diet of 'more', the amiable angel also withdraws it, and holds out the carrot of their limited 'happie state'. His sense of human appetite for happiness as a space to be filled—'enjoy | Your fill'—echoes God's 'Eate freely with glad heart; fear here no dearth' (VIII. 322), the stern reminder of limit disguised with generosity's open hand. No wonder Adam's nervous excitement mounts to the outburst of his question at the opening of book VIII. After trying to soothe away with reason Eve's anxieties about her dream, he seems to be having an intoxicating dream of his own.

The many narrators of *Paradise Lost* want to tell and teach what they know as if they were all trying to piece together a large puzzle. Each wants to approach the mysterious moment of creation and first causes. The epic speaker, Uriel, Sin, Eve, Adam, Raphael, Michael—all have their story, their piece. Yet in the course of the poem the mystery of origins turns into the secret of—in Adam's words about Eve—'so well to know | Her own' (VIII. 548–9). And the quiet moment of new creation comes when least expected, when Eve speaks the words necessary to calm a turbulent Adam, to halt his falling into a lonely 'Abyss of fears | And horrors', and to re-establish them together in a new moral balance.[66]

The distance come by the internalization of eyes and ears at the end of *Paradise Lost* is a freedom from external voices and eyes in the creation of Eve's original voice of penitence (X. 914–36), which balances acknowledgement of guilt with repentance and a request for forgiveness. Her voice erupts like a spring from the wandering underground river of Paradise and turns Adam from his weak resemblance of the angry Father to resemble more closely the forgiving Son. Coming from her who is pointedly not a talker in this poem, whom Christ finds not 'bold or loquacious', who confesses her sin in a brief line following Adam's twenty, the penitent burst that begins 'Forsake me not thus, Adam' disarms rigidity and sounds a new space of moral interiority. With the sentence of death hanging over them, Eve's inner ear is able to hear and create what is missing. Her modulation into a voice of her own marks the digressive progress and accomplishment of an epic that holds all in suspense, even death, until the hidden moment is ripe. The poem's and Eve's relation of interior and exterior worlds, of past and present, depends on a voice that sounds its way and is large but secret. Eve turns inward the grace and sumptuousness of her mazy exterior, her external *copia*, and produces the depth of penitence. By asking forgiveness in a speech for which she has no model, she plumbs and sounds—simultaneously feels, hears, and creates the sound of—fallen human experience. In this poem, to author a self means to judge and to choose alone and to create one's voice in a world whose inherent multiplicity presses to be devoured.

Paradise Lost leads us, although indirectly, for all the poem's examina-

[66] Kevis Goodman writes eloquently about the labour of Eve's speech that through her suffering transforms Adam's response and, through her own sympathy, awakens again his sympathetic feeling. As Goodman notes, through this speech in which she takes control of the responsibility for sinfulness and strives to move a rigid Adam they build 'their own bridge of sympathy against the giant work of Sin and Death' (431) and will be able to begin to extend a connection back to God. Kevis Goodman, ' "Wasted Labor"? Milton's Eve, the Poet's Work, and the Challenge of Sympathy', *ELH* 64 (1997), 415–46.

tion of loss to an experience of a find: we fall into the essential experience of creation, although writ small, in Eve's invisible, silent process of the creation of the words that will open Adam's eyes to his destructive anger and that reunites them in a new relation of balance. As the invocations remind us, the speaker opens his inner ear to receive inspiration; the fertile, creative mind graduates from hearing and being led only by exterior voices to hearing and listening for an inspired voice that lies within. The essential experience of creative thought for this blind speaker and poet is that of internal hearing, a form of reflection that hears what is missing and fills in the gap—hearing that, like God's brooding over the waters of the deep, creates new space and new worlds but in words. *Paradise Lost* meditates on preparation and wandering, on waiting and delay, and the evolution of a voice that knows so well its own. Like that of the wandering Israelites in the desert, Milton's path has been 'not the readiest way' (XII. 216). The transition from his prose career to epic leads through Eve's accomplishment, the difficult birth of a new idea embodied in a new voice. The pointedly graphic surgery of the rib's extraction, while it may anticipate later sacrificial warm wounds and 'life-blood streaming fresh' of mankind's saviour, suggests most immediately a special birth, unlike passive Sin's that substantiated as incestuous love Satan's shallow self-entrapment. The birth of a new idea and voice wrests from mankind 'Substantial life' nearest the heart (IV. 484–5).

SUSPENDED IN DIGRESSION

The poem leads Eve to internalize her *copia* and her appearance of being 'in herself complete, so well to know | Her own' (XII. 548–9). Milton's God, by contrast, externalizes himself through his creation. He fills Paradise until it resembles an overstuffed room in which the forbidden fruit seems an odd tease 'amid the choice | Of all tastes else to please thir appetite, | Though wandring' (VII. 48–50). As vines and streams wander in Paradise, so may human appetite—up to a limit. W. Gardiner Campbell has reminded us of the early presence in *Areopagitica* of this 'all bounteous king' who simultaneously showers 'With copious hand' (V. 640–1) and sets before man a 'provoking object' in order that satiety be a perfect tension between capacity and obedience, profusion and temperance:

> Wherefore did he create passions within us, pleasures round about us, but that these rightly temper'd are the very ingredients of vertu? . . . This justifies the

high providence of God, who, though he command us temperance, justice, continence, yet powrs out before us, ev'n to a profusenes, all desirable things, and gives us minds that can wander beyond all limit and satiety.[67]

Milton confronts the paradox that man's capacity to enjoy abundance requires the provocation of a limit to appetite set 'ever almost in his eyes' and the freedom to choose that bound to wandering. In order to choose obedience, the visible symbol of limit must become invisible as well, the meaning internalized—not the literal fruit.

Satan's self-consuming appetite for revenge will transform Eve's initial delight in 'answering looks', not voices, her delight in the balance of perfect reflection, into self-consumption. From her first delighted moment at the pool and experience of having her vision corrected at her ear, the poet's Eve dramatizes the Fall as a process of falling through shallow self-reflection or 'unexperienc't thought' into the deepest experience of internal reflection. As she mistakes Satan for a real serpent and the forbidden fruit for godhead, she falls but unlike Satan plunges through surfaces deep into guilt that becomes transformed into self-knowledge audible as sound from 'within'.[68] Renaissance physiology depicted the female exterior as the most delightful and dangerously permeable of the two sexes; her moist and cold interior spaces waited to be warmed and filled by male heat. The first woman naturally, then, may dramatize the human body's, and perhaps not least a poet's, sensitive 'trembling' ears,

[67] Milton, *Complete Prose Works*, vol. ii, 'Areopagitica', 527–8. The phrase 'a provoking object' occurs in an earlier passage: 'We our selves esteem not of that obedience, or love, or gift, which is of force: God therefore left him [Adam] free, set before him a provoking object, ever almost in his eyes; herein consisted his merit, herein the right of his reward, the praise of his abstinence' (*Complete Prose Works*, ii. 527. See Campbell, 'Paradisal Appetite and Cusan Food'.

[68] Recent work on Milton and the feminine include Tony Davies, ' "The Meaning, not the Name": Milton and Gender', in William Zunder and Suzanne Trill (eds.), *Writing and the English Renaissance*, (London: Longman, 1996), 193–212; Riggs, 'The Temptation of Milton's Eve'; Mandy Green, ' "The Vine and her Elm": Milton's Eve and the Transformation of an Ovidian Motif', *Modern Language Review*, 91 (1996), 301–16; Michael Wilding, ' "Thir Sex Not Equal Seem'd": Equality in *Paradise Lost*', in P. G. Stanwood (ed.), *Of Poetry and Politics: New Essays on Milton and his World*, Medieval and Renaissance Texts and Studies 126 (Binghamton, NY: Medieval and Renaissance Texts and Studies, 1995), 171–86; Donald M. Friedman, 'Divisions on a Ground: "Sex" in *Paradise Lost*', in Stanwood (ed.), *Of Poetry and Politics*, 203–12; Michael Lieb, ' "Two of Far Nobler Shape": Reading the Paradisal Text', in *Literary Milton: Text, Pretext, Context*, Diana Treviño Benet and Michael Lieb (eds.), (Pittsburgh, Pa.: Duquesne University Press, 1994), 114–32; Joseph Wittreich, ' "Inspir'd with Contradiction": Mapping Gender Discourses in *Paradise Lost*', in Benet and Lieb (eds.), *Literary Milton*, 133–79; John Leonard, *Naming in Paradise: Milton and the Language of Adam and Eve* (Oxford: Clarendon Press, 1990); Turner, *One Flesh*.

as open 'wickets' to insidious colonization by flatterers but also, when contemplatively turned within, to the self's interior space of understanding and will.[69]

In the solitary, hidden space of judgement like the innermost ear where we began this chapter, man finds or loses his balance. The poem's interrelated images of scales, of listening and eating, of spaces that fill and empty—even Raphael's account of angelic digestion—reflect the drama of interiority as one of self-knowledge and the acknowledgement of limit. Eve's interior growth into self-recognition occurs through becoming separated—in her devilish dream and through her plan for efficient gardening—from the arms of Adam's 'grateful digressions' that held them together in a balance of reciprocity. What is balanced needs nothing added or removed. When she upsets that balance, tempted by Satan to substitute transgression for their 'digressions', she falls trying to consume knowledge as filling, as ballast to balance herself alone.

Eve's fall into the birth of human depth prepares for the virgin birth of 'the Great Son' who knows how to wait and to match the Father 'me' for 'me' (III. 173–82 and 236–49).[70] The final lines of *Paradise Regained*—'hee, unobserv'd, | Home to his Mothers house private return'd'—recapitulate the hidden movement of *Paradise Lost*, which takes place in shadow and digression behind the cover of epic extravagance. Eve usefully leads Milton home 'unobserv'd' and 'private' to the terse confidence of the Son. God cedes his power to the Son as his voice modulates into the Son's new sound and as the luscious garden that represents a fine line between full and excess modulates into the wilderness. The Son's

[69] On Renaissance conceptions of female physiology, see, for example, Kate Aughterson (ed.), *Renaissance Women: Constructions of Femininity in England*, (London: Routledge, 1995), ch. 2, 41–66; Thomas Laqueur, *Making Sex: Body and Gender from the Greeks to Freud* (Cambridge, Mass.: Harvard University Press, 1990); Jonathan Sawday, *The Body Emblazoned: Dissection and the Human Body in Renaissance Culture* (London: Routledge, 1995).

[70] Empson, *Milton's God*, first brought to my attention the ringing repetition of 'me' in the Son's speech. Many critics have seen lines of connection between Eve and the Son: see Kerrigan, *The Sacred Complex* esp. 186–7; Richard Corum, 'In White Ink: *Paradise Lost* and Milton's Ideas of Women', in Julia M. Walker (ed.), *Milton and the Idea of Woman*, (Urbana: University of Illinois Press 1988), 120–47; less directly, David Robertson, 'Soliloquy and Self in Milton's Major Poems', in Stanwood (ed.), *Of Poetry and Politics*, 59–77; and Patricia A. Parker's chapter on Milton in *Inescapable Romance*. On Eve as representative of a 'new heroism' celebrated by Milton, one characterized by virtues traditional commended to females such as patience and suffering, see John C. Ulreich, ' "Argument Not Less But More Heroic": Eve as the Hero of *Paradise Lost*', in Charles W. Durham and Kristin A. Pruitt (eds.), *All in All: Unity, Diversity and the Miltonic Perspective*, (Selinsgrove, Pa.: Susquehanna University Press, 1999), 67–82.

quiet sound of moral aristocracy and sufficiency, like Eve's discovery of penitence, reflects Milton's creation of the private voice of moral authority. The Son, but first and more subtly 'our mother Eve', reforms the rigid law, and sound, of the Father by internalizing and containing the pressures of abundance and visibility of this poem. Submissive, she will yield her story of interiority to the Son and to Samson. Milton claims the whole epic landscape and a politics which models itself on such extravagant, public lines as his beloved native ground of youthful instruction, as England's nostalgic past, and as an overgrown, outgrown territory of voices. Behind a dazzling visual profusion of a mind that seems to be 'remembering and repeating', this Protestant epic of a blind poet sounds a model of heroism that is subtly audible.[71]

[71] Schwartz, *Remembering and Repeating*, esp. 27 and 92–104.

PART III

Strategic Self-Sounding: Mystery, Malice, and Mastery of a Voice

5
Feminine Disguise in *The Hind and the Panther*

> Much malice mingl'd with a little wit
> Perhaps may censure this mysterious writ,
> Because the Muse has peopl'd *Caledon*
> With *Panthers, Bears,* and *Wolves,* and Beasts unknown,
> As if we were not stock'd with monsters of our own.
>
> (*The Hind and the Panther,* III. 1–5)[1]

The narrator of *Paradise Lost* leads us to loss although away from ends, announcing in the last lines a new beginning of wandering. Dryden will observe in *The Discourse of Satire* that Milton's epic subject is 'not that of an Heroique Poem; properly so call'd: His Design is the losing of our Happiness; his Event is not prosperous, like that of all other Epique Works'; but in the digressive texts we turn to by Dryden, as in the *Anniversaries* earlier, the poet writes if not epic then at great length in defensive and aggressive self-portraiture with a voice that knows, like Milton's narrator, 'the losing of our Happiness' and knows, although hidden behind Donne's Mosaic voice and Dryden's beast hides, the difficulty of prospering.[2] In these last two texts there is no garden, except perhaps the salad shared by the Hind and the Panther. The blade of execution that has fallen already at the middle of the *Anniversaries,* which reappears obliquely with new meaning in Marvell's estate poem, hovers in *The Hind and the Panther* whose debates and stories do not resolve difference but only keep physical violence at bay. The blade also reappears deep inside the *Discourse of Satire* through a report that the wife of public executioner Jack Ketch, a notorious butcher, praised her husband's

[1] All citations to Dryden's *The Hind and the Panther* are to *The Works of John Dryden,* vol. iii, ed. Earl Miner (Berkeley and Los Angeles: University of California Press, 1969), and are included parenthetically by part and line number in the text.

[2] *Discourse Concerning the Original and Progress of Satire,* in *The Works of John Dryden,* vol. iv, ed. A. B. Chambers and William Frost (Berkeley and Los Angeles: University of California Press, 1974), 14–15.

skill 'to make a Malefactor die sweetly'—an ironic foil for the satirist's bloodless skill 'that separates the Head from the Body, and leaves it standing in its place'.[3]

Milton's biblical Adam and Eve wandering to found not Rome but a private 'paradise within' hardly resembled, in 1667, the passionate heroes of one of Dryden's heroic dramas, nor did they conform to the current tastes of Restoration culture for visibility, extravagance, and play-going, especially for witty comedy of sexual banter cynical about Puritan morality. That same year, in which England suffered an embarrassing defeat by the Dutch that ended their three-year war and brought to a head escalating criticism of the court, also saw young John Dryden publishing new work in several modes: *Annus Mirabilis: The Year of Wonders, 1666*, a long poem celebrating England's naval victory of the preceding year, Charles II as father of his people, and the Fire of London as prophetic of the city's phoenix-like rise to power; the plays *Secret Love*, a high-toned pastoral romance, and his adaptation with William Davenant of Shakespeare's *The Tempest* that featured a sensuous sister for Miranda, a secret lost heir of Mantua raised innocent of females, and Sycorax as Caliban's sexy sister; and registered in August, the month that Milton registered his epic poem in blank verse, Dryden's first major piece of literary criticism, *An Essay of Dramatick Poesie*, which celebrated English drama and championed rhyme in tragedy as not only 'natural' but 'more effectual than blank Verse', heroic couplets as 'the noblest kind of modern verse'.[4] Created poet laureate in the following year and becoming the prolific arbiter of literary modes and values for his era, Dryden would have a complex relationship to Milton and his epic that would include transforming Milton's blank verse into a five-act opera in heroic couplets. In the preface to *Fables* (1700) shortly before his death, the former laureate will include Milton, his professional acquaintance ('Milton has acknowledged to me, that *Spenser* was his original'), in a literary lineage of Chaucer and Spenser, one of the family lines of poets among whom Dryden traces his own poetic fathers.

At least since *Annus Mirabilis*, Dryden had practised the control of narrative closure through his 'loose' periods and digressions—syntactic and narrative strategies of wandering and self-display to which he draws

[3] *Discourse Concerning the Original and Progress of Satire*, in *The Works of John Dryden*, vol. iv, ed. A. B. Chambers and William Frost (Berkeley and Los Angeles: University of California Press, 1974), 71.

[4] 'An Essay of Dramatick Poesie', in *The Works of John Dryden*, vol. xvii, ed. Samuel Holt Monk (Berkeley and Los Angeles: University of California Press, 1971), 3–81, 68, 74.

the reader's attention.[5] His image in the prefatory letter to *Annus Mirabilis* of the writer's faculty of wit or imagination that, 'like a nimble Spaniel, beats over and ranges through the field of Memory, till it springs the Quarry it hunted after' becomes a recurring figure in his work for creative thought as a delightful hunt of wandering within the well-stocked mind of the poet.[6] The epigraph from Dryden's 'The Life of Plutarch' that opens the Introduction to this book continues into a description of digressive thought as part of the pleasures for both writer and reader of the imagination's chase for game. Dryden there imagines the learned mind of a great poet or a great historian like Plutarch as so abundantly filled with treasures that the writer cannot help but overflow the bounds of his story, dropping 'riches' by the way:

> The best quarry lies not always in the open field: And who would not be content to follow a good Huntsman over Hedges and Ditches when he knows the Game will reward his pains? But if we mark him more narrowly, we may observe, that the great reason of his frequent starts, is the variety of his Learning: He knew so much of Nature, was so vastly furnish'd with all the treasures of the mind, that he was uneasie to himself, and was forc'd, as I may say, to lay down some at every passage, and to scatter his riches as he went:[7]

By 1687, however, as the voices of the hind and the panther, the poet speaks for both hunted and hunter and appears 'to scatter his riches' in order to send his readers over a hedge onto a false trail or into a ditch. Susan Stewart describes digression as a movement that opens narrative and personal closure 'from the inside out'; and Dryden's late work will reflect a shift in the meaning of being on the 'inside'—from the world of court and government to the fluid home and interiors of a mind become infinitely expansive.[8]

[5] Morris Croll, *Style, Rhetoric, and Rhythm* (Princeton: Princeton University Press, 1966), 327, referred to the 'loose' sentences which are 'always periodic in the proper sense' of Browne and Dryden. Others have observed how Dryden draws attention to the wayward nature of his prose, beginning in the Preface to *Annus Mirabilis* ('But to return from this digression to a further account of my poem . . .'. See *The Poems of John Dryden*, ed. James Kinsley (London: Oxford University Press, 1958), i. 46). In the words of one recent assessment, 'By the middle of his career, digression had become one of the most telling marks of Dryden's strongly purposeful style', behind which the poet 'constructed superbly shaped literary instruments'. See Steven N. Zwicker, 'Dryden and the Dissolution of Things: The Decay of Structures in Dryden's Late Writing', in Paul Hammond and David Hopkins (eds.), *John Dryden: Tercentenary Essays*, (Oxford: Clarendon Press, 2000), 308.

[6] Dryden, *Works*, i. 53.

[7] *Ibid.* xvii. 277.

[8] Susan Stewart, *On Longing: Narratives of the Miniature, the Gigantic, the Souvenir, the Collection* (Baltimore: Johns Hopkins University Press, 1984), 30, describes how digression 'stands in tension with narrative closure. It is narrative closure opened from the inside out. It holds the reader in suspension, or annoyance, for it presents the possibility of never getting back, of remaining forever within the detour'.

Dryden's conversion to Rome had become a subject of comment since the poet was seen going to mass in the company of his sons and Nell Gwyn in January of 1686.[9] Speculation over the motive for Dryden's conversion was rife from the beginning, and *The Hind and the Panther* suggests how sensitive to the scandal of insincerity Dryden had become in the months following the conversion as he mounted a defence of the integrity of his new faith. Entered in the Stationers' Register on 27 May 1687, almost twenty years after the publication of *Paradise Lost*, Dryden's *The Hind and the Panther* appeared in a highly charged, hostile environment. It occasioned a flood of abusive pamphlets: the readers greeted it not unlike the boorish sectarian beasts at the 'wat'ring place' who stared at the Hind, 'Survey'd her part by part, and sought to find | The ten-horn'd monster . . . | Such as the Wolfe and Panther had design'd' (I. 536–8). As the laureate's long-awaited defence of his conversion to Roman Catholicism and of James II's strategic Declaration of Indulgence, the poem faced a readership as unindulgent as can be imagined. Hardly surprising, then, is its heavy armour of confrontational preface, of fabular, oriental mystery, and 'nocturnal howlings' from 'bestial citizens' which dramatically distinguish the poem from the tones of vernal mildness and thanksgiving being orchestrated to celebrate James's project.[10] Here is a depiction less of toleration than of violence barely restrained.

[9] This well-known rumour reported in Evelyn's *Diary* for 19 Jan. 1686 is the first known reference to Dryden's conversion. See John Evelyn, *The Diary of John Evelyn*, ed. Esmond Samuel De Beer, 6 vols. (Oxford: Clarendon Press, 1955), iv. 497.

[10] Note, for example, the opening of 'A Poem Occasioned by His Majesties Most Gracious Resolution Declared in his Most Honorable Privy Council, March 18, 1686 | 7, for Liberty of Conscience':

> What heav'nly beam thus antedates the spring
> And summer's warmth with autumn's fruits doth bring.
> That spreads new life throughout Great Britain's isle
> And, making the most sullen tempers smile,
> Does all the jarring factions reconcile?

Galbraith M. Crump (ed.), *Poems on Affairs of State*, vol. iv (New Haven: Yale University Press, 1968), 102–4. Addresses of thanksgiving from the sects—from Baptists and Anabaptists, Presbyterians, Independents, Quakers, Congregationalists, and Nonconformists—filled the *London Gazette* from 14 April 1687 to 21 June 1688; they were finally replaced by congratulations on the birth of the Prince of Wales. For a contemporary survey of the addresses, see John Oldmixon, *The History of Addresses. By one very near a kin to the author of the Tale of a Tub. Diu multumque desideratum* (London, 1709), ch. vi, 105–55. Much commented upon as the phenomenon of the day, the addresses were parodied in such pamphlets as 'The Humble Address of the Atheists, or the Sect of the Epicureans', signed from 'the Devil-Tavern', 5 November 1688. Also sceptical in response to the 'fashion' of addresses and to the court's role in drafting them is George Savile, Marquis of Halifax, in

But the hostile atmosphere (as anticipated and real) presented the poet with interesting strategic and aesthetic terms which have not been sufficiently appreciated. The history of its reception, in fact, is a record of outrage and bewilderment that reaches from the barrage of contemporary parodies, through Johnson's disapproval of its mixed satiric and heroic modes, Saintsbury's reluctant pronouncement of its 'desultory' character, to C. S. Lewis's notorious remark that a design blending beast fable and theological controversy suggests a mind 'bordering on aesthetic insanity'.[11] Modern scholarship has been more energetic in appreciating the poem's historical and political context and the ways Dryden engaged the fabulist tradition, yet the poem still impresses as an extravagant jumble of poetic techniques and voices.[12] More than one scholar has stumbled over the poem's biblical and literary allusion, its historical, prophetic, and satiric vision, confessing with James Winn that 'Dryden must bear some of the blame for the long history of misreadings this difficult poem has endured'.[13] Its original readers, prepared for another well-honed attack along the lines of *Absalom and Achitophel*, found only an embarrassing 'New-converted Hero, Mr. Bayes' who 'hath subdued his Understanding' to zeal. They were rebuffed by the poem's savage darkness, by the extravagant unreason of a distracted author 'in the flower of his Romantick Conceptions', whose 'Brains, indeed, have been a long time used to Chimera's', capable only of 'Ornaments and Superfluencies of Invention and Satyr'. As one contemporary wrote in

'A Letter to a Dissenter, upon Occasion of his Majesties Late Gracious Declaration of Indulgence' (London: G. H., 1687, Wing H312); see esp. 4–5. See also *Calendar of State Papers, Domestic Series. James II*, iii: *June 1687–February 1689* (London: HM Stationery Office, 1972), paper no. 655.

[11] For the contemporary responses see Hugh Macdonald, *John Dryden: A Bibliography of Early Editions and of Drydeniana* (Oxford: Clarendon Press, 1939), 253–63; and Crump (ed.), *Poems on Affairs of State*, iv. 116–50. Samuel Johnson, *Lives of the English Poets*, ed. George Birkbeck Hill and Harold S. Scott, 3 vols. (Oxford: Clarendon Press, 1905), 'John Dryden', i. 380–3; George Saintsbury, *Dryden* (London: Macmillan, 1881), 79; C. S. Lewis, 'Shelley, Dryden and Mr. Eliot', in *Rehabilitations and Other Essays* (London: Oxford University Press, 1939), 8–9.

[12] See, for example, Earl Miner's notes in the California Dryden, iii. 320–459, esp. 340–6; also Mark Loveridge, *A History of Augustan Fable* (Cambridge: Cambridge University Press, 1998), 144–55; Anne Barbeau Gardiner, *Ancient Faith and Modern Freedom in John Dryden's The Hind and the Panther* (Washington, DC: Catholic University of America Press, 1998); Jayne E. Lewis, *The English Fable: Aesop and Literary Culture, 1651–1740* (Cambridge: Cambridge University Press, 1996); and Annabel Patterson's *Fables of Power: Aesopian Writing and Political History* (Durham, NC: Duke University Press, 1991), 95–105.

[13] James Anderson Winn, *John Dryden and his World* (New Haven: Yale University Press, 1987), 427.

1687, 'take away the Railing, and no Argument remains: so that one may beat the Bush a whole day, and after so much labour, only spring a Butterfly, or start an Hedg-hog'.[14] Like more recent students of the poem, they were uncomfortable with such ambiguous models of heroism as a hind (even if she is a church), a narrator at once confessional and viciously satiric, and a 'British Lyon' by the end demystified to the view of street gossips. 'What, do you make a fable of your religion?' a shocked Johnson asks Bayes in Montagu and Prior's 'The Hind and the Panther Transversed' (1687), the most influential contemporary attack; and so have wondered many.

The digressive narrator was seized on immediately by Montagu and Prior in their hastily composed send-up 'The Hind and the Panther Transversed to the Story of the Country Mouse and the City Mouse', which appeared within two months of Dryden's poem. In their spoof, Dryden as Bayes boasts that he has borrowed but elevated and heightened Horace's simple fable of the mice: 'Now, whereas Horace keeps to the dry naked story, I have more copiousness than to do that, egad. Here I draw you general characters and describe all the beasts of the creation; there I launch out into long digressions and leave my Mice for twenty pages together; then I fall into raptures and make the finest soliloquies, as would ravish you. Won't this do, think you?'[15] To many of Dryden's readers to this day, his eerie beast-churches which only meet and begin to speak at the end of a first part of over 500 lines, and which are interrupted periodically by the reflections of a confessional narrator, won't 'do' at all.

Montagu and Prior mock Dryden's 'long digressions' and easy 'raptures' in 'obedience to his new mother Hind'; and they gaily contrast his smooth profusion designed 'for the ladies' with the rough, virile lines of Milton whom 'a man must sweat to read'.[16] One popular theme of contemporary response, in fact, was the susceptibility of Dryden's conscience to wifely wish and female art—'his fond uxorious vice'.[17] A typical anonymous pamphlet scolded Dryden for falling prey 'To Midianitish

[14] Martin Clifford, *Notes upon Mr. Dryden's Poems in Four Letters to Which are Annexed Some Reflections upon the Hind and the Panther. By Another Hand* (London, 1687, Wing C4706), 18–19.

[15] Charles Montagu and Matthew Prior, 'The Hind and the Panther Transversed to the Story of the Country Mouse and the City Mouse', in Crump (ed.), *Poems on Affairs of State*, iv. 124–5.

[16] Ibid. 134.

[17] The phrase appears on p. 2 of *The Weesils. A Satyrical Fable, Giving an Account of Some Argumental Passages Happening in the Lion's Court about Weesilion's Taking Oaths* (London, 1691), attributed by Wing to Tom Brown.

Gods and Wives', and associated the 'soft bewitching Arts' of *The Hind and the Panther* with the decadent wiles of feminized Egypt, Babylon, and Balaam.[18] By associating the tantalizing delays of digression with 'the ladies' and the Whore of Babylon, Dryden's critics turn their own bewilderment with the poem into a portrait of a weakened and wandering laureate and feminize their prey. But unwittingly they describe his game. For after the Glorious Revolution, Dryden will assume often this cover of the subordinate gender, as well as syntactic subordination and digression, to wrest control over his own closure.

The numerous editions of Aesop and other fabulists in the period suggest their popularity and a perception of these tales as 'both plain and devious' among a wide range of readers.[19] When Montagu and Prior dashed off *The Hind and the Panther Transversed* (1687) in response to Dryden's poem, they knew exactly what a fable should look like:

> They were first begun and raised to the highest perfection in the eastern countries, where they wrote in signs and spoke parables and delivered the most useful precepts in delightful stories. . . . All their fables carry a double meaning. . . . But this is his new way of telling a story and confounding the moral and the fable together.[20]

For a story to teach and delight while the characters devour each other, the moral must be clear; but in Dryden's 'Medley Offerings', who had won?[21] The simultaneous appearance in 1651 of Hobbes's *Leviathan* and of the first of John Ogilby's five Restoration editions of Aesop reflects the nervous politics of fable in an age when the human beast appears to require firm control and when only the simplest words and images can be trusted.[22] But Dryden's text refuses to close on a precept—it refuses to close at all.

[18] *The Murmurers* (London: R. Baldwin, 1689), 14.

[19] Lewis, *The English Fable*, 5. Mark Kishlansky has noted, 'from the 1550s not a decade passed without the publication of another English edition of Aesop. It was one of the most popular books in early modern England'. See 'Turning Frogs into Princes: Aesop's *Fables* and the Political Culture of Early Modern England', in *Political Culture and Cultural Politics in Early Modern England, Essays Presented to David Underdown*, eds. Susan D. Amussen and Mark A. Kishlansky (Manchester and New York, 1995), 338–60, 340.

[20] Montagu and Prior, 'The Hind and the Panther Transversed to the Story of the Country Mouse and the City Mouse', 118–45, 119–20.

[21] Lewis characterizes the moral of fables as 'cynical and pragmatic' (*The English Fable*, 20); the phrase 'Medley Offerings' appears in *The Revolter: A Trage-Comedy Acted between the Hind and the Panther, and Religio Laici* (London, 1687), 9.

[22] Lewis, *The English Fable*, 21. She argues that fables were concrete and moralistic in a way that circumvented the 'official hostility to figuration' characteristic of the Interregnum government and later of scientific and philosophic debate within the Royal Society. The popularity of fables in the late 17th century might reflect the way that their 'complex materiality' made them antidotes to a figural crisis that was also political and cultural (8). On the historical relations between politics and fable, see also Patterson, *Fables of Power*.

The contemporary reader had an instinct, though, for where the action was. And his nose for tracking the beast to its lair points in useful directions for thinking about this poem written so intensely into its historical moment. Dryden's contemporaries were well versed in the various languages and idioms of public discourse, in the allusive vocabulary from several decades of lampooning the laureate, and in the details of his current personal and political vulnerability. They may complain of groping in the dark, of feeling hoodwinked trying to navigate the unsteady ground of the poem. Yet their parodies, transversions, jingles, and admonitions to the laureate, when read together, reveal a coherent set of expectations to or around which Dryden must have been writing, and a consistent set of phrases and images from the poem—traces on the trail—which we can be sure the poet meant them to see. In an attempt to understand the poem's psychology and design, I propose working backward through this web of expectations and traces to the author at his task. With help from the contemporary responses, I hope to uncover the aesthetic and political materials, and choices, Dryden faced as he wrote the laureate's address of thanksgiving for James's Declaration.

If we track the poet to the literal centre of the poem, he holds up the words 'this mysterious writ' (III. 2). Under the official cover of court propaganda and the dreamlike aspect of fable, Dryden spins a complex representation from the inside, inside a beast's hide, of how the atmosphere of 1686–7 feels. At the same time, in this literary text he seems determined to conceal not only himself but, to some extent, the King, the central characters his readers would expect to find. We must ask, then, to what occasion is this poem addressed? Was Dryden leaving the representation of charity and mercy to the king and, as hired gun, flashing the threat of 'the arts of Craft and Violence', in the words of one reader? As a cornered man raises clouds of dust in the face of his pursuers to hide and gain time, or points away to the sky to divert their attention, so *The Hind and the Panther* functions like a smokescreen of distracting gestures. And at the climax of the Second Part, when the Hind looks up to the sky and says, 'She whom ye seek am I', we realize what the game is.

Those odd mothers, the four-footed churches, have made many uneasy; each like a negative image of the other, they suggest a world being viewed from the inside out. It is no accident that a poem which represents a historical moment as feeling like a world in negative, negative both as a reversal of light and dark and as of something crucially absent, introduces in its first part the image of God as 'darkness in th' abyss of light'. I suggest that this poem of hide and seek is written about, around, but irresistibly toward a crucial absence or vacuum, carefully enclosed, protected, and bridged by the suspended belief, like fable, of toleration. What is absent, I would argue, is the mystical light of the sun of Stuart monarchy, which blazed in *Astrea Redux* and lit up the sword of justice in *Absalom and Achitophel.*[23] In the confused finale of the Hind's fable, much remarked by disgruntled readers, which ends and re-ends, she looks ahead not only to the absence but to the extinction of James—at least on earth. By imagining the time beyond his death, the poem daringly erases the king and his Indulgence as if they had never been; no wonder the poet raises a protective mist of multiple endings, as if he had forgotten his original thought or were becoming senile. James will be translated to heaven, whence the Hind is also bound for her 'future state'. The final couplet, though speaking of the Hind, quietly grants a future to the deceased James of seventeen lines earlier—though not a future of this lifetime. Despite its religious and confessional sounds, the poem is intensely interested in, not heaven, but the here and now; and it imagines no such 'glorious Visions' of England's future state. By 1687, all that remains of Restoration heroism are two brief flashes. At the end of the second part, the comet's blaze of English Catholicism and of James's 'lambent easie light' serve only to 'Guild the brown horrour' and augur the night of the third part; they emphasize a false inversion of darkness to light, the void created by the sun's banishment. And into that void rushes violence—the beast of the apocalypse.

The poem leads its predators to dark empty spots which they rush to fill, first and most distractingly that of the 'Play-wright Laureate debaush'd', the subject of our first discussion. Instead of being alarmed by the beasts and rushing, too, I want to pause over the Hind and the Panther and their collusion in the poem. The second part, when they begin to talk, forms a curious interlude of relative calm which needs to be examined. Though not the actual centre of the poem, it serves as rather a fabulous moment of poise between the lurking, savage darkness of the narrator's bestiary of the first part and the prophetic darkness, climaxed by the grim pair of fables, of the third. And it introduces the churches, and the poem itself, as an uncanny balancing act of great verbal dexterity and darkening silence. Once the Hind and the Panther are tensely settled side by side indoors, civility almost breaks down, and so do their

[23] William Myers has argued that the poem demonstrates how Dryden is shifting faith from man to God, from the Stuart family to the Catholic Church (in *Dryden* (London: Hutchinson University Library, 1973), 120). Yet the shift seems of a more complex nature. The Church alone is not the 'broader base for his ideas' which Dryden needs.

differences as together they circle near—to enclose yet approach—a hushed void. Contemporary readers sensed a vacuum but could only describe it in feelings of being led down a false trail, finding what Thomas Heyrick called 'Beast Hides' covering straw.

By 1687 Dryden was in a position of political vulnerability quite new in his career.[24] He faced a different set of pressures, political and personal, from those which had produced the triumphant power of wit in *Absalom and Achitophel* or the unassailable authority of moderation and 'common quiet' of *Religio Laici.* The tone and strategy of *The Hind and the Panther*, which contemporary readers found so baffling, reflect this change. Yet Dryden was consistent in being outrageous. His boldness had been always to rewrite disadvantage as advantage, weakness as strength. If he could turn the disasters of 1666, like alchemy, into wonders prophetic of a new golden age, transform Charles II's profligacy into piety in the space of two opening lines, he could turn to advantage his conversion and his subsequent humiliations in the face of expected advancement. In the preface, Dryden's threat of moderation, coupled with slurs on the ingratitude of the sects, recalls similar claims for moderation in the prefaces to *Absalom and Achitophel* and *Religio Laici* where he simultaneously reaches for the surgical blade or the sword of Goliath. The tone is wearily superior, disciplinary, and provocative; he is controlling 'what I desire the reader should know concerning me', and not hiding his low opinion of the reader. The condescension of 'should know', the scolding of ''tis aim'd only at the refractory and disobedient on either side', and further teasing announcements which conceal more than they reveal, such as 'I will only thus far satisfie the Reader', establish the theme of discipline through frustration. I want to emphasize the tour de force of Dryden's boldness, his sleight of hand in aggressively keeping the hostile readers in the dark by announcing and, at the same time, withdrawing himself exactly when they assume he is most exposed. While the critics thought they had him covered, they failed to recall that the laureate's most brilliant writing had always been stimulated by opposition, and that exactly when the cause looked most hopeless did he feel freed to rewrite the terms—what he now does by late winter of 1686 and 1687. Only never before was his cause so much himself. In this rewriting of the Roman

[24] Work addressing this issue includes David Bywaters, '"Echo's of Her Once Loyal Voice": *The Hind and the Panther*', in *Dryden in Revolutionary England* (Berkeley and Los Angeles: University of California Press, 1991), esp. 9–10; and Steven N. Zwicker, *Politics and Language in Dryden's Poetry: The Arts of Disguise* (Princeton: Princeton University Press, 1984), 123–38.

mystery story, Dryden has claimed for himself, and significantly not for 'the plain good man', the privilege of feminine and Eastern inscrutability. Under the glare of the public gaze, Dryden's literary experiment is to be everywhere and nowhere, another 'darkness in the abyss of light'.

Challenged to test themselves against him, his enemies scurry to neutralize the poem's claims to authority and write over its mystery. Montagu and Prior pretend to lampoon only reluctantly what 'naturally falls into ridicule' like the village idiot—as if Dryden were, indeed, undergoing a gesture of humility and sacrifice in 'obedience to his new mother Hind'. Not only the 'bristl'd Baptist Boar' and the wolf with 'predestinating ears', but 'Sister Partlet with her hooded head' who 'would not pray a-bed' are so ridiculous they seem to demand attack, though they appear alerted against it. Yet the critics' embrace and the poem's seem to close around absences until it is only clear 'What vowels and what consonants are there'; the prey evaporates into thin air, like 'our air'y faith', thought 'winnowed well'—the poet's 'sparkles' as ignes fatui. And when Montagu and Prior defend their transversion by insisting 'there is nothing represented here as monstrous and unnatural, which is not equally so in the original', the adjectives suggest the enormity and danger of the beast they feel compelled to expose.

Sensing the wandering track of a wounded prey, the pamphleteers sharpened their quills and lost no time in aiming at every known assailable point. And there were many: the poet's conversion, his temptation to become a second Almanzor and 'fight single with whole Armies', his missed academic preferments, his unrealized epic ambitions now gradually overshadowed by Milton's accomplishment, his old liaison with Anne Reeves, and his unfinished exchange the previous year with Protestant bishop and controversialist Edward Stillingfleet over the Duchess of York's 'Royal Paper'. Just as Dryden's 'Defence' of Anne Hyde's conversion, with its masterful portrait of 'the answerer' whose 'cloven foot . . . appears from underneath the cassock', looks ahead to his own conversion paper, so Stillingfleet's heated reply anticipated those of Montagu and Prior, of Gould, Heyrick, and Brown. In writing *The Hind and the Panther*, Dryden anticipated and donned fictions such as the 'ductile soul' and 'Rebel to God', the quixotic 'Hector in controversy' or romantic hero charging armies of thistles; but he stepped out of them, leaving behind in his poem the outlines as teasing traces.[25] In frustration and disbelief, his readers kept shaking those beast hides.

[25] See Stillingfleet's 'An Answer to the Defence of the Third Paper', in *The Works of John Dryden*, ed. Sir Walter Scott, 18 vols. (London: William Miller, 1808), xvii. 252–77, esp. 253, 255.

In the preface to *The New Atlantis* (1687), Thomas Heyrick described how he had assumed of *The Hind and the Panther* that 'the utmost could be said for the Cause of the Hind was there, and if Troy was to be defended, it would be by the Hand of Such a Hero'. But instead of a 'dreadful Host', upon nearer approach he found 'Troops of Apes' led by the worst court advocate imaginable. Critics complained that Dryden's fable broke all the rules by being at once too long, too various, and without a moral.[26] For some, Dryden was the turncoat atheist become ranting prophet;[27] for others, he was 'An ordain'd Play-wright in the House of Prayer'[28] trying to compete with and steal from Milton.[29] Unable to miss the pressure of beastly violence and satire, the critics ridiculed the paranoid, 'hypochondriac author', afraid to step on the streets without drawing his sword, a wild-eyed fanatic such as James's Toleration was designed to temper, the King himself escaping only with faint praise.[30] Indeed, as one anonymous observer wrote,

> Now sure he cannot fail of a supply
> From a rich mother 'fated ne'er to die'?
> But how can he receive it from the cowls,
> Who likens their beloved nuns to owls?
> Nor can the sov'reign hand reward his tongue,
> Who counts it his prerogative to wrong.[31]

The poet's conversion for material reward is assumed, and his bitter mood has not been missed. Being 'out in his Politicks', the poet 'hath not recommended his Religion, as He was wont to do his Plays, by Civility, Insinuation, good Language . . . for the English being a good-natur'd

[26] 'What in that Tedious Poem hast thou done, | But cramm'd all Aesops Fables into one', charged Robert Gould in 'The Laureat. Jack Squabbs History in a Little Drawn, Down to his Evening, from his Early Dawn' (London, 1687, Wing G1421).

[27] 'And I see no reason, Mr. Bayes, after you have traded somewhat longer in Parable, & allegory, but that you may step in among their [the Turks'] Minor Prophets'. Thomas Brown, *The Reasons of Mr. Bays Changing his Religion. Considered in a Dialogue between Crites, Eugenius, and Mr. Bays* (London: S.T. , 1688, Wing B5069), 2.

[28] *The Revolter. A Trage-Comedy*, 3.

[29] (Bayes:) 'I writ this line for the ladies. The little rogues will be so fond of me to find I can yet be so tender. I hate such a rough, unhewn fellow as Milton, that a man must sweat to read him. Egad, you may run over this and be almost asleep'. Montagu and Prior, 'The Hind and the Panther Transversed to the Story of the Country Mouse and the City Mouse', in Crump (ed.), *Poems on Affairs of State*, 134.

[30] See, for example, *The Revolter. A Trage-Comedy*, 2, 13; and Clifford, *Notes upon Mr Dryden's Poems*, 29, 31–2.

[31] 'On the Author of *The Hind and the Panther*', ll.12–17, in Crump (ed.), *Poems on Affairs of State*, iv. 145.

People, are sooner won by good Words than Blows'.[32] From the 'Blows', the unreasoned violence of the poem, the critics recoiled; yet the violence they had registered was necessary for Dryden to rewrite the terms of authority. He gained the necessary distance to become mysterious by assuming the stance of the barking, apocalyptic spectre who 'rails at all before him, and is fed | Hyena-like, by tearing up the dead'.[33]

The author attacked every recognized political faction except his own, the moderate Catholics. And the poem seems to be preparing a departure as if in the light of 'certain knowledge' that 'the Conflagration is at hand'.[34] As Tom Brown saw it, there was no going back: 'The worthy Gentlemen that have set him upon the Heroick design of writing the *Hind and Panther* (for I must beg Mr. Bays's pardon if I am so unmannerly as not to believe every thing he says in his Preface) . . . have cut off all hopes of a retreat from him; the back doors are shut, but the passage before is open enough, and the way to Meccha and Constantinople as easie to be found as ever'.[35] The identification of pope and cannibal-Turk, papist and 'Musselman', the superimposition of Rome onto a monstrous East, was a fixture of the anti-Catholic literature and political cartoons. When he converted Dryden began a new life as the 'mighty Mohammed's hail fellow'.[36] The 'Land of Nod' first wandered by the 'murth'rer Cain' was incarnated in the beastly Whore of Babylon on whose forehead was 'a name written, mystery'. As a Roman Catholic, Dryden was inventing a new voice of mystery; and, as in any mystery story, characters are missing, there are unexplained events, and frustrating, inexplicable gaps of knowledge.

[32] Clifford, *Notes upon Mr Dryden's Poems*, 33.

[33] Brown, *The Reasons of Mr. Bays Changing his Religion*, p. 8 of the preface.

[34] Ibid. 3.

[35] Ibid. p. 8 of the Preface.

[36] See, for example, not only *Poems on Affairs of State*, vol. ii (ed. Elias F. Mengel, Jr., 1965) and iii (ed. Howard H. Schless, 1968), but also British Museum, *Catalogue of Prints and Drawings in the British Museum. Division I: Political and Personal Satires*, i: *1320–April 11, 1689* (London: The Trustees, 1870). For discussion of anti-Catholicism in early modern English texts, see Alison Shell, *Catholicism, Controversy, and the English Literary Imagination, 1558–1660* (Cambridge: Cambridge University Press, 1999), and Arthur F. Marotti (ed.), *Catholicism and Anti-Catholicism in Early Modern English Texts* (Houndmills: Macmillan 1999).

At the conclusion of his 'Defence' of the Duchess's paper, Dryden taunts Stillingfleet by scoffing at this time-honoured marriage of Rome and the East as a fantasy of 'the common people' ('Our author knows he has all the common people on his side, and they only read the gazettes of their own writers . . . and the Turk and Pope are their sworn enemies'), playfully tracing the association to a hymn by zealot Robin Wisdom, which begins: 'Preserve us, Lord, by thy dear word; | From Turk and Pope defend us, Lord'. *The Works of John Dryden*, ed. Scott, xvii. 250–1.

A parallel between *The Hind and the Panther* and *Absalom and Achitophel* has been sensed by Sanford Budick who notes, 'The same politico-exegetical impulse which produced the stream of David–Absolon applications which ultimately resulted in Dryden's *Absalom and Achitophel* also generated the literature of horn and beast applications which was to eventuate, in complex ways, in *The Hind and the Panther*'.[37] Since the Reformation, anti-papal tracts had cartooned Rome as 'this filthy Babylonish Trull' and 'Scarlet Whore', which in one broadside was contrasted to the Church of England as a pleading Queen Esther.[38] From Spenser's Duessa and Lucifera up to Restoration polemics, the blood-drinking Whore of Babylon was the ubiquitous Protestant depiction of the papacy. At the same time, Anglicans maintained a firm tradition of affinity with Christianity of the Eastern Church. The Reformation had no quarrel with the Orthodox East, and Anglican authority felt as ready to regulate its church by continuous Eastern practice as by primitive Christianity.[39] Andrewes, Laud, and Stillingfleet all attempted negotiations with Constantinople.[40] Thus the Anglican Panther, not Dryden, is a minotaur caught in her own maze, like 'a creature of a double kind, | In her own labyrinth she lives confin'd' (I. 402–3). As a 'meer mock Queen of a divided Herd' (I. 498), her upper body wields crozier and mitre showing 'affectation of an ancient line' (I. 397), but her lower body is stigmatized as beastly. Exploiting the emotion around Rome's, and Canterbury's, oriental connections, flashing the red alarm to frighten his enemies and make them show their horns, Dryden's feminine churches ventriloquized as beasts blur and reverse the identification of saint and whore. He piles up fables within his fable and adds creation and genealogy myths as well, using Eastern and feminine luxury and ambiguity to excite and elude definition. The guilty 'ever changeling' convert turns again, now into the copious fabulist skilled in sign and parable. The Hind may be ascetic in her tastes; but she is spectacularly

[37] Sanford Budick, *Dryden and the Abyss of Light: A Study of 'Religio Laici' and 'The Hind and the Panther'* (New Haven: Yale University Press, 1970), 204.

[38] See *Babel and Bethel: or, the Pope in his Colours* (London?, 1680), Wing B244.

[39] Aidan Nichols, *The Panther and the Hind: A Theological History of Anglicanism* (Edinburgh: T. & T. Clark, 1993), 73.

[40] P. E. More and F. L. Cross, (ed.), *Anglicanism: The Thought and Practice of the Church of England, Illustrated from the Religious Literature of the Seventeenth Century* (London: Society for Promoting Christian Knowledge, 1935), p. lxxii. Herbert Thorndike, a scholarly prebendary of Westminster under Charles II, articulated this enduring High Church theme of kinship with the East, 'which acknowledgeth not the Pope', in his monumental *Epilogue to the Tragedy of the Church of England* (1659). See *The Theological Works of Herbert Thorndike*, vols. i–vi (each vol. in two parts) (Oxford: J. H. Parker, 1844–56).

verbal, of Jesuitic stamina (although she admits that Jesuits 'can equivocate', II. 45), and her turning the Protestant charge of Catholic sexual misconduct and Eastern hedonism back against the 'Lady of the spotted muff', a thrust crucial to their very feminine exchange, rewrites and remystifies the Rome-Meccha story as catty female gossip. Under protection of the feminine beast, Dryden takes the Roman and the Eastern veil.[41]

Before we move into the twilight of the second part, whose voluble spiritualist summons the rest of the poem with a look to the skies, we need to acknowledge another Roman presence in the poem. We have described one set of associations with his new Roman connection which Dryden was exploiting to rewrite the terms of his defence. He baffled his critics with Eastern profusion, repelled and distanced them with the female predator and negative mystery of the apocalyptic beast. But the connections between the feminine and 'Mr. D. the Romanist' are more complex; they include not only the feminine beast but an 'ancient mother', the exiled, pious hero and a bloody conqueror. We might ask ourselves why the poem's narrator and both of the beasts regularly allude to *The Aeneid*.[42]

The Hind and the Panther are not the only females or mothers in the poem; they are preceded by a pagan mother and goddess of love in epigraphs on the title page: '*Antiquam exquirite matrem*' ('Seek your ancient mother') and '*Et vera, incessu, patuit Dea*' ('The true goddess is revealed by her grace of movement'). After all, Dryden's first 'Ancient Mother' was the Rome of Augustus Caesar and its literary masters. Virgil, Horace, and Ovid were preoccupied with origins and authority, with transformations and destiny. The Virgilian passages in the poem recall Aeneas as the invader bringing war to Latium, who finally yields to his own bloodlust. Through the voices of the Hind and the Panther, we hear Evander and Turnus (II. 309, III. 766–80), and we see the boding birds sent to Juturna (II. 701–13).

[41] Earl Miner notes that 'Dryden does enjoy playing upon the fact' that 'the Hind and the Panther are feminine', but he says no more on the effect of their femininity in the poem (see *Dryden's Poetry* (Bloomington: Indiana University Press, 1967), 150). He has viewed the three parts as a historical vision extending from the evolution of religious controversy in the past (the first part), to the present debate (the second part), and thence to prospects for the future of the English churches (the third part). See Miner, 'The Significance of Plot in *The Hind and the Panther*', *Bulletin of the New York Public Library*, 69 (1965), 446–58.

[42] See, however, Steven Zwicker's discussion of *The Hind and the Panther* in *Politics and Language in Dryden's Poetry*, esp. 153–5.

Virgil is given an oddly feminine aspect in this poem, from the elusive women of the epigraphs to the way we experience Aeneas as the violator of a people. The feminine, and Virgil's epic, are associated throughout with the mysteries not only of religion but also of violence, with tradition and grace but also with the spectre of invasion and conquest which underlies the weaker animal's investment in disappearance through the metamorphoses and ambiguity of fable. Although the Hind is 'milk-white' and the Panther's fur is silky, they express not milky softness but tensed vigilance. As feminine creatures, they are constantly 'panting', vulnerable, and hunted; they complexly focus the poem's sense of precariousness and disguise. In this poem, the Protestant fear of Catholic conquest turns into the Catholic fear of persecution and, in turn, into the author's own experience and expectation of attack.

Protective, distracting 'arma' haunt Dryden's poem of hide and seek. As Dryden's translation ten years later will emphasize, driving the epic are 'haughty Juno's unrelenting Hate' and 'angry Pallas with revengeful Spleen'—conniving, gossiping, vengeful goddesses. The gossip and politics of 'Heav'nly Minds' have dictated the labours of Hercules, moulded and menaced Aeneas' destiny. Deities compete to find swords for the hands of their favourites, and Aeneas' heavenly mother must scheme to protect him. What sword is the Hind putting in Dryden's hand; in what veil does she wrap her son who needs protection? As royal policies pushed the country and its monarch into confrontations ever more reminiscent of the 1630s and 1640s, the only practical benefit left of Dryden's new religion was its mystery. When the poet speaks about Paul's 'obscurity', that 'He darkly writ', which 'is true apply'd to all' (II. 345), he adverts not only to the Gospels but to 'this mysterious writ' as well. As recent students of the poem have recognized, Dryden is evolving a different way of writing satire that looks ahead to the experience of disfranchisement and censorship and the final, major poems and literary translations of the 1690s.[43] The Hind steps forward to reveal herself, but Dryden is wrapped in Roman, indeed oriental and feminine, mystery like Aeneas in the mists of his heavenly mother. The beast of the apocalypse keeps the critics from coming too close.

Sixty lines into the poem, the narrator announces that he is leaving 'the shoar', piloted by Christ, to explore 'a better world'. Dryden has a poem to write, so *he* is not leaving this world; but he disappears in another

[43] Zwicker *Politics and Language*, 123–58; Bywaters, *Dryden in Revolutionary England*, 9–33.

sense. Interjected without preparation, when the scene of the poem is being carefully set, that odd digression stops the movement of the piece. It holds the beasts at bay, and announces *The Hind and the Panther* as a withdrawal, though not exactly a retreat to the spirit. Rather, the departure happens right before our eyes: the ground of the confession keeps evasively slipping away into plea, doubt, and question—'O teach me', 'Can I believe', 'Can I my reason to my faith compell', 'Can they', 'Could He', 'if he'. And the final couplet, 'Faith is the best ensurer of thy bliss; | The Bank above must fail before the venture miss' (I. 148–9), triumphantly declares its faith with the very terms of the accusation that Dryden had converted for personal gain. He effectively pulls the rug out from under the whole speech; the tone is impossibly opaque. The poet removes himself and his words from reach by mystifying, in a play of mutuality—by coupling—both defence and offence. The embrace that outwits his attackers' terms, as if nothing were there, prepares us for the cautious arms of goodwill and hospitality which enclose the fragile balance of the second part of waiting for levitation.

Neither the Hind nor the Panther expects to convert the other. Similarly, recent critics have observed that, as a Catholic, Dryden can no longer presume to persuade a Protestant nation. As a poet, however, he is free to use the Hind and the Panther to represent political affairs as a timeless vision of Aesopian fable.[44] In their confrontation, then, the Hind and the Panther, although opposing forces, actually fit together remarkably well and together anticipate a violent solution to an irresolvable debate. I suggest they talk towards and around this common knowledge, slowly unwrapping the veiled languages of ecclesiology, politics, and fable. Their initial catechism represents the illusion of reprieve from, and poise amidst, the enclosing landscapes, although they are moving inexorably from one to the other: from the global and historical bestiary—the panoramic sweep expected in an heroic poem—to the night of prophetic tales.[45] The embrace of 'good-will' at the end of the first part looks ahead to the final attempt at embrace towards the end of the second where the Catholic Church is daringly pictured as Joseph before his brothers in

[44] For example, Bywaters, *Dryden in Revolutionary England*, 22, 24–5; and Zwicker, *Politics and Language in Dryden's Poetry*, esp. 123–45.

[45] On the narrator's universal knowledge, of history and geography to navigation, commerce, chemistry, and astronomy, as among several signs of Dryden's epic project, see Rebecca Parkin, 'Heroic and Anti-heroic Elements in *The Hind and the Panther*', *SEL* 12 (1972), 459–66.

Egypt. She is one who 'With open arms, a kind forgiving face, | Stands ready to prevent her long lost sons embrace' (II. 640–1). The image of 'Joseph as . . . persecuted Catholicism now in a position to give succour to its betrayers, the Anglican "supplicants" ', has been described as 'a masterpiece of the unthinkable', which 'could only be a provocation' to an audience 'nurtured on Foxe's martyrs, with the recent revocation of the Edict of Nantes . . . as a formidable reminder'.[46] Yet provocation through the embrace of incongruity is the business of this poem. And the moments of open-armed goodwill become like two arms of a parenthesis enclosing the debate whose dance describes a pattern not only of connection but of collusion between the Hind and the Panther.

Phillip Harth has argued that the second part 'is essentially a long speech by the Hind, infrequently interrupted', and that 'it is very far from being a "balancing of ideas" '. This is not a formal debate, . . . It is a dramatic series of alternate speeches, a platform for the Hind, the Panther relegated to giving cues by asking the right questions'.[47] The 'sober' Hind is allotted 575 lines to the Panther's 73. D. W. Jefferson saw their dialogue as 'a game of skill whereby the Hind achieves one advantage, moral or dialectical, after another . . . .The Hind becomes a creation of wit', of eloquent smoothness and cunning.[48] I would argue that the debate of the second part exemplifies, if not a balancing of ideas, then a complex balancing act of another sort. I am not referring to the balance of suspended belief required to allow a predator to stroll with its prey and debate ecclesiology. More interestingly, the section produces what George Myerson calls 'an intense vision of the equalising force' of differing voices.[49]

The falling light of 'One evening' makes it sometimes hard to distinguish between the Hind and the Panther, like two faces of the same coin superimposed on each other. In the last stanza of the first part (I. 554–72), for example, referents for the personal pronouns become momentarily confused. The twilight of the second part suggests the odd possibility of

[46] D. W. Jefferson, 'The Poetry of "The Hind and the Panther" ', *MLR* 79/1 (1984), 32–44; see 32–3.

[47] Phillip Harth, *Contexts of Dryden's Thought* (Chicago: University of Chicago Press, 1968), 36, 273 ff. Other critics, such as Miner 'The Significance of the Plot', have noticed that the tongue of the Hind, while born dumb, 'is loosened, by whatever stimulus, to speak about five words to the Panther's one' (149).

[48] Jefferson, 'The Poetry of "The Hind and the Panther" ', 41.

[49] George Myerson, *The Argumentative Imagination: Wordsworth, Dryden, Religious Dialogues* (Manchester: University of Manchester Press, 1992), 98.

their complicity. And their complicitous talk raises the spectre of contemporary politics as the other, and complementary, face of ecclesiology. 'Pope and council' evoke 'Prince and Senate'; a 'Rebel' from the Church of 'spiritual Royalty' and a term like 'gospel-liberty' conjure up the threat of political rebellion and overthrow of the King ('Shall she command, who has herself rebell'd?'); while the issue of which church may call itself apostolic generates language about 'God-like descent' and 'Succession lawfull in a lineal course', the idiom of legitimate monarchy.

Their feminine confrontation consists of competitive storytelling. They compare notes and vie to rewrite past, present, and future versions of events and of each other. For instance, the second part begins hopefully with a reminder of common ground: they shared an enemy in the dissenting sects during the Popish Plot. Yet they recall the past by matching sarcastic comments ('four fair leggs', 'your own dear self'); and the Hind is the more catty:

> P: For, what e'er promises you have apply'd
> To your unfailing church, the surer side
> Is four fair leggs in danger to provide. (II. 12–14)
>
> H: Those toils were for your own dear self design'd
> As well as me; and, with the self same throw,
> To catch the quarry, and the vermin too,
> (Forgive the sland'rous tongues that call'd you so.) (II. 19–22)

As they reimagine history, not only their animosity but their well-matched skills, and even similarity, are established. Sober versus giddy, courteous versus calculating: the differences between the Hind and the Panther are complementary and interchangeable. Every seventeenth-century reader took for granted Dryden's manœuvre of imparting to the sleek, glittering Panther the luxury, appetite, and sexual incontinence of which the Catholics had been long accused, indeed by Dryden himself. Yet the 'sober Hind', not the giddy sensualist, talks without cease and most nearly loses her self-possession (at II. 394–401, and most strikingly at III. 261–305 and 639). The Panther rather listens silently, licks her jaws, and shows no more emotion after the Hind's tale than a healthy yawn. They represent mutually complementary styles of calculation and attack. Sharing historical and cultural background, including caricatures, the Hind and the Panther understand and complete each other. And they know their script, as did Dryden's contemporaries. The 'chat' reviews well-worn themes of the century's running debate between papist and Protestant, in print and pulpit, which had gained intensity since the

Popish Plot.[50] No wonder critics jumped with authority on the poet's 'twinkling arguments' and confidently dismissed them as coffee-house wit. They knew what such a debate should sound like, and this was an interlude of theatre.

As a balancing act of verbal and non-verbal comment by rival female performers, the debate allows Dryden to keep control of the tone by deflation and mystification. When the Hind lets slip one of her dangerously self-righteous remarks, 'For all have not the gift of martyrdome', the Panther's grin in the next line helps save the moment, as does her cool, bitten matter-of-factness, 'That men may err was never yet deny'd. | But, if that common principle be true, | That Cannon, Dame, is level'd full at you'. Confessing herself not a friend of 'long disputes' (with her lack of authority for language, she is at a disadvantage and eventually falls silent), the Panther nevertheless drawls sarcastically, 'I fain wou'd see | That wond'rous wight Infallibility'. Her dry style, even though 'salvage', becomes a vital comic relief to the Hind's patronizing and rather priggish self-control; the Panther's mockery, which sounds like Montagu and Prior, is superbly off-handed.

The Panther is used in other ways to balance the Hind and to suggest their relation. The word 'needfull', a significant echo from *Religio Laici*, comes under close scrutiny. The Hind refers to 'all the needfull points' and, again, 'ev'ry needfull point of truth', to which the Panther rejoins, 'Yet, Lady, still remember I maintain, | The Word in needfull points is onely plain' (II. 143–4). The Hind must sidestep the charge as casually as possible, 'Needless or needfull I not now contend', and thinks 200 lines before she uses the word again.

[50] Between 1685 and 1687, a flurry of almost indistinguishable pamphlets on the issue of truth and disguise in representations of the Catholic and Anglican churches was initiated by John Gother's, 'A Papist Mis-Represented and Represented, or, a Two-Fold Character of Popery' (London, 1685), which was swiftly attacked by Stillingfleet's 'The Doctrines and Practices of the Church of Rome Truly Represented, in Answer to a Book Intitled, A Papist Misrepresented and Represented'. (London, W. Rogers, 1686). At least eight responses followed. In his survey of the whole controversy, Protestant William Clagett summarily decried Gother's as 'a Book full of Cunning and Dissimulation', since popery cannot be promoted 'if it appear in its own shape. . . . It is necessary therefore, that the Religion, like the Prophet, should come to us in *Sheeps cloathing*, and the Heresie to be made look as Orthodox as is possible. . . . Popery is to be received as a very innocent harmless thing.' See William Clagett, *The Present State of the Controversie between the Church of England and the Church of Rome, or, An Account of the Books Written on Both Sides. In a Letter to a Friend* (London: The Basset etc., 1687, Wing C4390), 10. An excellent collection of contemporary materials on the religious controversy is Thomas Jones (ed.), *A Catalogue of the Collection of Tracts for and against Popery*, parts 1 and 2, Remains Historical and Literary Connected with the Palatine Counties of Lancaster and Chester, published by the Chetham Society, vol. 48 (Manchester: Chetham Society, 1859, 1865).

Warming to her story, the Hind asserts the authority of tradition through a simple, harmless tale that happened once upon a time:

> The good old Bishops took a simpler way,
> Each ask'd but what he heard his Father say,
> Or how he was instructed in his youth,
> And by traditions force upheld the truth. (II. 164–7)

The Panther, who if silenced in the debate is never fooled, catches the rhetoric and 'smil'd at this'; but except for two brief interruptions by the Panther, the Matron holds the field at lines 228–648 with an onslaught of words, arguing both sides. The 'fair Apostate' still functions, however, as the poem's acknowledgement of the Hind's (and of Dryden's own) self-righteous tendencies.

In the climax of the discussion about 'a living guide' necessary to interpret God's word, the Panther plays the disbelieving foil as cue for the next spectacle:

> Suppose, (the fair Apostate said,) I grant,
> The faithfull flock some living guide should want,
> Your arguments an endless chase persue:
> Produce this vaunted Leader to our view,
> This mighty Moyses of the chosen crew.
>
> The Dame, who saw her fainting foe retir'd,
> With force renew'd, to victory aspir'd;
> (And looking upward to her kindred sky,
> As once our Saviour own'd his Deity,
> Pronounc'd his words—*she whom ye seek am I.*) (II.389–98)

The Hind looks up to 'her kindred sky' and pronounces a version of the words of Christ in Gethsemane to the officers seeking to arrest him; the words also echo those of Aeneas in Carthage as he stepped like a miracle out of the cloud into view of his men and Dido: 'He whom you seek am I' (Dryden's translation, *Aeneis*, I. 834). The tone is impossibly opaque yet surely comic, and contemporary readers hearing the grind of stage machines parodied the line mercilessly. As one critic sensibly noted,

> 'She whom ye seek am I', is not a sufficient Warrant for the Church of Rome's claiming an Infallibility in all her Decrees; no more than a Mountebank is to be credited, who after a deal of Scaffold-Pageantry to draw Audiences, entertains them by decrying all others with a Panegyrick of his own Orvietan Balsom.[51]

[51] Clifford, *Notes upon Mr Dryden's Poems*, 24.

Is the debate, then, 'Scaffold-Pageantry' and the Hind a mountebank—or is the mountebank Dryden? Or is it James, and the 'Balsom' the Declaration of Indulgence? Do the poet's shrill allusions and wobbling tone suggest that the old classical and biblical drapery for the monarch is becoming monstrous or wearing thin? The curious parentheses around this climactic yet clearly risky moment acknowledge the risk by containing the words in protective, arresting arms. The words seem to echo out of the text like a voice from the past or a voice of hide and seek heard from a mist—the author calling to his pursuers. And Dryden uses the Panther, her 'amaz'd' gaze, not only to register the wobbling moment but to reinforce the biblical echo as quaint. Sounding like a translation, the awkward syntax of line 399 disturbs the solemnity: 'Nor less amaz'd this voice the Panther heard, | Than were those Jews to hear a god declar'd' (ll. 399–400). The adjective 'modestly' a few lines later, 'Then thus the matron modestly renew'd', quietly brings the high flight back to earth.

Our gaze is again directed to the skies at the end of the section for two blazes of light, the last in the poem as night takes over until the 'streaky light' of dawn peeps in at the end. While the Hind is speaking, 'A streaming blaze' breaks through the shadows, whose authority banishes temporarily 'wandring guilty' ghosts and prophetic, death-boding, 'obscene' birds: what the interlude of the second part has done. Then, at a turning point of the poem, and the only section carrying the trace 'Poëta loquitor', Dryden points up to the sky in recollection and suggests, I believe, that the falling light of contemporary politics and of his poem is paradoxically prefigured in the victorious 'lambent easie light'—too easie—which the poet marked in the night sky over the battlefield of Sedgemoor, but which, like James's victory, was only 'guild' for 'the brown horrour' of factionalism and hate engulfing all. The flickering but deceptive ease of that moment when James seemed to have opened up a bright future for himself with the conquest of Monmouth was coming to resemble a flash in the pan. For the comet of 1685 which is a sign of victory in the second part has become in the third part 'Your bloody Comet-laws' hanging over the heads of English Catholics.

This play of suspended light is an image for the flickering balance of debate in the second part, which in turn serves as a parenthical image of the protected, covert project of the whole. 'She whom ye seek am I': under the guise of catechism as feminine storytelling and revision of history, who is being sought? Whose absence is registered by the strain on Restoration panegyric, and what do these women know? For the answer to this mystery, we look to the second half of the poem, deceptively labelled its third part.

Once the beasts have taken a seat under the Hind's roof (under James's reign), the balance is upset, and they begin to say what is on their minds. In a fallen world, however, by definition no longer capable of being uncovered, the truth if out must be veiled: they gossip, not in catechism now but in fables. George Myerson has observed that fable's 'peculiar combination of the oblique and the direct, obliqueness of reference and directness of feeling', makes it a natural mode for communication when more direct exchange would be explosive. He thus neatly links the Hind and the Panther's decision 'to put their cases obliquely in the form of fables, and the fact that interest has become the issue'.[52] In fact, the shift Dryden outlines in his preface—from the high magnificence of heroic verse to the 'more free and familiar' vision of 'Domestick Conversation'—is the poem's explanation of itself: where the Hind and the Panther end, speaking in fables, is where Dryden had begun.

The author's announced descent from the heroic to fabular recalls the descending progress outlined in the creation myth of the first part from the easy, open arms of King Adam to the persecution of man by man. And that other fall, traced in the same myth, from the kindness of 'kings upon their coronation day' to 'pride of empire', suggests the pressure of a contemporary anxiety close to home: that James's current aggressive placement of Catholics into civil service posts betrays those who believed his promise of 1685 to protect the Anglican Church and non-Catholic rights and property. After all, what 'pride of empire' in seventeenth-century Europe can match the 'Gospel-sound diffus'd from Pole to Pole' of the Roman Church, whose 'wealthy Tides' threaten to invade every shore? Fears of its impending conquest fuelled the Popish Plot, the Exclusion Crisis, and continued opposition to a papist on the British throne. As the Hind herself notes, the hour of grace is past. What is left is destiny, the inevitable fall, and resort, to the veiled truth of fable, that alluring Eastern costume for once innocent truth which is specifically linked to the thinly cloaked truth of feminine 'chat' and gossip—what is 'sung in ev'ry Street'.

After the second movement as a balancing act absorbing and postponing violence,[53] the atmosphere of threat and darkness deepens. Just at the

[52] Myerson, *The Argumentative Imagination*, 106.

[53] Ibid. 82–113, discusses argument as dialogue based on the mutuality of difference, an imaginative and visionary mode like storytelling.

moment when the elaborate cloaking of this 'mysterious writ' seems to become most layered—fable within fable—the layers, like clouds, gently part as if onto a simple scene at last, 'a wholesome tale'; the shade of the Redcross knight appears in the figure of James, 'who oftner drew his Sword, and always for the right' (III. 914). The common chat of gossips, however, proceeds to buzz around a dark morsel: as also the mild unsuspecting farmer, James II is eerily there and not there. The poem's suspension continues but sagging under a royal dead weight (III. 933). No blade, in fact, is drawn 'for the right', although the Hind brandishes what the Panther calls a 'double edg'd' rhetorical sword (III. 192) that becomes a blade of 'satyr' (III. 264), a 'shining weapon' that in anger she is tempted to use but draws back, like the royal lion, 'pleas'd with bloodless honours of the day' (III. 271). As the imagery of rising but immobilized aggression and anxiety attests, the world of this poem is waiting for resolution; and as the debate's self-enclosed embrace hints, the Hind and the Panther seem to know what will happen all along. The two madams peer into the future to emphasize its coming—and they see much the same. In fact there is no mystery.

Will a commanding moral authority pierce the veils and clean up this 'Aegyptian Piece'? A heroic monarch to be represented as Aeneas, as Christ, the father and disciplinarian of his people—a David who, if reluctantly but necessarily, unsheathes the sword of justice on 'the offending age'? Unlike the character of David-Charles II at the end of *Absalom and Achitophel*, the king of Toleration in 1687 has no speech and no sword (except Curtana, 'that pointless clergy-weapon', II. 419–20). We are reminded of the existence of the 'British Lyon' throughout the poem but as a presence momentarily forestalling disaster, fear of the 'Lyon' has 'Scarce, and but scarce, from in-born rage restrain'd' the sects. Except for his 'awfull roar' in I. 530 which subdues the Hind's enemies to feign kinship, 'Whether for love or int'rest', his actions are those of curbing his own action and authority—arresting his roars, uncurling his mane, sheathing his paws—checks which bring to mind the suppressed howls and violence of the Wolf and Panther.

The anonymous author of *The Revolter* (1687) accuses the poet of not only 'a rambling Conscience' but a Roman, 'feminine' limpness with respect to Dryden's praise of James:

When he comes to the Panegyrick upon his present Majesty, wherein he had so transending a Subject, and ought tho it had been by way of Digression, to have expended the whole Treasure of his Genius. Heaven's! what a difference there is between the feminine Encomiums of Mr. D. the Romanist, upon his present

Majesty, and the ranting Raptures of Mr. D. the Independent upon a Monster of a Tyrant.[54]

While never having allowed the laureate to forget his early 'Heroic Stanzas' for Cromwell, Dryden's critics correctly sensed in his portrayal of this Stuart monarch an indirection or reserve in tone, which they characterized as 'feminine'. The 'free and familiar' fusion of beast fable, Scripture, and Virgil contributes to this poem's oblique portraiture by gossip—fable as rumour. The poem enfolds a domestic portrait along with an indictment of literary and literal plainness and of its royal spokesman. 'Sung in ev'ry Street' like the Hind's fable, a certain 'Domestick' pair hover behind the uneasy family resemblance of the Hind and the Panther: one popularly figured as both hero and child-devouring Catholic beast ('do't as readily as Turkish mute'), the other represented as murderous whore and late-converted saint.[55]

The fervent hopes of 1685 for the sacredness of the 'Royal Word', a belief in the promise of trust and 'Plain Dealing' delivered with James's opening Declaration to Council, are waning in Dryden's poem. An ungrateful monarch has not acted on his promises either to Anglican pigeons or even at least to one of his 'tender chickens'. Dryden's disappointed hopes for an academic post at Eton or a 'Dublin gown' were one popular explanation of his conversion—an angry fist at the Anglicans—while the poem's incivility was ascribed to continued disappointment under James. He had suffered ridicule yet emerged with no reward from a king who had been busy placing other Catholics in choice public posts. In the winter and spring before publishing his poem, he aspired to but was overlooked for both the wardenship of All Souls and the presidency of Magdalen College; for both posts James endorsed undeclared or non-Catholics.[56] In the latter case, the royal mandate to appoint not Dryden but a young, disreputable Anthony Farmer, neither a professed Catholic nor a good Protestant and later formally reviewed and judged unqualified, was signed ironically the very day after the king issued his Declaration—no indulgence for Dryden.[57]

[54] *The Revolter. A Trage-Comedy*, 23.

[55] This caricature of James, Duke of York, popular around the time of the Popish Plot, appears, for example, in the Whig satire 'Popish Politics Unmasked' (1680), in Mengel (ed.), *Poems on Affairs of State*, II. 381–90.

[56] See Roswell Ham, 'Dryden and the Colleges', *Modern Language Notes*, 49 (1934), 324–32; J. A. W. Bennett, 'Dryden and All Souls', *Modern Language Notes*, 52 (1937), 115–16; and Steven N. Zwicker, 'The Paradoxes of Tender Conscience: Dryden's *The Hind and the Panther* and the Politics of Religious Toleration', *ELH* 63 / 4 (1996), 851–69.

[57] John Miller, *James II: A Study in Kingship* (Hove: Wayland, 1977), 171.

As if the word 'plainness' had now become also its opposite, both the Hind and the Panther claim plainness and honesty as their peculiar virtues, obfuscation and artifice the method of the other side. The Hind uses plainness to attack the dissident Protestant sects: 'With Texts point-blank and plain he [the Rebel] fac'd the Foe: | And did not Sathan tempt our Saviour so?' (II. 162–3). And in defending the necessity of a 'living guide' to clarify the efforts of the Bible's 'sacred Pen-men', she argues that no text is safe from malicious predators: 'No written laws can be so plain, so pure, | But wit may gloss, and malice may obscure' (II. 318–19). At the same time, she claims for herself and her monarch all that is plain, honest, and open: he possesses 'an honest open Breast' to read, she an 'honest meaning and an open breast' (II. 678); she offers 'plain simplicity of love' (III. 31) along with her 'plain fare', 'homely board', and 'a wholesome Tale' told 'in homely stile', and her canons are distinguished by their 'words so plain'.

The Hind's fluttering veils around plainness clearly prepare for the final portrait of the 'Patron'. But they also invoke the spirit of another well-born lady of recent notoriety and hardly 'milk-white', whom Dryden had been busy ventriloquizing as a 'plain' heart the year before: Anne Hyde, the first wife of James, then Duke of York. The Hind's long, rather histrionic speech of renunciation, 'fame, that darling fame' (III. 279–305), sounds troublingly like Dryden's version of the Duchess of York as religious martyr who suffered

> loss of friends, of worldly honours and esteem, the defamation of ill tongues, and the reproach of the cross,—all these, though not without the strugglings of flesh and blood, were surmounted by her; as if the saying of our Saviour were always sounding in her ears, 'What will it profit a man to gain the whole world, and lose his soul!'[58]

Reputedly licentious both before and after her marriage, Anne Hyde had been viciously portrayed by Marvell twenty years earlier in *The Last Instructions to a Painter* as the jealous, large-rumped poisoner of Lady Denham. This exceedingly spotted shade, roughly transformed to a saint by conversion—whose voice Dryden ventriloquized from beyond the grave in his 'Defence'—is incorporated into, yet shadows, the Hind like the Panther. And the mountebank selling them all is the restless, complex voice of that other struggling 'new convert'. The poet's feelings of betrayal, loneliness, and martyrdom may haunt each of the portraits. He

[58] *The Works of John Dryden*, ed. Scott, xvii. 209.

has been fighting for the ladies of his monarch, the Duchess and the Church; but, like them, he needs a protector. And such vulnerable emotions are naturally displaced to, safely distanced and even derided in, mysterious feminine voices.

At the beginning of the third part, the poet's reference to Spenser's *Mother Hubbard's Tale* and the carelessly sleeping and naked 'British Lioness' not only invokes an extreme image of royal oblivion and shameful self-exposure, carefully distanced by its femininity.[59] In changing the sex of Spenser's lion, which had been safely male in 1591 but was so no longer, Dryden suggests the poets' similar calculation and project. He is promising a climactic fabular portrait of James. But instead of the 'Warlike Prince' and Herculean figure of *Threnodia Augustalis* (1685), a monarch 'ripen'd for a Throne'—the great naval commander receiving from Neptune 'The Fasces of the Main', his 'whole life . . . a continuous series of heroic actions'[60]—*The Hind and the Panther* concludes with an anticlimax, an anti-hero, and an absence.

This rather simple 'Plain good Man' owns fowl. He will not punish evil troublemakers on his property, keeps his favourites on starvation rations, and embodies mild and reasonable moderation presupposing a reasonable world, while the preface and poem have eloquently testified to another reality. In fact this mild Patron conceivably eats the 'poor Domestick Poultry' which are 'Not overstock't, but barely for his use'. After all for what use *are* chickens? Fed by his own hand, presumably these are the nuns and clergy, but why not include such poor 'Domestick' staff as the laureate himself? Some twenty lines earlier, a vision of the farmer's dining table is conjured and the issue of his diet raised. He does not like the 'pamper'd Pigeons' for food; their rank 'Flesh was never to the Table serv'd'. But if not theirs, in this poem of salivating carnivores where a 'Lenten sallad' is a joke, then whose? Why raise the spectre, even delicately, of the Master's eating flesh when, at the height of the Popish Plot, this Catholic prince had been caricatured plotting to devour 'Babes'

[59] As has been noted before, Spenser's 'lion', discovered by the Ape and the Fox, is pointedly male:

> Lo where they spide, how in a gloomy glade,
> The Lyon sleeping sly in secret shade,
> His crown and sceptre lying him beside,
> And having doffed for heat his dreadful hide:
> Which when they saw, the Ape was sore afrayde, ...
> Edmund Spenser, *Mother Hubbard's Tale*, ll. 951–5.

[60] From the dedication to the Duke of York of *The Conquest of Granada*, in *Selected Dramas of John Dryden*, ed. George R. Noyes (Chicago: Scott, Foresman, 1910), 3.

pettitoes, cut large with arms and legs', commanding an army of villains who entertained themselves with 'black inhuman banquets of the night'?[61]

And James's final command of toleration, like the fantastic suspension of tensions in the debate, only postpones the return of the bloodthirsty Buzzard and more dining. By imagining James's death so as to look beyond it, the poem quietly, startlingly, levitates 'this Indulgent Lord' out of the poem where he is an embarrassment. He is summoned into view only to be rather hurriedly dismissed to heaven. Through levitation and angel voices he escapes the feeding of the world below; his absence becomes a vacuum which the violent Buzzard will move instantly to fill. With all of the Virgilian echoes—as one critic noted, with all of Dryden's 'Ulyssean Eloquence'—where is the hero? As suggested earlier, when the Hind stretches for her high note of 'She whom ye seek am I', she is out of her range, and she and the Panther know it. Through their talk, they are constantly testing, correcting, and refining the vision of this poem. The Virgilian hero of the allusion wobbles as well because it is not clear what he is doing there. In fact 'pious Aeneas' does not belong—except in parentheses. He constitutes yet another absence but, like that of the author, in the form of suspension and mystery waiting for a new incarnation.

While sensing the eerie tension of suppressed violence in *The Hind and the Panther*, Dryden's contemporaries found themselves, their prey, and their predictable savage mockery written into the poem. Their responses reflect a state of suspended frustration because they could finally never account for what the poem might be doing—only for what it failed to accomplish. Thomas Heyrick's conclusion, that Dryden's poem seemed 'a piece of mortification', designed to damage equally the poet's and the Hind's cause by making both look as foolish as this 'mock Elephant' of a poem, summarizes the way Dryden allowed his critics to grasp certain real elements without comprehending the whole.[62] Even today, *The Hind and the Panther* proves 'a piece of mortification'—for the reader.

The seventeenth-century readers complained of an 'over-hasty' and feminine extravagance and indirection, illogical digressions, and exoticism. Dryden played on the orientalism of the beast fable to dramatize his, and the poem's, turn towards and engagement with Rome as a locus

[61] See 'Popish Politics Unmasked', in Mengel (ed.), *Poems on Affairs of State*, ii. 381–90, esp. ll. 95–100.

[62] Thomas Heyrick, 'To the Reader', preface to *The New Atlantis: A Poem in Three Books with Some Reflections upon the Hind and the Panther* (London, 1687, Wing H1754).

of spiritual, epic, and fabular—of Eastern—mystery. He drew on the orientalism of the monstrous female Babylon riding on the beast of Revelation to put the Hind and the Panther in charge of the revelations of the poem, its gradual unveiling.

The Hind and Panther's debate of the second part, which appears to constitute the middle of the poem, its hopeful moment of reprieve from violence, embraces contraries, encloses nothing except itself, and is literally *not* the centre. *The Hind and the Panther*'s well-announced structure of three parts, with its implication of the disinterested middle, is like an exotic dance which veils the poem's steadily shifting ground between dualities—day to night, light to dark, outside to inside, public talk to personal feeling, epic to fable, presence to absence. In its parenthetical, self-enclosed but not central, position, the debate on ecclesiology is an expression of the risk of the poem itself and of the Restoration's monarchy suspended as a kind of parenthetical statement, the most fabulous interlude of all, enclosing the final moments of an old world being embayed by the pack. But with *The Hind and the Panther* Dryden is exploring not only a public vision of contemporary religious politics but the private question of 'Where do I go from here?' The world of the poem is presented and experienced as a kind of déjà vu that the creator has left to his pursuers sniffing his tracks to finish off as they wish. Meanwhile under cover of a twilight moment he is making a necessary shift into commitment to various forms of obscurity: religious mystery, literary ambiguity, and the possible prospect of disenfranchisement. The image of launching and sailing alone 'into the deep' will come to assume the heroic ambitions of epic.

The beastly feminine East inspiring the poem's twilight confusion of the Hind and the Panther raises a protective mist of negative mystery. The Antichrist presides over a void. Through indirection and displacement, the poet is able to express his complex feelings of vulnerability, of disappointment and anger at the same 'mighty James' who, in the final weeks before the poem's publication, was being celebrated in 'fanatical thanksgivings'. As the powerless take revenge often by singing their gossip in the streets in a veiled form that turns a calculated obliqueness into a pointed finger, so Dryden in his fable makes sure the interesting question is not who are the attackers, because the answer is everyone, but who is defending the barnyard? Simultaneously he announces the failure of such a figure and throws a feminine blush over the gap. The poem becomes its own ancient mother of protection. By this time, the laureate's uncertainty about his direction and his need for cover in difficult days have led him to a reconsideration of the heroic in terms of the literary modes of digression and fable. His experience of being the hunted prey, of having faithful trust scorned and invaded, has become 'thrown', like a ventriloquist's voice, into the feminine, maternal beasts who equally threaten and hide, horrify and protect.

6

The Obscure Progress of Satire in Dryden's Late Preface

> Besides, the Nature of a Preface is rambling; never wholly out of the Way, nor in it.
>
> Dryden, preface to *Fables Ancient and Modern*, (1700)

The *Discourse Concerning the Original and Progress of Satire* is one of the most intriguing and least appreciated of Dryden's critical texts. The sources of Dryden's formal remarks on satire have been amply documented;[1] and while the *Discourse* has been characterized as 'the most important contemporary English discussion of formal verse satire',[2] it is also deplored as 'fragmentary, poorly organized, frequently ambiguous, and conventional in the extreme'.[3] The odd proportions of the essay, its digressiveness and sheer length, and the poet's complex and ambivalent relations with his patron, Charles Sackville, the sixth Earl of Dorset—relations written directly and obliquely into the fabric of the *Discourse*—have not been attended to. Students of this text have remarked its length and noted the hyperbolic praise of Dorset, lavish even by the standards of that age;[4] but the undercurrent of hostility toward Dorset has not been

[1] See particularly the notes to *The Discourse of Satire* in *The Works of John Dryden*, iv: *Poems 1693–1696*, ed. A. B. Chambers and William Frost (Berkeley and Los Angeles: University of California Press, 1974), 513–86. All citations to the *Discourse of Satire* are to this edition and are included parenthetically by page and line number in the body of the text. On Dryden's theory and practice of translation, see most recently Paul Hammond, *Dryden and the Traces of Classical Rome* (Oxford: Oxford University Press, 1999), 143–50, and 179–92 for reflections on the poet's translations of Juvenal.

[2] Howard D. Weinbrot, *The Formal Strain: Studies in Augustan Imitation and Satire* (Chicago: University of Chicago Press, 1969), 65 ff. See also Mary Claire Randolph, 'The Structural Design of the Formal Verse Satire', in Bernard N. Schilling (ed.), *Essential Articles for the Study of English Augustan Backgrounds* (Hamden, Conn.: Archon Books, 1961), 271–5.

[3] Alvin B. Kernan, *The Plot of Satire* (New Haven: Yale University Press, 1965), 6.

[4] Brice Harris has written that 'John Dennis and John Dryden share with each other the questionable honor of having written two of the longest, most effusive, and most saccharine dedicatory epistles that Dorset ever received—Dennis, before his *Miscellanies in Prose and Verse* (1693); Dryden, in his *Discourse*'. *Charles Sackville, Sixth Earl of Dorset: Patron and*

recognized, nor have many readers wondered why the poet's translations of Juvenal and Persius should have been the occasion for his longest dedication and critical essay.[5]

The length and the tone of its dedication are not the only features to demand attention. The *Discourse* seems unusually digressive, and the poet draws repeated attention to his digressiveness. Do the length and structure of the essay reflect Dryden's easy authority, or are they signs of a careworn and ageing poet?[6] Is Dryden's overbearing, garrulous presence in the *Discourse* the mark of a writer who has come to put less pressure on the formal character of his writing, or are the essay's length and

Poet of the Restoration (Urbana: University of Illinois Press, 1940), 188. Stanley L. Archer, 'John Dryden and the Earl of Dorset' (Ph.D. thesis, University of Mississippi, 1965) offers a fairly standard response to the *Discourse*: 'Its length is not matched by uniform quality. The essay has never been a favorite with critics or with general readers. It has been criticized as digressive, unoriginal, and extravagant in praise of the patron to the point of bad taste. . . . Surely Dryden neither organized nor revised with care. He has more than the usual number of digressions and at times appears weary of the effort that the writing cost him. . . . It is the most valuable dedication ever addressed to Dorset' (194). For a recent perspective, see Michael Seidel, 'Satire, Lampoon, Libel, Slander', in Steven N. Zwicker (ed.), *The Cambridge Companion to English Literature 1650–1740* (Cambridge: Cambridge University Press, 1998), 33–57.

[5] Critics have demonstrated how Dryden, under the protection of translation, loosed his 'Unsafely just' satirical rage 'by Proxy' on the government of William in the Juvenal and Persius translations. See, for example, Kirk Combe, 'Clandestine Protest against William III in Dryden's Translations of Juvenal and Persius', *Modern Philology*, 87 (1989), 36–50; and Rachel Miller, 'Physic for the Great: Dryden's Satiric Translations of Juvenal, Persius, and Boccaccio', *Philological Quarterly*, 68 (1989), 53–75. In ' "Complying with the Times": Dryden's *Satires of Juvenal and Persius, 1693*', *Eighteenth-Century Life*, 12 (1988), 76–87, James Anderson Winn has pointed to passages in the *Discourse* which should be read 'as a covert set of instructions for decoding the translations' (81). But Winn has not pressed further what he calls 'a shocking disparity' between the tone of Dryden's suggestions to Dorset about ways the government might support the arts and the tone of such translations as Juvenal's *Third Satire*, 'where a "Government" some readers would equate with the one Dorset now served is cursed as "base" ' (80).

[6] Dryden coyly alluded in the *Discourse* to the 'tattling Quality of Age . . . which is always narrative' (16, 2–3); but he had also begun to allow age to qualify himself for the disillusioned, defiant authority of experience, the dramatic stance struck in the preface to *Don Sebastian* (1690): 'Having been longer acquainted with the Stage, than any Poet now living, and having observ'd how difficult it was to please. . . . I am not yet arriv'd to the Age of doating. . . . At least, if I appear too positive; I am growing old, and thereby, in possession of some experience, which men in years will always assume for a right of talking. Certainly, if a Man can ever have reason to set a value on himself, 'tis when his ungenerous Enemies are taking the advantage of the Times upon him, to ruin him in his reputation. And therefore for once, I will make bold to take the Counsel of my Old Master *Virgil. Tu, ne cede malis; sed, contrà, audentior ito*'. *The Works of John Dryden*, vol. xv, ed. Earl Miner (Berkley and Los Angeles: University of California Press, 1976), 65, 71, 72. The line of Virgil is from the *Aeneid*, 6, 95. 143–4 in Dryden's translation: 'But thou, secure of Soul, unbent with Woes, | The more thy Fortune frowns, the more oppose'.)

digressive structure strategic efforts to distract attention from the personal and political anxieties that accompanied all the former laureate's publications after the Revolution, and in particular from his relations with the Earl of Dorset, a powerful aristocratic patron with whom Dryden had enjoyed a long, and at times difficult, relationship?[7]

In the preface to *Fables Ancient and Modern* from which I have drawn my epigraph, without missing a beat in the middle of a long paragraph comparing Ovid and Chaucer, Dryden acknowledges his habit of 'rambling' in prefaces, which he says he learned from 'honest Montaign'.[8] The reference to Montaigne's self-exploratory, experimental essays, and their 'honest' author, suggests that the 'pre-' or 'beforehand' nature of prefaces, literally 'a saying beforehand', resembles in its quality of freedom from formal demands the open space for self-representation created by Montaigne. The Frenchman claimed to eschew artifice, yet the essays are highly figurative and grow increasingly sceptical; they are hardly artless confession. As Montaigne has shown us about the nature of his self, Dryden suggests, the 'way' of communication of the self to a reader does not run directly forward but moves gradually, variably, involving and demanding what appear to be byways. The preface, as a space and as the undefined matter of what needs to be said 'beforehand', distinct from the main text, offers to the writer something of the same space and opportunity for evolving self-portraiture as Montaigne had created.

I would like to suggest that the digressive structure of Dryden's dedicatory epistle to Dorset and essay on satire is purposeful and skilfully designed to communicate a critique, but one whose force exists only as a hint of resemblance embedded in a digressive argument: only in the teasing, oblique representation that the essay's digressiveness can permit and enfold, not as a direct fact. The aggressive length, ambiguity, and meandering, even difficult, progress—closely related to what Dryden calls the dark, obscure, or cloudy writing in Persius (53. 12, 22–3, 30–2)—constitute a deliberate strategy to guide the reader circuitously toward a highly unflattering portrait of Dorset and William and Mary's court of reformed manners and morals, carefully lodged at the centre of the essay in the oddly prolonged trial between Horace and Juvenal. Horace, the court poet, is brought before the author's personally orchestrated tribunal and

[7] On the institution of literary patronage in the Restoration and Dryden's patrons, see Dustin Griffin, *Literary Patronage in England, 1650–1800* (Cambridge: Cambridge University Press, 1996).

[8] *The Works of John Dryden*, vol. vii, ed. Vinton A. Dearing (Berkeley and Los Angeles: University of California Press, 2000), 31.

tried with a witty, wicked hostility that, if only indirectly, must touch Dorset, who early and repeatedly in the essay is compared as satirist to Horace in their correction of human 'Follies' (first at 6. 19–20), who is crowned 'King of Poets' (9. 31) (by the man whose laurels Dorset had removed) and, as Lord Chamberlain and a member of the Privy Council, holds the highest office of the civil government of William's court, after the Lord Steward.[9] The Lord Chamberlain's office, as Dryden reminds Dorset while crowning him 'King of Poets', is that most concerned with literary censorship designed to protect 'the Decency and Good Manners of the Stage' and 'restrain the licentious insolence of Poets and their Actors' (9. 35–7). Even while Dorset's satire is praised in the initial quarter of the text specifically addressed to his patron, Dryden cautiously introduces the notion of a competition; in fact, the world of the *Discourse* is revealed to be harshly competitive.[10] The contest is then suggested more firmly in the climactic third quarter where Dryden contrasts the satirical writing of Horace, who is presented as muzzled 'court Slave' and sycophant, with the 'more vigorous', driving, and 'manly wit' of Juvenal[11] who versifies 'in spite', since 'the World with Writing is possest'. After all, Dryden has not translated for this volume the satires of Horace; he has rendered those of Juvenal who wrote 'Difficile est Satyram non Scribere' as he looked about Rome, revolted by the vistas of corruption:

> No Age can go beyond us: Future Times
> Can Add no Farther to the present Crimes.
> Our sons but the same things can wish and do;
> Vice is at stand, and at the highest flow.
> Then Satyr spread thy Sails, take all the Winds can blow.
>
> (*Satire I*, ll. 220–4)

[9] Harris, *Charles Sackville, Sixth Earl of Dorset*, 119.

[10] A hint that the two men were perceived as competitors in satire during the final decade of Dryden's laureateship appears in the anonymous poem 'Advice to Apollo, 1678', published in *Poems on Affairs of State* (1697). An example of the early tributes to Dorset's skills as a satirist, the poem finds the aristocrat easily the better writer, recommending that Dryden return to composing plays 'without one word of sense' (cited in Archer, 'John Dryden and the Earl of Dorset', 126–7).

[11] The insistence on the 'masculine' quality of Juvenal's wit echoes repeated references in Dryden's work to his own strength as a writer as 'masculine vigour' and to censorship as castration—for example, in the prefaces to *Don Sebastian* and *Cleomenes*, the prologue to *Amphitryon*, ll. 1–ll, and Dryden's translation of Juvenal's *Satire III*, ll. 75–88. See also John Robert Moore, 'Political Allusions in Dryden's Later Plays', *PMLA* 73 (1958), 36–7.

The result of the contest is a withering, emasculating portrait of Horace. Dryden, who aligns his pleasure and temperament with that of Juvenal, his fellow exile, takes his laurels back—and spreads his sails.

Dryden not only pairs Dorset with Horace as stylists of satire in praising Dorset's work (6. 19–22, 70. 22 ff., 71. 26–8); he pairs William and Augustus. After quietly preparing for Augustus' appearance in the essay by quoting lines from Horace's epistle to Augustus (*Epistles* II:1) describing the law of the Decemviri, which made libel a capital offence (32. 26–34, 33. 1–3), Dryden launches into a digression about Augustus' seizure of power and his need to restore the law of the Decemviri to protect himself from lampooners. The parallels to William are clear:

> When Horace writ his Satires, the Monarchy of his Cæsar was in its newness; and the Government but just made easie to the Conquer'd People. They cou'd not possibly have forgotten the Usurpation of that Prince upon their Freedom, nor the violent Methods which he had us'd, in the compassing of that vast Design: . . . but they must be patient, where they had not power. . . . Propriety was generally secur'd; and the People entertain'd with publick Shows, and Donatives, to make them more easily digest their lost Liberty. (66. 14–36)

Vocabulary such as 'the Conquer'd People', 'Usurpation', 'that vast Design', and 'lost liberty' as Jacobite interpretation of the Glorious Revolution would not be lost on the seventeenth-century reader of the *Discourse*—and to whom could they have been more transparent than to Dorset? Under the shadow of Augustus read William of Orange, encouraged to make England his conquest, who took by force the title of king which had belonged by birth and inheritance to James II, and in whose usurpation the people of England were forced to acquiesce.[12]

The figure of trial and judgement and the dichotomies it insists on—in favour or out, Whig or Tory, true or false, life or death—seem an experience the essay is obsessed with, an image comprehending Dryden's own irreversible banishment. As a response to a world, and a life, severed by factionalism, where survival depended on the ability to find freedom in the play of disjunction, might not digression represent the experience and assimilation, the encompassment, of discontinuity? Might not real political strains between Dryden and Dorset have served imaginatively to focus Dryden's resentment into a vision of a reality, and a text, constantly breaking and reorganizing, creating unlikely juxtapositions and heroes?

[12] For a discussion of Dryden's translation of Virgil's *Aeneid* as 'sustained political meditation', see Steven N. Zwicker, *Politics and Language in Dryden's Poetry* (Princeton: Princeton University Press, 1984), 177–205.

This chapter reviews the evidence that poet and patron took separate political paths in the 1680s and were estranged temporarily, particularly by the issue of Catholicism. The tale of a complex friendship that endured over several decades and to the end of Dryden's life is embedded, however, in a richer narration.

Since he himself had served as laureate for twenty years, in the pay of two kings, Dryden's past progress, more than Dorset's present post, must be at issue in his rejecting the court poet. Might the protracted contest between Horace and Juvenal and the unusual fury of Dryden's attack on Horace be evidence of the emotional effort required for the poet voluntarily to distance himself—publicly and psychologically—from his own former life at court, while not letting it go? In the *Discourse* Dryden looks back over a long career, his treatment not only after the Revolution but also from enemies within the circle of noble wits at the court of Charles II, and at his treatment by two Stuart kings who showed, at best, uneven attention to the laureate's stipend. One of the stories he tells through the digressions of the *Discourse* is of a court and patronage system that failed to provide him with the financial leisure to 'please himself',[13] to write the national epic that he had announced as a project at least as early as the dedication to *The Conquest of Granada* (1672).[14] As David Bywaters has rightly perceived, the prominent digression on epic in the first quarter of the essay is no accident; Dryden presents himself

> not as the displaced hireling of a discredited court, but as the rightful heir of a transcendent literary tradition. By neglecting him, William's England has . . . robbed itself of the chance of standing in that tradition alongside Renaissance Italy and Augustan Rome.[15]

[13]
Our author by experience finds it true,
Tis much more hard to please himself than you:
And out of no feigned modesty, this day
Damns his laborious trifle of a play: . . .
Prologue to *Aureng-Zebe* (1675), 1–4.

[14] In *John Dryden and his World* (New Haven: Yale University Press, 1987), James Winn suggests that Dryden's 'desire to secure the leisure to write in nondramatic forms' was probably one of the motives, besides his need for political protection and general financial aid, that led to his brief courting of Rochester and Sedley in the early 1670s (243–8). At that point, Dryden's position at court and finances were weakened by the resignations of York and Clifford and by the decline of the fortunes of the King's Company to which he had been tied as house playwright and shareholder since 1668.

[15] David Bywaters, *Dryden in Revolutionary England* (Berkeley and Los Angeles: University of California Press, 1991), 140. Much has been written of Dryden's overriding ambition to write a heroic poem. See, for example, Reuben A. Brower, 'Dryden's Epic Manner and Virgil', in H. T. Swedenberg, Jr. (ed.), *Essential Articles for the Study of John Dryden*, (Hamden, Conn.: Archon Books, 1966), 466–92; and H. T. Swedenberg,

In the *Discourse* is a clear, carefully placed account of literary hopes disappointed by a factious, illiberal court world neglectful of poets—of the modern epic hero as literary artist forced to set himself sail with rage, like 'some side wind or other', to accomplish the 'Extraordinary Undertaking'.[16] I think that Dryden's reasons for a self-consciously difficult, obscure 'progress', like the disputed circumlocutory 'progress' of satire which he struggles to advance to clarity, are political and aesthetic, and his working out a new relationship between the two pressures—launching the banished Stuart exile as epic hero—mark the *Discourse* and the translations it introduces as an important transition between Dryden's original writing before the Glorious Revolution and his work of the 1690s. The technique of digressiveness is one Dryden would employ with ever-increasing mastery in the *Dedication of the Aeneis* (1697) and the *Preface to the Fables* (1700) to become a figure for the mature poet's freedom to be at home with the passions and a genuine way of seeing 'the filaments of connection among disparate subjects and, in turn, a way of structuring an argument'.[17]

Written and published in 1692, the year of writing his last play (*Love Triumphant*), the *Discourse* represents a turning point in Dryden's career. He needed to find a way to address the issues of politics he felt most deeply about without danger of censure, and at the same time he needed to evolve a new, authoritative literary voice out of political disenfranchisement; digressiveness provided, politically, a strategy of evasion and, psychologically, a comfortable ambiguity. Furthermore, it was an aesthetic of independence and virtuosity signalling freedom from the authorities who have rejected him, while allowing the poet still to make claims on their support. While not letting go of his long-standing connections to and expressed affection for either Dorset or Horace, Dryden

Jr., 'Dryden's Obsessive Concern with the Heroic', in Daniel W. Patterson and Albrecht B. Strauss (eds.), *Essays in English Literature of the Classical Period Presented to Dougald MacMillan*, (Chapel Hill: University of North Carolina Press, 1967), 12–26. In *Dryden's Classical Theory of Literature* (Cambridge: Cambridge University Press, 1975), 158, Edward Pechter suggested that it is 'virtually impossible to exaggerate the power of this ambition', once characterized by Swedenberg as 'obsessive'. Swedenberg was referring to 'how consistently Dryden tended to view the variety of poetic forms he employed as related in some way or other to the epic form'.

[16] This figure for the indirectness of digression as a 'side wind', which appears in the *Dedication of the Aeneis*, is reminiscent of Davenant's description of the unpredictable, self-directive progress of learning in his preface to *Gondibert* (1650) as 'not Knowledge, but a continu'd Sayling by fantastick and uncertaine windes toward it' (J. E. Spingarn (ed.), *Critical Essays of the Seventeenth Century*, vol. ii (Oxford: Clarendon Press, 1908), 7, 26–7).

[17] Zwicker, *Politics and Language in Dryden's Poetry*, 62.

seems momentarily to declare his independence from exactly their central authority—to create the image of surpassing them in moral and literary power—by writing circles around them.[18]

POET AND PATRON: AMBIVALENCE AND COMPETITION

In the 1660s and 1670s, the early years of Dorset's patronage of Dryden, the poet maintained loyalty to the first Earl of Clarendon, Edward Hyde, who was impeached and exiled in 1667, and to his children. Dryden was also unswerving in his commitment to James, Duke of York, whose first wife was Clarendon's daughter Anne Hyde. Dorset, on the other hand, maintained close friendships with men who became Clarendon's and Dryden's enemies: Buckingham, Sedley, and Rochester. The poet was beaten in Rose Alley in December 1679, possibly at Rochester's behest because of the Earl's belief in Dryden's authorship of the anonymous manuscript circulated first in November 1679, 'An Essay upon Satire', which had lampooned Rochester and Dorset (including a tasteless account of Dorset's recently deceased wife), King Charles, and Sedley. According to Winn, the piece was 'pretty clearly' written by the Yorkist John Sheffield, Earl of Mulgrave, with perhaps some corrections by Dryden.[19] A cousin of Dorset, but distant from him, Mulgrave had taken Dorset's place as Dryden's patron by the mid-1670s.[20] Whether Dorset held Dryden responsible for the poem is not known, but contemporaries often attributed the poem to Dryden; and what appear to be references to it occur in an anonymous attack on Dryden's conversion, evidently written in 1686 and most commonly attributed to Dorset, to which I return below.

While serving as Dryden's patron, Dorset became increasingly attached to Dryden's arch-rival, playwright Thomas Shadwell.[21] By 1682

[18] Judith Sloman has rightly noted that by the time Dryden writes the *Dedication of the Aeneis*, he is defending the courtier, Virgil, against charges of servility and inconsistency, 'making us see how the court poet's heightened self-consciousness is essentially another facet of the qualities we respect in his art' (*Dryden: The Poetics of Translation* (Toronto: University of Toronto Press, 1985), 35). The compromise of accommodation is made up for by the 'involutions' of artistic intentions—'calculation can provide its own sort of literary interest' (34).

[19] Winn, *John Dryden and his World*, 326, 328.

[20] 'Dryden probably made up his mind to ally himself with Mulgrave during the winter of 1673–74', suggests Winn (ibid. 254). In 1676 the poet dedicated the published text of *Aureng-Zebe* to his new patron.

[21] Charles II's current, and Dorset's former, mistress, the actress Nell Gwynn, wrote a letter in June 1678 to Lawrence Hyde reporting court gossip which linked Dorset and Shadwell as drinking cronies: 'My lord of Dorscit apiers wouse in thre munthe, for he drinkes aile with Shadwell and Mr. Haris [Henry Harris, actor] at the Dukes house all day long' (Harris, *Charles Sackville, Sixth Earl of Dorset*, 75–6).

he was Shadwell's chief patron and, by 1689, had him crowned poet laureate, having been required to dismiss Dryden from that post. The laureateship was a reward for Shadwell's anti-popery and his exclusionist associations during the late 1670s and 1680s, politics which Dorset shared. Before Shadwell's death of an overdose of opium in November 1692, less than a month after the publication of the *Discourse*, the new laureate had used his position to obstruct the production of work by a now impoverished Dryden, for example by ensuring that Dorset banned Dryden's prologue to *The Prophetess* (1690) and in the winter of 1691–2 by delaying the production of Dryden's play *Cleomenes*, evidently complete by October 1691, which Dryden needed for financial reasons to see produced immediately.[22] Shadwell succeeded in stalling the play's appearance until the spring of 1692. As *Cleomenes* was being readied finally, on 9 April 1692 Queen Mary instructed Dorset to prohibit performance, fearing that it contained dangerous political comment, and 'Shadwell may have been the moving force behind this prohibition'. The bann was lifted a week later and the play staged, although Narcissus Luttrell reported that potenially offensive passages had been removed.[23]

Dorset's second marriage in 1685 to Lady Mary Compton ended in her death from smallpox after six years, but it brought Dorset under the influence of the anti-Catholic Comptons for the rest of his life.[24] (His wife's uncle Henry Compton, the staunchly Protestant Bishop of London—'the Sagan of Jerusalem' in *Absalom and Achitophel*—was the only bishop eventually to sign the invitation to William of Orange.) Early in 1688, Dorset lost his commission as Lord Lieutenant of Sussex, which he had held since 1670, when he refused to question potential members of Parliament concerning their vote on repeal of the Test Act and other measures proposed by the Crown. Thereafter he abandoned a position of

[22] An anonymous contemporary observed, 'Shadwell had never been Laureat in his latter days but by being an early rake, and fixing his reputation with Dorset, Sidley, and the rest'; and Oldys had heard 'that Dorset, Sedley and others of those idle wits would write whole scenes for' Shadwell (see Harris, *Charles Sackville, Sixth Earl of Dorset*, 125–6). In the dedication to Dorset of *The Squire of Alsatia* (1688), Shadwell boasts that most of his comedy had been written at Copt Hall, the country estate of the earls of Middlesex, where he had been received as one of the family (ibid., 140).

[23] Winn, *John Dryden and his World*, 453.

[24] For a brief account of the politics of the Comptons, see G.E.C., *The Complete Peerage*, ed. H. A. Doubleday and Lord Howard de Walden, vol. ix (London: St Catherine Press, 1936), 679–82; and *The Dictionary of National Biography*, ed. Sir Leslie Stephen and Sir Sidney Lee, vol. iv (London: Geoffrey Cumberlege, Oxford University Press, 1949), 899–903, 905. The influence of the Comptons appears to have developed into a rather aggressively controlling power over Dorset and his children. See Harris, *Charles Sackville, Sixth Earl of Dorset*, 117.

careful neutrality: in June 1688, he sat with other Protestant lords at the Trial of the Seven Bishops, thereby assuring their acquittal; and in November with Henry Compton he accompanied Princess Anne in her flight from the King to the camp of William of Orange. While Dorset did not sign the invitation to William, he was one of the principal peers who, after James's flight on 11 December, 'assisted in the management of affairs until the following February when the crown was offered to William and Mary'.[25] The day after they ascended the throne, Dorset accepted the office of Lord Chamberlain as reward for his support.

While Dorset was working against James, Dryden had converted to Catholicism, probably late in 1685 or early the following year, after decades of political and family ties with recusants.[26] In the winter of 1686–7, Dryden wrote of his Catholicism in *The Hind and the Panther.* The poem precipitated a torrent of abuse including 'The Hind and the Panther Transvers'ed to the Story of the Country Mouse and the City Mouse' (1687), written by Dorset's protégés Charles Montagu and Matthew Prior (see Chapter 5).[27]

Among the pamphlets attacking Dryden's poem appeared one in July 1688 entitled *Religio Laici, or a Lay-Man's Faith, Touching the Supream Head and Infallible Guide of the Church: in Two Letters to a Friend in the Country* and bore on the title page the initials 'J.R., a Convert of

[25] Harris, *Charles Sackville, Sixth Earl of Dorset*, 115–17.

[26] His connections to the Duke of York, Sir Thomas Clifford, and Henry Bennet, first Earl of Arlington, were well known; but within the family lay another influential network. Philip Howard, Elizabeth Dryden's second cousin, was a Dominican priest who later became a cardinal. When Catherine of Braganza came to England in 1662, Howard was among her priests and became her Grand Almoner in 1665. Philip Howard's brothers were also Catholics, and one of them, Henry, who became Earl of Norfolk in 1677, was part of an influential group of Catholics based at the court of the Queen Mother. William Cecil, the father of Dryden's mother-in-law Elizabeth Cecil Howard, was a Catholic, and Elizabeth Cecil may have been as well. The religion of Dryden's wife is not known, but she was at least sympathetic to Catholics, if not one herself. See Winn, *John Dryden and his World*, 121–4.

[27] 'The Hind and the Panther Transversed' is reprinted in Galbraith M. Crump (ed.), *Poems on Affairs of State*, vol. iv, (New Haven: Yale University Press, 1968), 118–45. Archer notes another attack on Dryden's Catholicism which hints at Dorset's displeasure. In a letter from Charles Montagu to George Stepney, dated 14 Apr. 1687, occurs an epigram which compares Dryden to Oates: 'The Church of Rome on ours Reprisals makes, | For Turncoat Oates, she Turncoat Dryden takes' (159). After Montagu writes that he has shown the Earl of Dorset some of Stepney's verses on the new converts, a passage occurs which is suggestive about the authorship of the epigram: 'I have not the time and leasure yet to set to an Epistle . . .; in the Mean Time I will give you some of our Epigrams. For our Heads have layn much in that way of late, and they may serve for some Recompense for those you sent us on the French King' (160). Four epigrams follow, including the one above. Archer judges that the 'our' of 'our Epigrams' and 'our Heads' refers to Montagu and Dorset.

Mr. Bays's'.[28] Near the end of the first and shorter letter, a highly abusive poem on Dryden is quoted which begins, 'Thou Mercenary Runnegade, thou Slave . . .'[29] The authorship of the poem has never been established, but Dorset is the only figure to whom it has been attributed. The poem appeared in a letter dated 20 April 1686 from John Newton of the Inner Temple to Arthur Charlett, Fellow of Trinity College, Oxford, so that, in fact, it was written in response not to *The Hind and the Panther* but to the laureate's conversion.[30]

At the end of the First Letter, 'J.R'. acknowledges Dryden's power of satire, unmatched by any except 'that unknown (but supposed) worthy Author, that writ to him upon his (at last) turning Roman Catholick', after which he quotes the poem.[31] Harris admits that the meter, tone, and wit 'uncomfortably' resemble those of Dorset,[32] and Dorset would have had motivation. Given his hatred of Catholicism and the Duke of York, his possibly still smouldering resentment of 'An Essay upon Satire', it is not hard to imagine how the combination of Dryden's conversion and work of court propaganda,[33] in service of the man and religion Dorset opposed, might have inspired at least one burst of passionate disgust and cynicism from the patron against his old client. Into such a relatively obscure pamphlet Dorset's abuse might be tucked—to be released a year after Dryden's poem was published, the year Dorset himself took a public stand against James (probably judging the risk had become minimal), and only four months before the Glorious Revolution. Both Hugh Macdonald and Harris have rejected the possibility of Dorset's authorship, on the questionable grounds that Dorset was at this time assisting Dryden financially. The poem in question, however, was published in 1688 and probably written earlier, while Macdonald and Harris refer to the event of 1689, when Dorset, as Lord Chamberlain, was forced to remove Dryden from his posts and, as compensation for the loss of an

[28] Wing No. R30.

[29] The poem is reproduced in *The Poems of Charles Sackville, Sixth Earl of Dorset*, ed. Brice Harris (New York: Garland Publishing, 1979), 18–19, entitled 'To Mr. Bays'.

[30] Ibid. 18.

[31] 'J. R.', *Religio Laici*, 8.

[32] Harris, *Charles Sackville, Sixth Earl of Dorset*, 123.

[33] Early in 1686 James II published a pamphlet containing two brief statements, alleged to have been written by Charles II, concerning his death-bed conversion, and a third, similar statement by Anne Hyde, James's first Duchess. Bishop Edward Stillingfleet attacked these 'Royal Papers' as fabrications and offensive Catholic propaganda; as state laureate, Dryden participated in the anonymous counter-attack, *A Defence of the Papers Written by the Late King of Blessed Memory, and Duchess of York* (London: H. Hills, 1686), whose title page includes the phrase 'By Command'. The critical concensus is that Dryden produced at least the defence of the Duchess's paper; some scholars believe he composed or had a hand in all three. See Winn, *John Dryden and his World*, 612 n. 85.

annual salary of £300, made him a generous gift of money. Between 1686 and 1689 the tables had turned: in 1689 Dorset was established in a position of power and, at the expense of the poet's misfortune, could afford gestures of reconciliation. There is evidence that Dorset may even have tried to keep Dryden in office on the condition of certain terms—most likely that he return to the Church of England—which Dryden refused to accept.[34] Whatever happened at the time, in the *Discourse* Dryden seems to be engaged not only in a literary debate but as well in a personal conversation, perhaps ongoing, in which he wanted to have the last word.

Safely installed as Lord Chancellor, Dorset was ready to forgive and forget;[35] but having been humiliated by his patron's new court, Dryden would have had cause for continued resentment. His description of his own temper in the *Discourse* as 'naturally vindicative' (60: 1) and reference in the *Dedication of the Aeneis* to the '*genus irritabile vatum*' which defers but never forgets vengeance[36] are suggestive. Even if Dorset were friendly to Dryden in the 1690s, as we have reason to believe he was, the aristocrat's tendency to strategic neutrality and the comfortable—even corrupted—good nature of privilege kept him also at the service of others not as friendly.[37] It is not difficult to see how Dryden used the figures of

[34] On the cancel leaf of one of the thirty-five extant copies of Dryden's *King Arthur* (1691), where a portion of the dedication to Halifax appears, is the following parenthetical material, suppressed in the cancel leaf of all other copies: 'But not to offend the present Times, nor a Government which has hitherto protected me (and by a particular Favour wou'd have continued me what I was, if I could have comply'd with the Termes which were offered me), I have been oblig'd so much to alter the first Design, and take away so many Beauties from the Writing, that it is now no more what it was formerly, than the present Ship of the *Royal Sovereign*, after so often taking down, and altering, to the Vessel it was at the first Building'. (Archer, 'John Dryden and the Earl of Dorset', 172–3. See also Fredson Bowers, 'Dryden as Laureate: The Cancel Leaf in "King Arthur" ', *TLS* (10 Apr. 1953, 244.)

[35] Throughout the 1690s Dorset showed signs of renewed friendship and respect, support acknowledged by Dryden both in the *Discourse* and in the *Dedication of the Aeneis* (see *Essays of John Dryden*, ed. W. P. Ker (Oxford: Clarendon Press, 1990), ii. 239. 15–23). For example, 'Of the one hundred plates which adorned the handsome subscription edition of Dryden's *Works of Virgil* (1697) and for which subscribers paid five guineas per plate to have their arms and names inserted, Dorset's household accounted for five: . . . Dorset was thus responsible for subscriptions totalling twenty-five guineas' (Harris, *Charles Sackville, Sixth Earl of Dorset*, 198). In a letter of November 1699 to Elizabeth Steward, Dryden reports that he has shown Dorset and Montagu poems from his manuscript of the *Fables* and they 'are of opinion that I never writt better'. He says he has 'had the honour of a visite from the Earl of Dorsett, & din'd with him' (*The Letters of John Dryden, with Letters Addressed to him*, ed. Charles E. Ward (Durham, NC: Duke University Press, 1942, 123–4).

[36] Dryden, *Essays*, ii. 173. 19.

[37] Nearly all the offices of which he had oversight as Lord Chamberlain were his to bestow or sell, and Dorset's undisguised 'place-selling' for personal gain provoked satiric attacks from outraged Tories. See William J. Cameron (ed.), *Poems on Affairs of State*, vol. v (New Haven: Yale University Press, 1971), 100–9. I am grateful to Michael Werth Gelber for this point.

Horace and Juvenal in the *Discourse* to explore these personal, social, and professional issues. Dependent on Dorset for general and specific support against enemies at court, but angry and compelled to take revenge over the way his work has been censored before production[38] and he himself made the object of scorn, Dryden announces his retirement and isolation in the *Discourse* as well as in the Juvenal translations and original verse of the 1690s, such as 'Eleonora', 'To my Dear Friend Mr. Congreve', and 'To Sir Godfrey Kneller'.[39] He may claim a willingness to leave behind an age to 'reap each other in lampoons'; but he may not have been entirely ready to let go, hence, the complexities and obscurities of the *Discourse*. The posture of the philosophical satyr turning to retirement is contradicted by the forceful, totally dominating and domineering presence who effortlessly exhibits his authority in every possible literary field, making personal, professional, and political statements while telling us he can say nothing.

PRAISE AND BLAME: DRYDEN'S 'EPISTLE' TO DORSET

The first quarter of the *Discourse* sets the tone of authoritative familiarity with the Lord Chancellor and all of literature. Reflecting a technique of digression which will be characterized in the *Dedication of the Aeneis* as a deliberately inexact, 'loose and, as I intended it, epistolary' method,[40] the epistle shows an unhurried Dryden launched on a challenging tour of a difficult landscape. He gives signs throughout that the topography and the journey are interesting because *he* is, that there will be numerous temptations to dawdle and admire (but he knows enough to avoid 'a flat

[38] According to Moore, 'Political Allusions', 36–7, for example, *King Arthur, Don Sebastian*, and *Love Triumphant* were cut before production. In the preface to *Don Sebastian*, Dryden boasts of Dorset's critical approbation and protection, but in that same year, 1690, the Lord Chamberlain was forced to ban Dryden's 'Prologue' to Betterton's *The Prophetess* because of its ridicule of William's Irish Wars, the English soldiers, and Mary's government. The production of *Cleomenes*, as discussed above, was first delayed by Shadwell's efforts and then prohibited by Dorset following an order from Mary. Though the Lord Chamberlain had read the play and returned it without alteration, he could do no more; it was Lawrence Hyde, uncle to the Queen (and son of Dryden's controversial early patron, the first Earl of Clarendon) and created Earl of Rochester in 1682, who insisted on the play's innocence.

[39] In the *Discourse*, for example, even his discussion of Persius' stoic 'tranquility of Mind' becomes part of Dryden's rhetoric of retirement, of 'Virtue lodg'd at home, and afterwards diffus'd in her general Effects, to the improvement, and good of Humane Kind'. Now it is not Dryden who is exiled: 'Passion, Interest, Ambition, and all their Bloody Consequences of Discord and of War, are banish'd' from this philosophy (56: 16–17).

[40] Dryden, *Essays*, ii. 179. 1–2.

of thought'): there is a new model for an English epic poem and a new critical method; the blocking 'Rubbish' of bad lampooners is confronted and removed, and the 'Under-wood' of satire is distinguished from the 'Timber-Trees'; various species of poetry are noted and discussed in passing.

This epistle is about writing and literature, and the focus of interest is not Dorset but Dryden. The landscape is quickly revealed as the complex and dangerous grid of a political world with Dorset on the inside and Dryden fixed at the edges, alternately praising, scolding, thanking, and complaining. Praise and blame were important imaginative modes for Dryden, and certainly the guide through the *Discourse* is busy dispensing both. If Dryden and his 'Cause' have been displaced at court, he seems to hold court or audience here with a royal sense of spread. A judge, he hands down sentences. The panegyric is particularly complicated and clouded in tone through a recurrent stylistic device, such that praise is dispensed by indicating the threat of dangers narrowly missed.

The labyrinth of contradicting, ambivalent statements becomes focused and intensified as it becomes a portrait of the servile court satirist. Dryden reverses the value of inside and outside: his experience of censorship—of being muzzled and castrated—is displaced, transferred to the compromised courtier, and Dryden is freed to set sail on a sea of scorn. As suggested earlier, the reality was no doubt more complicated—he still considered Dorset a friend and patron, and Horace, along with Virgil, was a master. Still, the crucial reversal he had experienced, the chilling executive power that turns 'in' to 'out', becomes a figure for other dichotomies Dryden systematically creates in the *Discourse* by setting up competitions between writers and genres, setting them against each other to separate the weak from the strong, the noble 'wit' from the self-made genius, the tepid from the impassioned. Even the age-old twin aims of poetry, instruction and delight, are marshalled into the competitive ring. Dryden turns banishment from the court into a position of strength from which he can tell a story about his heroic denial to compromise. In so doing, he ultimately incorporates the 'dexterous' blade of dichotomy in the more complicated and philosophical response of digression.

The *Discourse* was published 'during the wealthiest and most influential period of Dorset's life'.[41] Dryden begins by saying that 'The Wishes and Desires of all Good Men, which have attended your Lordship' have been 'accomplish'd' with an abundance of good fortune 'you have so

[41] Harris, *Charles Sackville, Sixth Earl of Dorset*, 188.

long deserv'd', which would include his recent appointments within William's government. The relationship between deserving and receiving 'Honours and Dignities' is immediately introduced as problematic by an author who not only had lost an appointment (when Dorset gained one) but was himself subject to shame and dishonours and indignity. Immediately, the phrase 'all good Men' suggests there may be others, and with 'from your First appearance in the World', 'at length accomplished', and 'so long deserv'd', the sentence emphasizes an ordeal and triumph out 'in the World' of politics. In fact, a few pages later, Dryden recalls this first sentence and gives its sentiments a quarter turn, just enough to flash a hint of bite in the teasing urbane banter:

> Mankind that wishes you so well, in all things that relate to your prosperity, have their intervals of wishing for themselves, and are within a little of grudging you the fulness of your Fortune: They wou'd be more malicious if you us'd it not so well, and with so much generosity. (7: 28–32)

One hears Dryden's 'grudging' presence in the 'Mankind' that wishes something 'for themselves' and 'wou'd be more malicious' if not assured that the Lord Chancellor readily shares his good fortune.

In the second sentence, Dryden closes in on those not included in 'all good Men', as he continues his praise which proves a path through formidable woods: 'no Factions, tho irreconcilable to one another', 'not united in their Affection to you', the negatives pile up in difficult celebration.[42] Plunged into this world without introduction or comment, the reader is presumed to know these factions and deem nothing to be more natural than for factions to raise their head exactly in the midst of unqualified praise. Perhaps, Dryden implies, there is no such thing as simple, unqualified praise in this world. Soon after, the praise is again complicated by negatives, this time raising the spectre of 'Enemies' and 'hate' and of Dorset's freedom from such evils of public life through the unflattering, even insulting, possibility of his utter non-existence to some people: 'you neither have Enemies nor can scarce have any; for they who have never heard of you, can neither Love or Hate you' (4. 7–9). Here is a mixed kind of praise whose eloquence primarily evokes danger. Dryden wastes no time in suggesting the obstacles—enemies, factions, hate—which others not as fortunate as Dorset, such as the author himself, may face, and suggesting that the Earl's support is required to overcome these obstacles.

[42] Winn has pointed out that Dryden used double negatives and qualifying conditional tenses to praise, and at the same time indicate scepticism, as early as the 1662 poem 'To my Honour'd Friend, Dr. Charleton' (*John Dryden and his World*, 133–4).

The disturbing double negatives continue their halting, circular progress. Dryden suggests an elevating comparison between Dorset and the Roman emperor Titus Vespasian, but in fact the comparison implies that Dorset is not as universally known or as powerful. Titus Vespasian was better able to help those who depended on him: 'He had greater Ability of doing Good, but your Inclination to it, is not less'. The writer addresses his strongest ally at a court hostile to his person and art; but even the country's most powerful patron was unable to find him a sinecure. The difficult syntax of negatives twists about this failure to ease mental suffering with the suggestion of lost days and sleepless nights: 'And tho' you could not extend your Beneficence to so many Persons, yet you have lost as few days as that Excellent Emperour; and never had his [Titus Vespasian's] Complaint to make when you went to Bed, that the Sun had shone upon you in vain, when you had the Opportunity of relieving some unhappy man' (3. 12–17). That 'unhappy man' is, of course, Dryden.

In short, from the first words, 'wishes and desires', Dryden is speaking of his own wishes. He is dispensing praise and blame and asking for help, though in a complex, defensive, and belligerent manner. One curious passage near the beginning where Dryden seems to be scolding Dorset opens, 'Good Sence and good Nature, are never separated' (5. 11), a phrase whose 'never' sounds ominous in this *Discourse* where to separate, to split apart, is the order of business; the poet is making statements in order to turn on them—sentences become grist for their own mill—or to turn off them like a highway running into detour.[43] He goes on to say that good nature, for which his patron has been acclaimed, is the natural result of exercising 'right Reason', which makes allowance for human imperfection and forgives. Dryden may be chiding his patron with holding no firm standards for distinguishing, or being too lightly reconciled to, bad behaviour or bad poetry.[44] On the other hand, what follows also

[43] The 'never' of 5.11 prepares for the introduction of 'The best Good Man, with the worst-Natur'd Muse' (6.13), Rochester's bow to Dorset's 'poynted Satyrs' in 'An Allusion to Horace'. The phrase is not 'an Insolent, Sparing, and Invidious Panegyrick', as Dryden claims in an odd gesture of outrage for his patron over a poem whose central target for attack is Dryden. When the poet discusses Juvenal later on, he prefers him to Horace because he is angry. The muse of satire is not known for being good-natured.

[44] In the dedication to Mulgrave of *Aureng-Zebe* (1676), Dryden praises him for inviolable constancy to his friends which is matched by an equal resolution against his enemies:

'The Italians have a proverb to that purpose, "To forgive the first time, shows me a good Catholic; the second time, a fool"' (cited in George McFadden, *Dryden, the Public Writer 1660–1685* (Princeton: Princeton University Press, 1978), 166).

sounds like Dryden being impatient with Dorset for not having taken a more 'Elevated' view of his old friend's conversion, one of the 'errors' which should not be allowed to overshadow 'those things' in Dryden 'which are somewhat Congenial' to Dorset and have always deserved a look of pleasure:

'Tis incident to an Elevated Understanding, like your Lordships, to find out the errors of other men: But 'tis your Prerogative to pardon them; to look with Pleasure on those things, which are somewhat Congenial, and of a remote Kindred to your own Conceptions: And to forgive the many Failings of those, who with their wretched Art, cannot arrive to those Heights that you possess, from a happy, abundant, and Native Genius: . . . (5: 18–25)

In the course of the essay, Dryden will imply that he with his 'Wretched Art' scales heights more substantial than the 'natural' peaks of privilege.

The account of Dorset possessing, like Shakespeare and Homer, the 'inborn' heights of 'a happy, abundant, and Native Genius' sets the tone of the panegryic of the next few pages on Dorset the supreme poet, Dryden's master, where, as even Harris admits, 'the outlines of truth begin to waver'.[45] As early as the poem to Sir Robert Howard in 1660 and more recently in the ode 'To the Pious Memory of . . . Anne Killigrew' of 1686, Dryden complimented other writers without debasing his own professionalism, a distinction he so often insisted upon. He praises them for their natural 'native sweetnesse'—'That your Lordship is form'd by Nature for this Supremacy, I cou'd easily prove'—which seems to flow as easily as bird song without toil or study: 'This Success attends your Lordship's Thoughts, which wou'd look like Chance, if it were not perpetual. . . . If I grant that there is Care in it, 'tis such a Care as wou'd be ineffectual, and fruitless in other Men' (24. 28–32). Such an emphasis on Dorset's 'good nature', by all evidence correct, disqualifies him, as we shall see, from the furies that possess the satirist. Nature can be violent, satire has a bad-natured muse, and the image of the gold of Dorset's thoughts ('you go not out of Nature for any of them') makes memorable not the precious substance but a scatological process by which it is brought to light: 'but [it] lies so hidden, and so deep, that the Mines of it are seldom found; but the force of Waters casts it out from the Bowels of Mountains, and exposes it amongst the Sands of Rivers' (24. 24–7) As noblemen and noblewomen are born into privilege, so are they born into poesy ('So wert thou born into a tuneful strain, | An early, rich, and inexhausted vein', Killigrew ode, ll. 27–8), and with that said, a private irony

[45] Harris, *Charles Sackville, Sixth Earl of Dorset*, 199.

or condescension seems quietly managed; the 'adorn' | 'born' rhyme in the Killigrew ode may tactfully suggest the limits of this type of genius:

> Such noble vigour did her verse adorn,
> That it seemed borrowed where 'twas only born.
> (ll. 75–6)

The same emphasis on 'inborn' and 'adorn' characterizes the description of Dorset who 'excels all others, in all the several parts of Poetry which you have undertaken to adorn' (5. 30–1). He is godlike, kinglike, as necessary to poets as the 'daily Course of ordinary Providence' to the world, '(I may almost say)' Dryden inhales with mock caution on such panegyric heights. Dorset is a natural phenomenon but not as a writer—for it becomes clear he does not actually write much, or as much as a professional like Dryden who is kept waiting for 'sufficient Copy to Transcribe'. Even the godliness is soon tarnished by indolence. Jehovah rested on the seventh day as if he knew Virgil's wisdom 'that even Fame . . . acquires strength by going forward'. In fact, by the end of the first quarter of the *Discourse*, Dryden will be arguing—or threatening—that Dorset's fame in future ages will depend not on 'those Honours to which your Birth has intitl'd you', not on inborn merit or achieved rank and power, but on his written work. Rather than proffer a ticket to fame, Dryden intimates that it may be beyond Dorset's reach: other powerful patrons, Augustus and Richelieu, 'wou'd willingly have been' poets, but were not. Dryden meditates on the crucial relationship between fame, writing, and 'Honours and Dignities'—he and his life's work now on the defensive. Hence, the odd, emphatic declaration, ''Tis no shame to be a Poet, tho' 'tis to be a bad one'. The embarrassing, malignant figure of the bad or indifferent poet and the 'Multitude of Scriblers' evoked early, the 'Cattel' of bad poetry branded 'on this Buttock, or that Ear', threaten throughout the *Discourse* as pretenders who overwhelm the field and must be exposed.

For the prize of fame, Dryden pits political authority against the arts and sciences in all ages—'Great Genius'—which forms its own international, apolitical line of succession and development. Early in the essay, Dorset is 'the Sun' (4. 13), a figure which leads to an elaboration of that conventional image of godlike royalty in a busy paragraph where Dryden figures prominently as 'a First Discoverer' who not only saw Dorset rise in the east but 'bespoke you to the World'. But soon Dorset is dropped altogether as subject; Dryden stops bespeaking him to the world as the focus becomes the Making of a Great Poet, the movement from the 'Ambition of a Writer' to the skill, the heroic journey, Dryden's career:

'When thus, as I may say, before the use of the Loadstone, or knowledge of the Compass, I was sailing in a vast Ocean, . . .' He looks back as a master who can now talk about learning 'the Rudiments of Poetry', being then 'without Name, or Reputation' (he now has both). By implication, Dorset and Dryden have 'risen' together, one 'naturally' as a talented man of rank and wealth; the other, without the benefits of birth and privilege, has raised himself by work and genius.

Dryden pictures himself as the autodidact, set to school by necessity, taught only by foreign sources—the ancients and the rules of the French stage. As demonstrated literally by Dryden's relegating the rules for 'a Modern Satire' to the back of the *Discourse*, the rules of an art give ground in this essay to genius, to a vast humanistic accumulation of learning acquired through self-directed study, and to long practice of an art. The disenfranchised literary genius and professional is both born, like Homer, and self-made, like his epic hero. Not only does Dryden emphasize that he has studied all 'Arts and Sciences, all Moral and Natural Philosophy', but when he comes to describe who in England would be capable of writing the epic poem for which he has advanced a new 'Model', 'a rude draught' given to the world, the portrait sounds suspiciously like himself. It combines 'Genius', conversancy in the 'Philosophy of Plato', invention, judgement, memory and 'knowledge of the Liberal Arts and Sciences, and particularly, Moral Philosophy, the Mathematicks, Geography and History'; such is a 'born Poet'. He then uses the word 'arise', the movement of the sun of Dorset—'if such a Man, I say, be now arisen, or shall arise'—bringing the sun or born genius around from Dorset to his 'Discoverer'.

Dorset is named 'the King of Poets' and 'by an undisputed Title' (unlike William). This honour, however, is tossed off in a relative clause buried in a description of how Dryden, as 'Counsellour bred up in the knowledge of the Municipal and Statute Law', will explain the limits of Dorset's power. By overlaying Dorset's political post as Lord Chamberlain with the 'inborn' literary role of 'King of Poets', he can shift more easily from titled honours to greatness of person ('But I mean not the Authority, which is annex'd to your Office: I speak of that only which is inborn and inherent to your Person', 10: 2–4). Dryden describes a potentially subversive, apolitical greatness, of inherent supreme moral authority, of a divine right of moral kingship which can tell the difference between the true and false coin, genuine and 'clip't' poetry.[46] On that

[46] Silver coins clipped within the circle around the king's head were not legal tender.

ground, Dryden can attack Dorset person to person, so to speak, by attacking his moral laziness for not restraining 'the licentious insolence of Poets and their Actors, in all things that shock the Publick Quiet, or the Reputation of Private Persons', and even for participating in them. Dryden's digression in distinguishing Dorset's poetry from 'Spurious Productions' hints that he would have been able to spot Dorset's writing even in unacknowledged places, such as previously circulated, anonymous satiric attacks:

> I can farther add with truth (though not without some vanity in saying it) that in the same Paper, written by divers Hands, whereof your Lordship's was only part, I could separate your Gold from their Copper: And tho I cou'd not give back to every Author his own Brass, . . . yet I never fail'd of knowing what was yours, and what was not: And was absolutely certain, that this, or the other Part was positively yours, and cou'd not possibly be Written by any other. (10. 16–25)

While still in a panegyric mode, Dryden suggests that he has not forgotten satire, his ostensible subject. Dorset's writing is the 'most perfect Model' of satire in English. This absolute judgement is placed in the middle of a curious set of paragraphs mixing attack and praise, and an ominous chiding through Dryden's conditional tenses and characteristic sly use of 'almost' and 'sometimes': 'This, I think, my Lord, is a sufficient Reproach to you; and shou'd I carry it as far as Mankind wou'd Authorise me, wou'd be little less than satire. And, indeed, a provocation is almost necessary, in behalf of the World, that you might be induc'd sometimes to write' (8. 20–4)[47] His first example of compliment, what he himself calls 'an insolent, sparing, and Invidious Panegyrick', is by the Earl of Rochester, and the problem with the remark, says Dryden, is that it unjustly separates the man from the poet, the person from his writings. In this *Discourse*, where the reader finds it difficult to sort out the lines of concern of the 'man' as opposed to those of the 'poet'—who is speaking for whom—the distinction seems to be a charged one, part of the confusing grid of the world of political satire, where persons are attacked and where 'good Nature', despite what Dryden says about Dorset, seems to have no role—certainly not for Juvenal.

[47] Dryden's praise is often troubled by conditional and subjunctive tenses (see n. 42 above) and hedging qualifiers. For example, he says that Dorset lays his thoughts so close together 'that were they closer, they wou'd be crowded, and even a due connexion wou'd be wanting' (25. 15–16). The sentence's energy becomes preoccupied with the specter of a failure which becomes more vivid than the success Dryden began to praise. 'You are always bright, even almost to a fault, by reason of the excess'. The words 'even almost' effectively weaken the 'always'.

In this context—panegyric veering into satire—Dryden scolds Dorset for not writing enough, for being too complacent; as a man of rank, Dorset can certainly afford to be. In the earlier dedication of *An Essay of Dramatick Poesie*, the poet had first, conventionally, urged Dorset to write more, but the tone of the remarks of 1692 is stubbornly sharper. The message is that Dorset's friends not so fortunately placed are oppressed by Dorset's own kind, 'those Noble Characters of Men of Wit and Pleasure about the Town' (9. 3–4). In the first of several references to Buckingham, Dryden alludes to the Duke's attack in the *Rehearsal* against whose 'prose and doggrel' Dryden will not defend 'my Poetry'. This part of the *Discourse* is thick with Dryden's preoccupation with libel and feelings of political impotence. But to save appearances—and draw attention away from his politics—the appeal to Dorset takes the form of a scolding of his patron (whose writings are 'the most perfect Model' of satire) for ignoring his public duty of writing more and thereby stifling the production of the garbage now in circulation. A confusing taunt appears when he says that Dorset needs to 'refresh' his 'Character' with 'somewhat of extraordinary'; perhaps it has become dull and tarnished by his constant, silent association with the likes of Shadwell or other 'dull Makers of Lampoons'. Finally, there is suggested a direct relationship between writing 'on behalf of the World' and writing on behalf of one's own reputation—the first ultimately stemming from the second—between writing and anger from provocation ('indeed, a provocation is almost necessary ... that you might be induc'd sometimes to write'). Dorset does not write enough because he has compromised; as we will come to see, Dryden is also making an implication about Dorset's manhood, so risky that the rest of the *Discourse* wraps protective circles around it.

When Dryden finally announces that he has arrived at 'my present Business' of the origin and development of satire 'among the Romans' and of the 'Nature of that Poem' and 'this New Way of Version which is attempted' in his translation (26), he just as deliberately sidesteps satire. He barely takes a breath when, without explanation or apology, he perversely begins the next paragraph on still another digressive note—'The most Perfect Work of Poetry, says our Master Aristotle, is Tragedy' (26. 29–30)—and veers back to unfinished business with the heroic poem, the subject of the major digression of the first quarter.[48] He had outlined a

[48] An example of similar toying with the reader occurs in his discussion of the verse of satire towards the end of the essay. 'Had I time, I cou'd enlarge on the Beautiful Turns of Words and Thoughts; which are as requisite in this, as in Heroique Poetry it self', he says (84. 14–16), implying that he does not have the time and will skip the subject. In the next

design for the Christian English epic which he himself would have written had patronage been forthcoming. Now, as if in afterthought, he must correct that first literary authority, Aristotle, and complete the argument that epic, rather than tragedy, is 'certainly the greatest Work of Human Nature' (a theme he will return to in a much fuller digression in the *Dedication of the Aeneis*). This assertion is proved by the fact that fewer have attempted it than have attempted drama, since tragedy requires 'a less and more confin'd Knowledge: moderate Learning, and Observation of the Rules is sufficient, if a Genius be not wanting' (27. 19–21). As to the qualifications for a writer of epic, Dryden had given them at length, but now adds a study of Homer and Virgil, Aristotle and Horace, Vida and Bossu, and the Italian and French critics. All of this 'does not particularly concern Satire', he throws out at the end and hastens on, again, 'to my present business'. Dryden breezily appears to drop epic for the time being and dissociates what he was doing from the factious contentions of 'the Critiques on either side' about their preference for 'this or that sort of poetry', as he also claims later that his observations on Persius, Horace, and Juvenal, unlike the in-fighting for favourites of 'the Modern Critiques', are characterized by disinterestedness (though, confusingly, he admits to judging finally by his personal taste).

One is provoked to ask why does this propaganda about epic greatness—the learnedness of its writer, the difficulty of its form and themes, the exceptional nature of its heroes—emphatically precede and delay the discussion of satire? Such a digression can only make satire look less glamorous: without a hero, a difficult journey, or the tradition of learning. The unavoidable implication seems to be, keeping in mind Dryden's finishing touch—his idea for an epic which he is only prevented from writing because of lack of support—that Dryden could and should be writing epic now (he does all but begin before our eyes), that his present business of writing about satire is, in fact, another example of the long digressions of his career, the many low roads away from that high road, and that, with his qualifications and authority so insistently demonstrated throughout the *Discourse*, he must inevitably infuse whatever project he takes on with something of the epic. He does not hesitate to remind us of the labour he has put into the translations which were 'so difficult an Undertaking', especially of Persius ('who has cost me more labour and time, than Juvenal', 50. 36, or, speaking of the obscurity of

sentence, prolonged over eight lines, he unhurriedly slips into a discussion of 'turns'—'With these Beautiful Turns I confess my self to have been unacquainted, till about Twenty Years ago, in a Conversation which I had . . .'.—that takes several leisurely pages.

Persius, 'so, he [Casaubon] went through his laborious Task, as I have done with my difficult Translation', 54. 30–2). Satire is 'a Poem of a difficult Nature in it self, and is not written to Vulgar Readers' (54. 20–1), and Dryden's readers are not allowed to forget the labour of the obstacle course which is the *Discourse*, both for writer and reader: 'I am now arriv'd at the most difficult part of my Undertaking'; 'I am now, my self, on the brink of the same Precipice'; 'I wish I coul'd as easily remove that other difficulty which yet remains'; 'But I have already wearied my self, and doubt not but I have tir'd your Lordships Patience'; 'But I have said enough, and it may be, too much on this Subject. Will your Lordship be pleas'd to prolong my Audience, only so far, till . . .'; 'I am still speaking to you, my Lord; though in all probability, you are already out of hearing. . . . But I am come to the last Petition of Abraham. . . .' There is a journey and a hero not hurrying to get home.

THE 'MIXT' AND OBSCURE PROGRESS OF SATIRE

For the next quarter of the essay where he is committed to tracing the origins of satire 'as a Species of Poetry', Dryden draws most heavily on Casaubon's *De Satyrica Graecorum Poesi et Romanorum Satira* (Paris, 1605); he also used Casaubon's 1605 edition of Persius for his translations. Descending as he does from epic, Dryden seems immediately dismayed by the task of disentangling his genre from its 'deprav'd' origins in cursing, railing, and invective. To separate satire from satyr, 'that mixt kind of animal', and to elevate it beyond association forever with the 'Common Audience' who 'soon grow weary of good Sense', he must dramatically enter the 'War' of the critics on the side of Casaubon and against Julius Scaliger. But what is most interesting for our purposes about this laborious section of the *Discourse* is not the dialectic between Casaubon and Scaliger but rather our experience of the discussion as a series of manœuvres that, in fact, go nowhere at all—stop and start, retreat and advance—as the author drags us along in his steps and gives us the illusion of overhearing him noisily think out loud.

> But I am afraid he [Casaubon] mistakes the matter, and confounds. . . . The Reason of my Opinion is this. . . . Yet since it is a hard Conjecture, that so Great a Man as Casaubon should misapply what Horace writ . . . I will not insist on this Opinion. . . . For, Indeed, when I am reading Casaubon, on these two subjects, methinks I hear the same Story told twice over with very little alteration. Of which Dacier takeing notice. . . . But what is yet more wonderful, that most Learned Critique takes notice also. . . . A strange likeness, and barely possible: But the

Critiques being all of the same Opinion, it becomes me to be silent, and submit to better Judgments than my own.

But to return to the Grecians . . . I am to take a View of them first, and see if there be any such Descent from them as those Authors have pretended. (30: 29–33: 10)

Here we have Dacier making out that. . . . It may possibly be so; but Dacier knows no more of it than I do. (42: 36–43: 7)

When Dryden finally manages to establish the independence of Roman satire from Greek traditions, he makes another one of his self-dramatizing progress reports, this time likening himself to one who has been swimming underwater and is coming up for air: 'Thus, my Lord, I have at length disengag'd my self from those Antiquities of Greece; . . . I am now almost gotten into my depth; at least by the help of Dacier, I am swimming towards it' (36. 3–8).[49]

Dryden has just laboured with the critics to dissociate spleen from that species of poetry he calls 'Noble' satire. (We remember the earlier association of 'noble' with 'good nature' in Dryden's description of Dorset.) He has established that an author to write 'Noble' satire must have 'purg'd himself from those splenetick Reflections' that generate invective, as Horace seems to have done through the *Odes* and *Epodes*. Dryden repeats this point when he begins to judge the relative merits of Horace and Juvenal, from which contest he pointedly excludes the *Odes* and *Epodes* because many were written 'Satirically, against his private enemies. . . . But Horace had purg'd himself of this choler, before he enter'd on those Discourses which are more properly call'd the Roman Satire:' (58. 32–59. 3).[50] Satire, then, is of the nature of moral philosophy, says

[49] In the prefatory letter to 'Eleonora' (1692), addressed to the Earl of Abingdon, Dryden uses the image of swimming to contrast the experience of being with and without inspiration. He dramatizes his temporary reprieval from ill health as having 'only gain'd a Rock by hard swimming'; but when he becomes the inspired priest of Apollo, the godlike fury sweeps him along happily with 'double strength' like a swimmer in a tide: 'the weight of thirty Years was taken off me while I was writing. I swom with the Tyde, and the Water under me was buoyant' (*The Poems of John Dryden*, ed. James Kinsley, vol. ii (London: Oxford University Press, 1958), 582).

[50] In the *Dedication of the Georgics* four years later, when his brooding over age, ill health, and loss of potency as a writer had darkened, Dryden gives perhaps a more honest assessment of Horace. In that *Dedication*, Horace's satires are seen as the product of his descending powers, of loss of boldness and increased caution, when he had come to be more 'a Philosopher and a Critick than a Poet' (*The Works of John Dryden*, vol. v (Berkeley and Los Angeles: University of California Press, 1987), 138. 15–16). Again, loss of spleen seems to mean loss of manhood. Horace's genius is pictured as 'still rising' in the first and second book of *Odes*, but he 'came not to his Meridian 'till the Third: After which his Judgment was an overpoize to his Imagination' (138. 12–13).

Dryden, by which he means that Horace corrects 'the Vices and the Follies of his Time' and gives rules for a happy life (59. 5–6). In the course of discussing Horace and Juvenal, however, Dryden reverses his position and has Juvenal ride first in triumph as the 'greater poet, I mean in Satire', whose spleen unpurged 'raises mine' and gives the reader 'the Pleasure of Concernment in all he says'. The connection between spleen, boldness of imagination, and poetry—hinted at in Dryden's earlier ambiguous nagging over Dorset's laziness and in the description of his own self-made 'rising', then vigorously denied in his discussion of the origin and nature of satire—becomes an aesthetic for a Jeremiah, the fury of vision.

THE PRIZE OF SATIRE

In the middle of the *Discourse*, then, its argument appears to shift; the footwork becomes particularly bewildering around the poor figure of Horace. Robert Elliott has commented on 'the tortuous progress of the essay, the reluctance to come to judgment', as Dryden is forced 'into considering problems of genre', a 'consciousness on his part of the aesthetic problems' of comparing two such different satirists as Horace and Juvenal.[51] Both Elliott and Pechter remark that Dryden finally settles for 'a multiple conclusion';[52] and while it is true that Dryden says he is declaring a draw among Juvenal, Horace, and Persius—'Let these Three Ancients be preferr'd to all the Moderns; as first arriving at the Goal: Let them all be Crown'd as Victours' (75. 27–9)—the sentence continues by insisting on the inevitable reality of pre-eminence, that someone must be favoured and first, and he sends them off riding in a triumphal procession out of our view, with Juvenal leading. To see how the balance shifts to Juvenal requires a close look at the contest for best satiric poet that Dryden gradually, digressively organizes between Horace and Juvenal, Persius summarily dismissed. As we have noted, Dryden insists on his attempt to remain impartial, vows to avoid the error of those critics who favour whomever they have spent most time translating. On the other hand, he wants to avoid the error of levelling critics who automatically favour a 'Poor Man, right or wrong' and who conclude without a hearing that a rich man must be 'an Oppressor'. The brief digression that moves from critical to legal judgement and to Sir Matthew Hales (or Hale)

[51] Robert C. Elliott, *The Power of Satire: Magic, Ritual, Art* (Princeton: Princeton University Press, 1960), 116–18.

[52] Pechter, *Dryden's Classical Theory of Literature*, 28–9.

seems to suggest the impossibility of impartiality in the present age and leave us with the sense that even the most upright judge works inevitably on a bias:

> I remember a saying of K. Charles the Second, on Sir Matthew Hales, (who was doubtless an Uncorrupt and Upright Man) That his Servants were sure to be Cast on any Trial, which was heard before him: Not that he thought the Judge was possibly to be brib'd; but that his Integrity might be too scrupulous: And that the Causes of the Crown were always suspicious, when the Priviledges of Subjects were concern'd. (50: 10–17)

According to Roger North, Chief Justice Hale of the King's Bench was scrupulous in his morals and well known for his suspicion of money and privilege and his bias toward the people, a 'warping to plebeianisme', such that 'a greasy cap, had allwais the better of a modish perruque'. His vast learning and knowledge of past proceedings of his court, however, meant 'he never would judg against the crowne against his knowledge, and president was much for the advantage of the prerogative'.[53] Is the writer suggesting that the judge of the contest to follow is one for whom the causes of the Crown, now William III's, are 'always suspicious' when the privileges of subjects, such as Dryden, are concerned? Before long, in fact, Dryden will drop the pretence of being impartial and will judge which poet gives him the most pleasure.

After remarking that Horace, once purged of choler, does not attack particular sects and persons but corrects vices and follies, Dryden launches into a digression about lampoons—the kind of work he has just said Horace does not do—and which he had earlier in the *Discourse* castigated at some length as beneath the dignity of 'noble' satire. Nobility as it is associated with the court has become suspect, however, and Dryden has prepared for the presentation of satire in the image of Juvenal: Jeremiah howling in the wilderness. Suddenly there are two justifications for lampoons, and in both Dryden seems to be seriously invested. Lampoons are indeed 'a dangerous sort of weapon . . . for the most part Unlawful'; but they are not wholly without value.

The first instance when lampoons may be justified is personal revenge for abuse from another, a topic which gives Dryden the opportunity to expound on the abuse he has suffered and his 'Christian' forbearance. The second case that justifies writing against particular persons is the 'Publick Nuisance'. Here, confusingly, he says that Horace, like Persius

[53] Roger North, *Notes of me: The Autobiography of Roger North*, ed. Peter Millard (Toronto: University of Toronto Press, 2000), 164–5, 170.

and Juvenal, has, after all, written against individuals in his satires; and Dryden is most emphatic about this 'Duty' which is 'absolutely of a Poet's Office to perform'. And now he performs that duty, though he seems to be launched into a digression: what follows is moral outrage against bad lampooners because they are a public nuisance and give satire a bad name. Dryden is required to pretend that he, perfectly disinterested, is often forced against his will to read bad lampoons—'when they come in my way, 'tis impossible sometimes to avoid reading them'—and as exclamation marks explode on the page the personal basis of his vehemence becomes clear. He is angry first at the incompetence of the lampooners to pick the right subject, angry over the injustice of being the wrong person 'stabb'd'; second, his is the competitive artist's scorn at the clumsiness of the botched job, granted the wrong subject: 'But, good God, how remote they are in common Justice, from the choice of such Persons as are the proper Subject of Satire! And how little Wit they bring, for the support of their injustice!' (60. 20–3). He continues the diatribe until his anger is spent and 'I have removed this Rubbish'.

Beginning again the comparison of Horace and Juvenal which was interrupted almost immediately by the digression on lampoons, Dryden wants to give the prize 'in my particular Opinion' to Horace for instruction and to Juvenal for delight (61. 6–12). Why does the discussion of the two poets then extend over fifteen pages? To give Juvenal the first prize, Dryden has created a situation where he must justify valuing delight over instruction, and these traditional terms must be recharged with new political and personal meaning: delight takes on the qualities of self-made, great-souled genius and the transport of 'swimming with the tide' of poetic fury, of excellence not due to aristocractic origins ('though but second in degree') but irresistibly vigorous, while instruction is only esteemed like titles and high rank and is not capable of inspiring transport.

Additionally, the government of William and Mary had come to endorse a reformed world of domesticity and marriage, of manners, sentimentality, and civil contracts in what D. W. R. Bahlmann called 'the moral revolution of 1688'.[54] For his entire career Dryden had defended the moral pleasures of poetry, and 'Versification and Numbers' as giving

[54] D. W. R. Bahlman, *The Moral Revolution of 1688* (New Haven: Yale University Press, 1957). See also Shelley Burtt, *Virtue Transformed: Political Argument in England, 1688–1740* (Cambridge: Cambridge University Press, 1992); and Leo Braudy, 'Unturning the Century: The Missing Decade of the 1690s', in Elaine Scarry (ed.), *Fins de Siècle: English Poetry in 1590, 1690, 1790, 1890, 1990*, (Baltimore: Johns Hopkins University Press, 1995), 63–93.

'the greatest Pleasures' (64. 27–8) of all, the craft behind poetic licence that achieves a poetic sublime. To split apart for judgement the Horatian functions of poetry, to teach and to delight—to create 'Horace our Minister of State in satire, and Juvenal of our private Pleasures' (66. 4–5)—is to reflect the separation created by the court of William and Mary with their campaign against vice, their suspicion of the passions, and emphasis on instruction in art. Early in the *Discourse* Dryden secures the connection between the office of Lord Chamberlain and the government's promotion of virtue and 'Good Manners': 'As Lord Chamberlain, I know, you are absolute by your Office, in all that belongs to the Decency and Good Manners of the Stage' (9. 33–5). Thus when Horace's style of satire is praised as the best 'for amending Manners', and Dorset complimented, 'you see I have preferr'd the Manner of Horace, and of your Lordship, in this kind of Satire' (71. 26–7, 35), the praise sounds ambiguous since both Horace and Dorset are associated in their good manners with the court that has been censoring Dryden's work.

Dryden emphasizes that he is presenting an opinion, his particular taste 'which I set not up for a Standard to better Judgments'. At the same time, he becomes defensive of his taste and 'Moderation' as what 'all unbiass'd Readers' will agree with. The *Discourse* throughout is both self-defence and a trial and judgement of those who have judged against him. Courtroom vocabulary turns his 'Opinion' into high drama:

> To such Impartial Men I must appeal: For they who have already form'd their Judgment, may justly stand suspected of prejudice; and tho all who are my Readers, will set up to be my Judges, I enter my Caveat against them, that they ought not so much as to be of my Jury. Or, if they be admitted, 'tis but Reason, that they shou'd first hear, what I have to urge in the Defence of my Opinion. (61: 19–25)

For a while he dilates on Horace's great skill as a teacher of virtue, but this moment of poise is strictly temporary. He soon shifts the balance, as if he had gone too far or become bored with his praise, and the rest of the discussion is a wild see-saw of giving and taking away praise all around to hide his preference for Juvenal. The diatribe against Horace is now launched, however, and he never recovers. The delight Dryden gets from Horace is 'but languishing', his 'salt' is 'insipid', his wit 'faint'. Juvenal's thoughts are more elevated, and he is 'on the gallop', whereas Horace ambles. Horace's low style matches 'groveling' subject matter; he is 'a Temporizing Poet, a well Manner'd Court Slave, and a Man who is afraid of Laughing in the right place: who is ever decent because naturally servile' (65. 21–3).

Suddenly, in mid-paragraph, he says he has ended the comparison 'before I was aware'; but he has not finished. As the reader knows by now, such signals may be deliberately misleading. Instead he begins some crucial footwork about the relative merits of the two aims of poetry. After all the protestations of impartiality, Dryden's critical debate is turning into politics: an attack on tyranny, the court, and courtiers. Juvenal has 'more of the Commonwealth Genius' which means, in this context, 'he treats Tyranny, and all the Vices attending it, as they deserve, with the utmost rigour: And consequently, a Noble Soul is better pleas'd with a Zealous Vindicator of Roman Liberty; than with a Temporizing Poet' (65. 17–21). Dryden distinguishes between, on the one hand, a pale, civic 'Honour'—the poetry of instruction being honourable like a Cabinet post—and, on the other, favour or liking, the pleasure of 'Concernment' raised by a lone, angry voice like Juvenal's:

> For if we make Horace our Minister of State in Satire, and Juvenal of our private Pleasures: I think the latter has no ill bargain of it. Let Profit have the preheminence of Honour, in the End of Poetry. Pleasure, though but second in degree, is the first in favour. And who wou'd not chuse to be lov'd better, rather than to be more esteem'd [especially if those who dispense the honors are dishonorable]? (66: 4–9)

Such a declaration for pleasure over instruction in virtue clearly rejects the court's current fashion for moral teaching in literature. With this distinction between public instruction and private pleasures, Dryden condemns staid 'Honours and Dignities' of state and claims preeminence through the favour he obtains on his own merits as a poet that gives private, if not public, pleasure. (He would like to be not only 'the first in favour' but also 'esteem'd', and the implication is that in his own country it is impossible to be both.) The break-up, juggling, and rearrangement of values within these few sentences seems a key moment in the *Discourse*, an important statement that needs to be made, after which the tension in the essay begins to wane, though a quarter of the text remains, and Dryden is not finished with Horace.

The line of argument is now a bit tangled, and the author does not seem particularly concerned to untangle anything—the blur is more comfortable: 'But I am enter'd already upon Another Topique; which concerns the particular Merits of these two Satirists [what other topic?]. However, I will pursue my business where I left it [what business?] and carry it farther than that common observation of the several Ages, in which these Authors Flourished' (66. 10–14). What follows, in fact, is a digression on Augustan politics. Presented in a language which calls to mind the 'conquest' by William III, it intensifies the negative connotations of Horace as tainted court product.

As if suddenly remembering that he writes to a patron whom he has crowned king of satire and associated from early in the essay with Horace (6. 19–20), and perhaps afraid of having gone too far at this point, Dryden appears to begin a mild attempt to reclaim the poetic status of Horace by praising his 'fine Raillery': 'still the nicest and most delicate touches of Satire consist in fine Raillery. This, my Lord, is your particular Talent, to which even Juvenal could not arrive' (70. 21–3). (The language of 'most delicate touches' recalls the vaguely condescending references early in the *Discourse* to the 'secret graces' and 'peculiar graces' of Dorset's writing, which Dryden claimed to be struggling to imitate; his 'imitation' now turns the feather-tickling touch into a mock-execution.)

The attempt to give Horace back some ground leads to a climactic final disjunction. From 'fine Raillery' Dryden takes up the image of satire whose 'correction' tickles rather than hurts; as in the preface to *Absalom and Achitophel*, where this description of painless satire ended with the drastic recommendation of 'an act of oblivion' for the patient, so Dryden here is but a short step to decapitation: 'Yet there is still a vast difference betwixt the slovenly Butchering of a Man, and the fineness of a stroak that separates the Head from the Body, and leaves it standing in its place' (71. 8–11). Dryden is quoting trade talk by the wife of hangman Jack Ketch (notorious for having bungled the execution of Monmouth, among many others). In what does this 'vast difference' consist except in managing that moment of unreality when what looks like life is death, praise blame? In the whirl of distracting gestures, Dryden claims to hope that his character of Zimri in *Absalom and Achitophel* may be a good example of 'a Malefactor' made to 'die sweetly', as opposed to 'a bare hanging', being 'not bloody' but 'ridiculous'. The masterful achievement of, for a moment, maintaining satire as an execution that only tickles, of deadly revenge as 'the Jest' gone round, and a libeller 'of Great Crimes' as one who 'began the Frolick' requires keeping the pace dizzy. The reader feels his own head has been severed when the head or crown of a sentence, as it were—the substance of what has been said—hovers in the air yet, denied an existence, cleanly separated from the body of words on the page.

At this point Dryden seems to favour Horace and make a last attempt to resuscitate him from earlier injuries. From images of aesthetic decapitation, it is but a short step to the standard topoi of the medicinal effects of satire: Horace becomes 'a Pleasant Cure' leaving all limbs intact, while Juvenal amputates. The tentative gain, however, is a tease; the balance, if it had momentarily tipped towards Horace, begins immediately to swing back to Juvenal. Dryden's torture of what is left of Horace is not over yet: 'This Manner of Horace is indeed the best; but Horace has not executed it, altogether so happily, at least not often', he says, and begins to jab again, pile up the faults. The raillery is actually 'insipid', his tickling not successful at all, Horace descends to puns—'he has no fine Palate who can feed so heartily on Garbige' (73. 6–7). Perhaps nervous still about his treatment of Horace and wanting to be done with the business, he wearily brings in, for Horace's defence or as farewell words of unexciting praise, the opinion of Dacier whom he quotes at length, after which he dismisses Horace with an impatient wave of relief: 'Let Horace go off with these Encomiums, which he has so well deserv'd' (75. 21–2).

DISJUNCTION AND THE WANDERING HERO

I have examined the *Discourse Concerning the Original and Progress of Satire* as a piece of writing at least as artful as it is critical, an assumption suggested by its aggressive length and digressiveness. And I have suggested that the essay's chief values are to be discovered in the movement of its prose: the evolution of a rich but 'loose epistolary' style based on digression, which allows Dryden the appearance of an expansive, inadvertent, informal manner while he strategically relocates centre stage in a complex, disturbing way—because the world he is describing is complex and disturbing. Constantly splitting apart at the seams, it severs patron from client and civil servant from office at a stroke of the clumsy axe of faction. Safe progress in such a world becomes an obscure progress, one which must accommodate the detours required by sudden disjunctions of reality, when the earth splits under one's feet—a progress of digression which is both political and aesthetic, which turns a radical break into an epicentre of meaning about which collect and wrap reverberating, protective circles of commentary. The figure of arbitrary trial and judgement and its butchering dichotomies—in and out of favour, Whig or Tory, true or false, the scapegoat and the quietly unpunished—seem an organizing shock that the digressions of the *Discourse* repeat, mock, and attempt to transcend.

In the years immediately preceding the Glorious Revolution, especially after Dryden's conversion, the poet and his patron of long standing went separate political ways and their friendship was probably strained. The most popular and influential lampoon published in response to the laureate's Catholicism and to his long, complex poem of 1687 was written by Dorset's protégés, as were lesser taunts; Dorset himself possibly composed one of the more literate and vicious short poems of abuse. By 1689 their positions with respect to the centre of power had reversed. Dorset, whose lord lieutenancy had been revoked by James in January 1688, had become a minister in England's first cabinet as a reward for his anti-Catholicism and role in William's ascent. Because of his conversion, Dryden was forced to the margins: he lost the government position and salary he had held for twenty years, while his Jacobite sympathies meant the constant reality of government censorship.

The writer of the *Discourse* could not have forgotten these events. He seems to be reminding his patron of, and recalibrating, the disturbing shocks which have sent him to the edge of the political map by sending a few back to the centre. Under the cover of inadvertency and digression, the poet rambles into turning the worst charges levelled against himself, of court flunky and turncoat, onto Horace. He also associates William and Mary's campaign against vice and their promotion of art as moral instruction with the Roman court satirist and, thence, with the current government's Lord Chamberlain and 'King of Poets' whose satire, like Horace's, demonstrates exquisite good manners and fine raillery. More deeply embedded in the *Discourse* are hints of partisanship and moral complacency that clash with the image, which Dryden also affirms in the *Discourse*, that Dorset enjoyed as a generous and graciously tolerant Maecenas. At the essay's epicentre of judgement is the executioner's block, and there collects the emotion generating the digressions. There Dryden recalls how he dealt with his old enemy Buckingham-Zimri; and there he judges Horace and Juvenal who are, at one level of imagination, Dorset and Dryden: he contrasts the delicate satire of manners with the angry satire of the exile who carries moral passion and authority. The contest is startlingly erratic and finally abitrary. The verdict is, in fact, partisan.

The *Discourse* and the translations of the satires of Juvenal and Persius form an interesting transitional moment between the original plays and poems of Dryden's career within the court of Charles II, and the concentrated work of poetry and translation to which he turned in the last years of his life. The digressiveness of the *Discourse* gives the sense of a mind released, on the ramble, one 'so richly cultivated that the reader is rewarded at every turn with fresh prospects of literary knowledge and insight',[55] and it allows Dryden the freedom, not constricted by the theatre's demands, to include those 'many things, which not only please, but are real beauties in the reading' but which, as he says in the 'Dedication of the Aeneis', would appear absurd upon the stage'.[56] The ramble, however, is also a deliberate tour of a landscape or grid in which threats and dangers loom from the first words. In the course of explaining and defending why he is translating satire rather than writing an epic poem, Dryden achieves in his prose an epic freedom and mastery of movement that allows him to navigate in and out of dangerous waters unscathed while leaving behind unmistakable signs of his political, critical, and artistic presence.

Dryden must have played to the readers' speculations as to whether, at this point, he felt the personal and strategic need for a conclusive, public statement about satire, and he speaks as its authority through study and its master through practice, who was leaving the increasingly bleak field to lesser lights in order to engage with the grandest achievements of the ancients, leaving London for Rome as Umbricius left Rome for the country. The suggestions of leave-taking, vague business elsewhere, are epic echoes of an interrupted and endless voyage, the hero and his prose always wandering. Digressiveness, as both disjunction and progress, becomes a stylistic reflection, and an encompassing, of all the important conflicts in the world of the *Discourse*: the relationships between epic and revenge, praise and blame, patron and poet, king and subject, 'in' and 'out' open at the seams under the pressure of public and psychological disenfranchisement, and the achievement of a voice in which 'the Majesty of the Heroique' is not only 'mix'd' with but ultimately encompasses 'the Venom of the other' will become, in his late prose, a reflection of Dryden's mastery of the gaps.

[55] Bywaters, *Dryden in Revolutionary England*, 107.

[56] Dryden, *Essays*, ii., 161. 25–7.

Epilogue: Wandered too far? Swift's Monstrous Voice

Read all the Prefaces of Dryden,
For these our Criticks much confide in,
(Tho' meerly writ at first for filling
To raise the Volume's Price, a Shilling.)
(Jonathan Swift, 'On Poetry, A Rapsody' (1733), ll. 251–4)

This book has been exploring how writers of the seventeenth century used digressive writing to create a powerful literary voice. The digressions of these narrative voices elude attack and connect pieces of a fallen world, and all have 'a beast in view'.[1] At the end of the century, the digressive ease in Dryden's great prefaces, which Swift swipes at in his poem above, distracts the reader from the remarkably busy hunter, his chase and his game, but Swift responds to their menace. In these concluding pages I want to follow where the digression appears to unravel in Swift's attack on the 'moderns' and on one modern in particular. In 1704 *A Tale of a Tub* took London by storm. At the start of a new century this disorderly, exuberant, and angry text looked back over literary productions of the late seventeenth century and forward toward a world of increased and increasingly digressive writing, and of textual and psychic fragmentation.

Scholarship has been fruitful with respect to *A Tale* which was published together with *The Battle of the Books* and *A Discourse Concerning the Mechanical Operation of the Spirit*, comprising what Ian Higgins calls

1 All, all, of a piece throughout;
Thy Chase had a Beast in View.

John Dryden, 'The Secular Masque' (1700), ll. 86–7. Momus speaks, the god whom Swift in *The Battle of the Books* refers to as 'the Patron of the Moderns' (l. 239).

'a baroque miscellany book on abuses in religion and learning'.[2] Students of this hallucinatory text have emphasized Swift's advocacy of his mentor, Sir William Temple, and of the ancient writers whom Temple defended in a pamphlet war against 'moderns' Richard Bentley and William Wotton. Readers have noted Swift's attack on Hobbes's mechanistic paradigm, on the Royal Society's aims and projects, and his participation in seventeenth-century satire on Puritan enthusiasm, in anti-Quaker, anti-atheist, and anti-popery polemics.[3] I intend to focus

[2] Ian Higgins, *Swift's Politics: A Study in Disaffection* (Cambridge: Cambridge University Press, 1994), 96. Higgins has emphasized that *A Tale* 'is very much the cultural product of the contemporary pamphleteering tradition and writings on affairs of state' (96). Readers have explored Swift's relation to Erasmus, Rabelais, Cervantes, Montaigne, and the tradition of Renaissance scepticism; his response to the aesthetic, political, and scientific debates of the time. See, for example, Clarence M. Webster, 'Swift's *A Tale of a Tub* Compared with Earlier Satires of the Puritans', *PMLA* 47 (1932), 171–8, and 'Swift and Some Earlier Satirists of Puritan Enthusiasm', *PMLA* 48 (1933), 1141–53; Phillip Harth, *Swift and Anglican Rationalism: The Religious Background of 'A Tale of a Tub'* (Chicago: University of Chicago Press, 1961); Jay Arnold Levine, 'The Design of *A Tale of a Tub* (with a Digression on a Mad Modern Critic', *ELH* 33 (1966), 198–227; Maureen Quilligan, *The Language of Allegory; Defining the Genre* (Ithaca, NY: Cornell University Press, 1979), 136–45, who considers *A Tale* as a parody of allegorical reading of the Bible; and Michael Seidel, *Satiric Inheritance: Rabelais to Sterne* (Princeton: Princeton University Press, 1979), 169–200. Everett Zimmerman, *Swift's Narrative Satires: Author and Authority* (Ithaca, NY: Cornell University Press, 1983) and Ronald Paulson, *Theme and Structure in Swift's 'Tale of a Tub'* (New Haven: Yale University Press, 1960) both discuss the influence of Montaigne on *A Tale*, while Zimmerman and Eugene R. Hammond, 'In Praise of Wisdom and the Will of God: Erasmus' *Praise of Folly* and Swift's *A Tale of a Tub*', *Studies in Philology*, 80 (1983), 253–76, look at Erasmus' paradoxical encomium as a model for Swift. For Alan S. Fischer, however ('An End to the Renaissance: Erasmus, Hobbes, and *A Tale of a Tub*', *Huntington Library Quarterly*, 38 (1974), 1–20), Swift's parody so impatient of deception signals the end of a rather luxurious tradition of Renaissance paradox or at least shows the 'dark side of paradox' (10). See also Marcus Walsh, 'Text, "Text", and Swift's *A Tale of a Tub*', *MLR* 85 (1990), 290–303, on *A Tale*'s relation to the heated debate about interpretation of scripture in the 1680s; John Sitter, *Arguments of Augustan Wit* (Cambridge: Cambridge University Press, 1991), 155–62; Joseph M. Levine, *The Battle of the Books: History and Literature in the Augustan Age* (Ithaca, NY: Cornell University Press, 1991); Warren Montag, *The Unthinkable Swift: The Spontaneous Philosophy of a Church of England Man* (London: Verso, 1994), 86–123; and Clement Hawes, *Mania and Literary Style: The Rhetoric of Enthusiasm from the Ranters to Christopher Smart* (Cambridge: Cambridge University Press 1996), esp. 101–25. David Bywaters has argued persuasively for the *Tale*'s anticlerical force. David Bywaters, 'Anticlericism in Swift's "*Tale of a Tub*" ', *SEL* 36 (1996), 579–602.

[3] With his essay 'Upon Ancient and Modern Learning', Temple had entered a long-standing debate but responded specifically to Thomas Burnet's *Sacred Theory of the Earth* and Fontenelle's *Digression sur les anciens et les modernes*. See J. E. Spingarn, *Sir William Temple's Essays on Ancient & Modern Learning and on Poetry* (Oxford: Clarendon Press, 1909), 2–42; for a historical discussion of the debate, see Levine, *The Battle of the Books*, and most recently Joseph M. Levine, *Between the Ancients and the Moderns: Baroque Culture in Restoration England* (New Haven, Yale University Press, 1999), in which he discusses Dryden's relationship to the controversy, 35–109. A recent discussion of Swift's allegory and his 'patrician' attack on the 'plebeian' Puritans is Hawes's chapter in his *Mania and Literary Style*, 101–25.

on the feeling that Swift directs against digressions and their famous recent advocate; my topic is what Johnson called 'Swift's perpetual malevolence to Dryden'.[4] John Boyle, fifth Earl of Cork and Orrery, observes that Swift in *A Tale of a Tub* 'never loses the least opportunity of venting his keenest satir against Mr. Dryden, and consequently loads with insults the greatest, although the least prosperous, of our English poets'.[5] Two paragraphs later, he adds, 'rancour must be very prevalent in the heart of the author, who could overlook the merits of Dryden, many of whose dedications and prefaces are as fine compositions, and as just pieces of criticism, as any in our language'.[6]

Swift's 'malevolence' and 'rancour', I suggest, detect and reconfigure as madness an emotional underworld beneath the high authority and extravagant digressions of Dryden's late discursive voice: a body inventive of fathers, full of pride, self-vindication and self-pity, and melancholy fears of disease and old age. *A Tale*'s parodic embodiment of Dryden's 'malevolence' is the disruptive, deformed body of the modern book that speaks through the voice of a Hack who wanders uncontrollably into digressions: a rootless voice for a body wounded in the modern war of words. The Hack belongs to a 'Brotherhood' of proudly original 'Moderns' who claim to have equalled and surpassed all of their fathers. As a result he and his digressions have become unmoored to bob loose in a dangerous sea, figures for a permanent condition of dislocation from ancient sources of physical and mental health and fertility. Swift's parody formally severs the digression from the parent line of narrative, and the disinherited figure becomes the 'modern' story. Once turned loose by Swift to make extended journeys around ever-larger chasms of discontinuity, the digression becomes available to embody voices like that of the distracted son and wounded body, Tristram Shandy, in a world whose linear pressures of thought and reproduction, and other domestic engines, have become as dangerous as cannon.

[4] Kathleen Williams, *Swift: The Critical Heritage* (New York: Barnes & Noble, 1970), 200. With few recent exceptions, no one has mused on the large imaginative space which Swift allows Dryden to occupy in this work. See, however, Robert Phiddian, *Swift's Parody* (Cambridge: Cambridge University Press, 1995), particularly 127–32. See also Ian Higgins, 'Dryden and Swift', in *John Dryden (1631–1700): His politics, His plays and His poets*, ed. Claude J. Rawson and Aaron Santesso, forthcoming from the Unversity of Delaware Press.

[5] John Boyle, *Remarks on the Life and Writings of Dr. Jonathan Swift*, ed. João Fróes (Newark: University of Delaware Press, 2000), Letter XXIII, 300.

[6] Ibid., 300–1.

THE BODY AND MADNESS

Digressive Voices opened with an image of seventeenth-century texts as battlefields, and the satiric preface of *A Tale of a Tub* sets a deadly scene: penetrating Wits and a Leviathan ready to overturn Church and State, 'Danger hourly increasing' and 'Offensive Weapons' ready to be drawn for 'immediate Execution', to distract which the Hack launches his distracted text. Frank Boyle observed that 'Swift sees in the intellectual violence of scientific revolutions', which the Hack links to modern progressive literary culture, 'the same potential for human violence that is associated with political and religious revolutions'.[7] Indeed images of emotional and physical violence and disease fill this text designed to expose the distorted body behind an intellectual madness that has fathered 'all those mighty Revolutions, that have happened in Empire, in Philosophy, and in Religion' (171).[8] From the pushing and shoving of bodies for air in the first lines (a fight for space that recalls Satan's sensitivity to 'narrow room'; see Chapter 4), through the rending of pages, coats, and gaps in the text, to the flaying of a woman and stripping of a Beau, from the imagination 'at Cuffs with the Senses' to common sense 'Kickt out of Doors', *A Tale*'s embattled narrator conveys the violent world of the 'Stage-itinerant' productions and 'engines' of 'the Societies of Gresham and of Will's' (64). Among the aggressive 'Writings of our Society', the narrator reserves for parody and special mention several works by Dryden, including the laureate's long prefaces, his beast fable *The Hind and the Panther*, and the production and distribution of his complete *Virgil*, which appeared to emphasize the project as a complex whole of many parts.

Dryden's career had spanned the second half of the century; and he not only survived but rose to the top, 'to a certain Degree of Altitude' above the crowd, which the narrator of *A Tale* deems necessary for 'those Orators who desire to talk much without Interruption' (56). Dryden indeed had to 'press, and squeeze, and thrust, and climb'. But he rose, too, on the ladder 'of Faction and of Poetry' (62) by enfolding the

[7] Frank Boyle, *Swift as Nemesis: Modernity and its Satirist* (Stanford, Calif.: Stanford University Press, 2000), 145; see also 101.

[8] Jonathan Swift, *'A Tale of a Tub' To Which is Added 'The Battle of the Books' and the 'Mechanical Operation of the Spirit'*, ed. A. C. Guthkelch and D. Nichol Smith, 2nd edn. (Oxford: Clarendon Press, 1958). All citations of Swift's *Tale* and the *Battle of the Books* are from this edition and are indicated parenthetically by page numbers in the text.

disparate occasions available to his pen into the creation of a voice in verse and prose, whose multiplicity of offensive and defensive fronts may have cost him the unwritten epic he mourned. Instead he created a flexible instrument of work, a voice from and about the work of writing—an invention distinct yet inseparable from his individual labours.

While known for 'sluggishness in conversation' and a lack of style in dress, self-described and mocked by critics as saturnine—'Nor wine nor love could ever see me gay; | To writing bred, I knew not what to say'—Dryden on paper proved for his enemies a maddeningly arrogant and elusive wit.[9] The poet's talent for writing himself or the King out of a tight spot, writing best when against all odds, produced work based on covering one's tracks and showing a tantalizing, seductive textual surface that confidently invites yet resists a blow. The voice of the Hack and his madness reflect the paradox of Dryden's written voice and the maddening impact on Swift of a sound so immensely cultured, confident, and controlled, whose culture offers glimpses of, yet adroitly steps aside from acknowledging, the rawest passions engaged. It is Dryden's unacknowledged rawness, as a model of the barely concealed beastliness of the modern professional pen, that Swift attempts furiously to upend and expose in his *Tale* whose surface is deliberately shocking, spattered and torn by interaction with the human body.[10]

Swift was not the only reader of that voice who yearned to deflate it. Dryden once claimed that 'More libels have been written against me, than almost any man now living';[11] indeed literary caricatures of Dryden were numerous and notorious throughout his career as Macdonald's bibliography and volumes of contemporary satires such as *Folio Verse Relating to Dryden 1681–1699* or *Poems on Affairs of State* confirm.[12] Published after the poet's death, Swift's attack perpetuates a tradition of criticism and satire of the laureate established early in the Restoration and that included a brutal physical beating in 1679. The personal satires

[9] Samuel Johnson, *Lives of the English Poets*, ed. George Birbeck Norman Hill and Harold Spencer Scott, 3 vols. (Oxford: Clarendon Press, 1905), i. 397.

[10] On Swift's relationship to the body, see Carol Houlihan Flynn, *The Body in Swift and Defoe* (Cambridge: Cambridge University Press, 1990), and Richard Braverman, 'Satiric Embodiments: Butler, Swift, Sterne', in James E. Gill (ed.), *Cutting Edges: Postmodern Critical Essays on Eighteenth-Century Satire* (Knoxville: University of Tennessee Press, 1995).

[11] *The Discourse of Satire*, the California Dryden, iv, 59.

[12] *Folio Verse Relating to Dryden 1681–1699*, Drydeniana XIII (New York: Garland, 1975); George de F. Lord (gen. ed.) *Poems on Affairs of State; Augustan Satirical Verse, 1660–1714*, 7 vols. (New Haven: Yale University Press, 1963–75); Hugh Macdonald, *John Dryden: A Bibliography of Early Editions and of Drydeniana* (Oxford: Clarenden Press, 1939).

viciously attacked the poet's body, too—specifically his stature and his physical and speaking mannerisms—in order to puncture and deflate through mimicry what were perceived as Dryden's inflated claims and high tone of authority. The mad Hack of *A Tale* contains Swift's frenzy to uncover and punish, as vulnerable and impotent, a body that Swift places and exposes for abuse at the centre of Dryden's labyrinth, his mysterious voice:

as far as brevity will permit, I have recollected, that the shrewdest Pieces of this Treatise, were conceived in Bed, in a Garret: At other times (for a Reason best known to my self) I thought fit to sharpen my Invention with Hunger; and in general, the whole Work was begun, continued, and ended, under a long Course of Physick, and a great want of Money. (44)

The voice in Swift's parody coyly expands under the pretence of having no space ('as far as brevity will permit') and, while full of self-advertising, reveals only depleted bodily resources. The sharpness of invention proves to be hunger pangs.

The image of a weak and clumsy or an exhausted body and brain characterizes earlier attacks on Dryden designed to explode the confidence and control of his written voice. Rival dramatist Thomas Shadwell first attacked the new laureate in the preface to Shadwell's play *The Sullen Lovers* (1668); and in *The Humorists* (1671) he created the first theatrical parody of Dryden as Drybob, 'A Fantastick Coxcomb' frantically proud of his poor wit. In contemporary slang a drybob referred to an act of intellectual and physical impotence. In December 1671 George Villiers, second Duke of Buckingham, attacked Dryden as Mr Bayes in *The Rehearsal*, in which a naively bombastic and physically clumsy Bayes eagerly shows two friends, Mr Johnson and Mr Smith, a rehearsal of an inane heroic drama he has composed, madly praising himself and his incomprehensible work in an attempt to elicit their approval. According to an early editor of Dryden, Buckingham took pains to instruct the actor who played Dryden to mimic exactly the laureate's gestures, dress, and speech when reciting passages from the plays: 'Dryden was notoriously a bad reader, and had a hesitating and tedious delivery, which, skilfully imitated in lines of surpassing fury and extravagance, must have produced an irresistible effect upon the audience'.[13] Buckingham attempted

[13] Brian Fairfax, *Memoirs of the Life of George Villiers, Second Duke of Buckingham*, introd. to George Villiers, Duke of Buckingham, *The Rehearsal*, ed. Edward Arber (London: Constable and Co., 1927), 17. Fairfax quotes from a life of Dryden by Robert Bell.

to ridicule the poet's professional skills and intelligence by making a farce of his speaking voice and physical mannerisms.

In his prefatory poem to the second edition of *Paradise Lost* (1674), Marvell refers to Dryden, 'the Town-Bayes', as a plodding workhorse of a dramatist who 'like a Pack-Horse tires without his Bells' of rhyme that keep him shuffling (ll. 47–8). The comparison of rhyme and fashionable laces (both pleasing to vulgar taste) in Milton's reported permission to Dryden to 'tag my points' and stage *Paradise Lost* as an opera in heroic couplets reappears in Marvell's contrast of Milton to his rhyming successors like Dryden: 'Their Fancies like our bushy Points appear, | The Poets tag them; we for Fashion wear' (ll. 49–50), Marvell ambiguously condemning his own fancies dressed in couplets.[14] In 1675–6, in 'An Allusion to Horace', the Earl of Rochester attacked Dryden's prolific rhyming to please the playhouse 'Rabble'—'the heavy Masse, | That stuffs up his loose Volumes must not passe' (ll. 8–9)—and he mocked the laureate's failed attempts in his plays to match with 'a dry Bawdy bob' the court wits' sexual potency and aristocratic obscenity. Rochester, Shadwell's patron, heightened the physical caricature of Drybob into 'Poet Squab', connecting Drybob's impotency of brain and body to a short, round stature and blunt manner. Shadwell's 'The Medal of John Bayes' appeared in 1682 as the Whig response to Dryden's 'The Medall'; and as we observed in Chapter 5, *The Hind and the Panther* elicited a flood of personal abuse and accusations of a wit gone mad, most famously Montagu and Prior's 'transversion' that revived Mr Bayes and his friends Johnson and Smith.

Enemies had mocked Dryden's ambition to be at once novel yet a voice of the ancients and his rapid, enormous productivity and pride in that fertility yet wide literary borrowing. They derided his pride in personal mastery of the couplet, and they ridiculed with zest his perpetual indigence and apparent willingness as a result to write for any political cause in any genre or to please any low taste of the playhouse, particularly with his creation of the heroic drama characterized by bombast of heroes, feelings, settings, forms—*The Conquest of Granada* in ten acts and two parts. Dryden's daring, whether in heroic drama, in a satire like 'Absalom and Achitophel', or in his beast fable, prompted enemies to caricature him as a bard gone snarling mad. The 1681 pamphlet 'Second a Bull-Dog. Or a

[14] Sartorial images were commonplace not only in controversy about stylistic ornament but also in the polemical literature on religion in the 1680s, as Higgins notes, *Swift's Politics*, 117. The 'bushy points' used to satirize Dryden in 1674 reappear in Swift's allegorical tale to describe the deviance and excess of spiritual error.

short Reply to Absalom and Achitophel' wastes no time in turning Dryden into a mad dog, his 'Brains infected sure':

> In pious times when Poets were well bang'd
> For sawcy Satyr and for Sham-Plots hang'd
> A Learned Bard, that long commanded had
> The trembling Stage in Chief, at last run mad,
> And Swore and tore and ranted at no rate.[15]

But Swift turns the 'Modern' wit more disturbingly mad. He observes a relation between Dryden's digressions and the laureate's theory of literary fathers and genealogies, articulated in *A Discourse of Satire*, the dedicatory epistle to his *Aeneis*, and the preface to *Fables*, whereby the ancients reappear within the souls of modern heirs. But in the authority of Dryden's modern digressions and expansive vision, Swift finds not a new Virgil but the opposite: a wandering, false son, a Hack whether in the form of 'True Critick' or modern wit, disconnected from any one father but ready to claim many, a turncoat 'Jack of all faiths'[16] and all fathers, not to mention all 'God-fathers':

> And indeed, it seems not unreasonable, that Books, the Children of the Brain, should have the Honor to be Christned with variety of Names, as well as other Infants of Quality. Our famous Dryden has ventured to proceed a Point farther, endeavouring to introduce also a Multiplicity of God-fathers; which is an Improvement of much more Advantage, upon a very obvious Account. 'Tis a Pity this admirable Invention has not been better cultivated, so as to grow by this time into general Imitation, when such an Authority serves it for a Precedent. Nor have my Endeavours been wanting to second so useful an Example: But it seems, there is an unhappy Expence usually annexed to the Calling of a God-Father, . . . (72)

In Swift's view Dryden's characterization of the relationship between ancient and modern writers as that between fathers and sons, while not new, was powerfully pitched to legitimate the poet and his chosen sons and dispossess others of the right of inheritance. Dryden's claims to fathers allowed him to step around the divide between ancients and moderns; but his supreme confidence in literary inheritance (and prominent

[15] Henry Care, 'Towser the Second, a Bull-Dog. Or a Short Reply to "Absalom and Achitophel"' (London, 1681), first item in *Folio Verse Relating to Dryden, 1681–1699*, no page numbers.

[16] See Galbraith M. Crump (ed.), *Poems on Affairs of State: Augustan Satirical Verse, 1660–1714*, iv: 1685–1688 (New Haven: Yale University Press, 1968), 'To Mr. Dryden', 78, l. 79.

display of godfathers with the *Virgil*) stands in contrast to the complete absence of fathers at the heart of Swift's text.[17]

At the conclusion of the passage quoted above, which ends with the Hack's proving unable to procure a single godfather for his child, the allegorical parable of *A Tale of a Tub* opens s. ii with an odd blur of emotion. The parable tells the story of the death of a father who leaves behind three orphaned sons. Into the turgid world of *A Tale* already harsh and malicious by the second section—where textual children are extinguished by Time's sharp teeth, nails, and scythe and threatened by 'terrible Wits'—Swift raises the spectre of a child's pain at abandonment by a parent but only to disperse it through the satiric reversal of a story of sons who leave their father through disregard of his will. *A Tale* colours the rootless disjunction of the modern book, whose writers claim to have left behind the authority of the ancients, with both an orphan's bewildered abandonment and the children's proud severance of their own roots.

Swift does not forget that Dryden used themes of physical generation and inheritance, birth and rebirth in *Absalom and Achitophel* and 'MacFlecknoe' to mock his enemies with grotesque representations of fatherhood and resemblance. In Dryden's poems offspring become a litmus test exposing the essential moral or poetic legitimacy or illegitimacy of the parent. David-Charles II's godly, abundant fertility and handsome offspring contrast with Achitophel-Shaftesbury's restless 'pigmy body', hinted madness, and a son 'Got while his soul did huddled notions try' and 'born a shapeless lump, like anarchy'. Political deviance that threatens the body politic reproduces itself as physical anarchy, 'a shapeless lump'. Flecknoe says that Shadwell 'alone my perfect image bears, | Mature in dullness from his tender years', and the words 'fog' or 'fogs' and 'dullness' recur with numbing effect to describe Shadwell as an oblivion, a nothing, an emptiness made physical as a 'mountain belly' and 'large bulk' that is but 'a tympany', a swelling or tumour (*OED* 1) 'of sense'.[18]

A Tale attempts to turn that grotesque relation of disease, physical bulk, and empty sense back on Dryden and the moderns, reflected in the

[17] On Dryden's representation of lines of literary inheritance, see particularly David Bruce Kramer, *The Imperial Dryden: The Poetics of Appropriation in Seventeenth-Century England* (Athens: University of Georgia Press, 1994), and Jennifer Brady, 'Dryden and Negotiations of Literary Succession and Precession', in Earl Miner and Jennifer Brady (eds.), *Literary Transmission and Authority: Dryden and Other Writers*, (Cambridge: Cambridge University Press, 1993), 27–54.

[18] John Dryden, *The Poems of John Dryden*, i: *1649–1681*, ed. Paul Hammond (London: Longman, 1995), 334.

mirror of their digressions. More importantly *A Tale* notably lacks fathers yet focuses on the physical 'protuberances' that produce a biological relation of fathers and children and in the swelling digressions that seem to mimic a promise of biological life but produce only the misshapen, ephemeral children of 'our Illustrious Moderns'. The Hack's gradual loss of direction but frantic desire to keep speaking suggests a disinherited voice in search of a body of origin—a genealogy more substantial than the 'True Critick' possesses who descends 'in a direct Line from a Celestial Stem, by Momus and Hybris, who begat Zoilus, who begat Tigellius, who begat Etcætera the Elder, who begat B—tl—y, and Rym—r and W—tton, and Perrault, and Dennis, who began Etcætera the Younger' (94). Suddenly, narrative's most ancient storyline is disjointed and wandering—become repeated generations of etcetera.

Angered by what Swift portrays as a turncoat, self-dramatizing author who attempts to cover a vengeful temperament, emptiness of conviction, and a complete rupture from tradition—despite public deference to the classics—with digressions in which he claims to be persecuted for piety but blessed with a wealth of literary fathers, *A Tale of a Tub* explodes the digression from a rhetorical move into a psychological device. Swift's own 'rancour' enables him to detect the anger, the aggressive, competitive pressures, the emotional, even irrational, underworld of Dryden's digressions, and to link the modern author to an array of other breathless underworld modern visionaries whom he characterizes as disordered at their core. Demonized, like a wandering soul in hell, with a crippled emotional body exposed, Swift's digression becomes a figure of thought that winds around and hides an interior void of sense and history: the movement conceals yet reveals a profoundly bewildered state of disconnection from the deepest sources of self.

'MY NEAR RELATION'

Dryden's extensive reading and translation of classical writers had only deepened in the 1680s and 1690s: his introduction to a new version of Plutarch's *Lives* (1683) carried 'an apostrophe to the ancients that is as enthusiastic and unqualified as anything in Sir William Temple',[19] and by the time of the prefaces to *Aeneis* and *Fables*, the ancient authors have become invincible. What is more important, they are also Dryden's

[19] Levine, *The Battle of the Books*, 273–4.

poetic relations. While the disenfranchised laureate addressed his readers in the 1690s from the isolation and ignominy of domestic exile, he managed to end his career in a comfortable 'house' of fables—not in fragments as his miscellany of translations might suggest but within personally fitted and spacious dimensions. Into this house, he gathers relations ancient and modern:

> Milton was the Poetical Son of Spencer, and Mr. Waller of Fairfax; for we have our Lineal Descents and Clans, as well as other Families: Spencer more than once insinuates, that the Soul of Chaucer was transfus'd into his Body; and that he was begotten by him Two hundred years after his Decease. Milton has acknowledg'd to me that Spencer was his Original; and many besides my self have heard our famous Waller own, that he deriv'd the Harmony of his Numbers from the *Godfrey of Bulloign* which was turn'd into English by Mr. Fairfax. But to return: Having done with Ovid for this time, it came into my mind, that our old English Poet Chaucer in many Things resembled him. . . .[20]

A superbly confident, exclusive tone characterizes this written voice, a tone about the triumph from political persecution of exclusive, inviolable literary authority and temperament derived from a direct, familial connection with early writers of genius like Chaucer: 'I found I had a Soul congenial to his, and that I had been conversant in the same Studies'.[21] Swift challenges Dryden's tone with the voice of a mad orphaned relation who belongs to a fatherless 'Fraternity' (63).

Dryden's bravado about multiple literary fathers becomes in Swift's parody an anxiety of the modern author about legitimacy as a poet-son, rather than a 'pack-horse', in the face of increasing pressures from the press and the print market for novelty and quantity of production. The figure of Bayes in *The Rehearsal* and 'The Hind and the Panther Transversed' portrays Dryden as a playwright who struggles to be heard and to be unique, who claims absolute originality yet is tied to his commonplace book and his audience's low tastes. His necessity to write for money, even as a civil servant, prompted the scorn of aristocrats like Rochester who in 'The Allusion to Horace' deigned to advise Dryden to write more slowly and painstakingly: 'Scorne all Applause the Vile Rout can bestow, | And be content to please those few, who know' (102–3). Rochester, like Milton, could afford to 'loathe the Rabble' and name his chosen few, but Dryden hardly could as he often lamented. When the Glorious Revolution deprived him of a court post the necessity of sup-

[20] John Dryden, *The Works of John Dryden*, vol. vii, ed. Vinton A. Dearing (Berkeley and Los Angeles: University of California Press, 2000), 25.

[21] Ibid. 40.

porting himself by his art initially demanded a return to writing plays as well as an indefatigable production of work to be marketed by Tonson.

The aristocrat John Boyle, in a passage quoted earlier, describes Dryden as 'the greatest, although the least prosperous, of our English poets', and as something like a spinning compass 'bewildered' by politics, impoverishment, and the need to write for all comers. 'I am willing to imagine', he notes indulgently, 'that Dryden, in some manner or other, had offended my friend Dr. Swift, who, otherwise, I hope, would have been more indulgent to the errors of a man oppressed by poverty, driven on by party, and bewildered by religion'. Dryden's 'translation of Virgil', Boyle continues, 'was a work of haste and indigence: Dryden was equal to the undertaking, but unfortunate during the conduct of it'.[22] Although the poet felt exploited by Tonson, Dryden was quick to market his work and to develop genres such as the poetic miscellany that proved popular among buyers but that Swift caricatured in *A Tale* as a taste for 'Ollio's, Fricassées and Ragousts'. Anthony Ashley Cooper, third Earl of Shaftesbury and grandson of Dryden's Achitophel, was 'also very fond of petulantly carping at Dryden', in the words of Joseph Warton, and ridiculed in 1711 'the ingenious way of miscellaneous writing'. Cooper, like Swift, equates the licentious, ignorant mixture of elements in writing with hapless bastard children that must fend for themselves by being novel. He lampoons modern writers who no longer feel obliged to obey 'strict laws and rules of composition . . . 'Twas a yoke, it seems, which our forefathers bore, but which, for our parts, we have generously thrown off. In effect, the invidious distinctions of bastardy and legitimacy being at length removed, the natural and lawful issue of the brain comes with like advantage into the world'.[23]

A Tale is launched with the commonplace that books are 'Children of the Brain'; but the instability of books and brains, of child and parent, in Swift's 'orphaned text' is hardly commonplace.[24] Anger and aggression galvanize this restless brainchild that Swift never acknowledged publicly.[25]

[22] Boyle, *Remarks*, Letter XXIII, 300–1. Boyle seems to reproduce exactly Swift's assessment, in his letter to Thomas Beach quoted earlier, of indigent Dryden forced to write hastily and sloppily.

[23] Anthony Ashley Cooper, third Earl of Shaftesbury, *Characteristics of Men, Manners, Opinions, Times, Etc.*, ed. John M. Robertson, 2 vols. (Gloucester, Mass.: Peter Smith, 1963), ii. 157.

[24] See Phiddian, *Swift's Parody*, ch. 7 (140–71), '*A Tale of a Tub* as an orphaned text.'

[25] David Nokes, *Raillery and Rage: A Study of Eighteenth Century Satire* (Brighton: Harvester, 1987); Alan D. Chalmers, *Jonathan Swift and the Burden of the Future* (Newark: University of Delaware Press, 1995).

Swift appears to project himself into the physical book, into the 'hapless' abandoned child of a wandering brain, and the Hack reels in perpetual motion estranged between religious allegory and digressions in a quixotic yet claustrophobic whirl. Among the characters and prospects of his journey, the monster of them all is the disjunctive modern book composed in parts, in fits and starts—all manic talk, voluminous length, and sudden gaps or 'chasms'—which, for Swift, no literary figure had come to represent so much as Dryden.

Swift's anger at Dryden was clear to other eighteenth-century readers besides Boyle; and the fact of their distant family relation was well known. In a letter of 12 April 1735 to Thomas Beach, Swift calls Dryden 'my near relation'—draws him exaggeratedly close only to push him away with condescension as indigent and pathetic, a slogging breadwinner that 'I have often blamed as well as pitied. He was poor, and in great haste to finish his plays, because by them he chiefly supported his family, and this made him so very incorrect'.[26] In Swift's 'Fragment of Autobiography', in reference to his paternal uncle Mr Dryden Swift, he notes in parentheses, '(called so after the name of his mother, who was a near relation to Mr. Dryden the poet)'. The relation in fact was not that close: Swift's grandmother, born Elizabeth Dryden, was a niece of Dryden's grandfather Sir Erasmus Dryden (d. 1632), who was a son of John Dryden of Canons Ashby, Northamptonshire (d. 1584), Dryden's great-grandfather and Swift's great-great-grandfather. The writers were second cousins once removed.[27] Crucial for Swift's 'malevolence' toward Dryden, however, may be the fact that the paternal grandfather whom Swift venerated, Thomas Swift, Elizabeth's husband, was an Anglican and Royalist vicar who had been persecuted harshly by the Puritans. The laureate, on the other hand, had descended from a line that produced quite vocal Puritans. In the 'Autobiography', Swift's father remains a shadowy, unfortunate figure who made an 'indiscreet' marriage, from which his son suffered lifelong, and who died young. But the 'Autobiography' feelingly commemorates at length the selfless heroism of the grandfather who had lost everything in the civil wars and died before the Restoration when he would have been rewarded for his sufferings and restored to his land and livings:

[26] *The Correspondence of Jonathan Swift*, ed. F. Elrington Ball, 6 vols. (London: G. Bell and Sons, 1910–14), vol. v. 162, 452–3. Cited in Irvin Ehrenpreis, *Swift, the Man, his Works, and the Age* (Cambridge, Mass.: Harvard University Press, 1962), i. 5.

[27] See P. D. Mundy, 'Dryden and Swift: Their Relationship', *Notes and Queries*, 147 (July–Dec. 1924) 243–4, 279–80, 334.

> This Thomas was more [later: much] distinguished by his courage, as well as his loyalty to K. Charles the 1st, and the Sufferings he underwent for that Prince, more than any person of his condition in England. . . . He was plundred by the roundheads six and thirty [in margin: some say above 50] times.[28]

His church livings were taken from him 'sooner than most other Loyall Clergymen upon account of his superior zeal for the King's cause, and his estate sequestred'; and according to one account, for a time in 1646 the profits of his preferment of Goodrich were turned over to his brother-in-law, the minister Jonathan Dryden, whose grandfather, Sir Erasmus, had secretly harboured and supported Puritan preachers.[29] The twinned movements of *A Tale of a Tub* conflate Dryden and his modern literary zeal of digression with the self-serving digression into zeal of sectarianism. Dryden's claims of having suffered for his Roman Catholic faith after what looked to his contemporaries like a mercenary rather than spiritual conversion, and his complaints about poverty and a lifetime of persecution, must have sounded particularly offensive to Swift when compared with the deprivations experienced by that man of unswerving conviction, Thomas Swift, at the hands of revolutionaries in whose government Dryden worked briefly and whose leader he had eulogized.

'The Epistle Dedicatory, to His Royal Highness Prince Posterity' is dated December 1697, and 'The Apology' claims that most of *A Tale* was written in 1696. At least one echo in *A Tale* and one in the *Battle of the Books*, however, suggest that Swift's 1704 volume included material in response to Dryden's *Fables Ancient and Modern* (1700), in whose preface Dryden presses most confidently his claims for literary genealogies and inheritance. The proud casual intimacy in the sound of Dryden's boast, 'Milton has acknowledged to me that Spenser was his original', seems recalled by Swift to attack Dryden's preface of heroic self-presentation: 'Our Great Dryden has long carried it as far as it would go, and with incredible Success. He has often said to me in Confidence, that the World would have never suspected him to be so great a Poet, if he had not assured them so frequently in his Prefaces' (131). In *The Battle of the Books*, Swift arranges a mock encounter between the hero of 'the Grubaean Sages' and his father Virgil whereby

[28] Jonathan Swift, *Miscellaneous and Autobiographical Pieces, Fragments, and Marginalia*, ed. Herbert Davis (Oxford: B. Blackwell, 1969), 189.

[29] Ibid. 190. On Erasmus Dryden's Puritan sympathies, see James Winn, *John Dryden and His World* (New Haven: Yale University Press, 1987), 4–5.

Dryden in a long Harangue soothed up the good Antient, called him Father, and by a large deduction of Genealogies, made it plainly appear, that they were nearly related. . . . Then, they agreed to exchange Horses; but when it came to the Trial, Dryden was afraid, and utterly unable to mount. (247)

The climactic failure of this mock-heroic encounter intends to puncture Dryden's claims in 1697 to be a Virgilian mouthpiece; but conceivably the passage recalls another, more disingenuous claim in 1700, within a complex, conflicted moment of self-deprecation and self-congratulation in the preface to *Fables*. Late in the long, continuous burst of the second paragraph, at a point when he begins to plead for the reader's indulgence of any literary imperfection on account of his body's ills, Dryden divides himself strikingly in two: into an aged body and a vital and observing mind ('when I was present'). He uses the image of an old man slowly mounting a horse in the presence of ladies to complain about his age and disabilities which, no sooner acknowledged, are reversed into a celebration of his perfect fluency in verse and prose and his extreme mental vigour:

I have added some Original Papers of my own; which whether they are equal or inferior to my other Poems, an Author is the most improper Judge; and therefore I leave them wholly to the Mercy of the Reader: I will hope the best, that they will not be condemn'd; but if they should, I have the excuse of an old Gentleman, who mounting on Horseback before some Ladies, when I was present, got up somewhat heavily, but desir'd of the Fair Spectators, that they would count Fourescore and eight before they judg'd him. By the Mercy of God, I am already come within Twenty Years of his Number, a Cripple in my Limbs, but what Decays are in my Mind, the Reader must determine. I think my self as vigorous as ever in the Faculties of my Soul. . . . What Judgement I had, increases rather than diminishes; and Thoughts, such as they are, come crowding in so fast upon me, that my only Difficulty is to chuse or to reject; to run them into Verse or to give them the other Harmony of Prose. I have so long studied and practis'd both, that they are grown into a Habit, and become familiar to me. In short, though I may lawfully plead some part of the old Gentleman's Excuse, yet I will reserve it till I think I have greater need, and ask no Grains of Allowance for the Faults of this my present Work.[30]

Dryden begins the passage as if to plead indulgence for his new work but in the process withdraws his plea because in fact there is no need. His language is about action: 'vigorous as ever', 'increases rather than diminishes', 'crowding in so fast', 'run them into Verse', 'long studied

[30] Dryden, *Works*, vii. 26–7.

and practis'd'. And within the next paragraphs Dryden distances himself from Virgil whom he characterizes as 'confined', 'phlegmatic and melancholic'; in the last months of his life, he finds a new heroic father in Homer. Homer is 'masculine' and fiery, 'more full of vigour' and 'copious', 'more suitable to my temper' than Virgil, he claims. The more ancient Greek represents infinite inventive energy and potency. Swift's allegory in *A Tale*, however, suggests that one does not change fathers like coats. Dryden's most profound, lifelong literary debt and relationship lay with Virgil; and in Swift's scene Dryden's small physical body and literary stature, compared with Virgil's power, are conflated and ridiculed once again as they had been in earlier satires featuring Drybob, Poet Squab, and Bayes.[31]

But in fact Dryden had been able 'to mount' and to transcend the fears of belatedness and depletion that haunt *A Tale of a Tub*. With his fable of genealogy he stepped around the conflict that had absorbed Sir William Temple and his protégé. Meanwhile Swift, who was born in the outpost of Ireland and had never known his father, whose mother early relinquished him into the care of others and moved to England, once claimed that his family were 'of all mortals what I despise and hate'.[32]

Dryden turned his mastery into the right to belong to a literary family and to name his ancestors and poetic heirs. And for his heir he chose in 1693 William Congreve—not his distant cousin Swift but Swift's former schoolmate in Ireland and junior by two years:[33]

> Oh that your Brows my Lawrel had sustain'd,
> Well had I been depos'd, if you had reign'd!
> The Father had descended for the Son;
> For only You are lineal to the Throne.
> ('To my Dear Friend Mr Congreve', ll. 41–4)

Congreve had collaborated with Dryden in the volume of *Juvenal and Persius* completed in 1692, contributed to the miscellany of *Examen Poeticum*, 1693, and been praised by Dryden for his translation of Homer.

[31] Dryden's relationship to Virgil has been the focus of a number of recent studies, most notably Paul Hammond's *Dryden and the Traces of Classical Rome* (Oxford: Oxford University Press, 1999), especially ch. 4; Steven N. Zwicker's 'Mastering Virgil', a paper delivered at the Dryden Tercentenary Conference sponsored by the Beinecke Library in cooperation with the Yale Center for British Art, New Haven, 5–7 Oct. 2000, as well as his *Politics and Language in Dryden's Poetry: The Arts of Disguise* (Princeton: Princeton University Press, 1984).

[32] Ehrenpreis, *Swift, the Man*, i, 3. In fact he visited and sent money to his mother until she died, and he was under the care of relations at his own death.

[33] On Congreve and Swift, see ibid. 132–3.

He had achieved instant fame in England with *The Old Batchelour*, his first play, which opened in January 1693, and for his second performed later that year Dryden wrote a commendatory poem published with the play in 1694, which briefly traces a progressive history of English theater that culminates in Congreve, a second Shakespeare whose 'genius must be born and never can be taught' (l. 60). Swift, too, had written a commendatory poem, 'To Mr Congreve', of over 200 lines, much longer than Dryden's, and had hoped to publish it with his former schoolmate's new comedy; but whether he ever sent it is unknown.[34]

About the same time, as the story goes, Swift had shown Dryden some of his early odes and been rebuffed.[35] The account, for which no hard evidence exists, that Swift's resentment stemmed largely from Dryden's discouragement of his relative's poetic ambitions was repeated in the eighteenth century by Theophilus Cibber, Deane Swift, and Joseph Warton.[36] In Cibber's version Dryden

> said to him with an unreserved freedom, and in the candour of a friend, 'Cousin Swift, turn your thoughts some other way, for nature has never formed you for a Pindaric poet'. . . . Swift perhaps was conscious, that he had not abilities to succeed in that species of writing; yet this honest dissuasive of his kinsman he never forgave. The remembrance of it soured his temper, and heated his passions, whenever Dryden's name was mentioned.[37]

Aged 30 by 1697, and 36 in the spring of 1704 when *A Tale* was published, Swift had been living in Ireland but desperately seeking preferment in England. He had abandoned his first Irish parish at Kilroot after one year because of the isolation and Presbyterian fanatics (1695–6). If Dryden traced his superiority to a genealogy of imagination, we cannot be surprised that Swift's troubled narrator ironically claims the opposite: a 'despotic Power' from being 'the freshest modern' and 'the last Writer'. In contrast to his cousin, Swift generates his fiction with a claim to be related to no one.

[34] Jonathan Swift, *Jonathan Swift*, ed. Angus Ross and David Woolley (Oxford: Oxford University Press, 1984), 612.

[35] See, for example, Ricardo Quintana, *The Mind and Art of Jonathan Swift* (London: Oxford University Press, 1953), 30; Sir Walter Scott, *The Life of John Dryden*, ed. Bernard Kreissman (Lincoln: University of Nebraska Press, 1963), 318.

[36] See Theophilus Cibber, *Lives of the Poets of Great Britain and Ireland, to the Time of Dean Swift*, 5 vols. (London: R. Griffiths, 1753), v. 97–8; Deane Swift, *An Essay on Dr. Swift's Life and Character* (London: C Bathurst, 1755), 117; and Joseph Warton, *Essay on the Genius and Writings of Pope*, 3rd edn., 2 vols. (London: J. Dodsley, 1772–82), ii. 312–13 n., names Elijah Fenton, Orrery's tutor, as his source.

[37] See Cibber, *Lives of the Poets*, 97–8.

The Irish cousin's study of the laureate has taught him to ventriloquize digression as the arrogant, imperial confidence of belonging to a narrative more than the 'native' story does. In 'A Digression in Praise of Digressions', not only are Author and Reader 'nations'; the modern book resembles a besieged state like Ireland as well as a hapless child: 'Digressions in a Book, are like Forein Troops in a State, which argue the Nation to want a Heart and Hands of its own, and often, either subdue the Natives, or drive them into the most unfruitful Corners' (144)—perhaps those Irish 'Corners' that Swift feared, like Kilroot. Section vii bristles with other military images of the Moderns who attempt to control the rowdy and physical 'native' body of talk: for example, 'the Army of the Sciences hath been of late with a world of Martial Discipline, drawn into its *close Order*' and 'the Arts are all in a *flying* March, and therefore more easily subdued by attacking them in the *Rear*' (145). Yet Swift uses Ireland, the country from which he wanted early to escape, as Dryden used the exile of Roman Catholicism, to invert anxiety about origins and belatedness. Dryden had evolved a personal mythology of authority—of an original, primitive Church and Word with lines that reached back to Augustan Rome and which extended East to the ancient mystery of fable. Swift arms his text with a different kind of primitive power: the mystery of anonymity and an outsider's physical crudity and irreverence which shocked and captured his English audience. Curiosity indeed 'affords the firmest Grasp' (203), and the raw 'Native' made the 'troops' his prisoners: as Atterbury noted on 1 July 1704, 'Nothing can please more than that book doth here at London'.[38] *A Tale of a Tub* enjoyed three editions in 1704, a fourth in 1705, and a fifth, enlarged edition in 1710.

Swift's rage at Dryden's succession to an exalted lineage of fame seems to find a focus in the *Virgil*, the poet's climactic hymn to the ancients. And the target of that rage is not the translation but the physical product and its fanfare of publication: the mysterious collection of loose parts to be assembled and the host of protective, well-wishing 'God-fathers', the subscribers. The *Virgil* is introduced towards the close of 'To His Royal Highness Prince Posterity' which is dated December 1697:

> I do therefore affirm upon the Word of a sincere Man, that there is now actually in being, a certain Poet called John Dryden, whose Translation of Virgil was lately printed in a large Folio, well bound, and if diligent search were made, for ought I know, is yet to be seen. (36)

[38] Williams, *Swift: The Critical Heritage*, 36.

To undercut the mystique of the publication as a timeless work destined for a long life, Swift's Hack mimics the caution of the new scientific experimenters unwilling to rely on ancient testimony, who insisted instead on the verifiable truth of individual experiences recorded in a specific moment of observation. Dryden's massive achievement had been issued in August, and after several pages within the preface a numinous date, 'this present month of August, 1697', surfaces without explanation. The event is a focal point for this disjunctive text because the translation was sold in an elaborate format of parts designed to announce its importance and complexity—and its politics.[39] Frost and Dearing have described the mystique of parts surrounding the folio first edition:

> The book was sold unbound, and constituted a sort of kit complete with assembly instructions, a set of *Directions to the Binders how to place the Several Parts of this Book.* These directions, bewildering in their seeming illogic, are placed, prophetically, at the bottom of a page otherwise devoted to errata, which were testily drawn up by Dryden himself. Unsurprisingly, not all copies are bound in accordance with the directions, perhaps because some first owner yearned for a better, or any, logic in the ordering of parts, or perhaps because the directions were not encountered until the end of the book's fourth part'.[40]

The number and confusing assembly of the components suggested that this work was being christened and launched into a formidable world, one for which strict sequence was not appropriate and might even be a liability. The *Virgil* was also being launched into a financial market of select readers by 'the Modern way of Subscription' (137)—Swift's disdainful phrase. Such an inscrutable triumph of accident and manipulation, of the high aesthetic and the economic, hovers behind *A Tale of a Tub* as a disturbing imaginative structure to which Swift responds with his vision of parts in search of an order, a tale in search of an author, and a son in search of a father. Rather than a genealogy of heroes, *A Tale* offers anti-heroes. Swift leaves behind the Virgil but yearns for the 'Multiplicity of Godfathers' of 'Our famous Dryden'.[41]

[39] Zwicker, *Politics and Language in Dryden's Poetry*, ch. 6.

[40] *The Works of John Dryden: Poems, the Works of Virgil in English, 1697*, vols. v and vi, ed. William Frost and Vinton A. Dearing (Berkeley and Los Angeles, 1987), v. vii.

[41] 'But it seems, there is an unhappy Expense usually annexed to the Calling of a God-Father. . . . Where the Pinch lay, I cannot certainly affirm; but having employ'd a World of Thoughts and Pains, to split my Treatise into forty Sections, and having entreated forty Lords of my Acquaintance, that they would do me the Honor to stand, they all made it a Matter of Conscience, and sent me their Excuses' (72). The Hack's satiric voice of 'Pinch' and 'split' turns the pain of rejection into a fairy tale.

A VOID OF FATHERS

The voice of the Hack ventriloquizes the digression as a 'modern' state of disconnection from physical, literary, or spiritual fathers that makes orderly linear narrative no longer possible. With his narrator's increasingly desperate voice after Sect. VII, 'A Digression in Praise of Digressions', Swift unhinges the rhetorical figure from a central narrative and tosses voice and digressions out to wander like the orphaned and bewildered brothers of the parable. Section viii, called 'A Tale of a Tub', which should return us to the three brothers, is a digression on the Aeolists. Section ix is the 'Digression Concerning the Original, the Use and Improvement of Madness in a Commonwealth' (whose title echoes Dryden's *Discourse Concerning the Original and Progress of Satire*); ss. x and xi are both entitled 'A Tale of a Tub', but only in xi does the narrator pick up and drop for the last time the thread of Jack. Digressions take over the *Discourse of Satire* in 1693; they swell the 'Dedication of the *Aeneis*' in 1697, though Dryden in the *Discourse* had vowed, 'this is the last time I will commit the Crime of Prefaces' (16); and they swamp the allegory of the three brothers and take charge of *A Tale of a Tub.*

With the digression as a flapping figure whose connection to the parent narrative has snapped, Swift strings together Dryden with other fraudulent and dangerous modern phenomena and madmen: with modern critics of texts secular and sacred such as the 'brother modernists' William Wotton and Richard Bentley, who had praised the new philological scholarship on biblical texts of Father Simon, as had Dryden; with Hobbes's *Leviathan* and the positivist scientific endeavours and physical systems of the Royal Society represented by the work of Boyle and Newton; and not least with the dissenting religious sects.[42] Among the hundreds of tracts against Puritan zeal in a polemic tradition as old as the Reformation, one named *A Tale in a Tub* (1642) burlesques the Puritan sermon that deconstructs and inflates a line of biblical text, and the long subtitle makes the popular seventeenth-century association of religious nonconformity with lunacy on which Swift could draw: *or a Tub Lecture as it was delivered by Mi-Heele Mendsoale, an inspired Brownist and a most upright translator in a meeting house neere Bedlam, the one and twentieth of December last, 1641.* But the earlier pamphlet only emphasizes the

[42] On *A Tale of a Tub* as a response to the new science and to Newton, in particular, see Boyle, *Swift as Nemesis*, ch. 6, 'A Critical Theory of Air', 118–48.

labyrinthine fury of Swift's manic text that enters at its own risk so completely into the phenomenon it mocks.

While major philosophical disagreements separated Hobbes and Boyle, and while Dryden had shared with Swift a hatred of and talent for satirizing the dissident sects and a desire for an academy to codify rules of usage for English, Swift condemns them all without distinction as ungrateful sons and false fathers.[43] Their crime is self-promotion through the promotion of fraudulent offspring, grand systems of thought disguised as legitimate products of human reason: in Dryden's case, his huge beast fable's 'complete abstract' or his complete Virgil in many prefaces and parts or his exhaustive survey of satire's 'progress'. While briefly a member of the Royal Society, Dryden was hardly an experimental scientist, but *A Discourse Concerning the Original and Progress of Satire* promises an optimistic history of the progress of satire 'from its first Rudiments of Barbarity, to its last Polishing and Perfection' (76). The poet envisions a history of literary progress whereby writers build on and extend the achievements of their predecessors, Lucilius adding to Ennius, Horace to Lucilius, and Juvenal to Horace, 'since no Art, or Science, is at once begun and perfected, but that it must pass first through many hands, and even through several Ages' (73). The *Discourse* is replete with phrases like 'course of Time rather improves Nature, than impairs her' (11); ''tis possible some Great Genius may arise, to equal any of the Antients' (12); and of tragedy and satire, 'this Age and the last, particularly in England, have excell'd the Ancients in both those kinds' (12). In his critical contest for the prize of satire, Dryden also shows considerable investment in fame and 'the Prince Posterity'. The poet nudges his old patron, the Earl of Dorset, that 'Fame is in it self a real good' that 'acquires strength by going forward'.[44] Dryden's eagerness in the *Discourse* and elsewhere to claim the 'right of a first Discoverer' (4), to chart and lead the aesthetic progress of writing, makes him a zealot of the progressive brotherhood. And the disinherited, grotesque body and pointed non-progress of *A Tale* is Swift's mock relation and angry rejection of 'my cotemporary Brethren' (38).

The attempt to vaunt the brain too proudly over the body's life—and the modern intellect over ancient wisdom—leads to the physical and

[43] Hobbes had vigorously attacked Boyle's theory of air and the essentially optimistic, cooperative approach to intellectual order and to knowledge of God that Boyle's method implied. See Steven Shapin, *The Scientific Revolution* (Chicago: University of Chicago Press, 1996), 110–11. *The Discourse of Satire*, California Dryden, iv. 86.

[44] *The Discourse of Satire*, California Dryden, iv. 7.

mental disconnection, whether in a garret or an asylum, of lunacy. To disclaim fathers in the proud attempt to be the first father is to disconnect one's brain from the body's sources of reproductive life. Obsessively Swift draws attention with the wandering Hack and his digressions to the literal, the low, disorderly, and humbling physical ground, the body, proudly disregarded and immorally abandoned by the moderns' love of 'high' abstraction and orderly intellectual progress. In the 'Digression on Madness' Swift assails the degenerate 'Carcass of Humane Nature' by way of anatomy, and his target is the presumption of modern critics and the natural philosophers whose ambition is to anatomize nature or texts and uncover the invisible mechanical principles of design. The infamous passage that begins, 'Last Week I saw a Woman flay'd, and you will hardly believe, how much it altered her Person for the worse', reduces the analytical vision of the moderns to intellectual violence equal to the process of physical dissection that deforms the visible body and kills the invisible life. Swift equates the ambition and aggression of self-aggrandizing anatomists, whether in science or literary production, with that of military conquest and physical beating and reduces the desire to dominate to the explosion of sexual frustration. The mad emotional underground of the Hack and other modern wits begins in the lower body and erupts upstairs to the brain.

The uprooted digressions of the moderns point to an absence: there is no body and nobody there, only a diseased brain. The absence expresses the violent rupture perpetrated on the vision and values of Renaissance humanism by Puritan enthusiasm but even more urgently for Swift in 1704 by modern criticism, by natural philosophy, and by literary prefaces, digressions, and miscellanies that break up the integrity—and the body parts—of a book. In *A Tale of a Tub*'s passionate mimicry of scientific anatomy, the attempt to uncover an elusive inner core of disease and deformity bares the anatomist's own feverish desire to cut. When William Wotton complained in 1705 that 'our Tale-teller strikes at the very Root', he registered the intensity of the satiric surgeon's anger, which readers since have described as a loss of gravity in *A Tale*'s peculiar insistence on disconnection.[45]

Among Dryden's late works to which *A Tale* responds most completely is *The Hind and the Panther*. We have seen how Dryden's ability to articulate yet obscure feelings of vengeance, doubt, and loss through and

45 William Wotton, 'A Defense of the Reflections upon Ancient and Modern Learning', reprinted in *'A Tale of a Tub', to Which is Added 'The Battle of the Books' and the 'Mechanical Operation of the Spirit'*, 318.

around various voices—voices of the ancients, of beasts, of biblical personae—produced the complexity and distended form of a text like *The Hind and the Panther* which appeared in 1687 as a kind of dark madness like *A Tale*. Swift mocks Dryden's pretensions to encyclopedic learning compressed into the beasts' debate on ecclesiology, saying the poem was 'intended for a compleat Abstract of sixteen thousand Schoolmen from Scotus to Bellarmin' (69). As if not to be outdone, *A Tale* purports more ambitiously to be 'a faithful Abstract drawn from the Universal Body of all Arts and Sciences' (38). Where one text is a defence of Roman Catholic scriptural authority ('a seamless coat', II. 620) and the other of Anglican, both use allegory; both adopt the language of legal wills and estates for Christ's Testament—a commonplace, like sartorial images, in contemporary theological polemic—and both condemn the sectarians' habit of dissecting and disputing Scripture. Dryden's fable contains images of physical 'jarring' (II. 114) and the tortuous tearing and disintegration of texts, but the images could almost be Swift's. In Dryden's poem, as in Swift's *Tale*, biblical and literary texts are political battlefields, 'the Hungary' (II. 382) on which men stage wars of decimation and conquest. Although Swift drops all reference to Dryden after the fifth section, and though the Dean has other targets for his venom, Swift yokes Dryden, that Jack of all faiths, and his jarring fellow moderns with another excessive Jack—the ill-bred, disconnected, but inspired sectarian. He turns *The Hind and the Panther*'s fables back on Dryden in order to associate literary, political, and spiritual wandering and disjunction—and a fatherless, orphaned condition—with emptiness 'within':

> the Grubaean Sages have always chosen to convey their Precepts and their Arts, shut up within the Vehicles of Types and Fables, which having been perhaps more careful and curious in adorning, than was altogether necessary, it has fared with these Vehicles after the usual Fate of Coaches over-finely painted and gilt; that the transitory Gazers have so dazzled their Eyes, and fill'd their Imaginations with the outward Lustre, as neither to regard or consider, the Person or the Parts of the Owner within. (66)

While a self-proclaimed member of Grub Street, the Hack disparages his fraternity's unfortunate habit of hiding meaning, and themselves, within the vehicle of an elaborate textual surface whose tenor or subject seems permanently obscured. And the modern book in Swift's vision has become obscure and disjunctive less because it contains dangerous political observations, as Dryden had justified the obscurity in Persius' 'crabb'd' satires and, by implication his own, than because it disguises the lack of any subject at all. There is only the exhaustion of endlessly covering the gap and reinventing one's book as oneself or oneself as one's book—hence, according to Swift, Dryden's prefatory cries of weariness and drudgery.

In *A Tale*'s fixation on the role of air, vapours, and vacuity (and evacuation) in the human body and history, physicist and chemist Robert Boyle's recent, controversial study of the vacuum hovers as an emblem of the abhorrent emptiness behind the whole modern project.[46] Swift mocks the claims to reason that disguise a terrible void of knowledge and body signalled by the irrational pride and competitive drive at the heart of these grand schemes. The unknown at the heart of Boyle's experiments or Newton's *Principia* or Dryden's *The Hind and the Panther*—the exact cause of gravitation or the exact nature of 'inward substances' or the exact truth of Dryden's religious or political convictions—is the crucial chasm of absent knowledge or self-knowledge on which these proud towers of air stand. That void is covered by a rhetorical dodge or digressive stepping aside, by a fable within a fable, or by the assurance of Boyle and Newton that when we lack knowledge it is because we lack experiments.[47] When Swift ventriloquizes Dryden reinventing the story of his life in a continuous preface, verbs and adjectives stumble out in a negative progress toward that void: 'circumscribed', 'poor', 'unfortunate', 'worn', 'threadbare and ragged', 'broken', 'spent', 'ill cured', 'retire', and 'void of Offence'.

I have now altogether circumscribed my Thoughts and my Studies; and if I can bring it to a Perfection before I die, shall reckon I have well employ'd the poor Remains of an unfortunate Life. This indeed is more than I can justly expect from a Quill worn to the Pith in the Service of the State, in Pro's and Con's upon Popish Plots, and Meal-Tubs, and Exclusion Bills ... From an Understanding and a Conscience, thread-bare and ragged with perpetual turning; From a Head broken in a hundred places, by the Malignants of the opposite Factions, and from a Body spent with Poxes ill cured.... Four-score and eleven Pamphlets have I written under three Reigns, and for the Service of six and thirty Factions. But finding the State has no farther Occasion for Me and my Ink, I retire willingly to draw it out into Speculations more becoming a Philosopher, having, to my unspeakable Comfort, passed a long Life, with a Conscience void of Offence. (69–71)

[46] On the history of the air-pump controversey, see Steven Shapin and Simon Schaffer, *Leviathan and the Air-Pump: Hobbes, Boyle, and the Experimental Life* (Princeton: Princeton University Press, 1985).

[47] Shapin, *The Scientific Revolution*, ch. 2, 65–117.

Swift's syntax juxtaposes 'Conscience' and 'void' and encourages the reader first to read 'Conscience' as 'void'. The correction offered by the rest of the phrase simply emphasizes that what is intended to sound positive is an absence.

Swift has detected the emotion behind the exaggerated flattery and self-abnegation that propel the enormous digressions of a preface like the *Discourse* and has isolated and enlarged the unacknowledged feelings into madness. With his keen ear Swift has reproduced much of the sound of Dryden's written posture but transformed into one that hides an empty, not a mysterious, persona and text. Ears are protuberances that figure prominently in *A Tale* because they are the delicate, labyrinthine seats of receptivity—and of mimicry. The anonymous, disinherited condition of being an ear with no voice becomes translated into the disembodied voice of the Hack obsessed with textual bodies such as Dryden's which he attempts to hack to pieces. Ehrenpreis has noted Swift's formidable 'ear for talk', but here that ear has become a mouth, a cloven tongue, that cannot stop.[48]

In response to Dryden's lifelong invocation of fathers, Swift responds with a dark undercurrent in the parable and the narrator's voice of being bereft of a patriarch. But after his conversion, Dryden invokes also a mother, the mother Church; the first of his two Virgilian epigraphs to *The Hind and the Panther* is 'Antiquam exquirite matrem' (*Aeneid* 3. 96), 'Seek your ancient mother'. And in the absence of fathers, a frightening mother looms in Swift's volume, although not in *A Tale* but in *The Battle of the Books*: the 'malignant Deity, call'd Criticism'. A hideous mix of Milton's breeding Sin and Spenser's Errour, Criticism's Trinity includes her father and husband, Ignorance, at her right hand and her mother, Pride, on her left.[49] With an ass's head and no teeth to bite but a cat's claws, instead of the milk of human kindness she produces gall from an oversized spleen, traditionally the seat of melancholy and capricious feelings. Criticism's spleen was 'prominent like a Dug of the first Rate, nor wanted Excrescencies in form of Teats, at which a Crew of ugly Monsters were greedily sucking' an endless supply of ill temper (240). The 'poisonous dugs' of Errour likewise fed monsters of virulence; her vomit of

[48] In s. xi, the narrator dilates on ears as 'Protrusions of Zeal, or spiritual Excrescencies' revered among the sects, particularly among 'the devouter Sisters', as a sign of Grace 'as if they had been cloven tongues' (367). On Swift's 'ear for talk', see Ehrenpreis, *Swift the Man*, 201.

[49] *'A Tale of a Tub' to Which is Added 'The Battle of the Books' and the 'Mechanical Operation of the Spirit'*, 240.

books and papers suggested a poisonous press gone mad. Criticism is the descendant of Errour's den and of the hell of narcissistic self-absorption and malice that imprisoned Satan and gave birth to his brutally incestuous family at hell's gate in *Paradise Lost*, book II. Swift's modern wits appear to have substituted for the Christian Patriarch and humanist universe a hellish and regressive self-consumption, productive of volumes of gall and presided over by a matriarch but no muse, whose 'Eyes turned inward, as if she lookt only upon herself'—a void of spiritual insight filled with fury.

DIGRESSION AND EXILE IN A MODERN WORLD

In response to Dryden's confident claims to literary fathers and genealogy and against the pride of 'Modern Wits' in their progressive 'Empire of Reason', Swift counters with the lowly interior mechanisms and passions of the body. According to the Hack's theory of genius, the proud modern brain is one that has been shaken and overturned by vapours born in the lower body, which have collected, unacknowledged, and ascended like revolutionaries to induce a modern frenzy of ambition and delusion of conquest. The devious underground figure of earlier seventeenth-century digression, and the emotional life it carefully threaded, has emerged above ground as a body in crisis. The introduction about oratorical machines is crowded with bodies including the air, 'a heavy Body', and words, 'Bodies of much Weight and Gravity, as it is manifest from those deep Impressions they make and leave upon us'. Falstaff's words reduced to air, breath that he expended aggressively and retained defensively, protected his big body; now words have become bodies in their own right, while speakers' bodies grow indistinct. The Hack then quotes two lines of Lucretius about the power of words to wound. Swift supplies in a footnote Thomas Creech's translation: ' 'Tis certain then, that Voice that thus can wound | Is all Material; Body every Sound' (60). The body of the author, the body of the book, the bodies of sounds: the pressure of bodies in *A Tale* insist on the physical distortion perpetrated on human culture by the high-minded, disembodied, words of 'our Noble Moderns'. And with this angry body of his text, Swift delivers violence back.

By making digression the child of a topsy-turvy modern brain, 'the parent of all those mighty Revolutions, that have happened in Empire, in Philosophy, and in Religion', Swift has reinvented the revolutionary force of the rhetorical figure for a new age. The digressions of the rootless Hack represent a permanent anxiety about a lost or missed sense of relation. Swift stylizes the voice of digression as a modern voice of permanent dislocation and dispossession in a way that will enable Sterne to appropriate the figure for the voice of that great eighteenth-century digressor Tristram Shandy. Even more than *A Tale of a Tub*, *Tristram Shandy* is all digressions—and regressions. Sterne like Swift uses digressions to ponder the hard birth of a self, delicate relations between body and mind and the body and voice of a text, and the labyrinth of historical and literary continuity.[50]

Sterne, like Swift, associates as equally dangerous and potentially crippling the aggression of words, war, and sexuality, and he dramatizes the relation of digression's maddening frustration of narrative progress to a cautious, defensive postponement of sexual and self-definition. The traumatic intersection of intellectual and physical violence in Tristram's family, even before his birth, propels and shapes that digressive narration and keeps his stories open-ended. Ends in the sense of fulfilment of a desire or goal are like the guillotine of Tristram's window sash or the words that deliver Toby his second wound when Trim blasts forever his innocence about Widow Wadman. In the seventeenth century, the dangers that shaped digressive texts could be life-threatening including political execution, the fate of Stephen College and Algernon Sidney; by the time of Sterne, the dangers and battlefields have become domestic and personal ones that endanger reproduction and inheritance: not only economic but physical, intellectual, and psychological. Yet the violence of modernity's fraudulent 'engines and devices . . . second only to sex in supplying the metaphorical substance' of *Tristram Shandy* had cut Swift's narrator loose decades earlier.[51] George Puttenham's late sixteenth-century military 'Straggler', the *digressio* with which we began, by the eighteenth century looks like a permanent vagabond or refugee, more epistemological than political: an orphaned voice whose story has no

[50] On the relationship between Swift and Sterne, see J. T. Parnell, 'Swift, Sterne, and the Skeptical Tradition', *Studies in Eighteenth Century Culture*, 23 (1994), 221–42; and Melvyn New, 'Swift and Sterne: Two Tales, Several Sermons, and a Relationship Revisited', in Frank Palmieri (ed.), *Critical Essays on Jonathan Swift*, (New York: G. K. Hall, 1993), 164–86. See also John Mullan, 'Swift, Defoe, and Narrative Forms', in Steven N. Zwicker (ed.), *The Cambridge Companion to English Literature 1650–1740* (Cambridge: Cambridge University Press, 1998), 250–75, esp. 261 on Sterne's recuperation of the tradition of 'learned wit' for the novel.

[51] See Sigurd Burckhardt, '*Tristram Shandy*'s Law of Gravity', in Laurence Sterne, *Tristram Shandy*, ed. Howard Anderson (New York: Norton, 1980), 600.

end, whose protuberant shape suggests mental and physical deformity, but for whom words even in their violence have become the only medium of existence.

At the beginning of a century that sees the English novel off and running in a market of writers, booksellers, and readers, Swift anatomizes and derides the fatherless, fragmented body of the modern book. He caricatures yet promotes its romance as a frenetic, eccentric miscellany, a collection from commonplace books—a monster-show of 'Retailers of strange sights' whose authors employ a preface in front like a barker at the door. With his narrator he exposes the confessional, epistolary fictions and English picaresque of Dryden's rambling prefaces full of emotional journeys and private autobiographical detail. Swift's intense physical sensitivity fixes on the voice and missing body behind the fiction of printed 'Epistles, Advertisements, Introductions, Prolegomena's, Apparatus's, To-the-Reader's' (131) and conjures a physical immediacy, of an orphaned offspring tossed into the world on 'Accidents and Occasions'. His narrator's underworld of loss and disconnection becomes transposed above ground to physical pain and the attic of a darkened brain. The digression is at once demystified and given a new physical and psychological life under the pressure of Swift's competitive relation to Dryden. 'Malevolence' releases into centrifugal movement the parts of the new book: a wandering narrative voice in search of a home and a body, an accidental beginning and uncertain end.

Bibliography

ABATE, CORINE S., 'The Mischief-Making of Raphael upon Adam and Eve in *Paradise Lost*', *English Language Notes*, 36/3 (Mar. 1999), 41–54.

ALLEN, DON CAMERON, 'John Donne's Knowledge of Renaissance Medicine', *Journal of English and Germanic Philology*, 42 (1943), 322–42.

—— *Image and Meaning, Metaphoric Traditions in Renaissance Poetry* (Baltimore, MD: Johns Hopkins University Press, 1968).

ALLEN, MICHAEL, 'Divine Instruction: *Of Education* and the Pedagogy of Raphael, Michael, and the Father', *Milton Quarterly*, 26 (1992), 113–21.

ALPERS, PAUL J., *What is Pastoral?* (Chicago: University of Chicago Press, 1996).

ALTEGOER, DIANA B., *Reckoning Words: Baconian Science and the Construction of Truth in English Renaissance Culture* (Madison: Fairleigh Dickinson University Press, 2000).

Archer, Stanley L., 'John Dryden and the Earl of Dorset' (Ph.D. thesis, University of Mississippi, 1965).

ARMITAGE, DAVID, HIMY, ARMAND, and SKINNER, QUENTIN, (eds.), *Milton and Republicanism* (Cambridge: Cambridge University Press, 1995).

ASTON, MARGARET, 'English Ruins and English History: The Dissolution and the Sense of the Past', *Journal of the Warburg and Courtauld Institutes*, 36 (1973), 231–55.

AUBREY, JOHN, *'Brief Lives,' chiefly of Contemporaries, set down by John Aubrey, between the Years 1669 & 1696*, ed. Andrew Clark (Oxford: Clarendon Press, 1898).

AUERBACH, ERICH, *Scenes from the Drama of European Literature: Six Essays* (Gloucester, Mass: P. Smith, 1973).

AUGHTERSON, KATE (ed.), *Renaissance Woman: A Sourcebook. Constructions of Femininity in England* (London;: Routledge, 1995).

AUSTEN, RALPH A., *A Treatise of Fruit-Trees, Shewing the Manner of Grafting, Setting, Pruning, and Ordering of Them in All Respects . . .Together with the Spirituall Use of an Orchard: Held forth in divers Similitudes betweene Naturall & Spirituall Fruit-Trees: according to Scripture & Experience* (Oxford: Thomas Robinson, 1653).

AVELING, HUGH, 'The Catholic Recusancy of the Yorkshire Fairfaxes: Part 1', *Biographical Studies 1534–1829*, 3/2 (1955), 69–114.

—— 'The Catholic Recusancy of the Yorkshire Fairfaxes: Part 2', *Recusant History*, 4/2 (Ap. 1957), 61–101.

—— *The Catholic Recusants of the West Riding of Yorkshire 1558–1790*, Proceedings of the Leeds Philosophical and Literary Society, Literary and

Historical Section, 10/6 (Leeds, Printed for the Leeds Philosophical and Literary Society by Chorley & Pickersgill, 1963).

—— *Northern Catholics: The Catholic Recusants of the North Riding of Yorkshire* (London: Geoffrey Chapman, 1966).

Babel and Bethel: or, the Pope in his Colours (London?, 1680, Wing B244).

Bacon, Francis, *Of the Advancement and Proficience of Learning, or, The Partitions of Sciences, IX Bookes. (De dignitate et augmentis scientiarum),* trans. Gilbert Watts (Oxford: Printed by Leon. Lichfield . . . for Rob. Young & Ed. Forrest, 1640).

Bahlman, D. W. R., *The Moral Revolution of 1688* (New Haven: Yale University Press, 1957).

Bald, R. C., *Donne and the Drurys* (Cambridge: Cambridge University Press, 1959).

—— *John Donne: A Life* (New York: Oxford University Press, 1970).

Barilli, Renato, *Rhetoric,* trans. Giuliana Menozzi (Minneapolis: University of Minnesota Press, 1989).

Bartolovich, Crystal, 'Spatial Stories: The Surveyor and the Politics of Transition', in Alvin Vos (ed.), *Place and Displacement in the Renaissance,* Medieval and Renaissance Texts and Studies 132 (Binghamton, NY: Medieval and Renaissance Texts and Studies, 1995), 255–83.

Bate, Jonathan, *Shakespeare and Ovid* (Oxford: Clarendon Press, 1993).

Baumgaertner, Jill Peláez, 'Political Play and Theological Uncertainty in the *Anniversaries*', *John Donne Journal,* 13/1–2 (1994), 29–49.

Baxandall, Michael, *Giotto and the Orators: Humanist Observers of Painting in Italy and the Discovery of Pictorial Composition, 1350–1450* (Oxford: Clarendon Press, 1971).

Bell, Robert (ed.), *Memorials of the Civil War, Comprising the Correspondence of the Fairfax Family with the Most Distinguished Personages Engaged in That Memorable Contest,* vol. ii (London: R. Bentley, 1849).

Bell, Thomas, *The Anatomie of Popish Tyrannie* (London: Printed by Iohn Harison, for Richard Bankworth, dwelling in Paules Churchyard at the signe of the Sunne, 1603).

Bender, John and Wellbery, David E. (eds.), *The Ends of Rhetoric: History, Theory, Practice* (Stanford, Calif.: Stanford University Press, 1990).

Bennett, J. A. W., 'Dryden and All Souls', *Modern Language Notes,* 52 (1937), 115–16.

Bennett, Joan, *Sir Thomas Browne: A Man of Achievement in Literature* (Cambridge: Cambridge University Press, 1962).

Berry, Boyd, ' "Pardon . . . Though I Have Digrest": Digression as Style in "Salve Deus Rex Judaeorum" ', in Marshall Grossman (ed.), *Aemilia Lanyer: Gender, Genre, and the Canon,* (Lexington: University Press of Kentucky, 1998), 212–33.

Black, Joel Dana, 'The Second Fall: The Laws of Digression and Gravitation in Romantic Literature and their Impact on Contemporary Encyclopaedic Literature' (Ph.D. thesis, Stanford University, 1979).

BLESSINGTON, FRANCIS C., *'Paradise Lost' and the Classical Epic* (Boston: Routledge & Kegan Paul, 1979).

BOULTON, RICHARD, *The Works of the Honourable Robert Boyle, Esq; Epitomiz'd*, 4 vols. (London, Printed and are to be sold by Thomas Bennet . . . and John Wyat . . ., 1700).

BOWERS, FREDSON, 'Dryden as Laureate: The Cancel Leaf in "King Arthur" ', *Times Literary Supplement* (10 Ap. 1953), 244.

BOYLE, FRANK, *Swift as Nemesis: Modernity and its Satirist* (Stanford, Calif: Stanford University Press, 2000).

BOYLE, JOHN, EARL OF ORRERY, *Remarks on the Life and Writings of Dr. Jonathan Swift*, ed. João Fróes (Newark: University of Delaware Press, 2000).

BRADY, JENNIFER, 'Dryden and Negotiations of Literary Succession and Precession', Earl Roy Miner and Jennifer Brady (eds.) *Literary Transmission and Authority: Dryden and Other Writers*, (Cambridge: Cambridge University Press, 1993), 27–54.

BRAUDY, LEO, 'Unturning the Century: The Missing Decade of the 1690s', in Elaine Scarry (ed.), *Fins de Siècle: English Poetry in 1590, 1690, 1790, 1890, 1990* (Baltimore: Johns Hopkins University Press, 1995).

BRAVERMAN, RICHARD, 'Satiric Embodiments: Butler, Swift, Sterne', in James E. Gill (ed.), *Cutting Edges: Postmodern Critical Essays on Eighteenth-Century Satire*, (Knoxville: University of Tennessee Press, 1995).

British Museum, Dept. of Prints and Drawings, *Catalogue of Prints and Drawings in the British Museum Division I: Political and Personal Satires (no. 1 to no. 4838)*, i: *1320–April 11, 1689* (London, Printed by Order of the Trustees, 1870).

BRODY, MIRIAM, *Manly Writing. Gender, Rhetoric, and the Rise of Composition* (Carbondale: Southern Illinois University Press, 1993).

BROOKS, PETER, *Reading for the Plot: Design and Intention in Narrative* (New York: A. A. Knopf, 1984).

BROWER, REUBEN A., 'Dryden's Epic Manner and Virgil', in H. T. Swedenberg, Jr. (ed.), *Essential Articles for the Study of John Dryden*, (Hamden, Conn: Archon Books, 1966), 466–92.

BROWN, THOMAS, *The Reasons of Mr. Bays Changing his Religion. Considered in a Dialogue between Crites, Eugenius, and Mr. Bays* (London: Printed for S.T. . . ., 1688, Wing B5069).

—— *The Weesils. A Satyrical Fable, Giving an Account of Some Argumental Passages Happening in the Lion's Court about Weesilion's Taking the Oaths* (London, 1691, Wing B5077).

BROWNE, SIR THOMAS, *The Works of Sir Thomas Browne*, ed. Geoffrey Keynes, 4 vols. (Chicago: University of Chicago Press, 1964).

—— *The Major Works*, ed. C. A. Patrides (New York: Penguin, 1977).

BUCKINGHAM, GEORGE VILLIERS, DUKE OF, *The Rehearsal*, ed. Edward Arber (London: Constable and Co. Ltd., 1927).

BUDICK, SANFORD, *Dryden and the Abyss of Light: A Study of 'Religio Laici' and 'The Hind and the Panther'* (New Haven: Yale University Press, 1970).

—— *The Dividing Muse: Images of Sacred Disjunction in Milton's Poetry* (New Haven: Yale University Press, 1985).

BUHLER, STEPHEN M., 'Kingly States: The Politics in *Paradise Lost*', *Milton Studies*, 28 (1992), 49–68.

BURCKHARDT, SIGURD, '*Tristram Shandy's* Law of Gravity', in Laurence Sterne, *Tristram Shandy*, ed. Howard Anderson (New York: Norton, 1980).

BURDON, PAULINE, 'Marvell and his Kindred: The Family Network in the Later Years. The Alureds', *Notes and Queries*, 229 (Sept. 1984), 379–85.

BURTON, ROBERT, *The Anatomy of Melancholy*, ed. Nicolas K. Kiessling, Thomas C. Faulkner, and Rhonda L. Blair, 3 vols. (Oxford: Clarendon Press, 1989).

BURTT, SHELLEY, *Virtue Transformed: Political Argument in England, 1688–1740* (Cambridge: Cambridge University Press, 1992).

BYWATERS, DAVID, *Dryden in Revolutionary England* (Berkeley and Los Angeles: University of California Press, 1991).

—— 'Anticlericism in Swift's "Tale of a Tub" ', *Studies in English Literature 1500–1900*, 36 (1996), 579–602.

C., S., *The Art of Complaisance or the Means to Oblige in Conversation* (London, Printed for John Starkey . . ., 1673).

CALDWELL, TANYA, *Time to Begin Anew: Dryden's Georgics and Aeneis* (Lewisburg, Pa: Bucknell University Press, 2000).

Calendar of State Papers, Domestic Series, of the Reigns of Edward VI, Mary, Elizabeth, 1547–1580, ed. Robert Lemon and Mary Anne Everett Green (London: Longman, Brown, Green, Longmans, & Roberts, 1856).

Calendar of State Papers, Domestic Series, 1652–1653, ed. Mary Anne Everett Green, (London: Longman & Co., 1878).

Calendar of State Papers and Manuscripts, Relating to English Affairs, Existing in the Archives and Collections of Venice, and in Other Libraries of Northern Italy, xxix: *1653–1654*, ed. Allen B. Hinds (London: HM Stationery Office, 1929).

Calendar of State Papers, Domestic Series. James II, iii, *June 1687–February 1689* (London: HM Stationery Office, 1972), paper no. 655.

CAMPBELL, MARY BAINE, *Wonder and Science: Imagining Worlds in Early Modern Europe* (Ithaca, NY: Cornell University Press, 1999).

CAMPBELL, W. GARDNER, 'Paradisal Appetite and Cusan Food in *Paradise Lost*', in Kristin Pruitt McColgan and Charles W. Durham (eds.), *Arenas of Conflict: Milton and the Unfettered Mind* (Selinsgrove, Pa; London: Susquehanna University Press, 1997), 239–50.

CANTALUPO, CHARLES, ' "By Art Is Created That Great . . . State": Milton's *Paradise Lost* and Hobbes's *Leviathan*', in Margo Swiss and David A. Kent (eds.), *Heirs of Fame: Milton and Writers of the English Renaissance*, (Lewisburg, Pa: Bucknell University Press, 1995), 184–207.

CANTOR, H. V., '*Digressio* in the Orations of Cicero', *American Journal of Philology*, 52 (1931), 351–61.

CARE, HENRY, 'Towser the Second, a Bull-Dog. Or a Short Reply to "Absalom and Achitophel" ', in *Folio Verse Relating to Dryden, 1681–1699* (New York: Garland Publishing, 1975), no page numbers.

CARPENTER, RONALD H., *History as Rhetoric: Style, Narrative, and Persuasion* (Columbia: University of South Carolina Press, 1995).

CARRUTHERS, MARY J., *The Book of Memory: A Study of Memory in Medieval Culture* (Cambridge: Cambridge University Press, 1990).

CAVE, TERENCE, *The Cornucopian Text: Problems of Writing in the French Renaissance* (Oxford: Clarendon Press, 1979).

CHALMERS, ALAN D. *Jonathan Swift and the Burden of the Future* (Newark: University of Delaware Press, 1995).

CHAMBERLIN, JOHN S., *Increase and Multiply* (Chapel Hill: University of North Carolina Press, 1976).

CHAMBERS, ROSS, *Loiterature* (Lincoln: University of Nebraska Press, 1999).

CHAPPELL, WILLIAM, *The Preacher, or The Art and Method of Preaching* (London: Printed for Edw. Farnham, 1656).

CHARLAND, THOMAS MARIE, *Artes Praedicandi; contribution à l'histoire de la rhétorique au moyen âge* (Paris: J. Vrin, 1936).

CHARTIER, ROGER, *The Order of Books: Readers, Authors, and Libraries in Europe between the Fourteenth and Eighteenth Centuries*, trans. Lydia G. Cochrane (Stanford, Calif: Stanford University Press, 1994).

—— (ed.), *A History of Private Life*, iii: *Passions of the Renaissance*, trans. Arthur Goldhammer (Cambridge, Mass.: Belknap Press of Harvard University Press, 1989).

CHERWITZ, RICHARD A. (ed.), *Rhetoric and Philosophy* (Hillsdale, NJ: L. Erlbaum Associates, 1990).

CIBBER, THEOPHILUS, *Lives of the Poets of Great Britain and Ireland, to the Time of Dean Swift*, 5 vols. (London: R. Griffiths, 1753).

CICERO, MARCUS TULLIUS, *Pro Archia Poeta*, trans. N. H. Watts, Loeb Classical Library, 158 (Cambridge, Mass.: Harvard University Press, 1923, 1993).

—— *Brutus*, trans. G. L. Hendrickson, Loeb Classical Library 342 (London: W. Heinemann, 1971).

—— *De Oratore*, trans. E. W. Sutton, Loeb Classical Library 348–9 (Cambridge, Mass.: Harvard University Press, 1996).

—— *Ad. C. Herennium de ratione dicendi (Rhetorica ad Herennium)*, trans. Harry Caplan, Loeb Classical Library 403 (Cambridge, Mass.: Harvard University Press, 1954).

CIXOUS, HÉLÈNE, and CLÉMENT, CATHERINE, *The Newly Born Woman*, trans. Betsy Wing, foreword by Sandra M. Gilbert (Minneapolis: University of Minnesota Press, 1986).

CLAASEN, JO-MARIE, *Displaced Persons: The Literature of Exile from Cicero to Boethius* (Madison: University of Wisconsin Press, 1999).

CLAGETT, WILLIAM, *The Present State of the Controversie between the Church of England and the Church of Rome, or, An Account of the Books Written on Both*

Sides. In a Letter to a Friend (London: Printed for Tho. Basset, James Adamson, and Tho. Newborough, 1687, Wing C4390).

CLARENDON, EDWARD HYDE, EARL OF, *The History of the Rebellion and Civil Wars in England*, vol. v (Oxford: Clarendon Press; repr. Boston: Wells and Lilly, 1827).

CLARK, JAMES ANDREW, 'The Plot of Donne's "Anniversaries" ', *Studies in English Literature 1500–1900*, 30 (1990), 63–77.

CLARKE, M. L., *Rhetoric at Rome: A Historical Survey*, 3rd edn., rev. and new introd. by D. H. Berry (New York: Routledge, 1996).

CLERICO, TERRI, 'The "Amphibium" Poet: Phallic Identity in Marvell', *Criticism*, 34/4 (1992), 539–61.

CLIFFORD, MARTIN, *Notes upon Mr. Dryden's Poems in Four Letters to Which are Annexed some Reflections upon the Hind and the Panther. By Another Hand* (London, 1687, Wing C4706).

COIRO, ANN BAYNES, ' "To Repair the Ruins of our First Parents": "Of Education" and Fallen Adam', *Studies in English Literature, 1500–1900*, 28 (1988), 133–47.

COKAYNE, GEORGE E., *The Complete Peerage of England, Scotland, Ireland, Great Britain, and the United States, Extant, Extinct, or Dormant*, ed. H. A. Doubleday and Howard de Walden, vol. ix (London: St Catherine Press, 1936).

COLERIDGE, SAMUEL TAYLOR, *Coleridge's Miscellaneous Criticism* (Cambridge, Mass.: Harvard University Press, 1936).

—— *Coleridge on the Seventeenth Century*, ed. Roberta Florence Brinkley (Durham, NC: Duke University Press, 1955).

COLIE, ROSALIE L., *'My Ecchoing Song': Andrew Marvell's Poetry of Criticism* (Princeton: Princeton University Press, 1970).

—— 'All in Peeces: Problems of Interpretation in Donne's Anniversary Poems', in Peter Amadeus Fiore (ed.), *Just So Much Honor: Essays Commemorating the Four-Hundredth Anniversary of the Birth of John Donne*, (University Park: Pennsylvania State University Press, 1972), 189–218.

COLLETT, JONATHAN H., 'Milton's Use of Classical Mythology in *Paradise Lost*', *PMLA* 85 (1970), 88–96.

COMBE, KIRK, 'Clandestine Protest against William III in Dryden's Translations of Juvenal and Persius', *Modern Philology*, 87 (1989), 36–50.

Cook, Patrick J., *Milton, Spenser and the Epic Tradition* (Brookfield, Vt: Scolar Press, 1996).

Cooper, Anthony Ashley, third Earl of Shaftesbury, *Characteristics of Men, Manners, Opinions, Times, Etc.*, ed. John M. Robertson, 2 vols. (Gloucester, Mass.: Peter Smith, 1963), vol. ii.

CORTHELL, RONALD, 'The Obscure Object of Desire: Donne's "Anniversaries" and the Cultural Production of Elizabeth Drury', Arthur F. Marotti (ed.), *Critical Essays on John Donne*, (New York: G. K. Hall, 1994), 123–40.

CORUM, RICHARD, 'In White Ink: *Paradise Lost* and Milton's Ideas of Women' Julia M. Walker (ed.), *Milton and the Idea of Woman*, (Urbana: University of Illinois Press, 1988), 120–47.

CROLL, MORRIS W., *Style, Rhetoric, and Rhythm* (1966; repr. Woodbridge, Conn.: Ox Bow Press, 1989).

CROOKE, HELKIAH, *Mikrokosmographia: A Description of the body of man. Together with the controuersies thereto belonging. Collected and translated out of all the best authors of anatomy, especially out of Gasper Bauhinus and Andreas Laurentius* (London: William Jaggard, 1615).

CRUMP, GALBRAITH M. (ed.), *Poems on Affairs of State: Augustan Satirical Verse, 1660–1714*, iv: *1685–1688* (New Haven: Yale University Press, 1968).

CUMMINGS, ROBERT, 'The Forest Sequence in Marvell's "Upon Appleton House": The Imaginative Contexts of a Poetic Episode', *Huntington Library Quarterly*, 47 (1984), 179–210.

CURTIS, PAUL M., 'Byron's *Beppo*: Digression and Contingency', *Dalhousie Review*, 73/1 (1993), 18–33.

DAVIE, DONALD, *Purity of Diction in English Verse* (Oxford: Oxford University Press, 1953).

DAVIES, SIR JOHN, *The Poems of Sir John Davies*, ed. Robert Krueger (Oxford: Clarendon Press, 1975).

DAVIES, TONY, ' "The meaning, not the name": Milton and Gender', in William Zunder and Suzanne Trill (eds.), *Writing and the English Renaissance*, (London: Longman, 1996), 193–212.

DAVIS, NATALIE ZEMON, 'Women on Top: Symbolic Sexual Inversion and Political Disorder in Early Modern Europe' in Barbara A. Babcock (ed.), *The Reversible World: Symbolic Inversion in Art and Society*, ed. (Ithaca, NY: Cornell University Press, 1972), 147–90.

DEKKER, THOMAS, 'English Villanies, Eight Severall Times Prest to Death by the Printers . . . And because a companie of rogues, cunning canting Gypsies, and all the scumme of our nation fight here under their owne tottered colours: at the end is a canting dictionarie, to teach their language; with canting songs' (London: Printed by E.P. for Nicholas Gamage . . ., 1648).

DIPASQUALE, THERESA M., ' "Heav'n's Last Best Gift": Eve and Wisdom in *Paradise Lost*', *Modern Philology*, 95/1 (1997), 44–67.

DONAHUE, JENNIFER, 'Elizabeth Drury as Testimony: A Thomistic Analysis of Donne's "Anniversaries" ', *Ben Jonson Journal*, 5 (1998), 133–48.

DONKER, MARJORIE, *Dictionary of Literary-Rhetorical Conventions of the English Renaissance* (Westport, Conn.: Greenwood Press, 1982).

DONNE, JOHN, *Poems by J.D. with Elegies on the Authors Death* (London: Printed by M. F. for Iohn Marriot, 1633).

—— *The Variorum Edition of the Poetry of John Donne*, gen. ed. Gary A. Stringer (Bloomington: Indiana University Press, 1995–)

—— *Letters to Severall Persons of Honour*, ed. Charles Edmund Merrill, Jr. (New York: Sturgis and Walton Co., 1910).

—— *The Poems of John Donne*, ed. Herbert J. C. Grierson, vol. i (Oxford: Oxford University Press, 1912).

—— *John Donne: The Anniversaries*, ed. Frank Manley (Baltimore: Johns Hopkins University Press, 1963).

—— *John Donne's Sermons on the Psalms and Gospels, with a Selection of Prayers and Meditations*, ed. Evelyn M. Simpson (Berkeley and Los Angeles: University of California Press, 1963).

—— *Devotions upon Emergent Occasions, Together with Death's Duel* (Ann Arbor: University of Michigan Press, 1965).

—— *The Elegies and The Songs and Sonnets*, ed. Helen Gardner (Oxford: Oxford University Press, 1965).

—— *John Donne, Selected Prose*, selected by Evelyn Simpson, ed. Helen Gardner and Timothy Healy (Oxford: Clarendon Press, 1967).

—— *The Satires, Epigrams and Verse Letters*, ed. Wesley Milgate (Oxford: Oxford University Press, 1967).

—— *Letters to Severall Persons of Honour (1651): A Facsimile Reproduction*, introd. M. Thomas Hester (Delmar, NY: Scholars' Facsimiles & Reprints, 1977).

—— *John Donne: The Epithalamions, Anniversaries and Epicedes*, ed. Wesley Milgate (Oxford: Clarendon Press, 1978).

—— *Devotions Upon Emergent Occasions*, ed. Anthony Raspa (New York: Oxford University Press, 1987).

—— *The Anniversaries and the Epicedes and Obsequies*, ed. Paul A. Parrish et al. (Bloomington: Indiana University Press, 1995).

DRYDEN, JOHN, *A Defence of the Papers Written by the Late King of Blessed Memory, and Duchess of York, Against the Answer Made to Them* (London: Printed by H. Hills . . ., 1686).

—— *The Works of John Dryden*, ed. Sir Walter Scott, 18 vols. (London: William Miller, 1808).

—— *The Works of John Dryden*, ed. Sir Walter Scott, rev. and corrected by George Saintsbury, 18 vols. (Edinburgh: W. Paterson, 1882–93).

—— *Essays of John Dryden*, ed. W. P. Ker (Oxford: Clarendon Press, 1900).

—— *Selected Dramas of John Dryden*, ed. George R. Noyes (Chicago: Scott, Foresman, 1910).

—— *The Letters of John Dryden, with Letters Addressed to him*, ed. Charles E. Ward (Durham, NC: Duke University Press, 1942).

—— *The Works of John Dryden*, 20 vols., ed. Edward Niles Hooker, H. T. Swedenberg, Jr., et al. (Berkeley and Los Angeles: University of California Press, 1956–2000).

—— *The Poems of John Dryden*, ed. James Kinsley, 4 vols. (London: Oxford University Press, 1958).

—— *John Dryden: Four Tragedies*, ed. L. A. Beaurline and Fredson Bowers (Chicago: University of Chicago Press, 1967).

—— *John Dryden*, ed. Keith Walker (Oxford: Oxford University Press, 1987).

—— *The Poems of John Dryden*, 4 vols., ed. Paul Hammond and David Hopkins (London: Longman, 1995–2000).

DUNN, WILLIAM P., *Sir Thomas Browne: A Study in Religious Philosophy* (Minneapolis: University of Minnesota Press, 1950).

DUROCHER, RICHARD J., *Milton and Ovid* (Ithaca, NY: Cornell University Press, 1985).

DUSINBERRE, JULIET, *Virginia Woolf's Renaissance: Woman Reader or Common Reader?* (Iowa City: University of Iowa Press, 1997).

EARL, JAMES W., 'Eve's Narcissism', *Milton Quarterly*, 19/1 (1985), 13–16.

EHRENPREIS, IRVIN, *Swift, the Man, his Works, and the Age* (Cambridge, Mass.: Harvard University Press, 1962).

ELIOT, THOMAS STEARNES, *Selected Essays, 1917–1932* (New York: Harcourt, Brace and Company, 1932).

ELKINS, JAMES, *The Poetics of Perspective* (Ithaca, NY: Cornell University Press, 1994).

ELLIOTT, ROBERT C., *The Power of Satire: Magic, Ritual, Art* (Princeton: Princeton University Press, 1960).

EMPSON, WILLIAM, *Milton's God*, rev. edn. (London: Chatto & Windus, 1965).

—— 'Donne the space man', in *William Empson: Essays on Renaissance Literature*, ed. John Haffenden, vol. i (Cambridge: Cambridge University Press, 1993), 78–128.

ENGEL, WILLIAM E., *Mapping Mortality: The Persistence of Memory and Melancholy in Early Modern England* (Amherst: University of Massachusetts Press, 1995).

ENTERLINE, LYNN, *The Tears of Narcissus: Melancholia and Masculinity in Early Modern Writing* (Stanford, Calif.: Stanford University Press, 1995).

ERASMUS, DESIDERIUS, *On Copia of Words and Ideas* (Milwaukee, Wis.: Marquette University Press, 1963).

—— *Collected Works of Erasmus. Literary and Educational Writings*, ii: *De Copia. De Ratione Studii*, ed. Craig R. Thompson, *De Copia* trans. Betty I. Knott (Toronto: University of Toronto Press, 1978).

ERICKSON, LEE, 'Marvell's "Upon Appleton House" and the Fairfax Family', *English Literary Renaissance*, 9 (1979), 158–68.

ERICKSON, ROBERT A., *The Language of the Heart, 1600–1750* (Philadelphia: University of Pennsylvania Press, 1997).

ESTRIN, BARBARA L., *Laura: Uncovering Gender and Genre in Wyatt, Donne, and Marvell* (Durham, NC: Duke University Press, 1994).

EVANS, MARTIN J., *Milton's Imperial Epic: 'Paradise Lost' and the Discourse of Colonialism* (Ithaca, NY: Cornell University Press, 1996).

EVELYN, JOHN, *The Diary of John Evelyn*, ed. Esmond Samuel De Beer, 6 vols. (Oxford: Clarendon Press, 1955).

FAIRFAX, BRIAN, *Memoirs of the Life of George Villiers, Second Duke of Buckingham*, introd. to George Villiers, Duke of Buckingham, *The Rehearsal*, ed. Edward Arber (London: Constable and Co. Ltd, 1927).

FAIRFAX, SIR THOMAS, *Short Memorials of Thomas Lord Fairfax, written by himself*, ed. Brian Fairfax (London: Printed for Ri. Chiswell . . ., 1699).

FERGUSON, MOIRA (ed.), *First Feminists: British Women Writers 1578–1799* (Bloomington: Indiana University Press, 1985).

FERRY, ANNE D., *Milton's Epic Voice: The Narrator in 'Paradise Lost'* (Cambridge, Mass.: Harvard University Press, 1963).

FINCH, JEREMIAH, 'Sir Thomas Browne and the Quincunx', *Studies in Philology*, 37 (1940), 742–7.

—— *A Doctor's Life of Science and Faith* (New York: Henry Schuman, 1950).

FINEMAN, JOEL, 'Shakespeare's Ear', *Representations*, 28 (Fall 1989), 6–13.

FINKELSTEIN, ANDREA, *Harmony and the Balance. An Intellectual History of Seventeenth-Century English Economic Thought* (Ann Arbor, MI: University of Michigan Press, 2000).

FINUCCI, VALERIA, and SCHWARTZ, REGINA M. (eds.), *Desire in the Renaissance: Psychoanalysis and Literature* (Princeton: Princeton University Press, 1994).

FISCHER, ALAN S., 'An End to the Renaissance: Erasmus, Hobbes, and *A Tale of a Tub*', *Huntington Library Quarterly*, 38 (1974), 1–20.

FISH, STANLEY, *Surprised by Sin: The Reader in 'Paradise Lost'* (New York: St Martin's Press, 1967).

—— *How Milton Works* (Cambridge, Mass.: Harvard University Press, 2001).

FITZMAURICE, JAMES (ed.), *Major Women Writers of Seventeenth-Century England* (Ann Arbor: University of Michigan Press, 1997).

FLETCHER, ANGUS, 'The Image of Lost Direction', in Eleanor Cook et al. (eds.), *Centre and Labyrinth: Essays in Honour of Northrop Frye* (Toronto: University of Toronto Press, 1983), 329–46.

—— *The Transcendental Masque: An Essay on Milton's 'Comus'* (Ithaca, NY: Cornell University Press, 1971).

FLINKER, NOAM, *The Song of Songs in English Renaissance Literature: Kisses of their Mouths* (Cambridge: D.S. Brewer, 2000).

FLYNN, CAROL HOULIHAN, *The Body in Swift and Defoe* (Cambridge: Cambridge University Press, 1990).

FLYNN, DENNIS, *John Donne and the Ancient Catholic Nobility* (Bloomington: Indiana University Press, 1995).

Folio Verse Relating to Dryden 1681–1699, Drydeniana XIII (New York: Garland, 1975).

FONSECA, ISABEL, *Bury me Standing: The Gypsies and their Journey* (New York: Knopf, 1996).

FOUCAULT, MICHEL, *Language, Counter-Memory, Practice: Selected Essays and Interviews by Michel Foucault*, ed. and, introd. Donald F. Bouchard, trans. D. F. Bouchard and S. Simon (Ithaca, NY: Cornell University Press, 1977).

FRASER, ANTONIA, *Cromwell, our Chief of Men* (London: Weidenfeld and Nicolson, 1973).

FREER, COBURN, 'John Donne and Elizabethan Economic Theory', *Criticism*, 38/4 (Fall 1996), 497–520.

FREUD, SIGMUND, *The Standard Edition of the Complete Psychological Works of Sigmund Freud*, trans. James Strachey and Anna Freud (London: Hogarth Press, 1953–74).

FRIEDMAN, DONALD M., '*Comus* and the Truth of the Ear', in Claude J. Summers and Ted-Larry Pebworth (eds.), *'The Muses Common-weale': Poetry and Politics in the Seventeenth Century*, (Columbia: University of Missouri Press, 1988), 119–34.

—— 'Divisions on a Ground: "Sex" in *Paradise Lost*', in P. G. Stanwood (eds), *Of Poetry and Politics: New Essays on Milton and his World*, Medieval and Renaissance Texts and Studies, 126 (Binghamton, NY: Medieval and Renaissance Texts and Studies, 1995), 203–12.

—— 'The Lady in the Garden: On the Literary Genetics of Milton's Eve', *Milton Studies*, 35 (1997), 114–33.

—— 'Rude Heaps and Decent Order' in Warren Chernaik and Martin Dzelzainis (eds.), *Marvell and Liberty*, (Houndmills: Macmillan Press, 1999), 123–44.

FROULA, CHRISTINE, 'When Eve Reads Milton: Undoing the Canonical Economy', *Critical Inquiry*, 10 (1983), 321–47.

FRYE, NORTHROP, *Anatomy of Criticism: Four Essays* (Princeton: Princeton University Press, 1957).

GALLAGHER, PHILIP J., *Milton, the Bible, and Misogyny* (Columbia: University of Missouri Press, 1990).

GARDINER, ANN BARBEAU, *Ancient Faith and Modern Freedom in John Dryden's 'The Hind and the Panther'* (Washington, DC: Catholic University of America Press, 1998).

GEERTZ, CLIFFORD, *Works and Lives: The Anthropologist as Author* (Stanford, Calif.: Stanford University Press, 1988).

GIBB, MILDRED A., *The Lord General: A Life of Thomas Fairfax* (London: L. Drummond, Ltd., 1938).

GILLILAND, JOAN F., ' "Grateful Digressions" and Casual Discourse: Eve's Rapport-Talk', in Charles W. Durham and Kristin Pruitt McColgan (eds.), *Spokesperson Milton: Voices in Contemporary Criticism* (Selinsgrove, Pa.: Susquehanna University Press, 1994), 249–59.

GLENN, CHERYL, *Rhetoric Retold: Regendering the Tradition from Antiquity through the Renaissance* (Carbondale: Southern Illinois University Press, 1997).

GOLDING, ARTHUR, *The xv. Bookes of P. Ovidius Naso, entytuled Metamorphosis, translated oute of Latin into English meeter, by Arthur Golding Gentleman* (London: W. Seres, 1567).

GOODMAN, KEVIS, ' "Wasted Labor"? Milton's Eve, the Poet's Work, and the Challenge of Sympathy', *English Literary History*, 64 (1997), 415–46.

GOTHER, JOHN, 'A Papist Mis-Represented, and Represented, or, a Two-Fold Character of Popery' ([London], 1685).

GOTOFF, HAROLD, *Cicero's Eloquent Style: An Analysis of the 'Pro Archia'* (Urbana: University of Illinois Press, 1979).

GOUK, PENELOPE, 'The Role of Acoustics and Music Theory in the Scientific Work of Robert Hooke', *Annals of Science*, 37 (1980), 573–605.

—— 'Some English Theories of Hearing in the Seventeenth Century: Before and after Descartes', in Charles Burnett, Michael Fend, and Penelope Gouk (eds.), *The Second Sense; Studies in Hearing and Musical Judgement from Antiquity to the Seventeenth Century*, (London: Warburg Institute, University of London, 1991), 95–113.

—— *Music, Science, and Natural Magic in Seventeenth-Century England* (New Haven: Yale University Press, 1999).

GOULD, ROBERT, 'The Laureat. Jack Squabb's History in a Little Drawn, Down to his Evening from his Early Dawn' (London?, 1687, Wing G1421).

GRAHAM, ELSPETH, et al. (eds.), *Her Own Life; Autobiographical Writings by Seventeenth-Century Englishwomen* (London: Routledge, 1989).

GREEN, MANDY, ' "The Vine and her Elm": Milton's Eve and the Transformation of an Ovidian Motif', *Modern Language Review*, 91 (1996), 301–16.

GREENE, THOMAS M., 'Labyrinth Dances in the French and English Renaissance', *Renaissance Quarterly*, 4 (2001), 1403–66.

GREER, GERMAINE, et al. (eds.), *Kissing the Rod: An Anthology of Seventeenth-Century Women's Verse* (New York: Farrar Straus Giroux, 1988).

GREGERSON, LINDA, *The Reformation of the Subject: Spenser, Milton, and the English Protestant Epic* (Cambridge: Cambridge University Press, 1995).

GRIFFIN, DUSTIN H., *Literary Patronage in England, 1650–1800* (Cambridge: Cambridge University Press, 1996).

GUIBBORY, ACHSAH, ' "A Rationall of Old Rites"; Sir Thomas Browne's *Urn Buriall* and the Conflict over Ceremony', *Yearbook of English Studies*, 21 (1991), 229–41.

GUILLORY, JOHN, 'From the Superfluous to the Supernumerary: Reading Gender into *Paradise Lost*', in Elizabeth D. Harvey and Katharine Eisaman Maus (eds), *Soliciting Interpretation: Literary Theory and Seventeenth-Century English Poetry*, (Chicago: University of Chicago Press, 1990), 79–81.

—— 'Milton, Narcissism, Gender: On the Genealogy of Male Self-Esteem', in Christopher Kendrick (ed.), *Critical Essays on John Milton*, (New York: G. K. Hall, 1995), 194–233.

GUTCH, JOHN, *Collectanea Curiosa; or Miscellaneous Tracts, Relating to the History and Antiquities of England and Ireland, the Universities of Oxford and Cambridge, and a Variety of Other Subjects*, 2 vols. (Oxford: Clarendon Press, 1781).

HABER, JUDITH, *Pastoral and the Poetics of Self-Contradiction: Theocritus to Marvell* (Cambridge: Cambridge University Press, 1994).

HALE, JOHN K., *Milton's Languages: The Impact of Multilingualism on Style* (Cambridge: Cambridge University Press, 1997).

HALLEY, JANET E., 'Sir Thomas Browne's *The Garden of Cyrus* and the Real Character', *English Literary Renaissance*, 15/1 (1985), 100–21.

HAM, ROSWELL G., 'Dryden and the Colleges', *Modern Language Notes*, 49 (1934), 324–32.

HAMMOND, PAUL, *Dryden and the Traces of Classical Rome* (Oxford: Oxford University Press, 1999).

HARDING, DAVIS P., *The Club of Hercules: Studies in the Classical Background of 'Paradise Lost'*, Illinois Studies in Language and Literature, 50 (Urbana: University of Illinois Press, 1962).

HARRIS, BRICE, *Charles Sackville, Sixth Earl of Dorset: Patron and Poet of the Restoration* (Urbana: University of Illinois Press, 1940).

HARRISON, PETER, *The Bible, Protestantism, and the Rise of Natural Science* (Cambridge: Cambridge University Press, 1998).

HARTH, PHILLIP, *Swift and Anglican Rationalism: The Religious Background of 'A Tale of a Tub'* (Chicago: University of Chicago Press, 1961).

—— *Contexts of Dryden's Thought* (Chicago: University of Chicago Press, 1968).

HARTMAN, GEOFFREY, 'Milton's Counterplot', *English Literary History*, 25 (1958), 1–12.

HAVENSTEIN, DANIELA, *Democratizing Sir Thomas Browne: Religio Medici and its Imitations* (Oxford: Oxford University Press, 1999).

HAWCROFT, MICHAEL, *Rhetoric: Readings in French Literature* (Oxford: Oxford University Press, 2000).

HAWES, CLEMENT, *Mania and Literary Style: The Rhetoric of Enthusiasm from the Ranters to Christopher Smart* (Cambridge: Cambridge University Press, 1996).

HEAD, RICHARD, *The Canting Academy, or, the Devils Cabinet Opened: Wherein is shewn the Mysterious and Villanous Practices of that wicked Crew, commonly known by the Names of Hectors, Trapanners, Gilts, &c: to Which is Added a Compleat Canting-Dictionary, both of old Words, and Such as are now most in use . . .* (London: Printed by F. Leach for Mat. Drew . . ., 1673).

—— *The Life and Death of the English Rogue, or, his Last Legacy to the World . . .: to which is added an alphabetical canting dictionary, English before the canting* (London: Printed for Charles Passinger . . ., 1679).

HEFFERNAN, JAMES A. W., *Museum of Words: The Poetics of Ekphrasis from Homer to Ashbery* (Chicago: University of Chicago Press, 1993).

HEIDEMAN, MARGARET ASH, '*Hydriotaphia* and *The Garden of Cyrus*: A Paradox and a Cosmic Vision', *University of Toronto Quarterly*, 19 (1949), 235–46.

HENDRICKSON, G. L., 'The Origin and Meaning of the Ancient Characters of Style', *American Journal of Philology*, 26/3 (1905), 249–90.

HEYRICK, THOMAS, 'To the Reader', preface to *The New Atlantis: A Poem in Three Books with Some Reflections upon the Hind and the Panther* (London: Printed for the Author, 1687, Wing H1754).

HIBBARD, G. R., 'The Country House Poem of the Seventeenth Century', *Journal of the Warburg and Courtauld Institutes*, 19 (1956), 159–74.

HIGGINS, IAN, *Swift's Politics: A Study in Disaffection* (Cambridge: Cambridge University Press, 1994).

—— 'Dryden and Swift', in Claude J. Rawson and Aaron Santesso (eds.), *John Dryden 1631–1700: His Politics, His Plays, and His Poets* (Newark: University of Delaware Press, forthcoming 2003–4).

HILL, CHRISTOPHER, *The English Bible and the Seventeenth-Century Revolution* (London: Allen Lane, 1993).

HILL, GEOFFREY, *The Enemy's Country: Words, Contexture, and Other Circumstances of Language* (Stanford, Calif.: Stanford University Press, 1991).

—— 'Keeping to the Middle Way: The "Accurate Musicke" in Burton's Anatomizing of Worldly Corruptions', *Times Literary Supplement* (23 December, 1994), 3–6.

HIRST, DEREK, 'Samuel Parker, Andrew Marvell, and Political Culture, 1667–73', in Derek Hirst and Richard Strier (eds.), *Writing and Political Engagement in Seventeenth-Century England* (Cambridge: Cambridge University Press, 1999), 145–64.

—— and ZWICKER, STEVEN 'High Summer at Nun Appleton, 1651: Andrew Marvell and Lord Fairfax's Occasions', *Historical Journal*, 36/2 (1993), 247–69.

HOBBES, THOMAS, *Leviathan*, ed. Richard Tuck (Cambridge: Cambridge University Press, 1991).

HODGES, DEVON L., *Renaissance Fictions of Anatomy* (Amherst: University of Massachusetts Press, 1985).

HODGSON-WRIGHT, STEPHANIE, *Women's Writing of the Early Modern Period, 1588–1688: An Anthology* (New York: Columbia University Press, 2002).

HOLSTUN, JAMES, ' "Will you Rent our Ancient Love Asunder?" Lesbian Elegy in Donne, Marvell, and Milton', *English Literary History*, 54 (1987), 835–67.

HUGHES, RICHARD E., *The Progress of the Soul: The Interior Career of John Donne* (New York: Morrow, 1968).

HUNTLEY, FRANK LIVINGSTONE, 'Sir Thomas Browne: The Relationship of *Urn Burial* and *The Garden of Cyrus*', in Stanley E. Fish (ed.), *Seventeenth-Century Prose: Modern Essays in Criticism* (New York: Oxford University Press, 1971), 424–39.

—— *Bishop Joseph Hall 1574–1656* (Cambridge: D. S. Brewer, 1979).

—— '*The Garden of Cyrus* as Prophecy', in C. A. Patrides (ed.), *Approaches to Sir Thomas Brown: the Ann Arbor Tercentenary Lectures and Essays*, (Columbia: University of Missouri Press, 1982), 132–42.

IRIGARAY, LUCE, *Speculum of the Other Woman*, trans. Gillian C. Gill (Ithaca, NY: Cornell University Press, 1985).

JACOBUS, LEE A., *Sudden Apprehension: Aspects of Knowledge in 'Paradise Lost'* (The Hague: Mouton, 1976).

JEFFERSON, D. W., 'The Poetry of "The Hind and the Panther" ', *Modern Language Review*, 79/1 (1984), 32–44.

JOHNSON, GEORGE WILLIAM (ed.), *The Fairfax Correspondence: Memoirs of the Reign of Charles the First*, vol. i (London: R. Bentley, 1848).

JOHNSON, SAMUEL, *Lives of the English Poets*, ed. George Birbeck Norman Hill and Harold Spencer Scott, 3 vols. (Oxford: Clarendon Press, 1905).

—— *The Life of Sir Thomas Browne* in Sir Thomas Browne, *The Major Works*, ed. C. A. Patrides (New York: Penguin, 1977).

JONES, THOMAS (ed.), *A Catalogue of the Collection of Tracts for and against popery*, parts 1 and 2, Remains Historical and Literary Connected with the Palatine Counties of Lancaster and Chester, published by the Chetham Society, vol. 48 (Manchester: Chetham Society, 1859, 1865).

JONSON, BEN, *Ben Jonson*, ed. C. H. Herford and Percy and Evelyn Simpson, 11 vols. (Oxford: Oxford University Press, 1952).

—— *Ben Jonson*, ed. Ian Donaldson (Oxford: Oxford University Press, 1985).

JOOMA, MINAZ, 'The Alimentary Structures of Incest in *Paradise Lost*', *English Literary History*, 63/1 (1996), 25–43.

JUNIUS, FRANCISCUS, *The Literature of Classical Art*, i: *The Painting of the Ancients (De Pictura Veterum)*, ed. Keith Aldrich et al. (Berkeley and Los Angeles: University of California Press, 1991).

KAHN, COPPÉLIA, 'The Absent Mother in *King Lear*', in Margaret W. Fergusson, Maureen Quilligan, and Nancy J. Vickers (eds.), *Rewriting the Renaissance: The Discourses of Sexual Difference in Early Modern Europe* (Chicago: University of Chicago Press, 1986), 33–49.

KELLIHER, W. H. (ed.), *Andrew Marvell, Poet and Politician 1621–78: An Exhibition to Commemorate the Tercentenary of his Death* (London: Published for the British Museum by British Museum Publications, 1978).

KELLY, KATHLEEN, 'Narcissus in *Paradise Lost* and *Upon Appleton House*: Disenchanting the Renaissance Lyric', in David G. Allen and Robert A. White (eds.), *Traditions and Innovations: Essays on British Literature of the Middle Ages and the Renaissance*, (Newark: University of Delaware Press, 1990), 200–13.

KENYON, JOHN, 'Andrew Marvell: Life and Times', in R. L. Brett (ed.), *Andrew Marvell: Essays on the Tercentenary of his Death*, (Oxford: Published for the University of Hull by Oxford University Press, 1979), 1–35.

KERNAN, ALVIN B., *The Plot of Satire* (New Haven: Yale University Press, 1965).

KERRIGAN, WILLIAM, 'The Articulation of the Ego in the English Renaissance', in Joseph H. Smith (ed.), *Psychiatry and the Humanities*, iv: *The Literary Freud: Mechanisms of Defense and the Poetic Will*, (New Haven: Yale University Press, 1980), 261–308.

—— *The Sacred Complex: On the Psychogenesis of 'Paradise Lost'* (Cambridge: Harvard University Press, 1983).

KETTON-CREMER, R. W., *Norfolk in the Civil War: A Portrait of a Society in Conflict* (Hamden, Conn.: Archon Books, 1969).

KEYNES, GEOFFREY, *A Bibliography of Sir Thomas Browne, Kt. M.D.*, 2nd edn. (Oxford: Oxford University Press, 1968).

KIETZMAN, MARY JO, 'The Fall into Conversation with Eve: Discursive Difference in *Paradise Lost*', *Criticism*, 39/1 (Winter 1997), 55–88.

KIRK, DAVID MORRISON, 'The Digression: Its Use in Prose Fiction from the Greek Romance through the Eighteenth Century' (Ph.D. thesis, Stanford University, 1960).

KISHLANSKY, MARK A., 'Turning Frogs into Princes: Aesop's *Fables* and the Political Culture of Early Modern England', in Susan Dwyer Amussen and

Mark A. Kishlansky (eds.), *Political Culture and Cultural Politics in Early Modern England: Essays Presented to David Underdown,* (Manchester: Manchester University Press, 1995).

KNOESPEL, KENNETH J., 'The Limits of Allegory: Textual Expansion of Narcissus in *Paradise Lost*', *Milton Studies,* 22 (1986), 79–99.

KRAMER, DAVID BRUCE, *The Imperial Dryden: The Poetics of Appropriation in Seventeenth-Century England* (Athens: University of Georgia Press, 1994).

KRISTEVA, JULIA, *The Kristeva Reader,* ed. Toril Moi (New York: Columbia University Press, 1986).

—— *Black Sun: Depression and Melancholia,* trans. Leon S. Roudiez (New York, NY: Columbia University Press, 1989).

LABRIOLA, ALBERT, 'Milton's Eve and the Cult of Elizabeth I', *Journal of English and Germanic Philology,* 95/1 (1996) 38–51.

LANHAM, RICHARD A., *Analyzing Prose* (New York: Scribner, 1983).

—— *A Handlist of Rhetorical Terms,* 2nd ed. (Berkeley and Los Angeles: University of California Press, 1991).

LA PLANCHE, J., and PONTALIS, J.-B., *The Language of Psycho-analysis,* trans. Donald Nicholson-Smith (New York: Norton, 1973).

LAQUEUR, THOMAS, *Making Sex: Body and Gender from the Greeks to Freud* (Cambridge, Mass.: Harvard University Press, 1990).

LARRINGTON, CAROLYNE (ed.), *Women and Writing in Medieval Europe: A Sourcebook* (London: Routledge, 1995).

LEIBNITZ, JOHANN JACOB, Arnold Christoph, and Arnold, Christoph Molitor, *Inclutae Bibliothecae Norimbergensis Memorabilia* (Nuremberg: apud W. M. Endterum, & J. A. Endteriheredes, 1674).

LENNARD, JOHN, *But I Digress: The Exploitation of Parentheses in English Printed Verse* (Oxford: Clarendon Press, 1991).

LEONARD, JOHN, *Naming in Paradise: Milton and the Language of Adam and Eve* (Oxford: Clarendon Press, 1990).

Letters and Papers, Foreign and Domestic of the Reign of Henry VIII, 2nd edn., rev. and greatly enl. R. H. Brodie (London: HM Stationery Office, 1862–1920).

LEVIN, CAROLE, and SULLIVAN, PATRICIA A. (eds.), *Political Rhetoric, Power, and Renaissance Women* (Albany, NY: State University of New York Press, 1995).

LEVINE, JAY ARNOLD, 'The Design of *A Tale of a Tub* (with a Digression on a Mad Modern Critic', *English Literary History,* 33 (1966), 198–227.

LEVINE, JOSEPH M., *The Battle of the Books: History and Literature in the Augustan Age* (Ithaca, NY: Cornell University Press, 1991).

—— *Between the Ancients and the Moderns: Baroque Culture in Restoration England* (New Haven: Yale University Press, 1999)

LEWALSKI, BARBARA KIEFER, 'Innocence and Experience in Milton's Eden', in Thomas Kranidas (ed.), *New Essays on 'Paradise Lost',* (Berkeley and Los Angeles: University of California Press, 1969).

—— *Donne's Anniversaries and the Poetry of Praise: The Creation of a Symbolic Mode* (Princeton: Princeton University Press, 1973).

Lewalski, Barbara Kiefer, *Protestant Poetics and the Seventeenth-Century Religious Lyric* (Princeton: Princeton University Press, 1979).

—— *'Paradise Lost' and the Rhetoric of Literary Forms* (Princeton: Princeton University Press, 1985).

—— *Writing Women in Jacobean England* (Cambridge, Mass.: Harvard University Press, 1993).

Lewis, C. S., 'Shelley, Dryden and Mr. Eliot', in *Rehabilitations and Other Essays* (London: Oxford University Press, 1939).

Lewis, Jayne Elizabeth, *The English Fable: Aesop and Literary Culture, 1651–1740* (Cambridge: Cambridge University Press, 1996).

Lieb, Michael, ' "Two of Far Nobler Shape": Reading the Paradisal Text', in Diana Treviño Benet and Michael Lieb (eds.), *Literary Milton: Text, Pretext, Context,* (Pittsburgh, Pa.: Duquesne University Press, 1994), 114–32.

Liu, Yameng, 'The Making of Elizabeth Drury: The Voice of God in "An Anatomy of the World" ', *John Donne Journal*, 8 (1989), 89–102.

Loewenstein, Joseph F., *Responsive Readings: Versions of Echo in Pastoral, Epic, and the Jonsonian Masque* (New Haven: Yale University Press, 1984).

Long, Michael, *Marvell, Nabokov: Childhood and Arcadia* (Oxford: Clarendon Press, 1984).

Longinus, Cassius, *On the Sublime*, trans. with commentary by James A. Arieti and John M. Crossett (New York: E. Mellon Press, 1985).

—— 'Longinus: *On Sublimity*', trans. D. A. Russell, in D. A. Russell and M. Winterbottom (eds.), *Classical Literary Criticism* (Oxford: Oxford University Press, 1989)

Lord, George de Forest, et al. (eds.), *Poems on Affairs of State: Augustan Satirical Verse, 1660–1714*, 7 vols. (New Haven: Yale University Press, 1963–75).

Loveridge, Mark, *A History of Augustan Fable* (Cambridge: Cambridge University Press, 1998).

MacCaffrey, Isabel Gamble, *'Paradise Lost' as 'Myth'* (Cambridge, Mass.: Harvard University Press, 1959).

—— 'The Scope of Imagination in "Upon Appleton House" ', in K. Friedenreich (ed.), *Tercentenary Essays in Honor of Andrew Marvell,* (Hamden, Conn.: Archon Books, 1977), 224–44.

MacCallum, H. R., 'Milton and Sacred History: Books XI and XII of *Paradise Lost*', in Millar MacLure and F. W. Watt (eds.), *Essays in English Literature from the Renaissance to the Victorian Age,* (Toronto: University of Toronto Press, 1964), 149–68.

McCloskey, Donald N., *The Rhetoric of Economics* (Madison: University of Wisconsin Press, 1985).

McClung, William A., *The Country House in English Renaissance Poetry* (Berkeley and Los Angeles: University of California Press, 1977).

McColley, Diane Kelsey, *Milton's Eve* (Urbana: University of Illinois Press, 1983).

Macdonald, Hugh, *John Dryden: A Bibliography of Early Editions and of Drydeniana* (Oxford: Clarendon Press, 1939).

McDowell, Paula, *The Women of Grub-Street: Press, Politics and Gender in the London Literary Marketplace, 1678–1730* (Oxford: Clarendon Press, 1998).

McFadden, George, *Dryden, the Public Writer 1660–1685* (Princeton: Princeton University Press, 1978).

McKeon, Michael, 'Politics of Discourses and the Rise of the Aesthetic in Seventeenth-Century England', in Kevin Sharpe and Steven N. Zwicker (eds.), *Politics of Discourse: The Literature and History of Seventeenth-Century England,* (Berkeley and Los Angeles: University of California Press, 1987), 35–51.

Markham, Sir Clements R., *A Life of the Great Lord Fairfax, Commander-in-Chief of the Army of the Parliament of England* (London: Macmillan and Co., 1870).

—— *'The Fighting Veres': Lives of Sir Francis Vere, General of the Queen's Forces in the Low Countries . . .* (Boston: Houghton Mifflin and Company, 1888).

Marotti, Arthur F., *John Donne, Coterie Poet* (Madison: University of Wisconsin Press, 1986).

—— ed., *Catholicism and Anti-Catholicism in Early Modern English Texts* (Houndmills: Macmillan, 1999).

Martin, Catherine Gimelli, *The Ruins of Allegory: 'Paradise Lost' and the Metamorphosis of Epic Convention* (Durham, NC: Duke University Press, 1998).

Martindale, Charles, *John Milton and the Transformation of Ancient Epic* (Totowa, NJ: Barnes & Noble Books, 1986).

Martz, Louis L., *The Poetry of Meditation: A Study in English Religious Literature of the Seventeenth Century* (New Haven: Yale University Press, 1954).

Marvell, Andrew, *The Complete Works in Verse and Prose of Andrew Marvell,* ed. Revd Alexander B. Grosart, 4 vols. (London: Robson and Sons, printers, 1872–5).

—— *The Poems and Letters of Andrew Marvell,* ed. H. M. Margoliouth, 3rd edn., rev. Pierre Legouis with E. E. Duncan-Jones, 2 vols. (Oxford: Clarendon Press, 1971).

Maus, Katharine Eisaman, *Inwardness and Theater in the English Renaissance* (Chicago: University of Chicago Press, 1995).

May, James M., *Trials of Character: The Eloquence of Ciceronian Ethos* (Chapel Hill: University of North Carolina Press, 1988).

Mazzio, Carla, 'Sins of the Tongue', in David Hillman and Carla Mazzio (eds.), *The Body in Parts. Fantasies of Corporeality in Early Modern Europe,* (New York: Routledge, 1997).

—— 'The Melancholy of Print: in Carla Mazzio and Douglas Trevor (eds.), *Love's Labour's Lost', Historicism, Psychoanalysis, and Early Modern Culture,* (New York: Routledge, 2000), 186–227.

Meakin, H. L., *John Donne's Articulations of the Feminine* (Oxford: Clarendon Press, 1998).

Merton, Egon Stephen, *Science and Imagination in Sir Thomas Browne* (New York: Columbia University Press, 1949).

MILLER, JOHN, *James II: A Study in Kingship* (Hove: Wayland, 1977).

MILLER, RACHEL, 'Physic for the Great: Dryden's Satiric Translations of Juvenal, Persius, and Boccaccio', *Philological Quarterly*, 68 (1989), 53–75.

MILTON, JOHN, *The Works of John Milton*, ed. Frank Allen Patterson, 18 vols. of 21 (New York: Columbia University Press, 1931–8).

—— *Prose Selections*, ed. Merritt Yerkes Hughes (New York: Odyssey Press, 1947).

—— *Complete Poems and Major Prose*, ed. Merritt Yerkes Hughes (New York: Macmillan, 1957).

—— *The Complete Prose Works of John Milton*, gen. ed. Don M. Wolfe, 8 vols. (New Haven: Yale University Press, 1953–82).

MINER, EARL, 'The Significance of Plot in *The Hind and the Panther*', *Bulletin of the New York Public Library*, 69 (1965), 446–58.

—— *Dryden's Poetry* (Bloomington: Indiana University Press, 1967).

MONTAG, WARREN, *The Unthinkable Swift: The Spontaneous Philosophy of a Church of England Man* (London: Verso, 1994).

MONTAGU, CHARLES, and PRIOR, MATTHEW, 'The Hind and the Panther Transversed to the Story of the Country Mouse and the City Mouse', in Galbraith M. Crump (ed.), *Poems on Affairs of State, Augustan Satirical Verse, 1660–1714*, iv: *1685–1688*, (New Haven: Yale University Press, 1968), 124–5.

MONTAIGNE, MICHEL DE, *Complete Essays*, trans. Donald M. Frame (Stanford, Calif.: Stanford University Press, 1958).

—— 'The Essayes: or Moral, Politicke, and Militaire Discourses of Lo: Michaell de Montaigne', trans. John Florio, 3 vols. (1603; repr. London: J. M. Dent and sons, 1965).

MOORE, JOHN ROBERT, 'Political Allusions in Dryden's Later Plays', *PMLA* 73 (1958), 36–37.

MORE, P. E., and CROSS, F. L. (eds.), *Anglicanism: The Thought and Practice of the Church of England, Illustrated from the Religious Literature of the Seventeenth Century* (London: Society for Promoting Christian Knowledge, 1935).

MORRISSEY, LEE, *From the Temple to the Castle: An Architectural History of British Literature, 1660–1760* (Charlottesville: University Press of Virginia, 1999).

MOWL, TIMOTHY, 'New Science, Old Order: The Gardens of the Great Rebellion', *Journal of Garden History*, 13 (1993), 16–35.

MUELLER, JANEL, 'Women among the Metaphysicals: A Case, Mostly, of Being Donne for', in Arthur F. Marotti (ed.), *Critical Essays on John Donne*, (New York: G. K. Hall, 1994), 37–48.

MULLAN, JOHN, 'Swift, Defoe, and Narrative Forms' in Steven N. Zwicker (ed.), *The Cambridge Companion to English Literature 1650–1740*, (Cambridge: Cambridge University Press, 1998).

MULVEY, LAURA, 'Visual Pleasure and Narrative Cinema', *Screen*, 16/3 (1975), 8–18.

MUNDY, P. D., 'Dryden and Swift: Their Relationship', *Notes and Queries*, 147 (July–Dec. 1924), 243–4, 279–80, 334.

The Murmurers: A Poem (London: Printed for R. Baldwin, 1689).

MURRIN, MICHAEL, 'The Language of Milton's Heaven', *Modern Philology*, 74 (1977), 350–65.

MYERS, WILLIAM, *Dryden* (London: Hutchinson University Library, 1973).

MYERSON, GEORGE, *The Argumentative Imagination: Wordsworth, Dryden, Religious Dialogues* (Manchester: University of Manchester Press, 1992).

NARDO, ANNA K., 'Academic Interludes in *Paradise Lost*', *Milton Studies*, 27 (1991), 209–41.

NASHE, THOMAS, *The Works of Thomas Nashe*, ed. Ronald Brunlees McKerrow, 5 vols. (Oxford: Basil Blackwell, 1958).

NEW, MELVYN, 'Swift and Sterne: Two Tales, Several Sermons, and a Relationship Revisited', in Frank Palmieri (ed.), *Critical Essays on Jonathan Swift* (New York: G. K. Hall, 1993), 164–86.

NICHOLAS, SIR EDWARD, *The Nicholas Papers. Correspondence of Sir Edward Nicholas* (London, Printed for the Camden Society, 1886–1920), vol. 50.

NICHOLS, AIDAN, *The Panther and the Hind: A Theological History of Anglicanism* (Edinburgh: T. & T. Clark, 1993).

NICOLSON, MARJORIE HOPE, *The Breaking of the Circle: Studies in the Effect of the "New Science" upon Seventeenth-Century Poetry* (New York: Columbia University Press, 1960).

NOKES, DAVID, *Raillery and Rage: A Study of Eighteenth Century Satire* (Brighton: Harvester, 1987).

NORTH, ROGER, *Notes of me: The Autobiography of Roger North*, ed. Peter Millard (Toronto: University of Toronto Press, 2000).

NYQUIST, MARY, 'The Genesis of Gendered Subjectivity in the Divorce Tracts and in *Paradise Lost*', in Mary Nyquist and Margaret Ferguson (eds.), *Re-membering Milton*, (New York: Methuen, 1987), 99–127.

OLDMIXON, JOHN, *The History of Addresses* (London, 1709).

ONG, WALTER J., *Ramus, Method, and the Decay of Dialogue* (Cambridge, Mass.: Harvard University Press, 1958).

OVID, *Metamorphoses*, trans. Frank Justus Miller, rev. G. P. Goold, Loeb Classical Library, 42–3 (Cambridge, Mass.: Harvard University Press; London: 1994).

PAGE, WILLIAM (ed.), *The Victoria History of the Counties of England: A History of Yorkshire, North Riding*, 2 vols. (London: A. Constable, 1914).

PARKER, PATRICIA A., *Inescapable Romance: Studies in the Poetics of a Mode* (Princeton: Princeton University Press, 1979).

—— 'Eve, Evening, and the Labor of Reading in *Paradise Lost*', *English Literary Renaissance*, 9 (1979), 319–42.

—— 'Shakespeare and Rhetoric: "Dilation" and "Delation" in *Othello*', in Patricia Parker and Geoffrey Hartman (ed.), *Shakespeare and the Question of Theory*, (New York: Methuen, 1985), 54–74.

—— *Literary Fat Ladies: Rhetoric, Gender, Property* (New York: Methuen, 1987).

—— 'Fantasies of "Race" and "Gender": Africa, *Othello*, and Bringing to Light', in Margo Hendricks and Patricia A. Parker (eds.), *Women, 'Race', and Writing in the Early Modern Period* (London: Routledge, 1994), 84–100.

PARKER, PATRICIA A., *Shakespeare from the Margins: Language, Culture, Context* (Chicago: University of Chicago Press, 1996).

PARKER, SAMUEL, *A Reproof to the Rehearsal Transprosed in A Discourse to its Author* (London: Printed for James Collins . . ., 1673).

PARKIN, REBECCA, 'Heroic and Anti-heroic Elements in *The Hind and the Panther*', *Studies in English Literature 1500–1900*, 12 (1972), 459–66.

PARNELL, J. T., 'Swift, Sterne, and the Skeptical Tradition', *Studies in Eighteenth Century Culture*, 23 (1994), 221–42.

PATRIDES, C. A., ' "The Best Part of Nothing": Sir Thomas Browne and the Strategy of Indirection', in C. A. Patrides (ed.), *Approaches to Sir Thomas Browne. The Ann Arbor Tercentenary Lectures and Essays* (Columbia: University of Missouri Press, 1982), 31–48.

PATTERSON, ANNABEL, *Fables of Power: Aesopian Writing and Political History* (Durham, NC: Duke University Press, 1991).

PATTON, BRIAN, 'Preserving Property: History, Genealogy, and Inheritance in "Upon Appleton House" ', *Renaissance Quarterly*, 49/4 (Winter 1996), 824–39.

PAULSON, RONALD, *Theme and Structure in Swift's 'Tale of a Tub'* (New Haven: Yale University Press, 1960).

PAVORD, ANNA, *The Tulip: The Story of a Flower That has Made Men Mad* (New York: Bloomsbury Distributed by St Martin's Press, 1999).

PEACHAM, HENRY, *The Garden of Eloquence* (1593), facsimile reproduction, ed. William G. Crane (Gainesville, Fla.: Scholars' Facsimiles and Reprints, 1954).

PECHTER, EDWARD, *Dryden's Classical Theory of Literature* (Cambridge: Cambridge University Press, 1975).

PEPYS, SAMUEL, *The Diary of Samuel Pepys*, ed. Robert C. Latham and William Matthews, 11 vols. (London: HarperCollins, 1995).

PHIDDIAN, ROBERT, *Swift's Parody* (Cambridge: Cambridge University Press, 1995).

PLUTARCH, *Plutarch's Lives. The Translation Called Dryden's*, ed. Arthur Hugh Clough, 5 vols. (Boston: Little, Brown and Company, 1859).

POCOCK, J. G. A., *Politics, Language, and Time: Essays on Political Thought and History* (New York: Atheneum, 1971).

—— 'Texts as Events: Reflections on the History of Political Thought', in Kevin Sharpe and Steven N. Zwicker (eds.), *Politics of Discourse: The Literature and History of Seventeenth-Century England* (Berkeley and Los Angeles: University of California Press, 1987), 21–34.

PORTER, WILLIAM M., *Reading the Classics and 'Paradise Lost'* (Lincoln: University of Nebraska Press, 1993).

POST, JONATHAN F. S., 'Motives for Metaphor: *Urne-Buriall* and *The Garden of Cyrus*', in Jonathan F. S. Post (ed.), *Sir Thomas Browne*, (Boston: Twayne Publishers, 1987), 120–46.

PRICKET, ROBERT, *Times Anotomie, Containing The poore mans plaint, Brittons trouble, and her triumph, The Popes pride, Romes treasons, and her destruction* (London: George Eld, 1606).

PRINCE, F. T., *The Italian Element in Milton's Verse*, rev. edn. (Oxford: Clarendon Press, 1962).

PUTTENHAM, GEORGE, *The Arte of English Poesie* (London: Printed by Richard Field, 1589).

—— *The Arte of English Poesie: A Facsimile Reproduction* (Kent State, Oh: Kent State University Press, 1970).

QUILLIGAN, MAUREEN, *The Language of Allegory: Defining the Genre* (Ithaca, NY: Cornell University Press, 1979).

QUINT, DAVID, *Epic and Empire: Politics and Generic Form from Virgil to Milton* (Princeton: Princeton University Press, 1993).

QUINTANA, RICARDO, *The Mind and Art of Jonathan Swift* (London: Oxford University Press, 1953).

QUINTILIAN, *Institutio Oratoria*, trans. H. E. Butler, Loeb Classical Library, 124–7 (Cambridge, Mass.: Harvard University Press, 1995–8).

R., J., *Religio Laici, or a Lay-Man's Faith, Touching the Supream Head and Infallible Guide of the Church: in Two Letters to a Friend in the Country* (London: Printed for John Newton, 1688, Wing R30).

RADZINOWICZ, Mary Ann, *Milton's Epics and the Book of Psalms* (Princeton, NJ: Princeton University Press, 1989).

RAINE, JAMES, CLAY JOHN WILLIAM, *Testamenta Eboracensia; or, Wills Registered at York Illustrative of the History, Manners, Language, Statistics, &c. of the Province of York from the Year 1300 Downwards*, Publications of the Surtees Society London: J. B. Nichols, 1836–1999).

RAMUS, PETER, *Arguments in Rhetoric against Quintilian*, ed. James J. Murphy, trans. Carole Elizabeth Newlands (De Kalbe: University of Northern Illinois Press, 1983).

—— *Peter Ramus's Attack on Cicero, Text and Translation of Ramus's Brutinae Quaestiones*, ed. James J. Murphy, trans. Carole Newlands (Davis, Calif.: Hermagoras Press, 1992).

RANDOLPH, MARY CLAIRE, 'The Medical Concept in English Renaissance Satiric Theory: Its Possible Relationships and Implications', *Studies in Philology*, 38 (1941), 125–57.

—— 'The Structural Design of the Formal Verse Satire', in Bernard N. Schilling (eds.), *Essential Articles for the Study of English Augustan Backgrounds* (Hamden, Conn.: Archon Books, 1961).

RAYLOR, TIMOTHY, ' "Paradice's Only Map": A Plan of Nun Appleton', *Notes and Queries*, vol. 242 of the continuous series (NS, 44)/2 (June 1997), 186–7.

REBHORN, WAYNE A., *The Emperor of Men's Minds: Literature and the Renaissance Discourse of Rhetoric* (Ithaca, NY: Cornell University Press, 1995).

—— (ed. and trans.), *Renaissance Debates on Rhetoric* (Ithaca, NY: Cornell University Press, 2000).

REEVES, CHARLES ERIC, ' "Lest Wilfully Transgressing": Raphael's Narration and Knowledge in *Paradise Lost*', *Milton Studies*, 34 (1996), 83–98.

REGOSIN, RICHARD L., *Montaigne's Unruly Brood: Textual Engendering and the Challenge to Paternal Authority* (Berkeley and Los Angeles: University of California Press, 1996).

REVARD, STELLA P., *The War in Heaven: 'Paradise Lost' and the Tradition of Satan's Rebellion* (Ithaca, NY: Cornell University Press, 1980).

—— 'The Heroic Context of Book IX of *Paradise Lost*', *Journal of English and Germanic Philology*, 87 (July 1988), 329–41.

The Revolter: A Trage-Comedy Acted between the Hind and Panther, and Religio Laici, &c. (London, 1687, Wing R1206).

RICHARDSON, JONATHAN, father and son, *Explanatory Notes and Remarks on Milton's 'Paradise Lost'* (London: James, John, and Paul Knapton, 1734).

RICKS, CHRISTOPHER, *Milton's Grand Style* (Oxford: Clarendon Press, 1963).

RIGGS, WILLIAM G., 'The Temptation of Milton's Eve: "Words, Impregn'd/ With Reason" ', *Journal of English and Germanic Philology*, 94/3 (July 1995), 365–92.

ROBERTSON, DAVID, 'Soliloquy and Self in Milton's Major Poems', in P. G. Stanwood (ed.), *Of Poetry and Politics: New Essays on Milton and his World*, Medieval and Renaissance Texts and Studies, 126 (Binghamton, NY: Medieval and Renaissance Texts and Studies 1995), 59–77.

ROGERS, JOHN, *The Matter of Revolution: Science, Poetry, and Politics in the Age of Milton* (Ithaca, NY: Cornell University Press, 1996).

ROSENBERG, D. M., *Oaten Reeds and Trumpets: Pastoral and Epic in Virgil, Spenser, and Milton* (Lewisburg, Pa.: Bucknell University Press, 1981).

ROSENBLATT, JASON P., *Torah and Law in 'Paradise Lost'* (Princeton: Princeton University Press, 1994).

ROSS, ALEXANDER, *Medicus Medicatus, or, The physicians religion cured by a lenative or gentle potion with some animadversions upon Sir Kenelm Digbie's observations on Religio Medici* (London: Printed by James Young, and are to be sold by Charles Green . . ., 1645).

—— *Arcana Microcosmi, or, The hid secrets of man's body discovered in an anatomical duel between Aristotle and Galen concerning the parts thereof . . .* (London: Printed by Tho. Newcomb, and are to bee [*sic*] sold by John Clark . . ., 1651).

RØSTVIG, MAREN-SOFIE, 'In Ordine de Ruota: Circular Structure in "The Unfortunate Lover" and "Upon Appleton House" ', in K. Friedenreich (ed.), *Tercentenary Essays in Honor of Andrew Marvell* (Hamden, Conn.: Archon Books, 1977), 245–67.

RUSSELL, D. A., and WINTERBOTTOM M. (eds.), *Classical Literary Criticism* (Oxford: Oxford University Press, 1989).

SABINE, MAUREEN, *Feminine Engendered Faith: The Poetry of John Donne and Richard Crashaw* (Basingstoke: Macmillan, 1992).

SACKVILLE, CHARLES, *The Poems of Charles Sackville, Sixth Earl of Dorset*, ed. Brice Harris (New York: Garland Publishing, 1979).

SAINTSBURY, GEORGE, *Dryden* (London: Macmillan, 1881).

SANDYS, GEORGE, *Ovid's 'Metamorphoses', Englished, Mythologized, and Represented in Figures by George Sandys*, ed. Karl Hulley and Stanley Vandersall (Lincoln: University of Nebraska Press, 1970).

SAUER, ELIZABETH, *Barbarous Dissonance and Images of Voice in Milton's Epics* (Montreal: McGill-Queen's University Press, 1996).

SAVILE, GEORGE, Marquis of Halifax, 'A Letter to a Dissenter, upon Occasion of his Majesties Late Gracious Declaration of Indulgence' (London: Printed for G.H., 1687, Wing H312).

SAWDAY, JONATHAN, *The Body Emblazoned: Dissection and the Human Body in Renaissance Culture* (London: Routledge, 1995).

—— 'Self and Selfhood in the Seventeenth Century', in Roy Porter (ed.), *Rewriting the Self: Histories from the Renaissance to the Present*, (New York: Routledge, 1997), 29–48.

SCHEPER, GEORGE L., 'Reformation Attitudes toward Allegory and the Song of Songs', *PMLA* 89 (1974), 551–62.

SCHIESARI, JULIANA, *The Gendering of Melancholia: Feminism, Psychoanalysis, and the Symbolics of Loss in Renaissance Literature* (Ithaca, NY: Cornell University Press, 1992).

SCHLEINER, LOUISE (ed.), *Tudor and Stuart Women Writers* (Bloomington: Indiana University Press, 1994).

SCHOR, SANDRA, 'Reclaiming Digression', in Louise Z. Smith (ed.), *Audits of Meaning; A Festschrift in Honor of Ann E. Berthoff* (Portsmouth, NH: Boynton/Cook, 1988), 238–47.

SCHWARTZ, REGINA M., *Remembering and Repeating: Biblical Creation in 'Paradise Lost'* (1988; repr. Chicago: University of Chicago Press, 1993).

—— 'Through the Optic Glass: Voyeurism and *Paradise Lost*', in Valeria Finucci and Regina M. Schwartz (eds.), *Desire in the Renaissance: Psychoanalysis and Literature* (Princeton: Princeton University Press, 1994).

SCOTT, SIR WALTER, *The Life of John Dryden*, ed. Bernard Kreissman (Lincoln: University of Nebraska Press, 1963).

SEIDEL, MICHAEL, *Satiric Inheritance: Rabelais to Sterne* (Princeton: Princeton University Press, 1979).

—— 'Satire, Lampoon, Libel, Slander', in Steven N. Zwicker (ed.), *The Cambridge Companion to English Literature 1650–1740* (Cambridge; New York, NY: Cambridge University Press, 1998).

SHAPIN, STEVEN, *The Scientific Revolution* (Chicago: University of Chicago Press, 1996).

—— and SCHAFFER, SIMON *Leviathan and the Air-Pump: Hobbes, Boyle, and the Experimental Life* (Princeton: Princeton University Press, 1985).

SHARPE, KEVIN, *Remapping Early Modern England: The Culture of Seventeenth-Century Politics* (Cambridge: Cambridge University Press, 2000).

—— and STEVEN ZWICKER, N. *Politics of Discourse: The Literature and History of Seventeenth-Century England* (Berkeley and Los Angeles: University of California Press, 1987).

SHAWCROSS, JOHN T. (ed.), *Milton: The Critical Heritage* (New York: Barnes & Noble, 1970).

SHELDAHL THOMASON, T. KATHARINE, 'Marvell, his Bee-Like Cell: The Pastoral Hexagon of "Upon Appleton House" ', *Genre*, 16 (1983), 39–56.

SHELL, ALISON, *Catholicism, Controversy, and the English Literary Imagination, 1558–1660* (Cambridge: Cambridge University Press, 1999).

SIDNEY, SIR PHILIP (ed.), *Sir Philip Sidney*, ed. Katharine Duncan-Jones (Oxford; New York, NY: Oxford University Press, 1989).

SIMPSON, EVELYN MARY, *A Study of the Prose Works of John Donne*, 2nd edn. (Oxford: Clarendon Press, 1948).

SIMPSON, J. A., and WEINER, E. S. C. (eds.), *The Oxford English Dictionary*, 2nd edn., 20 vols. (Oxford: Clarendon Press: Oxford University Press, 1989).

SITTER, JOHN, E., *Arguments of Augustan Wit* (Cambridge: Cambridge University Press, 1991).

SKINNER, QUENTIN, 'Thomas Hobbes on the Proper Signification of Liberty', *Transactions of the Royal Historical Society*, 40 (1990), 121–51.

—— 'Moral Ambiguity and the Renaissance Art of Eloquence', *Essays in Criticism*, 44 (1994), 267–92.

—— *Reason and Rhetoric in the Philosophy of Hobbes* (Cambridge: Cambridge University Press, 1996).

—— *Liberty before Liberalism* (Cambridge: Cambridge University Press, 1998).

SLOANE, THOMAS O., 'Schoolbooks and Rhetoric: Erasmus's *Copia*', *Rhetorica*, 9/2 (Spring 1991), 113–29.

SLOMAN, JUDITH, *Dryden: The Poetics of Translation* (Toronto: University of Toronto Press, 1985).

SMITH, BRUCE R., *The Acoustic World of Early Modern England: Attending to the O-Factor* (Chicago: University of Chicago Press, 1999).

SMITH, NIGEL (ed.), *A Collection of Ranter Writings from the 17th Century* (London: Junction Books, 1983).

SPEED, ADOLPHUS, *Adam Out of Eden, or, An abstract of divers excellent experiments touching the advancement of husbandry . . .* (London: Printed for Henry Brome . . ., 1659).

SPINGARN, J. E., *Sir William Temple's Essays on Ancient & Modern Learning and on Poetry* (Oxford: Clarendon Press, 1909).

—— (ed.), *Critical Essays of the Seventeenth Century*, vol. ii (Oxford: Clarendon Press, 1908).

SPRAT, Thomas, *The History of the Royal Society of London* (London: Printed for J. Martyn . . ., and J. Allestry . . ., 1667).

STANFORD, Michael, 'The Terrible Thresholds: Sir Thomas Browne on Sex and Death', *English Literary Renaissance* 18 (1988), 413–23.

STEADMAN, John M., *Milton's Biblical and Classical Imagery* (Pittsburgh: Duquesne University Press, 1984).

STEPHENS, DOROTHY, *The Limits of Eroticism in Post-Petrarchan Narrative: Conditional Pleasure from Spenser to Marvell* (Cambridge: Cambridge University Press, 1998).

STEVENSON, JANE and DAVIDSON, PETER (eds.), *Early Modern Women Poets: An Anthology* (Oxford: Oxford University Press, 2001).

STEWART, STANLEY, *The Enclosed Garden: The Tradition and the Image in Seventeenth-Century Poetry* (Madison: University of Wisconsin Press, 1966).

STEWART, SUSAN, *On Longing: Narratives of the Miniature, the Gigantic, the Souvenir, the Collection* (Baltimore: Johns Hopkins University Press, 1984).

STILLINGFLEET, EDWARD, 'The Doctrines and Practices of the Church of Rome Truly Represented, in Answer to a Book Intitled, A Papist Misrepresented and Represented' (London: Printed for W. Rogers . . ., 1686).

STRONG, ROY, *The Renaissance Garden in England* (London: Thames and Hudson, 1979).

STUBBS, MAYLING, 'John Beale, Philosophical Gardener of Herefordshire. Part I. Prelude to the Royal Society (1608–1663)', *Annals of Science*, 39 (1982), 463–89.

SUMMERS, CLAUDE J., 'Donne's 1609 Sequence of Grief and Comfort', *Studies in Philology*, 89 (1992), 211–31.

SUMMERS, DAVID, *Michelangelo and the Language of Art* (Princeton: Princeton University Press, 1981).

SWAN, JIM, 'At Play in the Garden of Ambivalence: Andrew Marvell and the Green World', *Criticism*, 17 (1975), 295–307.

—— ' "Betwixt Two Labyrinths": Andrew Marvell's Rational Amphibian', *Texas Studies in Language and Literature*, 17 (1975), 551–72.

—— ' "Caesarian Section": The Destruction of Enclosing Bodies in Marvell's "Horatian Ode" ', *Psychocultural Review*, 9 (1977), 1–8.

SWANN, MARJORIE, *Curiosities and Texts: The Culture of Collecting in Early Modern England* (Philadelphia: University of Pennsylvania Press, 2001).

SWEDENBERG, H. T., Jr., 'Dryden's Obsessive Concern with the Heroic', in Daniel W. Patterson and Albrecht B. Strauss (eds.), *Essays in English Literature of the Classical Period Presented to Dougald MacMillan* (Chapel Hill: University of North Carolina Press, 1967), 12–26.

SWIFT, DEANE, *An Essay on Dr. Swift's Life and Character* (London: Printed for C. Bathurst, 1755).

SWIFT, JONATHAN, *The Correspondence of Jonathan Swift*, ed. F. Elrington Ball, 6 vols. (London: G. Bell and Sons, 1910–14).

—— *'A Tale of a Tub', to Which is Added 'The Battle of the Books' and the 'Mechanical Operation of the Spirit'*, ed. Adolph Charles Louis Guthkelch and David Nichol Smith, 2nd edn. (Oxford: Clarendon Press, 1958).

—— *Miscellaneous and Autobiographical Pieces, Fragments, and Marginalia*, ed. Herbert John Davis (Oxford: B. Blackwell, 1969).

—— *Jonathan Swift*, ed. Angus Ross and David Woolley (Oxford: Oxford University Press, 1984).

TANNER, JOHN S., *Anxiety in Eden: A Kierkegaardian Reading of 'Paradise Lost'* (New York: Oxford University Press, 1992).

TAYLER, EDWARD W., *Donne's Idea of a Woman: Structure and Meaning in 'The Anniversaries'* (New York: Columbia University Press, 1991).

THOMSON, P., 'John Donne and the Countess of Bedford', *Modern Language Review*, 44 (1949), 329–40.

THORNDIKE, HERBERT, *The Theological Works of Herbert Thorndike*, 6 vols. (Oxford: J. H. Parker, 1844–56).

THORPE, JAMES (ed.), *Milton Criticism: Selections from Four Centuries* (London: Routledge & Kegan Paul, 1951).

TREIP, MINDELE ANNE, *Allegorical Poetics and the Epic: The Renaissance Tradition to 'Paradise Lost'* (Lexington: University of Kentucky Press, 1993).

TURNER, JAMES GRANTHAM, *One Flesh: Paradisal Marriage and Sexual Relations in the Age of Milton* (Oxford: Clarendon Press, 1987).

ULREICH, JOHN C., ' "Argument Not Less But More Heroic": Eve as the Hero of *Paradise Lost*', in Charles W. Durham and Kristin A. Pruitt (eds.), *All in All: Unity, Diversity and the Miltonic Perspective*, (Selinsgrove, Pa.: Susquehanna University Press, 1999), 67–82.

VICARY, THOMAS, *The English-mans treasure: with the true anatomie of mans bodie . . . Whereunto are annexed many secrets appertayning to Chirurgerie, with . . . remedies for all diseases . . . with emplasters . . . potions and drinkes approved in phisicke. Also the rare treasure of the English bathes* (London: G. Robinson for J. Perin, 1587).

VICKERS, BRIAN, *In Defence of Rhetoric* (Oxford: Clarendon Press, 1988).

Vox Norwici: or, The Cry of Norwich, Vindicating their Ministers . . . (London: William Frankling, 1646).

WALLACE, JOHN M., *Destiny his Choice: The Loyalism of Andrew Marvell* (London: Cambridge University Press, 1968).

WALSH, MARCUS, 'Text, "Text", and Swift's *A Tale of a Tub*', *Modern Language Review*, 85 (1990), 290–303.

WALTERS, FRANK D., 'A Strategy for Writing the *Impossibilium*: *Aporia* in Sir Thomas Browne's *The Garden of Cyrus*', *Prose Studies*, 18/1 (Apr. 1995), 19–35.

WARTON, JOSEPH, *Essay on the Genius and Writings of Pope*, 3rd edn., corr., 2 vols. (London: Printed for J. Dodsley, 1772–82).

WATERS, LINDSAY, 'Milton, Tasso, and the Renaissance Grand Style and its Effect on the Reader', *Stanford Italian Review*, 2 (1981), 81–92.

WEBBER, JOAN, *Milton and his Epic Tradition* (Seattle: University of Washington Press, 1979).

WEBSTER, CHARLES, *The Great Instauration: Science, Medicine and Reform 1626–1660* (New York: Holmes & Meier Publishers, 1975).

WEBSTER, CLARENCE M., 'Swift's *A Tale of a Tub* Compared with Earlier Satires of the Puritans', *PMLA* 47 (1932), 171–8.

—— 'Swift and Some Earlier Satirists of Puritan Enthusiasm', *PMLA* 48 (1933), 1141–53.

WEINBERG, BERNARD, *A History of Literary Criticism in the Italian Renaissance*, 2 vols. (Chicago: University of Chicago Press, 1961).

WEINBROT, HOWARD D., *The Formal Strain: Studies in Augustan Imitation and Satire* (Chicago: University of Chicago Press, 1969).

WEISER, BRIAN, 'From Whitehall to Winchester: Charles II's Palaces', in Eveline Cruickshanks (ed.), *The Stuart Courts* (Stroud: Sutton, 2000), 203–13.

WHALER, JAMES, 'The Miltonic Simile', *PMLA* 46 (1931), 1034–74.

WHEELER, JAMES SCOTT, *The Making of a World Power: War and the Military Revolution in Seventeenth-Century England* (Stroud: Sutton, 1999).

WHITLOCK, BAIRD D. (*sic*), 'The Heredity and Childhood of John Donne', *Notes and Queries*, OS 204, NS 6 (1959), 257–62, 348–53.

WHITLOCK, BAIRD W., 'John Syminges, a Poet's Step-Father', *Notes and Queries*, OS 199, NS 1 (1954), 421–4, 465–7.

WILDING, MICHAEL, *Dragon's Teeth: Literature in the English Revolution* (Oxford: Clarendon Press, 1987).

—— ' "Thir Sex Not Equal Seem'd": Equality in *Paradise Lost*', in P. G. Stanwood (ed.), *New Essays on Milton and His World*, Medieval and Renaissance Texts and Studies 126 (Binghamton, NY: Medieval and Renaissance Texts and Studies, 1995), 171–86.

WILLIAMS, ARNOLD, *The Common Expositer: An Account of the Commentaries on Genesis, 1527–1633* (Chapel Hill: University of North Carolina Press, 1948).

WILLIAMS, KATHLEEN, *Swift: The Critical Heritage* (New York: Barnes & Noble, 1970).

WILLIAMS, RAYMOND, *The Country and the City* (New York: Oxford University Press, 1973).

WILSON, THOMAS, *The Arte of Rhetorique*, ed. Thomas J. Derrick (New York: Garland Publishing, 1982).

WINN, JAMES ANDERSON, *John Dryden and his World* (New Haven: Yale University Press, 1987).

—— ' "Complying with the Times": Dryden's *Satires of Juvenal and Persius*, 1693', *Eighteenth-Century Life*, 12 (1988), 76–87.

WISE, JAMES N., *Sir Thomas Browne's Religio Medici and Two Seventeenth-Century Critics* (Columbia: University of Missouri Press, 1973).

WITTREICH, JOSEPH, *Feminist Milton* (Ithaca, NY: Cornell University Press, 1987).

—— ' "Inspir'd with Contradiction": Mapping Gender Discourses in *Paradise Lost*', in Diana Treviño Benet and Michael Lieb (eds.), *Literary Milton: Text, Pretext, Context* (Pittsburgh, Pa: Duquesne University Press, 1994), 133–79.

WOTTON, WILLIAM, 'Defense of the Reflections upon Ancient and Modern Learning', repr. in Jonathon Swift, *A Tale of a Tub, to Which is Added 'The Battle of the Books' and the 'Mechanical Operation of the Spirit'*, ed. Adolph Charles Louis Guthkelch and David Nichol Smith, 2nd edn. (Oxford: Clarendon Press, 1958).

XENOPHON, *Memorabilia and Oeconomicus*, trans. E. C. Marchant, Loeb Classical Library, 89 (Cambridge, Mass.; London: Harvard University Press, 1979).

—— *Anabasis*, trans. Carleton L. Brownson, rev. John Dillery (Cambridge, Mass.: Harvard University Press, 1998).

YOUNG, BRIGADIER PETER, and HOLMES, RICHARD *The English Civil War: A Military History of the Three Civil Wars, 1642–1651* (London: Eyre Methuen, 1974).

ZIMMERMAN, EVERETT, *Swift's Narrative Satires: Author and Authority* (Ithaca, NY: Cornell University Press, 1983).

—— and HAMMOND, EUGENE R. 'In Praise of Wisdom and the Will of God: Erasmus' *Praise of Folly* and Swift's *A Tale of a Tub*', *Studies in Philology*, 80 (1983), 253–76.

ZWICKER, STEVEN N., *Politics and Language in Dryden's Poetry: The Arts of Disguise* (Princeton: Princeton University Press, 1984).

—— *Lines of Authority: Politics and English Literary Culture, 1649–1689* (Ithaca, NY: Cornell University Press, 1993).

—— 'The Paradoxes of Tender Conscience: Dryden's *The Hind and the Panther* and the Politics of Religious Toleration', *English Literary History*, 63/4 (1996), 851–69.

—— 'Dryden and the Dissolution of Things: The Decay of Structures in Dryden's Late Writing', in Paul Hammond and David Hopkins (eds.), *John Dryden: Tercentenary Essays*, (Oxford: Clarendon Press: 2000), 308–29.

—— 'Mastering Virgil', a paper delivered at the Dryden Tercentenary Conference sponsored by the Beinecke Library in cooperation with the Yale Center for British Art, New Haven, 5–7 Oct., 2000.

—— 'Early Modern Reading: Habits and Practices, Protocols and Contexts', *Eigo Seinen*, 148/2 (May 2002), 78–81.

Index

Note: **Emboldened** page numbers refer to chapters